Gridlock

Gridlock
Why Global Cooperation Is Failing When We Need It Most

Thomas Hale
David Held
Kevin Young

polity

First published in 2013 by Polity Press

Polity Press
65 Bridge Street
Cambridge CB2 1UR, UK

Polity Press
350 Main Street
Malden, MA 02148, USA

ISBN-13: 978-0-7456-6238-1
ISBN-13: 978-0-7456-6239-8(pb)

A catalogue record for this book is available from the British Library.

Typeset in 10.5 on 13 pt Swift
by Toppan Best-set Premedia Limited
Printed and bound in Great Britain by MPG Books Group Limited, Bodmin, Cornwall

For further information on Polity, visit our website: www.politybooks.com

Contents

Figures

Boxes and Tables

Boxes

Tables

Abbreviations

ABM	Anti-Ballistic Missile Treaty
ACV	armored combat vehicles
AIDS	Acquired Immune Deficiency Syndrome
ASEAN	Association of South East Asian Nations
ATT	United Nations Arms Trade Treaty
BCBS	Basel Committee on Banking Supervision
BIS	Bank for International Settlements
BWC	Biological Weapons Convention
CCM	Convention on Cluster Munitions
CD	Conference on Disarmament
CDM	Clean Development Mechanism
CERN	European Organization for Nuclear Research
CFCs	chlorofluorocarbons
CFE	Conventional Forces in Europe Treaty
CFSP	Common Foreign and Security Policy (EU)
CIA	Central Intelligence Agency (US)
CMF	Combined Maritime Forces
CMIM	Chiang Mai Initiative Multilateralization
CPSS	Committee on Payment and Settlement Systems
CSD	Commission on Sustainable Development
CSR	corporate social responsibility
CTBT(O)	Comprehensive Test Ban Treaty (Organization)
CWC	Chemical Weapons Convention
DDT	dichlorodiphenyltrichloroethane
DfID	Department for International Development
DRC	Democratic Republic of Congo
EC	European Community
ECOSOC	Economic and Social Council (UN)
EPA	Environmental Protection Agency (US)
EU	European Union

FAO	Food and Agriculture Organization
FATF	Financial Action Task Force
FDI	foreign direct investment
FMCT	Fissile Materials Cutoff Treaty
FSB	Financial Stability Board
FSC	Forest Stewardship Council
FTT	financial transaction tax
G5	Group of Five (France, Germany, Japan, UK, US)
G7/G8	Group of Seven/Eight (leading industrial nations)
G10	Group of Ten (Belgium, Canada, France, Italy, Japan, Netherlands, UK, US – and the central banks of Germany and Sweden)
G20	Argentina, Australia, Brazil, Canada, China, France, Germany, India, Indonesia, Italy, Japan, Republic of Korea, Mexico, Russia, Saudi Arabia, South Africa, Turkey, UK, US, EU.
GATS	General Agreement on Trade in Services
GATT	General Agreement on Tariffs and Trade
GDP	gross domestic product
GHG	greenhouse gas
GICHD	Geneva International Centre for Humanitarian Demining
GM	General Motors
GMO	genetically modified organism
HCFCs	hydrochlorofluorocarbons
HIV	Human Immunodeficiency Virus
IAEA	International Atomic Energy Agency
IAIS	International Association of Insurance Supervisors
IBRD	International Bank for Reconstruction and Development
ICBL	International Campaign to Ban Landmines
ICBM	intercontinental ballistic missile
ICC	International Criminal Court
ICG	International Crisis Group
ICISS	International Commission on Intervention and State Sovereignty
ICJ	International Court of Justice
ICTR	International Criminal Tribunal for Rwanda
ICTY	International Criminal Tribunal for the former Yugoslavia
IFF	International Forum on Forests
IFI	international financial institution
IGO	intergovernmental organization
ILO	International Labour Organization

IMB	International Maritime Bureau
IMF	International Monetary Fund
IMO	International Maritime Organization
INGO	international nongovernmental organization
IOPN	International Office for the Protection of Nature
IOSCO	International Organization of Securities Commissions
IPCC	Intergovernmental Panel on Climate Change
IPF	Intergovernmental Panel on Forests
ISAF	International Security Assistance Force
ISO	International Organization for Standardization
ITO	International Trade Organization
ITTA	International Tropical Timber Agreement
ITTO	International Tropical Timber Organization
IUCN	International Union for the Conservation of Nature
IUPN	International Union for the Protection of Nature
LDCs	least developed countries
LHC	Large Hadron Collider
MAP	Mutual Assessment Process
MEF	Major Economies Forum on Energy and Climate
Mercosur	Southern Cone Common Market (Latin America)
MNC	multinational corporation
MSF	Médecins sans Frontières
N-5	nuclear weapon states of the NPT regime
NAFTA	North American Free Trade Agreement
NASA	National Aeronautics and Space Administration
NATO	North Atlantic Treaty Organization
NGO	nongovernmental organization
NIE	newly industrializing economy(ies)
NIEO	New International Economic Order
NPT	Treaty on the Non-Proliferation of Nuclear Weapons
NWS	nuclear weapon state(s)
OAS	Organization of American States
ODS	ozone-depleting substances
OECD	Organisation for Economic Co-operation and Development
OPCW	Organization for the Prohibition of Chemical Weapons
OPEC	Organization of the Petroleum Exporting Countries
P-5	the five permanent members of the United Nations Security Council
PEFC	Programme for the Endorsement of Forest Certification
PRC	People's Republic of China
PRIO	Peace Research Institute Oslo

PTA	preferential trade agreement
R+D	Research and Development
R2P	Responsibility to Protect
RWP	Responsibility while Protecting
SALT	Strategic Arms Limitation Talks
SALW	small arms and light weapons
SARS	Severe Acute Respiratory Syndrome
SIPRI	Stockholm International Peace Research Institute
START	Strategic Arms Reduction Talks
TNC	transnational corporation
TRIMS	trade-related investment measures
TRIPS	Agreement on Trade-Related Aspects of Intellectual Property Rights
UCDP	Uppsala Conflict Data Program, Uppsala University
UK	United Kingdom
UN	United Nations
UNCED	United Nations Conference on Environment and Development
UNCTAD	United Nations Conference on Trade and Development
UNDP	United Nations Development Programme
UNEP	United Nations Environment Programme
UNESCO	United Nations Education, Scientific and Cultural Organization
UNFCCC	United Nations Framework Convention on Climate Change
UNFF	United Nations Forum on Forests
UNIDO	United Nations Industrial Development Organization
UN-REDD	United Nations Initiative on Reducing Emissions from Deforestation and Forest Degradation
US	United States
USAID	United States Agency for International Development
WA	Wassenaar Arrangement on Export Controls for Conventional Arms and Dual-Use Goods and Technologies
WCED	World Commission on Environment and Development
WHO	World Health Organization
WMD	weapons of mass destruction
WMO	World Meteorological Organization
WTO	World Trade Organization
WWF	World Wildlife Fund

Preface

The arguments in this book developed after the authors attended various lectures on why the outcome of the Copenhagen Climate Change Conference in 2009 had been so unsatisfactory. The question put by lecturer after lecturer was: why had the negotiations on climate change stalled? While the lectures were invariably engaging, they shared the questionable assumption that climate change negotiations could be understood sui generis and independently of wider geopolitical transformations. The questions about climate negotiations, however, could easily have been asked about the current state of trade, finance, nuclear proliferation, small arms, biodiversity and an array of other topics. In each of these areas international negotiations have either failed to make breakthroughs or have had only limited success.

The issue seems to be not why Copenhagen and subsequent climate negotiations have produced so little but, rather, why international negotiations in general are increasingly stalling in the face of growing differences among national interests, strident voices of leading and new emerging powers, and the sheer complexity involved in coming to agreement on issues that transcend national boundaries. Reflecting on these concerns, it seemed to us that the fundamental question was: why is a state of "gridlock" increasingly characteristic of international negotiations and organizations?

This book grapples with the causes and consequences of gridlock across leading sectors of international concern: security, the economy, and the environment. It develops a theory of gridlock and then explores it across these sectors. Having done this, the book ends by examining worrying scenarios of continued gridlock as well as pathways beyond it. The latter involve new kinds of political movements, institutional strategies of adaptation and more ambitious programs of the reform of global governance. But the way ahead is not clear and gridlock may yet remain the most pervasive feature of the global order.

Why does this matter? It matters because some of the most pressing global issues we face, from nuclear proliferation to global economic imbalances, and the degraded nature of our planet, will not be resolved unless new ways are uncovered for addressing them effectively and in such a manner that is representative of the diverse stakeholders they affect. As things stand, the global order is drifting into highly uncertain territory which, in sector after sector, may well involve cataclysmic moments which become the cause of a wider crisis affecting the life chances and life expectancies of people across the world. These are not worries for some remote future; they are concerns for the here and now. They imply some fundamental questions: what explains the development of gridlock in our international and transnational organizations and institutions, and how can these more effectively and legitimately address the global bads that threaten us, as well as the global goods we need for the development of our political and social lives?

This book has benefited enormously from the conversations the authors have had with each other in a diversity of places over the last two years. These have defined the theoretical framework we develop in this volume and how we apply it to the major sectoral issues examined. For the authors, at least, it has been a hugely productive discussion. The discussion has been added to in multiple ways by Kyle McNally. He has worked with us throughout, providing outstanding research support, detailed editorial contributions and a fine sense of the issues as they developed throughout the text. His overall contribution has been immense and we are deeply indebted to him. His academic achievements will stand out among the best as time evolves.

We are grateful to Robert O. Keohane and Jessica Green for thoughtful comments on parts of the manuscript, as well as to Irene Spagna, Danielle Stein, Troy Nichols, and Brent Ramsey for providing helpful research assistance at different stages of the project. We would also like to thank Jennifer Jahn, Neil de Cort, and Breffni O'Connor from Polity Press for turning our manuscript into the volume now in your hands, as well as the extraordinary Ann Bone for editing the text with skill and insight. For all worries about the future of publishing, it is striking how high the level of skill and dedication is in producing books and distributing them across the world remains. We are deeply appreciative of these efforts.

Tom Hale
David Held
Kevin Young

Introduction

The director of the European Organization for Nuclear Research (CERN) recently spoke proudly before a gathering of distinguished physicists to announce the discovery of a Higgs boson particle. This fundamental building block of our universe, the so-called "God particle," had been theorized by physicists in the early 1960s, but it took them another 50 years to prove its existence. His comments were brief, but he took care to stress the following to his audience: "It is a global effort, it was a global effort, and it's a global success" (BBC 2012). Behind this triumph of science lie four decades of coordinated intellectual and engineering efforts made possible by international cooperation. Finding the Higgs Boson required the work of thousands of scientists from across the globe working in concert toward a common goal. More specifically, work on the Large Hadron Collider (LHC), which made this discovery possible, involved research work from 608 institutes and universities, carried out by individuals representing 113 different nationalities. The LHC cost approximately £3.5 billion, which was paid for mostly by member and observing countries (20 European, and 6 others, respectively), with continuing research funded by those participating physicists and their organizations. The overhead costs for CERN, an intergovernmental organization founded in 1954, are proportionally distributed among the member countries according to their level of GDP considered in three-year cycles. This complex system of international collaboration has arguably produced one of the most profound discoveries that science can claim to date. Moreover, and simply put, it has been made possible by mechanisms of effective global collaboration.

This kind of success, in which countries work together to achieve a common goal through international institutions, is increasingly rare. The Higgs Boson discovery represents an exception to the rule of growing failure in global governance. Across a range of pressing global issues, countries have proven unable to cooperate effectively on issues of pressing global concern: the acute economic disparities across the globe, growing economic imbalances within and across countries, the lack of effective environmental governance in a world increasingly vulnerable to climate change, the proliferation of nuclear arms and the basic insecurities that persists from violent conflicts, to name just a few. To be sure, effective international cooperation has never been easy, but in recent years the problem seems to have grown worse, making the CERN success all the more remarkable. Why is this so?

This book seeks to answer that question – why and how current efforts to address the most pressing issues of our time seem to have stalled. The Earth has become a "smaller" place over the past century, as our individual and national fates are increasingly intertwined. Our world is now highly enmeshed as trade, finance, communication, pollutants, violence, and many other factors flow across borders and lock the well-being of countries and individuals into common patterns. This has created a system of structural global vulnerability; our actions directly affect the lives of others in distant corners of the world, and vice versa.

Collectively, the world community has sought to establish and maintain institutions that govern its common affairs. These take many forms, but by far the most important have been formal international agreements through which countries bind themselves, under international law, to negotiated commitments. These agreements are often supported by interstate organizations like the United Nations or the International Monetary Fund (IMF), which states create to manage issues or implement policies. Such organizations have mushroomed over the twentieth century. In 1909, 37 intergovernmental organizations existed; in 2011, the number of organizations and their various components had grown to 7,608 (UIA 2011).

Many of these institutions, like CERN, work quite well. Entities like the Universal Postal Union, the International Civil Aviation Organization, and the World Meteorological Organization (WMO) provide extensions of public goods offered by individual states, producing services that no party alone could attain on its own (Burnheim 1986: 222). Much of the day-to-day work of the UN specialized agencies and the technical or adjudicative functions of the World Trade Organization (WTO), IMF, and World Bank are similarly effective. By reducing the costs of complex coordination problems they create global public goods that are mutually beneficial for all participants.

Yet other international organizations and negotiations are wrought with seemingly intractable disagreements: multilateral negotiations in the WTO and the UN Security Council, for example. Preoccupied with questions of war and peace, rule-making and resource allocation, these bodies have always been highly politicized and confrontational. The starting premise of this book is that these perennial difficulties have taken on a new character. In our increasingly interconnected world, global problems, from climate change to financial market crises, call for increased collective and cooperative action, but multilateralism's ability to achieve this has eroded relative to the challenges it faces. Indeed, the massive growth in postwar institutions has begun to slow. Between 1990 and 2000, countries registered 406 new multilateral treaties with the UN Secretary General, as well as 12,566 bilateral ones. In the following decade, they submitted only 262 and 9,484 respectively.

This book focuses on the growing gap between our need for global solutions and the flagging ability of multilateral institutions to meet that need. This represents a breakdown of global cooperation that we call *gridlock*. As used in this book, the term refers to a specific set of conditions and mechanisms that impede global cooperation in the present day. The rise of new powers representing a more diverse array of interests makes intergovernmental agreement more difficult. The problems themselves have also grown harder as global policy issues penetrate ever more deeply into core domestic concerns. Existing institutions, created for a different world, have locked in dysfunctional decision-making procedures, while the proliferation of different organizations renders the institutional architecture ever more fragmented. Together these processes have blocked global cooperation even as we need it more.

We do not agree that gridlock is a complete explanation for all failures in global governance. Nor do we systematically test the basket of factors we term "gridlock" against alternative explanations. Instead, the book seeks to provide an innovative and systematic interpretation of the present challenges facing the multilateral system.

Three characteristics define our argument. First, we show how the multiple factors and pathways mentioned above combine to block cooperation. The drivers are many, but their outcome is the same: a "governance gap" in which crucial needs go unmet. Second, these common blockages can be observed across nearly all areas of global governance, not just within a single issue. In other words, gridlock is a general condition of the multilateral system. Third, the mechanisms we consider are historically contingent, specific to global governance today. Indeed, many are in part products of previous, successful efforts to cooperate across borders. In this sense, they can be thought of as "second order" cooperation problems. Over the postwar period, growing institutionalization has fed interdependence, and greater interdependence has in turn demanded more institutionalization. Through this cycle of *self-reinforcing interdependence*, multilateral institutions have helped create conditions that, ironically, now impede their effectiveness.

The Postwar Legacy

This is a book about the current state of a political system that traces its origins to the end of World War II. Our analysis therefore focuses on the challenges of the present and the near future with an analytic eye to the past. While the book explores international institutional developments prior to World War II, it is this war that provides the crucial backdrop to the story that is set out here. World War II was a calamitous moment not just in European history, but across the world. It reached across continents to create an axis of conflict that pitted countries against each other in a catastrophic war. The death and destruction was of a scale nearly impossible to comprehend, leaving Europe devastated and much of East Asia traumatized. The rise of Nazism and fascism in Europe created in its wake a horrific new form of industrial killing focused on Jews, political dissidents, and many minority groups. The Japanese invasions of China and Southeast Asia were marked by a trail of brutality, as was the march of Stalin's armies through the "bloodlands" between Moscow and Berlin (T. Snyder 2010). The other Allied forces also pushed the boundaries of violence; not only, for instance, in the fire-bombing of Dresden and Tokyo, but also in the first use of nuclear weapons, in Hiroshima and Nagasaki. In these cities men and women were going to work, children were playing, and "more human beings died at once than anyone thought possible" (Kingsolver 2001). World War II brought humanity to the edge of the abyss, yet not for the first time in twentieth-century history.

Politicians who gathered from 45 countries in San Francisco in 1945 were faced with the choice of either allowing the world to drift in the aftermath of the shock of the 1939–45 war, or to begin a process of rebuilding the foundations of their own societies and the international community. Having seen into the abyss, these individuals might have been tempted simply to defend the positions of their own countries and close the shutters on the rest of the world, as, indeed, many had in the 1930s. Yet they understood that doing so would simply reproduce the pattern of economic and political disaster that had spanned the first half of the twentieth century. Accordingly, they set about creating a world order that would be robust enough to sustain peace and economic prosperity. At the center of this vision was the drafting of the Charter of the United Nations which, in its preamble, emphasized that it could no longer be states alone that ordered the world for their own interests. Rather, it must be "We the peoples" who should be bound together in the United Nations.

The UN Charter affirmed the importance of universal principles, human rights, and the rule of law as the cornerstones of the new international order. Its drafters placed the irreducible moral worth of each and every human being at the center of their thinking, along with the principles of equal respect, equal concern and the priority of the vital needs of all people. In so doing, they rejected the view that human well-being can be defined by geographical or cultural location, that national or ethnic boundaries should determine the limits of rights or responsibilities for the satisfaction of basic individual needs, and that belonging to a given community must limit and determine the freedom of individuals. Accordingly, it was envisaged that the United Nations should foster tolerance across the world, develop friendly relations among nations based on respect for the principle of equal rights and self-determination, create unity in strength to maintain international peace and security, establish principles and the institution of methods that would prevent the use of armed force save in the common interest, and would build international machinery for the promotion of the economic and social advancement of all peoples (UN 1945). Such an expansive and radical idealism could only have been forged in a cataclysm on the scale of World War II.

It is, of course, commonplace to criticize the UN for the many ways it and the nations that created it have fallen short of these ideals. Subsequent chapters will discuss these at some length. Yet it would be utterly mistaken to underestimate the successes wrought by the UN system overall and the geopolitical stability that followed its foundation. The decades that followed World War II were marked by peace between the great powers, although there were many proxy wars fought out in the global South. This relative stability created the conditions for what now can be recognized as the almost unprecedented period of prosperity that characterized the 1950s onward. The UN is central to this story, although it is by no means the only important institutional innovation of the postwar settlement. A year prior to the founding of the UN, the Bretton Woods organizations were established in an effort to foster economic cooperation and a prosperous global economy: the IMF and the World Bank (previously the International Bank for Reconstruction and Development). The former focused on exchange rate stability and balance of payments assistance, while the latter on long-term economic development. A sister institution, the General Agreement on Tariffs and Trade (GATT), which would later develop into the WTO, committed countries to open their borders to foreign trade.[1] These institutions and many more specialized ones lay at the heart of postwar economic globalization. While the economic record of the postwar years varies by country, many experienced significant economic growth and living standards rose rapidly across many parts of the world. It was not just the West that was redefined by these developments; a global division of labor emerged which linked economic flows across large swathes of the world. In the wake of these changes, the world began to shift – slowly at first, but later more rapidly – from a bipolar toward a multipolar structure. By the late 1980s a variety of East Asian countries were beginning to grow at an unprecedented speed, and by the late 1990s countries such as China, India, and Brazil had gained significant economic momentum, a process that continues to this day.

The geopolitical stability engendered throughout the postwar years was a precondition for economic globalization, which subsequently transformed the way business and commerce were organized. Markets that were first and foremost domestic networks increasingly took on global dimensions. National economies became heavily enmeshed in the global system of production and exchange. Multinational corporations, many of which came to enjoy turnovers that dwarfed the GDP of even medium-sized nations, expanded across the globe. Financial markets exploded into a world of 24-hour trading, aided by competition between states eager to attract increasingly mobile capital flows. Economic globalization, with all its benefits and costs, winners and losers, came to embrace all regions and continents, and global interdependence deepened to a hitherto unknown degree.

Meanwhile, international cooperation proceeded at an impressive pace. Whereas once participation in the multilateral order was sporadic and tenuous, it became both more entrenched and regularized. The most obvious illustration of this is the rapid emergence of diverse multilateral organizations and transnational agencies. New forms of multilateral and global politics became established, involving states, intergovernmental organizations (IGOs), international nongovernmental organizations (INGOs), and a wide variety of pressure groups. The numbers of active IGOs and INGOs increased exponentially (UIA 2012). There was substantial growth in the number of international treaties in force, as well as the number of international regimes, formal and informal, altering the political and legal context in which states operated (Held et al. 1999: chs 1–2; Held and McGrew 2007: ch. 7). To this dense web of mechanisms of coordination and collaboration can be added the routine meetings and activities of the key international policy-making fora, including not only the UN and Bretton Woods organizations, but also the G-groups (the G5, G7, G20, etc.). Whereas in the middle of the nineteenth century there were just one or two interstate conferences or congresses per annum, the numbers increased into the many thousands each year (UIA 2012). Accordingly, states became enmeshed in an array of global governance systems and arrangements.

At the same time, new kinds of institutional arrangements have emerged alongside formal intergovernmental bodies (Hale and Held 2011). Networks of ostensibly "domestic" government officials now link with their peers across borders (Keohane and Nye 1971; Slaughter 2004b). Different kinds of actors, public and private, form partnerships with each other to tackle issues of mutual concern. And purely private actors have created an array of their own governance institutions, ranging from voluntary regulations to private arbitral tribunals (Büthe 2010). In some ways these new institutions show the adaptability and flexibility of global governance. But they also, we argue below, face significant limitations.

As forums for collaboration and engagement multiplied, they facilitated direct links between world powers, regardless of how explosive the rhetoric between them sometimes became, and opened the door for peripheral states to participate in the global order. Significantly, however, these institutions also embedded in their infrastructures and modus operandi the privileged positions of the 1945 victors. This was, arguably, a compromise needed to give incentives for great powers to participate in the new multilateral order.

Crucially, the success of global cooperation allowed for even greater economic and political transformations. Indeed, once the world started down this path, a self-reinforcing dynamic was created in which interdependence became increasingly institutionalized via interstate cooperation, and institutionalized cooperation created conditions under which globalization could deepen and accelerate, increasing interdependence. At the economic level, the spread of global markets and rapidly expanding economic opportunities created the basis for new powers to enter the world economy. The hierarchical centralized states of the Soviet Union and of Central and Eastern Europe, which could not adapt quickly enough to economic globalization, found themselves outmaneuvered by new patterns of invention, innovation, and investment. When the Cold War ended it was not only because of political pressure and the arms race, but also because of the growing stagnation of the Soviet economy and its satellite states. Economic globalization accelerated the conditions for Japan, South Korea, Taiwan, and later China and other parts of Asia to become major players in the global economy. And as they have done so, the level of interdependence linking all of us together has deepened profoundly.

These transformations have now come to alter the ability of states to cooperate multilaterally. That is, economic and political shifts in large part attributable to the multilateral order are now among the factors grinding that system into gridlock. We term these *second-order cooperation problems*. As new countries emerged to become economic forces in the global economy they sought new forms of political influence and voice. Over time the capacity of the US and Europe to secure or impose international agreements in areas such as trade or security became more difficult. Emerging countries not only wanted a stake in agenda setting and negotiations, they also had the power to get it. Thus, the ground was set for new demands for participation in global institutions and growing expectations of engagement. In many ways, the architects of the UN system could not have known how successful their institutional innovations would become.

However, despite the increase in international and transnational collaboration, the vested interests of the postwar victors remain firmly in place in the core institutional infrastructures of the multilateral order, such as the UN and the Bretton Woods organizations. Whereas once the entrenchment of these interests was key to their participation in building the postwar multilateral order, this dynamic became an obstacle to further multilateral developments as the world became more interconnected. Five states have retained effective control over the UN Security Council (a council comprised of ten nonpermanent members replaced every two years and five permanent members), yet the exclusive privileges of the permanent members (the P-5) are increasingly at odds with the changes in global power structures. All attempts to reform the position of permanent members have failed. In the case of the World Bank, convention dictates that the president is always from the United States, and even when there has been reform, the voting shares of the United States ensures that it retains veto power on all decisions – a privilege also enjoyed by the United States in the IMF.

At the same time, harder global problems have emerged that reflect the deeper level of interdependence made possible by previous cooperation. These problems involve the nature and form of the rule book of the global economy (global financial architecture, trade, investment and competition rules, intellectual property rights, and labor and migration rules), the sustainability of the planet (climate change, biodiversity and ecosystem losses, deforestation and water deficits) and the quality of life chances (global infectious diseases, conflict prevention, combating terrorism, and the fight against poverty) (see Rischard 2002). In other words, they are not merely the distant concerns of diplomats, but rather the basic dilemmas all societies face, penetrating deep into the daily lives of citizens everywhere. And as these new "intermestic" problems arise and new institutions are formed to deal with them (often only partially), the global institutional landscape has grown more crowded and fragmented. Perversely, this ad hoc proliferation of institutions has in some ways reduced our collective capacity to solve new problems as they emerge. Together, these mechanisms have led us to the present gridlock, and are likely to continue into the future.

Overview

The notion of gridlock is explored and more fully developed in chapter 1, which sets out the theoretical foundation for the story that follows. It begins by developing the concept of self-reinforcing interdependence sketched above, and identifies the key milestones in its institutional history. We argue that the previous successes of international cooperation, by facilitating peace and fostering economic linkages, have deepened interdependence to the point where international cooperation is now more difficult. Within this context, we identify four "roads to gridlock" that make up our core argument: growing multipolarity, harder problems, institutional inertia, and fragmentation. These are distinct but interrelated pathways to the present state in which demand for international cooperation exceeds the ability of the multilateral order to supply it.

The chapters that follow explore the onset of gridlock in three sectors of global governance: security, economy, and the environment. We conceive of governance problems as interrelated and overlapping across these different sectors. Indeed, the dynamic of self-reinforcing interdependence we identify in chapter 1 rests on this connection, as peace has facilitated economic linkages and growth, which have in turn created a greater need to manage our global commons. However, we examine each sector in a different chapter for analytic clarity. In each, we begin with the historical context for the institutionalization of global governance. Given the broad range of topics included, these histories are by no means exhaustive, but rather set out the background that is necessary to understand the emergence of gridlock. Having done this, each chapter then examines the causes and dynamics of gridlock that currently pervade existing institutional structures, decision-making, and governance outcomes. Our goal is not to prove, in a social scientific sense, that all the gridlock pathways are the only drivers of governance outcomes in each issue area. Rather, we argue that this basket of factors is responsible for many of the governance failures we see today, and that it is not possible to understand outcomes in each issue area without appreciating the role that these broad, general trends play.

Chapter 2 explores gridlock in the governance of global security. It evaluates the development of sovereignty, international law, human rights, and the general principles of the postwar order. Significantly, these developments gradually changed the meaning of security in the multilateral system. In broad terms the shift from "state security" to "human security" – an incomplete and contested trend – has rendered security issues increasingly interdependent and complex. At the same time, the chapter shows how the development of the UN and the entrenchment of the privileged positions of the 1945 victors have seriously handicapped solutions to traditional issues such as nuclear proliferation and arms control. It also shows how the emergence of harder, transborder problems from terrorism to failed states to piracy are unlikely to be adequately tackled within existing power structures and institutional arrangements. The intergovernmental nature of most security institutions comes into sharp tension with the intermestic issues they now face.

The global economy is taken up in chapter 3. The chapter begins by examining the evolution of postwar global economic governance, tracing the development of multilateral institutions governing international trade and finance. The story of postwar global economic governance is the story of self-reinforcing interdependence par excellence. Existing institutions solve some problems they were initially designed to address, but also fail to address problems which have emerged from the very global economic system they have enabled. Institutional fragmentation in global economic governance is rife; institutional inertia makes many international organizations slow to change even in the face of dramatic governance failures; harder problems have emerged which did not exist during earlier times, and yet the governance capacity to face these problems is weak and often highly ad hoc. Demand has far outstripped supply.

Chapter 4 focuses on efforts to manage our global environment. Since the 1970s scientists have recognized the cross-border and even global reach of environmental threats like air and water pollution, deforestation, species loss, and, perhaps most dangerous of all, human-made climate change. Bluntly put, it will not be possible to maintain our current standard of living, much less provide a better life for the billions who live in deprivation, without better ways to manage these global commons. The chapter shows how intergovernmental efforts to control environmental degradation have been weakened by the gridlock mechanisms. Environmental problems tend to be hard problems, penetrating deep into states to implicate the basic behavior of individuals and companies. They are even more characterized by multipolarity than other issues – China's GDP is half that of the US, but it emits more greenhouse gasses; Brazil, Indonesia, and Mexico each have more biodiversity than the US or Europe – and rich and poor countries tend to disagree over how to prioritize economic growth and environmental protection. Moreover, environmental governance has grown extraordinarily fragmented – there are now hundreds of environmental treaties, but no global regulatory body – hampering effective global policy.

Finally, we conclude in chapter 5 by exploring the overlapping nature of these developments. We argue that the mechanisms of gridlock overlap and affect one another across governance sectors, and that these sectors must be considered in relation to one another. The pathways to gridlock in each respective area of global governance vary, but there is a common result for each: gridlock is likely to continue to be pervasive. Indeed, the pathways to gridlock are likely to deepen in the immediate future. We recognize, however, that the state of gridlock which currently besets the multilateral order should not be conceived of fatalistically or as some inevitable set of processes. The potential exists to transcend this current impasse, and our contribution aims to illuminate the paths that have led us to where we are today, and also the roads and choices that may lie ahead. That said, the conclusion contains no list of (silver) bullet points through which policy-makers could, tomorrow, undo gridlock. Rather, the goal is to identify existing areas of institutional innovation and sources of political agency from which more effective global governance may spring.

Before proceeding it is important to clarify the status of our argument and its relation to existing work. Gridlock is a systemic, historically contingent, and compound argument. It runs against the fashion in both popular and academic writing to reduce social theories to a single soundbite, hypothesis, or factor. The urgency and nature of the current multilateral gridlock justify this departure. From a policy perspective, it is easy to see why. Soundbites make for good rhetoric, but rarely capture the nuance needed to make sense of global politics. At the same time, many analyses of global politics are written in issue "silos" that miss trends across issues or overlaps between them. Global public policy problems like climate change, nuclear proliferation, and global financial crises do not differentiate between discrete areas of academic enquiry.

Political scientists, in turn, tend to pursue general explanations for social phenomena across different times and places. The goal of social science is, after all, to explain the world through patterns and regularities, not just to treat history as "one damn thing after another." As we discuss in chapter 1, this project has been quite successful with respect to international cooperation. Over the last decades the academic literature has identified a wide range of conditions under which international cooperation is more or less likely, as well as the chains of cause and effect that lead to a certain outcome. We draw heavily on these theories in this book. However, we do not seek to explore the conditions that impede multilateral cooperation generally, but rather the conditions *currently* impeding multilateral cooperation. Our explanation therefore highlights a range of mechanisms especially connected to the here and now and to the recent past.[2] Such an approach is grounded in the importance of history – not simply because current problems demand a context in order to be understood, but also for more fundamental reasons. The fact that current gridlock is, as we argue throughout the book, the result, in part, of the existing institutions means that an adequate understanding of the problem is necessarily contextual and historically produced, rather than abstract and reducible to properties which might exist across time and place. In other words, we seek to apply the insights of political science to a specific, real-world problem, not to revamp our abstract, theoretical understanding of international cooperation.

The book, in overview, sits between two subgenres in the broader field of "world affairs" writing. The first may be described as the "global governance" literature, books that seek to explicate global challenges and propose solutions for them. This genre tends to tilt toward the more academic end of the spectrum. Examples include Jean-François Rischard's *High Noon: Twenty Global Problems, Twenty Years to Solve Them* (2002) or Thomas Weiss's *What's Wrong with the United Nations and How to Fix It* (2009). Some edited collections discuss various dilemmas of global governance, for example, *Globalization in Crisis*, edited by Barry Gill (2011).

The second genre is the much larger field of books that discuss global change, especially why and how the growing wealth and power of various non-Western countries will remake world order (or not). Prominent examples include Fareed Zakaria's *The Post-American World* (2008a), Parag Khanna's *How to Run the World* (2011) and *The Second World* (2008), Gideon Rachman's *Zero-Sum World: Power and Politics after the Crash* (2010), or Ian Bremmer's *Every Nation for Itself: Winners and Losers in a G-Zero World* (2012). Each of these books warns of the dire consequences a dearth of global leadership, or a contest for global leadership, will entail.

Beyond these broad trends, several books have explicitly confronted the failures of multilateralism in particular issue areas, often making broader points about international cooperation as well. Prominent examples include Amrita Narlikar's *Deadlock in Multilateral Negotiations* (2010), David Victor's *Global Warming Gridlock* (2011a), and David Humphreys' *Logjam: Deforestation and the Crisis of Global Governance* (2006). As just the titles of these works make clear, the failures of global governance warrant the type of systemic explanation we offer here.

Finally, and perhaps most importantly, we hope our arguments reach not just those who write books about global problems, but the people who confront them. It is crucial to acknowledge the debt our argument owes to the diplomats, activists, businesses, social movements, and other "practitioners" who work to provide the global public goods we so sorely need. These individuals are often all too aware of the challenges we discuss. Perhaps we can do no better than quote a Swedish diplomat reflecting on the challenges of organizing a global environmental organization in 1972:

> The world is divided into sovereign states that are not willing to give up their formal freedom of action. It is one of the ironies of history that the principle of national sovereignty . . . received its triumphal confirmation in the Charter of the United Nations at a time when the introduction of atomic weapons, the development of communications, rapid industrialization, and the awakening consciousness of environmental risks, made it unmistakably clear that all of humanity is interdependent and that the old concept of sovereignty is inadequate . . . Without strong new initiatives from their [specialized agencies'] respective principals they cannot be expected to achieve the effective interdisciplinary co-ordination of environmental endeavours that is now needed. (Quoted in Rowland 1973: 33–4)

1

Gridlock

Ambrogio Lorenzetti learned the virtue of effective governance by being born in Siena, in what is now the center of Italy, in 1290. His city had won its independence from the Church in 1167, and by 1169 had written a constitution that invested decision-making power in a council held accountable, under law, to a broadening proportion of the population. This government kept the peace, enforced the law, and invested in beneficent public works. Prosperity and culture followed. At a time when most of Europe was trapped in feudal misery, the Sienese – and their counterparts in Florence, Venice, and the other centers of what would become the Renaissance – flourished.

Lorenzetti was very clear on the causes of this success. Inside the Palazzo Pubblico, which anchors the unparalleled geometry of Siena's central square, he painted a series of room-sized frescos on both the promise of government (*The Allegory of Good Government*, *The Effect of Good Government on City Life*, *The Effect of Good Government on the Countryside*) and its peril (*The Allegory of Bad Government*, *The Effect of Bad Government on City Life*, and *The Effect of Bad Government on the Countryside*). Under good government the citizens look prosperous, harvests are rich, and even the pigs are plump. Under bad government, buildings have fallen into disrepair, citizens lie dying in the streets, and flames rise from the fields. No pigs can be seen.

The simple idea captured in Lorenzetti's paintings goes a long way toward explaining why polities with what we would now call "good governance" were the first to lead Europeans out of the Middle Ages.[1] That idea has reached its apogee (thus far) in the modern, liberal, social democratic state. By facilitating political conditions in which public needs can be articulated and collective solutions applied, and by balancing private gain and public good, the modern state has shown that the "effects of good government" can extend far beyond a city-state and its surrounding fields. And while the modern state, even in its law-based, constrained, and democratic form, is certainly capable of great wrongdoing, it is arguable that under no other set of institutions in the historical record have so many lived so well.

But some problems defeat even the best governments. In 1348 *Yersinia pestis*, a rod-shaped bacterium, entered Siena inside fleas carried on the backs of rats and inside the clothes of merchants trading with the cities of the eastern Mediterranean and Asia Minor. Within a matter of months more than half the city's population had died, along with, in just a few years, a third of all Europeans – including Lorenzetti himself (Bowsky 1964). Ironically, the speed and devastation of the Black Death were facilitated by the trade routes that had helped to make Siena and the other Italian cities wealthy (Benedictow 2004).

Today, many important policy problems are like the plague; they do not fit neatly into jurisdictional boundaries. And while our governments have (mostly) grown from city-states to nation-states, we do not have a global state – like the one envisioned by Lorenzetti's contemporary Dante in his *De Monarchia* (1312–13) – to tackle the many problems too big for any one country. So how can we bring the "effect of good government" to our globalized society?

Unlike in Renaissance Italy, our society has created a series of powerful tools to manage common problems beyond the state: multilateral institutions. These operate through a logic of intergovernmental cooperation. To solve joint challenges and provide public goods, governments must negotiate with one another to mutually adjust their policies so that the actions of one country help other countries realize their own objectives, and vice versa. A gives B a bit of what B wants, B gives A a bit of what A wants, and everyone is better off.

International institutions are both the products of this process and its facilitators (Keohane 1984). Cooperation is hard. What if one party goes back on their commitment? Or what if there is no clear standard by which to measure compliance? What if you simply can't ascertain whether your partners are complying or not? These kinds of doubts often discourage countries from making mutually beneficial deals. International institutions like the UN or the WTO serve to alleviate these problems in various ways. They act as forums to provide information about other countries' views and actions. They often monitor treaty commitments, like the International Atomic Energy Association's search for illicit nuclear weapons, or adjudicate and enforce them, like the WTO's dispute settlement mechanism. They also define and codify norms of appropriateness that help guide actors' behavior.

These functions help countries to cooperate and provide the governance structures needed in a world where risks – like fleas – spill easily across borders.

Fourteenth-century Europeans did not understand the epidemiology of the plague, but they did grasp that it could be spread from infected individuals to healthy ones. Once news of the plague reached a city, the inhabitants would typically bar the gates in a (usually futile) attempt to keep the sickness outside. But this meant that refugees from infected areas would just continue on to the next city, helping the plague spread. Imagine how history might have been different had the cities of northern Italy been able to coordinate their response through something like the World Health Organization (WHO), agreeing to contain infected individuals in a single geographic location. If Lorenzetti were painting today, he would have to title his fresco *The Allegory of Good Government and International Cooperation*.

The premise of this book is that this crucial political institution – institutionalized intergovernmental cooperation – is facing a period of crisis, which we term *gridlock*. Global governance has certainly never been easy, but it currently faces a new set of challenges. In this chapter we identify four mechanisms that have rendered multilateral cooperation increasingly difficult, four routes or pathways to gridlock. First, the diffusion of power from what used to be known as the industrialized world to the emerging economies has increased the number of actors who must agree – and the diversity of interests that must be accommodated – in order to achieve meaningful cooperation. Second, the institutional legacy of the postwar period has "locked in" policymaking processes that have now grown dysfunctional. Third, the easier items on the cooperation agenda have already been dealt with; yet deeper interdependence creates a need for more sophisticated, complex, and powerful institutions, which are harder to create. Fourth, a proliferation of institutions has led to fragmented "regime complexes" (Raustiala and Victor 2004) that can impede effective cooperation instead of facilitating it.

These reasons share, in part, a common origin. They are all to a significant extent consequences of previous, successful attempts to cooperate multilaterally. Over the last half-century, the postwar order has allowed for a cycle of deepening cooperation and globalization, a process of *self-reinforcing interdependence*. This process, along with other important factors such as technological innovation and the basic logic of capitalist expansion, has led to a deeper level of interdependence than has ever been experienced by the world, one that current multilateral institutions are less and less able to manage effectively. In other words, the postwar order has produced conditions, intended and unintended, which impede further cooperation even as they make it more necessary. The current situation of gridlock is thus not only historically contingent, but is also in crucial ways endogenous to the process of cooperation itself. As such, the four mechanisms highlighted in this chapter can be thought of as "second order" cooperation problems. Rather than stemming from the innate problems of cooperation per se, which are difficult enough, many current problems derive, at least in part, from the very fact of earlier cooperation.

The goal of this chapter is to illuminate the logic of each of these pathways to gridlock. Later chapters will demonstrate how they have made cooperation more difficult in specific policy domains, and indeed, how they can overlap and reinforce one another. Here, however, in the interests of clarity, they are presented as distinct causal pathways. The chapter proceeds as follows. First, we discuss the post-1945 settlement that established the basic institutional building blocks of the postwar order. The decision to establish bodies like the UN or the Bretton Woods institutions proved enormously significant, we argue. Though intimately tied to American power, these institutions also embodied the logic of negotiated international cooperation discussed above. Because they were useful ways for states to manage the challenges of interdependence, they persisted even following the relative decline in American hegemony in the 1970s. Indeed, they facilitated a process through which the world grew ever more institutionalized and interdependent. While conventionally we think of institutionalization as a response to interdependence, here we emphasize that it is also a cause. A relatively stable, peaceful, liberal global order facilitated the radical economic globalization of the postwar era, creating an unprecedented degree of interdependence, partially endogenous to the process of cooperation itself. Though this increase in economic interdependence over time was foreseen and desired by the institutional architects of the 1940s, they could not have imagined how deeply it would alter the world, especially in two unforeseeable ways. First, interdependence spread far beyond its original nexus among the advanced industrial democracies to encompass almost the entire world. Second, previously "domestic" issues like the environment, health, or policing increasingly spilled across borders, acquiring the attributes of interdependence. Indeed, interdependence has grown so pervasive that it has outstripped the traditional mechanism through which governance was "supplied" – state bargaining over institutionalized cooperation. This creates gridlock.

Building the Postwar Order

Before describing how the postwar order initiated a cycle of self-reinforcing interdependence and institutionalization, it is worth noting the monumental tragedy that created the conditions under which such an order could be constructed in the first place. As noted in the introduction, World War II, in which some 50 million people died, made clear the need for an institutionalized system of global governance to maintain peace and prosperity. Indeed, though of course the war had many causes, the weakness of global institutions for both collective security and economic stability was one of the biggest. Consider each in turn.

Following World War I, the victors – especially US President Wilson – attempted to create a system of collective security to ensure that the "war to end all wars" was just that. In creating the League of Nations, countries committed "to respect and preserve as against external aggression the territorial integrity and existing political independence of all Members of the League" (Article 10). But this commitment did not prove credible, for reasons of both design and implementation. The League operated under a principle of consensus, with all countries holding, effectively, a veto over substantive policy decisions (but not procedural matters). This meant that the very countries causing a problem could block efforts to address that problem. But even if the League had been better designed, it was unlikely to succeed because the world's strongest state never joined. President Wilson had lobbied his European allies to adopt a collective security arrangement, only to discover that his own Congress, dominated by isolationist Republicans, refused to join up. Deprived of American support, the League became a noncredible deterrent, and proved toothless against the aggression of the new fascist powers.

At the same time that the League was experimenting with a new form of collective security, global economic governance was in a period of transition and crisis. Prior to World War I, the British Empire had provided the functions needed to sustain economic globalization. British markets bought vast amounts of foreign products. British sterling, linked to gold, provided a stable currency of exchange. British capital financed growth from Patagonia to the Yangtze River Delta. British bankers acted as lenders of last resort to financially distressed markets. And, of course, British gunboats and soldiers eliminated any who threatened economic flows (Kindleberger 1986). These public goods were not provided altruistically; they benefited Britain, its factories, its workers, and its capitalists first and foremost. And cases like the Opium Wars, in which the UK forced the Chinese government to allow its people to buy the narcotic (grown in British-controlled India) so that the UK could balance its current account, showed exactly how vile the nexus of military power, economic interest, and colonial domination could be. And yet the aggregate effect of these policies was to sustain a globalized economic order of unprecedented proportions. The economist John Maynard Keynes described the world before World War I in terms we would find familiar today:

> The inhabitant of London could order by telephone, sipping his morning tea in bed, the various products of the whole earth, in such quantity as he might see fit, and reasonably expect their early delivery upon his doorstep; he could at the same moment and by the same means adventure his wealth in the natural resources and new enterprises of any quarter of the world, and share, without exertion or even trouble, in their prospective fruits and advantages; or he could decide to couple the security of his fortunes with the good faith of the townspeople of any substantial municipality in any continent that fancy or information might recommend. He could secure forthwith, if he wished it, cheap and comfortable means of transit to any country or climate without passport or other formality, could dispatch his servant to the neighboring office of a bank for such supply of the precious metals as might seem convenient, and could then proceed abroad to foreign quarters, without knowledge of their religion, language, or customs, bearing coined wealth upon his person, and would consider himself greatly aggrieved and much surprised at the least interference. (1920: 11–12)

After World War I this system became untenable. The war sapped Britain's capacity and willingness to pay the costs of empire. At the same time, the economic rise of countries like the United States and Germany had challenged Britain's ability to dictate global economic policy, just as the consequences of war reduced Britain's military capacity to enforce it. The functions required to maintain a global economy – open trade, stable exchange rates, basic macroeconomic management, etc. – went unmet.

As Kindleberger (1986) points out, the world's newly minted economic superpower, the United States, might have stepped into this role. But, as with the League of Nations, isolationist impulses concentrated in the Republican Party – which held power for most of this period – won out over internationalist ones. Instead of providing an open market for foreign goods, the United States raised tariffs. Instead of providing liquidity to countries in financial crisis, the United States demanded repayment of outstanding debt. And instead of using its bargaining leverage to push liberal policies on other countries, the United States looked away as country after country emulated it and adopted isolationist, "beggar-thy-neighbor" trade restrictions and currency controls. When the global economy largely collapsed in the 1930s, Britain was unable, and the United States unwilling, to do anything about it (Kindleberger 1986). The resulting worldwide depression laid the social and economic groundwork for extremist politics in Europe and, with it, World War II (see Polanyi 1944).

The victors of World War II were acutely aware of these earlier failings. Global governance had failed in the 1930s, and failed catastrophically. The isolationist policies of the US Republicans in the 1920s and 1930s were a major cause. Seeking to break from earlier patterns, the architects of the postwar order, largely from the Democratic Party, but also including internationalist, anti-communist Republicans, built an international system with an ambition forged in the horrors of the previous decade. The results, though flawed, have underwritten three generations of relative peace and prosperity for much of the world.

As we detail in chapter 2, multilateral approaches to security were institutionalized in organizations such as the United Nations, and expanded in the structures of an emergent body of international law. Whereas previous attempts at global security governance had failed, the United Nations succeeded in key respects. The participation of leading state powers gave the UN system a degree of legitimacy and credibility. However, the UN has not been the only forum for security governance. The tensions of the Cold War facilitated greater interaction between states, and this interaction led to bilateral treaties, regional security communities like the North Atlantic Treaty Organization (NATO) and the Association of South East Asian Nations (ASEAN), and a growing human rights regime that has gradually reshaped the meaning of security in significant ways.

The governance of the global economy was also subject, for the first time, to a set of rules and institutions which sought to generate the conditions for collective global economic prosperity through multilateral cooperation. Institutions such as the IMF, the World Bank, international trade agreements like the GATT, and the plethora of "transgovernmental" organizations that we discuss in chapter 3 represent the outcomes of such efforts. Between the end of World War II and the 1973 oil crisis, the world experienced one of the longest periods of global economic expansion on record. The result was a system of institutionalized cooperation that would set the stage for decades of peace and prosperity.

Explaining the Postwar Order: Hegemony versus Institutions

What explained this remarkable attempt at global governance, and its persistence? Could the project succeed where the victors of World War I had failed? Scholars have offered different explanations to these questions, but getting the answer right matters. We need to understand how international institutions have worked in the past in order to know how they have become gridlocked today, and how we might get around that condition in the future.

The conventional wisdom in the decades after World War II held that the multilateral order was fundamentally a product of American power. So-called "hegemonic stability theory" reasoned that only a superpower could provide the global public goods needed for peace and prosperity, deterring aggression and ensuring a smooth flow of global commerce. After all, as Kindleberger (1986) argued, British hegemonic leadership made the world economy function before World War I, and a lack of US leadership contributed to the Great Depression and World War II. Only when the US finally took up the mantle of global leadership following World War II was the world able to enjoy a peaceful and prosperous Pax Americana (Gilpin 1981). Whether this global order was equitable or just was considered beside the point. In this view, the fact that the British- and American-led systems worked best for the hegemons was necessary for the success of the system. Only the promise of material advantage could induce a powerful state to spend the blood and treasure needed to provide a stable global order. This theory, associated with the Realist school of international relations, held that the postwar order would succeed to the extent the United States retained the capacity and interest to make it succeed.

This view defined itself in contraposition to the idealistic, Kantian theories of international institutions that had been in vogue in the early twentieth century (see Carr 1946). Many observers at that time saw institutions like the League of Nations as a steppingstone toward a more cosmopolitan future in which war would be not just prevented but literally outlawed (as per the 1928 Kellogg-Briand Pact, which was signed by all the countries that would later engage in World War II). In contrast, the United Nations, with its decidedly non-idealistic Security Council, embodies the lesson that international law binds best when backed by power. Indeed, for the hardline Realist, law and institutions are merely superficial – true order comes only from the power behind them (Mearsheimer 1995).

Unfortunately, hegemony is as shaky a foundation for order as idealism, because power tends to shift. While the United States has remained peerless by conventional measures of state power, by the late 1960s its ability to maintain the global order was already being questioned. On the military front, the economic growth and increased conventional and nuclear forces of the Soviet Union created a global challenger to US power. A prolonged, strategically damaging war in Vietnam sapped US resources and morale, and raised questions about its ability to face down challenges across the world. The end of colonialism in Africa and Asia also created new regimes suspicious of Western power; they often oriented themselves toward Soviet or nonaligned foreign policies despite carrots and sticks from Washington. American economic hegemony was similarly coming into question. Facing enormous budget pressures, the US in 1971 abandoned its commitment to a strong dollar fixed to gold, effectively unraveling the postwar currency regime. This blow to the global economy was reinforced by the 1973 oil shock, in which the oil-producing cartel, the Organization of Petroleum Exporting Countries (OPEC) reduced supply to punish the United States for its support for Israel. Meanwhile, Europe and Japan had enjoyed a postwar economic boom that was bringing them closer to the United States in market size, with companies that were outcompeting US firms in key industries like automobiles. While the United States remained unquestionably the most powerful state in economic and military terms, its ability to coerce other states into a system of global order was reduced.

And yet, contra hegemonic stability theory, the central institutions of the postwar global order largely persisted through these shifts. Why? An important part of the answer lies in the nature of the multilateral postwar institutions. Just as the nineteenth-century system owed its creation to the British Empire, and served its interests, postwar institutions were of course shaped first and foremost by the United States. But, crucially, they also served the needs of a broader range of interests, and, because of their formal, law-based, and ultimately liberal nature, they even put some degree of constraint on the hegemon. The United States, in turn, accepted these constraints, in order to secure the compliance of others. Ikenberry's *After Victory* explains this bargain clearly: "The United States sought to take advantage of the postwar juncture to lock in a set of institutions that would serve its interests well into the future, and, in return, offered – in most instances quite reluctantly – to restrain and commit itself by operating within an array of postwar economic, political, and security institutions" (2001: 164).[2]

This logic of negotiated and institutionalized cooperation lies at the heart of our understanding of international institutions today, and Keohane's appropriately titled *After Hegemony* (1984) remains its clearest statement. For Keohane, international institutions are not mere screens for state power, and nor are they idealistic servants of the global public good (cf. Keohane and Martin 1995; Mearsheimer 1995). Rather, institutions are a tool states can use to solve a cooperation problem they otherwise could not. Consider a situation, such as trade, or disarmament, or the environment, in which the policy of one country affects the interests of another, and vice versa. This cross-border interdependence is the defining feature of the postwar era. Under these conditions, both countries may be better off if they adjust their policies in order to better accommodate the other. For example, if air pollution from a factory in one country is blowing across the border into its neighbor, which in turn has a factory spewing sludge into a river that flows downstream into the first country, scope for a deal exists in which both countries agree to limit pollution. In this simple example, there is likely to be limited need for an institution because countries can easily understand the problem and make a one-off deal to solve it. But the real world is of course far more complicated. Consider climate change, in which all 190-odd countries in the world contribute to the problem to different degrees. It is impossible to imagine each country simultaneously negotiating a deal with each other country to mutually restrict pollution. The transaction costs of such negotiations would be overwhelming. Instead, it makes far more sense for countries to come together in a central forum, in this case the UN Framework Convention on Climate Change, to negotiate a deal.

Institutions make bargains easier to strike for other reasons as well. They link "one-off" interactions into a longer-term process characterized by repeated interactions. If countries know they must negotiate with each other continuously into the future, they will be less likely to cheat on their past commitments. Doing so would hurt their reputation, making it more likely that other countries would not bargain with them in the future. Game theorists call this institution-induced incentive "the shadow of the future," and we can see its impact in, for example, trade rounds. Under first the GATT, and now the WTO, countries have locked themselves into an ongoing series of negotiations, so failing to comply with earlier deals will make other countries less likely to make concessions in the future.

In addition to linking past and future interactions, institutions help countries link issues together (Davis 2004). Countries may find that, for some issues, there is simply no scope for an international agreement on a given issue. Each country's minimum offer is just too high for the other to accept. When those kinds of intractable disputes can be credibly linked to other bargains, the incentives can change entirely. Again, trade is a quintessential example. If countries had to set tariff levels for only one product – especially a politically sensitive one – it would be hard for countries to make a deal. But if one country is able to trade, say, concessions on rice in exchange for increased reductions on cars, cooperation becomes much more likely. Within each dimension, there is no scope for a deal. But once the field of negotiation is expanded to include both issues, the logjam loosens.

But institutions do far more than simply ease the logistics of diplomacy. After a bargain is struck, institutions can help states make these deals credible – more than just words on paper. They precisely define what constitutes compliance and noncompliance. When questions of cheating arise, they can provide processes for resolving disputes and punishing violators. None of these functions are a panacea. For an institution to be effective, the states that create it have to *want* it to be effective, and design it accordingly. That will only happen when there are mutually advantageous deals to be struck. But even with those restrictions, international institutions can accomplish a lot. The WTO's dispute settlement mechanism, for example, has proven enormously successful at forcing countries to comply with their international trade obligations (chapter 3). Or consider the Montreal Protocol that committed countries to reduce ozone-depleting chemicals (chapter 4). Developing countries were only willing to sign on if rich countries were willing to share the replacement technologies their companies had developed. This was accomplished – to the mutual benefit of rich and poor countries, and their companies – through special international technology panels created by the treaty.

Finally, these "functional" explanations for institutions can become entrenched over time. As world politics grows institutionalized, institutional strategies increasingly become "rules of thumb" for policymakers (Schelling 1980), with both bureaucracies and individuals habituating themselves to multilateral processes. While none of this removes national interest or power politics from the equation, it does lead states to believe they will benefit, on average, from a system of "diffuse reciprocity" in which "wins" and "losses" balance out over time (see Ruggie 1993; Axelrod and Keohane 1985).

This view of institutions, while less dependent on raw power than the Realist perspective, still remains quite far from the idealistic, Kantian view of world politics rationalized by law. We would still expect the institutions created to serve powerful states' interests first and foremost, and indeed to serve the powerful interests within those states. When countries cannot agree on policy, no institution will force them into a deal. And few institutions can ever compel compliance from a state when its core interests lead it to go back on a deal. The postwar order, then, though not a mere veil for American power, was certainly a system designed to serve the needs of powerful countries and the powerful interests within those countries.

The Effect of the Postwar Order: Self-Reinforcing Interdependence

Institutionalist theory explains why states will create and maintain international institutions even in the absence of a hegemon, but only if they have an interest in doing so. What causes this "demand" for global governance (Keohane 1982)? The answer is interdependence, or "situations characterized by reciprocal effects among countries or among actors in different countries" (Keohane and Nye 1977: 7). In other words, if what happens in country A affects country B, and vice-versa, both countries may stand to gain by cooperating.

The most important change in politics since 1945 is that this condition – what happens in country A affects country B, and vice versa – has become omnipresent through a process of globalization. Globalization can be defined as a transformation in the spatial organization of social relations, an increase in their extensity, intensity, velocity, and impact. This process – or set of processes – generates transcontinental or interregional flows and networks of activity, interaction, and the exercise of power (Held et al. 1999). The result of these changes is a far deeper form of interdependence than was imagined by the creators of the postwar order. Already in the 1970s Keohane and Nye were referring to the phenomenon of "complex interdependence."[3] Three decades later, that extensive and variegated mutual dependency has only increased. As we argue below, it has reached a point at which the basic functionalist logic through which interdependence-based demand for global governance was supplied by cooperation between states has become far more difficult.

First, however, it is important to understand how interdependence got to this point. We argue that the success of the postwar order is a crucial yet often underappreciated element of this story. In the Keohanian logic described above, interdependence is what creates "demand" for international institutions. Here we want to emphasize that over time the causal arrow also flows the other way. Postwar institutions created conditions under which actors could benefit from forming multinational companies, investing abroad, developing technologies for global production chains, and other activities associated with globalization. These choices, combined with the expansionary logic of capitalism and basic technological innovation, changed the nature of the world economy, radically increasing dependence on people and countries from every corner of the world. This interdependence, in turn, created demand for further institutionalization, which states provided, seeking the benefits of cooperation, beginning the cycle anew. Throughout the postwar period, through the end of the Cold War and beyond, the world has enjoyed a period of *self-reinforcing interdependence* (figure 1.1).

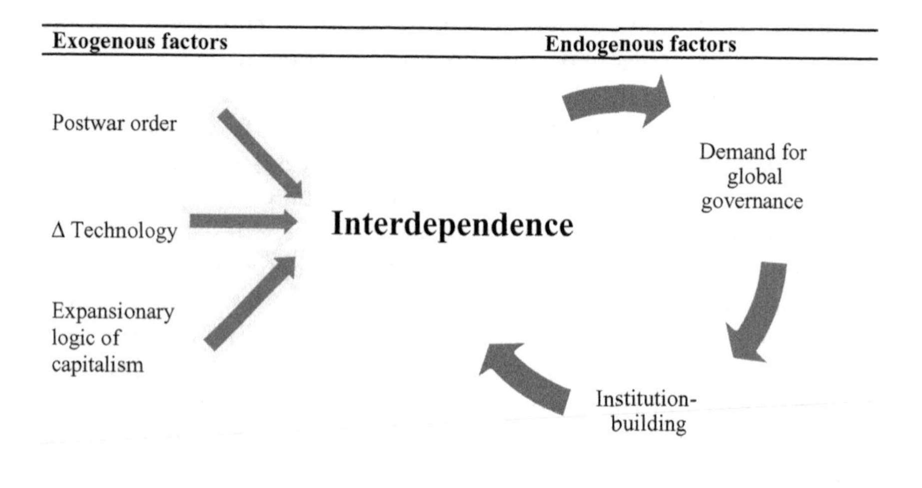

Figure 1.1 Self-reinforcing interdependence in the postwar period

Intended consequences: a global economy and a stable international order

This two-way, positive relationship between interdependence and institutionalization should not be surprising because building economic interdependence was an explicit part of the American postwar plan. Speaking at his inauguration in 1949, US President Harry Truman argued: "we must carry out our plans for reducing the barriers to world trade and increasing its volume. Economic recovery and peace itself depend on increased world trade." Two years earlier, Secretary of State George Marshall made a similar argument in a speech at Harvard, introducing the postwar reconstruction plan that would bear his name, stating, "It is logical that the United States should do whatever it is able to do to assist in the return of normal economic health in the world, without which there can be no political stability and no assured peace" (Marshall 1947). A geopolitical concern underlay these policies. The United States saw economic growth and liberalization as the best way to counter Soviet influence in Europe and in the developing world. A robust, linked world economy would therefore serve the core interests of the United States. The architects of the postwar order therefore explicitly hoped to bring the economies of the world – at least outside the Soviet bloc – closer together. But what are the actual mechanisms through which successful institutionalization promotes deeper interdependence? Here we identify several.

Many derive from the basic logic of a market economy. First, the postwar economic order gave companies an incentive to organize themselves multinationally, creating new stakeholders for liberal institutions (Milner 1987). Once barriers to trade and investment began to fall, companies seeking new markets for their goods rushed to expand abroad. In the immediate aftermath of the war, it was primarily American firms that had the resources to grow. But European and Japanese firms soon followed. When enough companies come to depend on global supply chains, globalization acquires a powerful constituency. Consider General Motors. The firm was such an American icon that its president, Charles Wilson, was appointed in 1953 to serve as Secretary of Defense. He is frequently quoted as stating at his confirmation hearings that "What is good for GM is good for the country." While the phrase has become a shibboleth for corporate influence in politics, Wilson actually said, "for years I thought what was good for our country was good for General Motors, and vice versa." The fates of the company and country were indeed linked. GM was the world's largest private employer at the time – with the vast majority of its employees in the US – and the first company to pay more than $1 billion in taxes (General Motors 1956). Today GM is still one of the world's largest companies, but it produces cars and trucks in over 30 countries. Of its 250,000 workers, 150,000 reside outside the United States (Besinger 2008).[4]

Second, corporate expansion was also closely linked to foreign direct investment. In 1970 global FDI flows totaled approximately $13 billion. By 2011, this figure had climbed to $1.5 trillion.[5] To put that into perspective, the global economy expanded to approximately 20 times its size during that period, yet FDI flows increased 113 times.[6] FDI is a particularly binding form of interdependence, because it represents a sunk cost. A company has an interest in global interconnectedness if its customers are in other countries, but it has an even stronger interest if its factories, R+D facilities, and managers are as well.

Third, much credit for globalization has rightly been given to technological advances. Tools invented for military or other applications (e.g. microprocessors, the Internet) have allowed businesses to communicate instantaneously at almost zero cost, organize data on a vast scale, and engage with customers in thousands of new ways. These capacities also underpin the globally distributed supply chains that have come to characterize an increasing share of the economy. However, it is important to realize that though the invention of the basic technology might have been unrelated to the global order, developing and applying it to global business only occurred because firms saw it was profitable to do so. Without the facilitative conditions of an institutionalized liberal order, companies would have had no reason to invest in the technologies and processes that we now know to have reshaped the world economy. Again, this process is characterized by path dependency. Once the technology exists to run a business globally, there will be more companies who come to depend on that kind of business model, and thus more political support for the liberal global order.

Finally, globalization has profoundly reshaped the division of labor, again in ways that reinforce interdependence. At the start of the industrial revolution, workers in wealthy countries were strong supporters of globalization because the world bought the products made in their factories. But globalization has turned these incentives on their head. The post-1945 global order allowed production to be shifted to lower wage countries, challenging industrial workers in developed countries to compete. It is no accident that much production shifted to countries where workers enjoyed fewer rights, and wielded less collective bargaining power. Industrial workers in developed countries have thus sometimes sought to oppose liberalization, believing that restrictions on trade would help keep manufacturing and jobs in the industrialized world. Shifts within the organized labor movement itself (such as the relative rise of public sector unions) and the declining political power of labor's protectionist elements weakened a further barrier to economic globalization (see Ellis and Smith 2007; Mosley and Uno 2007).[7]

All of these processes highlight how globalization, interdependence, and the set of liberal international institutions that undergirded them have reinforced one another in the decades since World War II. The point is not that international institutions have been the only cause of the dynamic globalization we experience today. As mentioned above, changes in the nature of global capitalism, including breakthroughs in transportation and information technology, are obviously critical drivers of interdependence. However, all of these changes were allowed to thrive and develop because they took place in an open, peaceful, liberal, institutionalized world order. By preventing World War III and another Great Depression, the multilateral order arguably did just as much for interdependence as microprocessors or email (Mueller 1990; O'Neal and Russett 1997).

Unintended consequences: new powers and new issues

Deepening interdependence was a logical consequence of the liberal institution-building that followed World War II. But other aspects were perhaps unforeseen. These unintended consequences have been as much a part of endogenous interdependence as growing economic linkages, widening its scope in two ways: the number and type of countries implicated and the range and depth of issues covered.

First, the world economy has become, more than ever before, a global economy. Following the war, interdependence was largely a characteristic of the West and Japan, and global output was concentrated in those countries. In 1960 the high-income OECD countries made up 75 percent of global GDP, and as recently as 2000 they still accounted for 78 percent. Today, that figure is 63 percent. The United States, in turn, went from making up 38 percent of global GDP in 1960 to just 22 percent today.[8] Similar shifts can be seen clearly in figure 1.2.

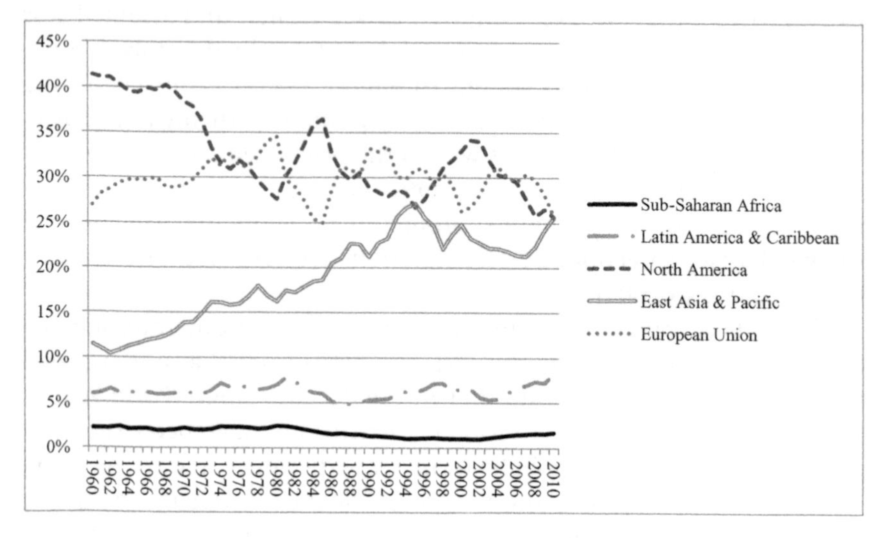

Figure 1.2 Changing contributions to global GDP by region

Source: World Bank World Development Indicators.

While the postwar order was meant to create a market-based world economic system open to all who would play by the rules, it was unclear that such a system would allow for such a massive shift of industrialization and economic growth from the United States and Europe to the emerging economies of the global South. For example, over the last half-century, East and Southeast Asia have more than doubled their share of world GDP and increased per capita income at an average growth rate almost two and a half times that in the rest of the world (see Quah 2008). The result has been not just a deepening of interdependence, but a widening of the phenomenon beyond the core of advanced countries. It is difficult to overstate the magnitude of this change, or its importance for global politics. Countries' fates are linked not just to one or two neighbors, but to a wide array of countries spanning the globe. Moreover, these interdependencies are no longer confined to a single group of countries (e.g. the West, or industrialized democracies) but to a diverse range of economies, regime types, and cultures.

Of course, economic might has not diffused evenly throughout the world. Rather, a key feature of this shift is the emergence of new powers, countries like China, India, and Brazil, whose economies are likely to rival and then surpass those of Japan, European countries, and even the United States in the medium term, although such predictions always contain significant uncertainty (World Economic Forum 2012: 3). This rising multipolarity, combined with globalization, is a powerful driver of interdependence, because it increases the number of powerful countries whose consent is required for cooperation, while simultaneously decreasing the leverage of any one country – even the most powerful – to compel a certain outcome. Put simply, the number of "veto players" (Tsebelis 2002) in global governance has increased. The rise of new powers and the widening of interdependence are of course caused by many factors. But, as with economic globalization, a stable, peaceful liberal global order has been a key enabling condition.

First, and most directly, the liberal order has allowed those developing countries with the capacity to take advantage of global economic flows to do so. For strong developmental states like Japan, the East Asian "tigers," and, of course, China, this global economic context has been crucial. Each of these states adopted an export-led growth strategy, using disciplined, educated workforces and state direction of investment to attract foreign capital for increasingly advanced manufacturing processes. This industrial strategy, which has brought more human beings out of poverty than ever before in human history, simply would not have been possible without a global context in which relatively underdeveloped states could take advantage of a thriving, open global market.

Second, other types of states have also benefited from an institutionalized world economy. A secure trade in natural resources and agricultural products has led to transformative growth in Brazil and allowed Russia to maintain an outsized presence in global trade. India, though less cohesive and less developmentalist than its neighbors to the east, has been able to exploit its natural advantages in linguistic skills, education, and historical linkages to become a global presence in service-related fields ranging from backroom operations and call centers to cutting edge software development and medicine. Again, none of this would have been achievable without the institutionalized certainty that current conditions of economic globalization have provided.

Third, the importance of the geopolitical stability created by the postwar order cannot be underestimated. Historically, rising powers have typically set off arms races. The postwar order has been remarkably different. By reducing the possibility of interstate war, international institutions have allowed many states to rise peacefully. Europe and Japan rebuilt their war-torn economies under the aegis of

American military protection. Far from threatening American interests, their growth reinforced them. Countries like South Korea, Brazil, Mexico, and South Africa have all grown into potent economies without provoking more established powers into trying to keep them weak.

Opinion is, of course, more divided in the case of China. Zheng Bijian, a prominent foreign affairs expert connected to Chinese policymakers, has described China's trajectory as a "peaceful rise," a usage employed by the government itself. Others are less sanguine, arguing that regardless of China's public statements, its true policy is one of *taoguang yanghui* ("hide brightness, cultivate shadow"), or concealing its true strength and intentions while it grows. The basic point, however, remains. The United States, Japan, Europe, and other established powers have not sought to hamper China's rise by attacking its economy. Instead, they have actively encouraged China's growth and engagement in the world economy. China, in turn, has not hinted that it wishes to radically overhaul the global order, and, indeed, why would it? Although it wishes to maintain a military option with respect to Taiwan and islands in and around its territorial waters, China stands to gain little from disrupting the system from which it benefits so immensely.

In addition to implicating new countries, contemporary interdependence has also come to characterize a wider swath of issues. Again, part of this shift is attributable to the success of postwar cooperation. The founders of the postwar order could not have foreseen how a liberal international architecture would combine with changes in technology and mobility to give what were once considered domestic problems a global dimension. The principal concern of the postwar order was international peace (defined as nonconflictual maintenance of the status quo) and moderated economic liberalism. But the interdependence this system created has had deep implications across the entire range of political issues, even topics once thought to be local concerns.

Consider how the rise in global mobility has affected how we keep ourselves healthy. Diseases deriving from unsafe animal handling practices (e.g. swine or avian flu) can now be carried across the world in a matter of days. The safety of a child in London depends on the sanitation procedures used by a chicken farm in Vietnam; the health of the American public depends on public health programs in Mexico. Or consider another issue of basic security – protecting civilians from extremist groups. While such groups have always used violence against civilians to push political goals, the way networks like al-Qaeda are able to recruit members, gather resources, and coordinate deadly attacks from anywhere in the world makes them especially dangerous.

The global mobility of capital, which far exceeds the mobility of labor, has led to transmission effects which are even more striking. In 2008–2009, mortgage defaults in the United States led to a global financial crisis that spread to affect every country in the world, with powerful local effects. Such effects have set back global welfare goals such as the Millennium Development Goals considerably, and have had negative effects on vulnerable groups. The enrollment of children in primary school, for example, suffered from these events – with the hardest effect on young girls (ILO 2009; World Bank 2009b).

Perhaps the most vivid new issue to fall under the logic of interdependence is our common home. Nearly 70 years of breakneck industrialization, facilitated by economic globalization, has put humanity within reach of exhausting the planet's capacity to sustain life as we know it. The ability of each of us to enjoy clean air, clean water, and a safe climate increasingly depends not just on our own actions, or on those of our neighbors or fellow citizens, but on the actions of each of the Earth's 7 billion inhabitants. This creates a new and powerful form of interdependence – the tragedy of the commons – which the founders of the global order could not conceive of in 1945.

Note also that the increasing range of issues characterized by interdependence compounds the first unintended consequence, the spread of interdependence to include a host of new countries. When more issues matter in a global context, even medium or small countries have a chance of becoming a "superpower," or at least a veto player, in something, even if in conventional economic and military terms they remain relatively undeveloped. For example, in chapter 4 we will see how relatively small tropical countries used their status as the world's greatest possessors of tropical forests to block global regulation of deforestation. Because wealthy countries came to care about rainforests, a country like Malaysia found itself in a strong bargaining position. Keohane and Nye (1977) termed this relationship "asymmetric interdependence" – when one party needs another more than that party needs them – and note it as a key power resource. As the range of issues affected by interdependence increases, the chances that previously unimportant countries will gain this kind of leverage also increase, flattening the global distribution of power even further.

The core of self-reinforcing interdependence lies in the globalization of the world economy, in the intended and unintended consequences of the postwar order. But as we have discussed, issue areas affect each other in profound ways. Economic connections could only take place in a context of peace between the great powers. In turn, by catalyzing the growth and diffusion of industrialization, economic linkages generated new kinds of interdependencies, such as the management of the global commons. Moreover, within the non-economic realms, other processes of self-reinforcing interdependence were at work. In security, for example, the normative changes inspired by the UN Charter, the Universal Declaration of Human Rights, and other elements of the postwar order led to a gradual shift in how we perceive security (chapter 2). Instead of caring just about the preservation of borders, our concerns now touch on how governments treat their own citizens, linking us together far more deeply. Similarly, environmental issues have undergone a step-change from merely cross-border problems like transboundary air pollution, to truly global ones like climate change. The actions of anyone, anywhere, now truly affect everyone, everywhere. The postwar institutions helped to create this new world, but they were not built for it.

Roads to Gridlock

For all these reasons, globalization, interconnectedness, and interdependence weigh much more heavily on politics than they did in 1945. The need for international cooperation has never been higher. Yet the "supply" side of the equation, institutionalized state cooperation, has stalled. We identify four reasons for this blockage, four pathways to gridlock: multipolarity, institutional inertia, harder problems, and institutional fragmentation (summarized in table 1.1). Each pathway can be thought of as a growing trend that embodies a specific mix of causal mechanisms. These mechanisms of gridlock are at least in part products of previous cooperation, and so can be understood as "second-order" cooperation problems. Therefore, they are qualitatively different from the cooperation problems faced in 1945 or in the decades that followed. They are not alternatives to existing theories of international cooperation – the bargaining logic described above – but rather as a supplement to them.

For clarity we present the gridlock mechanisms as distinct causal pathways. However, it is important for our argument to recognize the ways in which contemporary problems in global governance build upon each other. Ours is a compound argument in at least three respects. First, gridlock is characterized by "equifinality," which means

Table 1.1 Pathways to gridlock and their mechanisms

Pathway	Mechanism
Growing multipolarity	1 Increased transaction costs 2 Exacerbated legitimacy dilemma 3 Divergence of interests
Institutional inertia	1 Formal lock-in of decision-making authority 2 Entrenchment of cognitive and organizational focal points
Harder problems	1 Extensity: scope of problems has increased 2 Intensity: problems penetrate more deeply into societies
Fragmentation	1 Increased transaction costs 2 Inefficient division of labor 3 Excessive flexibility

that the same outcome – multilateral failure – can have several possible causes (Ragin 1987; Mahoney 2000; Braumoeller 2003). We highlight four possible pathways to gridlock – growing multipolarity, institutional inertia, harder problems, and fragmentation. Some of these pathways may be more important than others in specific instances. For example, multipolarity is more important in multilateral trade negotiations than in financial governance (chapter 3). Fragmentation is particularly pervasive in global environmental governance (chapter 4), but is less central to the causes of gridlock in security governance (chapter 2). Nonetheless, the multiplicity of factors impeding effective global governance is an important element of gridlock.

Second, and related, we argue that gridlock is a product of conjunctural causation. It is not just that each mechanism individually contributes to gridlock in an additive fashion (although they do). The pathways also overlap and interact to erect barriers to cooperation that are greater than the sum of their parts. For example, in environmental politics institutional inertia and multipolarity both limit successful cooperation in their own right. Inertia has replicated dysfunctional decision-making processes and multipolarity has broadened the range of preferences that must be accommodated (chapter 4). But in security, the combination of institutional inertia and increasing multipolarity has had an even stronger effect, locking in hierarchies like the permanent members of the UN Security Council that are increasingly at odds with the contemporary distribution of power (chapter 2).

Finally, the gridlock mechanisms do not just block multilateral processes through their additive and compound effects, they also help to drive each other, further exacerbating the problem. Harder problems like financial regulation, for example, have been divided up into manageable sub-problems and delegated to technocratic bodies (chapter 3). But this strategy in turn led to an increase in fragmentation that later undercut the effectiveness of global governance.

In sum, the impact of the gridlock mechanisms on cooperation is multiple, conjunctural, and compound. The complexity of these causal pathways is another reason why this book takes a holistic approach to understanding failures in multilateralism. To grasp the full nature of the problem we need to look beyond mono-causal explanations. As we show in chapter 5, for example, these features of gridlock have consequences for how contemporary global governance challenges might be solved; the different pathways require different solutions and there is no "silver bullet."

Growing multipolarity

In 1946 the UN General Assembly had 51 member states. Decolonization, the end of the Soviet Union, and self-determination movements have since added 142 more, for a grand total of 193. Of course, many of these countries carry little weight in global politics. But even if we look only at the countries that matter a great deal, that list has grown considerably since 1945. Back then, as hegemonic stability theory argued, the United States mattered far more than anyone else. The UK remained influential in the design of global economic institutions, and the Soviets had to be negotiated with on the security front, but the total number of actors to coordinate for most issues could be counted on one hand. Deals were relatively easy to make. Just two decades later, the economic landscape was radically different, with Western Europe and Japan quickly regaining the economic ground lost during the war. Today, of course, in the wake of the 2008–9 crisis, the list of countries has grown longer still. As noted above, interdependence has widened to cover a much larger swath of the world than ever before.

The so-called "rise of the rest" (Zakaria 2008b) is, in historical terms, simply a return to normal. It is also, without hyperbole, one of the greatest successes in the history of human betterment. Hundreds of millions of people in dozens of countries are leading much longer, richer, fuller lives than their predecessors (see Held and Kaya 2007). However, the argument in this book is that the successes of yesterday spawn the challenges of tomorrow. As emerging economies become wealthier, this increases multipolarity in the world, creating three specific barriers for international cooperation. First, it increases the transaction costs of negotiating agreements. Second, to overcome these costs, countries must increase delegation to institutions, and centralization within those institutions, to achieve effective cooperation, potentially raising concern about their fairness. Third, the increasing prominence of a diverse range of countries has led to a divergence in the interests of the countries that matter most in world politics, shrinking the space for mutually beneficial deals. Consider each of these mechanisms in turn.

First, the problem of transaction costs. At the most basic level, the more countries there are around a negotiating table, the more work is needed to figure out what kind of deal suits everyone. As anyone who has witnessed a multilateral forum can attest, these transaction costs can be substantial barriers to cooperation.

The transaction costs associated with large groups also change the incentives for leadership on behalf of individual actors. Mancur Olson's landmark book, *The Logic of Collective Action*, introduced a truism into the study of politics: "the larger the group, the less it will further its common interests" (1965: 36). His reasoning was as follows. In small groups, each individual has a good chance of getting a decent share of the fruits of the group's collective labors. He or she also knows that their contribution to the shared task will determine whether there are any fruits at all. But when too many are involved, any one individual's gains reduce accordingly, eventually becoming so small as not to be worth the effort. This is especially true if the individual knows other people will produce the benefit anyway, no matter what he or she does. After all, the individual's contribution is negligible in such a large group. Unfortunately, everyone else knows this too. The result is that things don't get done, even if everyone wants them.

Olson was mostly concerned with groups of individuals, but students of global politics have applied his ideas to multilateral diplomacy. A common critique of the UN climate negotiations is that they simply involve too many countries. David Victor, for example, has argued: "One of the chief strengths of the UN system – that it involves every nation on the planet – is a huge liability for global warming. By working in large groups, UN talks are often held hostage to the whims of even small players" (2011b).

Though the transaction costs stemming from the 300 percent increase in states over the last 70 years are large, they are not insurmountable. Indeed, this is exactly how international institutions like the UN can facilitate cooperation. National politicians, especially in the US, like to criticize the UN as a waste of money, but think about how much more money would be wasted coordinating diplomacy without a universal forum.

However, to provide the information and coordination that can facilitate intergovernmental cooperation, even in large group settings, international institutions must often centralize authority. The "rational design" literature in international relations notes that as the number of actors increases, institutions will need to become more centralized to make policy coordination more efficient (Koremenos et al. 2001). We see this in settings like trade negotiations or climate talks, where a small group of countries typically negotiate a deal among themselves on the sidelines of a meeting before bringing it to the full plenary.

Third, increasingly multipolarity means more power for countries that are often very different from the established powers economically, culturally, and politically. Table 1.2 compares the group of states that were world economic leaders in 1960 with those that can be considered leading economies in 2010. At the start of the postwar

Table 1.2 Comparison of world economic powers of 1960 with world economic powers of 2010

Year	Country	GDP/capita (2000 US$)	Life expectancy at birth
1960	United States	13,723	69.8
	European Union*	6,077	69.4
	Japan	7,775	67.7
	Standard deviation	*4,015*	*1.1*
2010	United States	37,329	78.2
	European Union	19,359	79.7
	Japan	39,972	82.9
	China	2,426	73.3
	India	794	65.1
	Brazil	4,716	73.1
	Standard deviation	*17,728*	*6.3*

*Average for future EU members.
Source: World Development Indicators 2011.

period the leading countries were remarkably similar, though the United States was significantly richer than the war-devastated economies of Europe and Japan. In 2010 the richest economies were two orders of magnitude richer, on a per capita basis, than the countries they must now coordinate economic policy with. It should therefore come as no surprise that these countries pursue a wider range of interests. This is probably the most important way in which rising multipolarity challenges cooperation. The countries that must agree are not just greater in number, they disagree more sharply.

Consider the economic realm. Britain and the United States had sharp disagreements about the way the international financial institutions (IFIs) should be run (see chapter 3). But ultimately these were squabbles between countries with similar domestic institutions and similar economies. Even when those institutions were discarded in the 1970s, the range of actors that mattered to the global economy – North America, Western Europe, and Japan – were all wealthy, liberal, market democracies. Today, the list of countries to be coordinated includes rich and poor, liberal and illiberal, industrial, postindustrial, and agricultural and resource-based economies. These divergent conditions produce different national interests and different agendas. Consider intellectual property rights and medicines. Western countries, whose pharmaceutical firms invest billions in research, have argued for strong patent protections. Countries facing wide-scale disease challenges, like South Africa, have made a moral case for less stringent requirements, and countries like Brazil or India, where companies mass-produce generic drugs, have an economic interest in the production of generic rather than patented drugs. These same countries, in turn, have demanded strong intellectual property protections for their plant life, arguing that foreign companies have copied compounds found in indigenous flora and resold them as medicines. Given this divergence of interests, it is a small wonder that intellectual property rights remain a perennial sticking point of international negotiations.

Or consider the new realm of global environmental governance, in which the divergence of interests between the North and the South is perhaps the dominant theme. It is not difficult to understand why a country like Germany will make different policy choices over environmental protection and economic growth than a country like India might. Even though India will suffer much more from environmental degradation, especially climate change, than Germany will, it is also far more constrained in what it can do about it. A deal on mutually beneficial policy adjustment is therefore difficult to reach.

Even in the security realm, interests have shifted in a way that makes deals harder to strike. The postwar world was defined by the struggle between the United States and the Soviet Union. At first glance it seems as if the world could not have been more divided and conflictive. But the Cold War bifurcation was actually remarkably successful at aligning most of the other countries in the world (even those officially within the Non-Aligned Movement) along the East–West axis, imposing a kind of tense stability. It even brought China and the United States together against the common Soviet foe. And even though the interests of the Western and Eastern blocs diverged, they in fact shared a fundamental interest in avoiding nuclear war. The basic deal of the Cold War – if you don't try to end the world, I won't either – proved remarkably resilient (although it was difficult to know this at the time).

The end of the Cold War removed this strict ordering of interests, and the relatively easy bargaining it facilitated. Today even the closest of allies within the NATO alliance disagree about military actions, for example in Iraq or Libya. For example, the US-led coalition that invaded Iraq in 2003 had the strong support of Britain but not of France. The Libyan intervention was led by Britain and France, with strong reservations from Germany, which did not support resolution 1973 (that authorized military action), while the US remained content to follow a policy of "leading from behind." The other members of the Security Council had even more divergent views.

Finally, the cultural diversity among countries should also be considered. On the one hand, it seems plausible that the globalization of communications has promoted greater intercultural understanding. But this is by no means inevitable. Hedley Bull argued that far from the globalization of communication easing understanding and the translation of ideas between peoples, it seems to have highlighted what it is that people do not have in common and find dislikable about each other (1977: 127). Either way, it seems clear that our capacity to understand one another and bargain effectively has not simply been enhanced by globalization in some sort of teleological convergence of worldviews. Instead, cultures retain central elements of their distinctiveness and can react negatively to global trends (Held et al. 1999: ch. 7). One example has been the global debate over gay rights. In 2008, a joint French-Dutch resolution was submitted to the UN General Assembly condemning the persecution of same-sex relations, the first time the global body had considered the issue. In response, the Arab League submitted an opposing resolution. Neither was passed. In 2011, South Africa submitted a request to the UN Human

Rights Council that a report be prepared to document violations of gay people's human rights, which was adopted 23–19 after bitter debate. Aside from South Africa, none of the other African members of the Council voted for the resolution, though Burkina Faso and Zambia abstained. In Asia, only Japan, South Korea, and Thailand voted in favor of the report. Eastern Europe was more positive, with only Russia and Moldova opposing. And every single member state in Europe and the Americas voted in favor. When the report was presented on March 7, 2012, several Arab and African states walked out.

In sum, emerging multipolarity has, ironically, increased the need for cooperation, by widening the bounds of interdependence to a new set of countries. But it has also made that cooperation less likely by raising the transaction costs of global deals and, most importantly, broadening the range of interests that must be accommodated.

Institutional inertia

In the most minimal version of International Relations institutionalist theory, international law and international institutions are tools for cooperation between states. By creating rules, monitoring their implementation, and (more rarely) enforcing them, international institutions help make countries' agreements more credible. They provide information about interests and expectations. And they implement programs and policies with varying degrees of autonomy. The exact form an institution takes is a product of the needs its creators want to address, their interests, and the bargain they strike. In this logic, when one of these factors changes – the underlying problem, the interests of the parties, their bargaining power – institutions should change too.

In practice, of course, institutions can be "sticky." Stickiness can be a useful quality in institutions, for example when constitutions "lock in" the rights of a minority against the whims of the majority. But it can also lead to dysfunction, for example in the case of constitutions that empower privileged minorities over others. Many conceptions of stickiness have been put forward, ranging from the structuralist view that institutions of authority perpetuate themselves, to the more behavioralist view that institutions create stakeholders vested in their preservation, and embody the sunk costs of shared expectations, information, and practices that can only be shifted at some price. Whatever the mechanism, Steven Krasner

(1984) suggests we think about political institutions as following a pattern of "punctuated equilibria." Institutions are created in foundational moments to deal with the needs of that time, and reflect the attendant constellations of power and interests. But these later shift, creating a mismatch between institutions and the conditions on which they depend. Secular shifts in those conditions stretch this incongruence to the point of crisis, destroying the existing institutions and allowing a new set more attuned to the changed conditions to take their place.[9]

In addition to both exogenous and, per our argument above, endogenous shifts in power and interests, Keohane and Nye (1977) offer a second endogenous explanation of how international institutions can become detached from the underlying conditions which gave rise to them. The creation of an institution will affect the surrounding norms, networks, and practices that (alongside the underlying constellations of power and interests) affect institutional outcomes. In this view, power over outcomes may be determined by "organizationally dependent" attributes, such as a vote in the General Assembly, or in trade rounds, where – in theory, if not in practice – the votes of all countries are weighted equally. The best example is perhaps the UN Security Council, in which the veto power of the existing P-5 – that is, a characteristic of the existing institution – stands as the greatest barrier to much-needed reform.

The key question is thus whether an institution is sticky enough to perform its function, but not too sticky to keep pace with the world around it. For the last several decades, the postwar order has managed this balancing act surprisingly well. It has outlasted both structural shifts like decolonization and the end of the Cold War, and moments of panic like the 1973 oil crisis or the military interventions of the 1990s. Our argument is that the governance gap between the existing multilateral order and the public goods needed is now dangerously large. So too is the divergence between the constellations of power and interests engrained in our key institutions and the realities they must govern. In other words, existing institutions are not just sticky, they have become stuck.

We highlight two common mechanisms generating this inertia. First, the formal, treaty-based nature of many of the postwar institutions makes them cumbersome to change. As mentioned above in the context of the Security Council, once power is formally vested in a certain institutional arrangement, that institution then has additional power to defend the status quo. In addition to the Security Council, this is common in the IFIs. The IMF, for example, was established through the leadership of the United States, at a time when the US was the world's undisputed hegemon. Thus the IMFs voting structure is highly favorable to the United States, which can always veto decisions, including decisions to reform voting rules. Moreover, many transnational financial governance institutions have their origins in informal pacts between Western Europe, Japan, and North America in the 1970s and 1980s. As a consequence, many European powers have a disproportionate degree of representation within these institutions, allowing them more control over decision-making than the current configuration of economic power or population would warrant.[10]

Second, institutions are more than just specific rules of the game for world politics. They also serve as focal points for actors' expectations, beliefs, and practices (Schelling 1980). After 60 years, these can congeal. For instance, the development of the Treaty on the Non-Proliferation of Nuclear Weapons (signed in 1968) gave special standing to a group of powers called nuclear weapon states (NWS), effectively the five permanent members of the Security Council. These states were the ones that developed the capacity for nuclear weaponry first. While the treaty explicitly states that nuclear disarmament is a long-run objective of these countries, in reality it reinforced and legitimated the privileged position of the NWS. Few, if any, believed that these nuclear powers would disarm and from this followed both the dynamics of the nuclear arms race and the attempt by new powers to further their nuclear capacities. Expectations became sedimented around the facts of power in such a way that there was no effective challenge by the parties to the treaty to the ownership of nuclear arms by the P-5. In short, the treaty created a solution that gave nuclear powers incentives to participate in its arrangements, and yet over time has contributed to a set of expectations and beliefs which effectively entrench the status quo. This is just one example of the way in which institutions all too often establish not only formal rules but also informal norms and beliefs; although the former define how institutions proceed in principle, the latter create a path dependency which is difficult to undo.

Harder problems

One of the key ways in which contemporary interdependence differs from postwar interdependence is that current transborder problems are often inherently harder to address from a policy standpoint.

Climate change is more difficult to solve than transborder air pollution. Intellectual property regimes are more difficult to define and agree than schedules of mutual tariff reductions. And it is more challenging to protect human security than to defend a line of fortifications across central Europe.

There are two ways in which problems have gotten harder. First, as argued above, different kinds of problems, issue areas that previously fell neatly into national boundaries, have become subject to the logic of interdependence. Moreover, old and new problems alike now penetrate deeper into societies, requiring larger policy adjustments – more shifts from what the domestic equilibrium might be – to achieve cooperation. We can think about these shifts as increases in the *extensity* and *intensity* of transnational problems (Held et al. 1999). Consider each in turn.

Extensity refers to the "stretching of social, political and economic activities across frontiers such that events, decisions and activities in one region of the world can come to have significance for individuals and communities in distant regions of the globe" (Held et al. 1999: 15). This condition now characterizes a bewildering array of policy issues. Mortgage regulation in Florida determines the safety of bank deposits in Iceland. Emissions in China determine the survival of low-lying island states such as Tuvalu. Educational opportunities in Pakistan affect the physical security of bus passengers in London. Rosenau (1997) coined the term "intermestic" to characterize this new class of policy issue, and it is hard to think of any important topic that cannot be thought of in these terms. In other words, almost all policy areas today have become increasingly *extensive*.

Intensity, in turn, captures the idea that "connections across frontiers are not just occasional or random, but rather are regularized such that there is a . . . growing magnitude of interconnectedness, patterns of interaction and flows" across borders (Held et al. 1999: 15). Some of this shift can be seen in that quantitative increase in various global economic and social flows. But qualitative differences are likely even more important examples of the growing intensity of interdependence. Consider the realm of world trade. For much of the postwar era, trade negotiations focused on reducing tariff levels on manufactured products traded between industrialized countries. These negotiations had large economic implications for the producers and consumers of the products under negotiation. Lowering tariffs might bring more jobs and profits to competitive producers and take them away from noncompetitive ones, even as they brought down the cost of products for consumers. The impact of the trade deal, however, was largely limited to these basic distributional questions. But once tariffs had been reduced, firms found that many other aspects of regulation, such as divergent environmental and safety standards (or lack thereof), made it difficult to trade across borders. These issues are much harder to negotiate over, because the basic distributional question – who wins and who loses – has become compounded with other policy issues, some of which touch on basic social principles.

Consider the trade in genetically modified organisms. Farmers in North and South America, where there are relatively few regulations on usage of GMOs, have made wide use of these products. Regulators in Europe, in contrast, have been more concerned about their potential implications for health and biodiversity. Both of these stances are legitimate choices that polities might choose, and they reflect different attitudes toward environmental risk in Europe and the Americas. But in a globalized world, there is pressure to harmonize these choices. In a dispute brought by producers in the United States, Canada, and Argentina, the WTO forced Europe to lift its ban on imports of American beef treated with hormones (Sands and Peel 2012).

Fragmentation

The last path to gridlock highlights the ways existing fragmented and inadequate systems of multilateral cooperation can stifle the supply of stronger governance solutions. International organizations have mushroomed since the end of World War II. According to the *Yearbook of International Organizations*, in 1951 (the first year after World War II for which data are available) there were 123 intergovernmental organizations and 832 international nongovernmental organizations. In 2011 those figures increased to 7,608 and 56,834, respectively. This trend is seen in key issue areas like the environment, around which nearly 700 agreements have been negotiated (UNEP 2012), and trade, where we have seen the number of preferential trade agreements climb to 319 (WTO 2012). At the same time, as noted above, in many areas of economic and environmental governance, a proliferation of transnational (non-intergovernmental) institutions have emerged that involve components of states or private actors. These are discussed extensively in chapters 3 and 4, but less so in the security chapter, as states have worked to maintain their control over that issue area (even as the nature of the threats has followed a similar trend of privatization and transnationalization).

The density and complexity of global governance has both positive and negative effects on outcomes (Biermann et al. 2009; Raustiala and Victor 2004; Alter and Meunier 2009). A diversity of institutions can allow for productive experimentation and healthy competition between competing regulatory approaches (J. Cohen and Sabel 1997). It can allow for a wider range of actors to participate in global governance by creating specialized fora that account for divergent preferences. This flexibility can also help make global governance more adaptive and increase the speed at which solutions are adopted.

These advantages come with trade-offs, however. Fragmentation can lead to a regulatory "race to the bottom" in which policy coordination is undermined by jurisdictional competition. This can result in significant regulatory uncertainty and transaction costs for actors, like multinational corporations, that operate across borders. Furthermore, allowing groups with divergent preferences to create their own arrangements can preclude the possibility of policy convergence over the long term, even if it would be unlikely in the short term. Moreover, new institutions are not necessarily productive. Some research on new transnational institutions in the forestry sectors suggests that institutions are created in order to be functionally idle and hollow, without significant power or purpose, all the while giving the appearance that something is being done to address the global public policy problem at hand (Dimitrov 2005; see also chapter 4 below). And fragmentation can render global governance arrangements excessively "clubby," undercutting their representativeness and, typically, their ability to address the needs of weaker countries.

These problems have been discussed in the international relations literature (e.g. Bierman et. al. 2009; Haas 2004). Here we focus on how existing fragmentation can impede further attempts at global coordination. In many ways, this network of institutions provides the kind of issue-specific flexibility that is necessary for addressing the highly variegated governance challenges that the world faces. Yet collective action is also harder under conditions of institutional fragmentation, for a variety of reasons.

First, weak coordination among institutions, either because of competing jurisdictions or simply due to communication difficulties, means that collective governance can be logistically difficult. As we noted above, a chief advantage of international institutions is that they allow an enormous amount of diplomacy to be conducted efficiently in the context of a multilateral forum. Institutions also act as focal points to bring actors' attention to a certain set of issues and make them the subject of deliberation. This effect is reduced, however, if there are too many fora in which actors engage and interact. Importantly, a proliferation of institutional bodies may also diffuse the political will needed to push countries to reach a cooperative agreement. While awareness of global governance problems is arguably rising, even most of the educated public is rather unaware of the detail of how global policies are actually carried out. Marginal and weak institutions can therefore provide opportunities for national leaders and the bureaucracies of existing international institutions to point to things that they are doing, thereby relieving pressure on them and thus on demand to generate more ambitious plans for reform. It is easier to grandstand when there are so many "stands" available.

Second, a diversity of institutions means that various elements of a problem can be divided into discrete tasks. When this division of labor is efficient, institutional complexity may be advantageous. But it can also be the case that such flexibility will lead to redundancy and navel-gazing. When there is a network of slightly different institutions, the reflex response to a given policy problem is for each institution to provide a contribution to the policy problem at hand based on their own specialization. The consequence is that many small, specific problems may be tackled, but large, overarching ones remain unresolved and may even grow, all the while giving the appearance that the problem is being resolved. To be sure, there is nothing wrong with an advanced institutional division of labor; however some problems are of such a significant scale and magnitude that grander interventions are necessary. A collection of different institutions responding to a policy problem might in some cases succeed in changing the status quo, but not in actually moving to a new equilibrium.

The global governance of financial markets represents a case in point. There is no single institution that sets global standards for risk regulation, monitoring, and communication of common problems, but rather a complex web of institutions, both formal and informal, which govern financial markets in a loose and often ad hoc way. This arrangement reflects the informal way in which transnational institutions emerged to tackle particular problems as they have presented themselves since the 1970s (see chapter 3). This "tangled web" not only duplicates resources, but, more importantly, diffuses responsibility when things go awry, such as in the 2008–9 global financial crisis. The problem only multiplies when one considers that finance is but one area of the global economy, meaning there is no institutionalized oversight of, for example, the links between finance and trade.

Last, fragmented political institutions can also help actors escape institutional constraints altogether, by letting them pick and choose the ones most favorable to them. This forum-shopping can be seen in the intellectual property regime, where countries can choose between the rules of various organizations – including the WTO, WHO, Food and Agriculture Organization (FAO), Union for the Protection of New Varieties of Plants, and the World Intellectual Property Organization – to shape how they distribute benefits between producers and users. To some extent, of course, creating a variety of fora and arbitraging between them is "efficient" in that it ensures institutions are responsive to states' needs. However, the implication is that states' preferences are too divergent to share the same institution, which bodes ill for cooperation. Moreover, by creating and reinforcing an ever increasing list of institutions, states can undermine the utility of all institutions by increasing transaction costs and reducing any one institution's centrality in global politics.

Conclusion

International cooperation has always been difficult. Our argument in this book is that now, after 60 years of qualified success, it is increasingly difficult for a new set of second-order reasons. Gridlock does not characterize every aspect of global politics. Nor has every change in the international system led to gridlock. Nonetheless, for almost any crucial policy issue today, demand for international cooperation is growing even as supply grinds to a halt.

As we have argued in this chapter, the manner in which current global governance challenges are addressed is necessarily historically contingent on preceding institutional developments. As such, we begin each of the chapters that follow with a historical analysis of how existing institutional arrangements came into place, before examining the manifestations of current gridlock. We examine gridlock mechanisms with our analysis directed at both the operation of governance institutions and toward emergent new problems.

2

Security

Introduction

While addressing a gathering of world leaders at the United Nations San Francisco Conference in 1945, US President Harry Truman warned that the world was at a crossroads:

> You members of this Conference are to be the architects of the better world. In your hands rests our future. By your labors at this Conference, we shall know if suffering humanity is to achieve a just and lasting peace . . . With ever-increasing brutality and destruction, modern warfare, if unchecked, would ultimately crush all civilization. We still have a choice between the alternatives: The continuation of international chaos, or the establishment of a world organization for the enforcement of peace. (Truman 1945)

At the heart of the postwar security arrangements was the newly formed United Nations and the development of a new legal and institutional framework for international affairs. What is remarkable about these developments is that they came against the backdrop of catastrophic war and its devastating consequences for Europe and all those embroiled in it. The architects of the UN system could have decided to turn their backs on efforts of international collaboration in the wake of the collapse of earlier initiatives, notably the League of Nations, to establish an effective world organization for peace. Instead, they sought to reframe the international system and embed even the most powerful states in its structure; they set down incentives for the great powers to engage, while also creating avenues that gave voice to emerging states. While there were inevitable compromises as dominant sovereign interests were spliced together with universal concerns, the results were strong enough to give rise to some remarkable developments.

The UN system can legitimately claim some credit for preventing another world war, although of course many other factors were at work (see below). Set against the backdrop of the persisting tensions of the Cold War, the postwar order bound states together in a common framework. Though there were many serious conflicts, they did not develop into major global conflagrations. This basic stability became the foundation for unprecedented economic integration, which in turn created new challenges for regulation and institutional design. The security crisis of World War II catalyzed a degree of cooperation among states greater than ever before. As this cooperation was institutionalized, global interdependence grew yet further, resulting in ever more complex forms of connectedness that ultimately changed the meaning and nature of security. These trends are evaluated throughout this chapter.

Divided into two parts, the chapter first presents key historical developments in the evolution of the interstate system. We highlight significant developments that have affected the governance of global security in the twentieth century, including the early modern codification of sovereignty as effective power as well as later attempts to transform this into codes of rightful authority in accordance with a rule-based legal order. These attempts are linked to diverging conceptions of security, state-based versus human security, and to different ways of conceiving the global security system. More generally, this narrative illustrates the profound growth of interdependence in the interstate system after World War II. The interdependence constructed in the postwar years spliced together disparate interests into a collective security framework, gradually reaching a point where it developed into a highly complex institutional structure. This structure can be credited with many successes, chiefly the absence of war between the great powers. But this success has also given rise to a set of new challenges, which are taken up in the second half of this chapter.

The new world of complex security interdependence brought with it a range of challenges which the designers of the UN system could not have foreseen. These challenges span a series of pressing global concerns, including, but not limited to, emergent threats such as terrorism and cyber insecurity, and also persisting threats such as nuclear proliferation. Equally important, the very meaning of security has evolved. We are more and more concerned not just with what countries do to their neighbors, but with what they do to their own citizens. This shift, a kind of deepening moral interdependence, creates an additional and difficult set of transnational problems to solve.

The manner in which these types of challenges are addressed is, it is shown, contingent on preceding institutional innovations. While these innovations help create a problem-solving context for some issues, there are failures elsewhere. These are typically the result of the aggregated consequence of four "pathways to gridlock"; namely, the entrenchment of dominant powers resulting in institutional inertia, emerging multipolarity which makes consensus more difficult, harder (complex, intermestic) problems which challenge governance structures, and coordination failures resulting from fragmentation. The four pathways block the enhanced collective security governance required to meet the challenge of contemporary security threats – a governance system that takes account of the continuing transformation of sovereignty and security toward a human security paradigm. However, since this transformation is much more apparent in principle than in practice, existing security arrangements fall far short of what is needed.

CHANGES IN THE NATURE AND FORM OF SECURITY

The Interstate System

The world order as we know it today is the product of sovereign state interests spliced together with universal claims pertaining to human rights standards and democratic values – both of which are embedded in the institutional arrangements that connect the world and facilitate international cooperation. At the most fundamental level, this order is characterized by the interactions of sovereign states; however, throughout time the very meaning of sovereignty, and indeed security, has undergone significant change. The nature of the problems has changed, as interstate war becomes increasingly rare and other forms of violence arise. Equally important, the way we think about security has also evolved. Understanding this transformation is critical to understanding current gridlock in security arrangements, and to do so we must first take a step back in time.

Historical perspective pre–World War II

Traditional conceptions of state sovereignty were based on effective power – wherein might equals right. This notion constructed a system of world order that held state power supreme so long as a clear territory could effectively be ruled by a state and its flag flown (Krasner 1999). This order was codified by select European powers in the seventeenth century through various institutional arrangements. Alongside these innovations the world order became increasingly interconnected, and subsequently more interdependent.

The Peace of Westphalia in 1648 entrenched the state system of international organization through a series of treaties that were designed to limit hegemonic aspirations in Europe (Osiander 2001: 252–7). Building upon this foundation, the origins of global security governance can be observed in the Concert of Europe from 1815 to 1870, wherein European powers sought to maintain a stable balance of power through institutionalized cooperation. This system created a relatively peaceful environment in Europe for most of the nineteenth century (Kissinger 1994; George and Craig 1995). Stability was established through the Congress of Vienna, 1814–15, which created a system of regular conferences in which European powers could negotiate and solve disputes. The multilateral character of the Congress should not, however, be overstated, as it was comprised of an exclusive group of eight European powers (Great Britain, Russia, Austria, Prussia, France, Spain, Portugal, and Sweden), requiring that "smaller powers [had] to submit to their decrees without a share in their deliberations" (Scott 1909: 15). A further institutional innovation during the late nineteenth and early twentieth centuries includes the Hague Conferences, which created an additional formal platform for international powers to come together in negotiation and collaboration to mitigate security threats and the worst effects of war. The Hague Conferences of 1899 and 1907 are important for two reasons in particular. First, they included non-European powers – such as China, Japan, Turkey, Persia, and Siam – which necessarily allowed for greater participation and voice from less dominant states (CEIP 1920). Secondly, and most significantly, the Hague Conferences furthered a "legalistic approach to international disputes" (Weiss and Thakur 2010: 56–7). James Scott, who was the technical delegate of the United States to the 1907 Hague Conference, recognized both the limitations as well as the significance of this innovation in a lecture he gave in 1909: "A complete code was not outlined – it is doubtful whether custom and usage are ripe for codification – but important topics of international law were given the symmetry and precision of a code," manifest in the four titles of the first conference: "The Maintenance of General Peace, Good Offices and Mediation, International Commissions of Inquiry, International Arbitration" (1909: 2, 254–5). The institutionalizing function of this code and the international conferences should not be understated, as they built the foundation for greater collaboration among states. Scott, even then, stressed that this collaboration was catalyzed by greater interconnectedness among world powers (1909: 4–7). In fact, one can see that it was both a result, and a driver, of growing interdependence. As interconnectedness grew, security concerns were restructured into the evolving institutional design of global governance.

The institutionalization of global security can be understood as the intersection of two related processes: first, a generalized process of global military buildup, and second, increasing military interconnectedness. Interconnectedness connotes not only a dependence of nation-states upon each other, but also a growing recognition of intertwined fates. World War I highlighted that international governance "could not rely on the balance of power if the most extreme forms of violence against humanity were to be outlawed, and the growing interconnectedness and interdependence of nations recognized" (Held et al. 1999: 62). The wide-scale application of industrial technology to warfare – the machine-gun, the tank, the fighter plane, and chemical weapons – gave countries an unprecedented ability to harm one another. As these trends developed so too did the need for a more comprehensive system of governance. Security, per se, was quickly outgrowing a local focus and was taking on a more global character.

At the end of World War I this institutionalization took on a unique form in the League of Nations. Part of the Versailles Treaty, the League was an "effort to bring an end to war by doing away with the balance of power and creating a supranational international organization" (Mansbach and Rafferty 2008: 127). Ultimately, 63 countries accepted membership, although the US Senate – despite Woodrow Wilson's leading role in creating the League – refused to ratify the initiative, as noted in the introduction. Setting itself against the secret practices of traditional European statecraft, the League represented an aspiration for "a new and more wholesome diplomacy" (Wilson quoted in Held 1995). Building on the nineteenth-century Concert system's conception of regular conferences, it proposed a permanent apparatus for these, a system of conciliation and arbitration involving a judicial body (the Permanent Court of International Justice), and a system of guarantees linked to the *status quo post bellum* (Clark 1989: 150–2; cf. Zimmern 1936; Osiander 1994: ch. 5). Underpinning these innovations was a desire to establish "a community of likeminded nations," cooperating fully with one another and "settling their differences like reasonable men, enjoying peace under a law . . . which if need be they would pool their resources to enforce" (Howard 1981: 91).

The design and authority of the League was lacking in one crucial respect: the buy-in of leading world powers. For example, when Japan invaded Manchuria in 1933, the League took action, albeit after a painstaking and inefficient delay. The League's official response was to order Japan's departure from the region; however, rather than leave Manchuria, Japan decided to simply leave the League. Another test of the League's efficacy came in 1935 when Italy sent forces into Ethiopia in an attempt to colonize the territory and expand its reach on the African continent. This act was one of clear aggression and in egregious violation of articles set forth in the League of Nations, of which both countries were members. The international community at large, through the League, identified the action as illegal, explicitly named Italy as an aggressor nation and consequently attempted to impose sanctions for the transgression; this was the first act of its kind for the international community. However, the League's effectiveness could not match its ideals – in Ethiopia, Manchuria, or elsewhere. Although the League pioneered a model of international organization that would be of enduring significance, its aspirations were dashed and its fate sealed by the growing international tensions of the 1930s and the eventual outbreak of World War II (see, for example, Carr 1946; Hinsley 1963). There certainly seems to be an abundance of evidence to suggest that few states, particularly among the most powerful, were willing to surrender one of the most integral elements of the idea of sovereignty: the freedom to define friend or foe and to pursue either war or pacific policies toward them without limitation. The League's systems of discussion, arbitration, and guarantees were at too great a distance from the realities of power politics of the time – a reality where sovereignty as effective power continued to trump the universalist claims emerging in multilateral talks and organizations. While this arrangement failed ultimately to prevent another world war, it marks a significant development in the creation of a liberal order tasked with the management of global security governance; a system that would be revised and recreated at the end of World War II.

World War II

World War II created conflict and violence on a scale that had never been experienced before, and was an event that would drastically reshape the global order. As Hobsbawm puts it, it was a "global human catastrophe" (1994: 52). The scale of the war effort, of destruction and of human suffering was historically unprecedented. As war embraced Europe and the Far East, military hostilities raged across almost every single continent and ocean, excepting South America and Antarctica. Few of those states not engaged directly or indirectly in military combat could effectively remain neutral, since supplying the war effort of both the Axis (German, Italy, and Japan) and the Allied powers (United States, Britain, and France) required extensive sourcing. As McNeill notes, "transnational organization for war . . . achieved a fuller and far more effective expression during World War II than ever before" (1982: 356). But one of the most profound consequences of the war was the resultant transformation in the structure of world power. The year 1945 marked the end of Europe's global hegemony and confirmed the US and the Soviet Union as global superpowers. This structural transformation heralded dramatic consequences for the pattern of postwar global military and security relations.

In many ways the events of World War II can be understood as an overwhelming failure in the global management of security and conflict. The League of Nations sought to temper the primacy of the state with a more legalistic and egalitarian order. Sovereign interests proved intractable, however, and the system broke down. Attempts at rebuilding a pacific settlement at the end of World War II would need far more legitimacy and buy-in – something that could only be achieved through structural arrangements that gave dominant powers incentives to uphold them. Both the preceding efforts of global security governance and the respective experiences of world powers during World War II influenced the construction of the postwar settlement in significant ways – a construction that lasts to this day and is the foundation for multilateral cooperation.

Postwar Developments: From the UN to the Cold War

World War II illustrated, in an appalling way, the necessity of establishing an international order capable of maintaining a just peace and global stability. Inherent in the conception of such an order was a significantly qualified notion of state sovereignty. If a rule-based order was to have any chance, then unbridled sovereignty would need to be tempered by counterbalancing forces. To that end, the very idea of sovereignty became linked to the idea of legitimate, or rightful, authority; an authority that is both recognized and regulated by the international community. Such notions found early expression in the United Nations Charter, where sovereignty was both entrenched and balanced with certain obligations to the world at large.

Building the United Nations system

Article I explicitly states that the purpose of the UN is to "maintain international peace and security, and to that end: to take effective collective measures for the prevention and removal of threats to the peace . . ." (UN 1945). Moreover, Article I goes on to stress that peace would be sought and protected through principles of international law. It concludes with the position that the UN is to be "a centre for harmonizing the actions of nations in the attainment of these common ends." This is particularly important for the purposes of this chapter since it speaks to the deliberate, facilitated interdependence that was sought by the UN. Moreover, the focus on principles of international law emphasizes the significance of the formal institutionalization of such prevention and mitigation mechanisms. By facilitating integration in this way the UN sought to replace the tendency toward unilateral military action with collective action that could still preserve central aspects of state sovereignty (Ikenberry 2001). Maintaining global peace and stability serves the obvious purpose of limiting violence, but it was also a quintessential prerequisite for accelerating globalization across sectors outside of the immediate sphere of security concerns; trade, finance, and communication being the most prominent among them.

While the need to create such a unified system could not have been more salient in 1945, it is important to recognize that the institutional design of the UN reflected disparate interests among the leading states. These resulted from differing contexts in the history of global power. This divide is illustrated by European states and the United States. While not discounting the casualties experienced by the United States in the conflicts of the twentieth century, these paled in comparison to the level of deaths experienced by Europeans. Europe emerged from World War II with a visceral sense of destruction and eventual relief, whereas the US emerged as the world's leading superpower and with a sense of military triumphalism (see Weiss and Thakur 2010). Yet, despite these different experiences, the leading powers could come together to establish the UN system. Moreover, they were to use this system to reinforce their positions. The codification of US dominance and the protection of the interests of other major states within the multilateral order needs to be recognized when exploring the achievements and limitations that can accurately be assigned to the UN system and, more generally, to the postwar settlement.

The titanic struggles of World War I and World War II led to a growing acknowledgement that the nature and process of global governance would have to change if the most extreme forms of violence against humanity were to be outlawed, and the growing interconnectedness and interdependence of nations recognized. Slowly, the subject, scope, and very sources of the Westphalian conception of international regulations, particularly its conception of international law, were all called into question (Bull 1977: ch. 6; Held 1995: ch. 4). The image of international regulation projected by the UN Charter (and related documents) was one of "states still jealously 'sovereign'" but now linked together in a "myriad of relations"; under pressure to resolve disagreements by peaceful means and according to legal criteria; subject in principle to tight restrictions on the resort to force; and constrained to observe "certain standards" with regard to the treatment of all persons in their territory, including their own citizens (Cassese 1991: 256). Of course, how restrictive the provisions of the Charter have been to states, and to what extent they have been actually operationalized, are important issues. Before addressing them, however, leading elements of the Charter model (adapted from Cassese 1986: 398–400) should be sketched, as they highlight the shift from the nineteenth-century conception of sovereignty to a different model based on the UN: see box 2.1.

At the heart of this shift lies a conflict between claims made on behalf of individual states and those made on behalf of an alternative organizing principle of world affairs: ultimately, a community of all states, with equal voting rights in the UN General Assembly, openly and collectively regulating international life while constrained to observe the UN Charter and a battery of human rights conventions. However, this conflict is still far from resolved, and it would be misleading to conclude that the era of the UN Charter model simply displaced the Westphalian logic of international governance. The essential reason for this is that the Charter framework represents, in some notable respects, an extension of the interstate system, even though it modified it in important ways.

The Cold War

The promise of the UN was constrained almost from its inception by the Cold War. While World War II and the fight against the Axis forces had united much of the world, it was a tenuous unity produced by a brutal common enemy at war. Thus, when the dust began to settle,

Box 2.1 The UN Charter model

1 The world community consists of sovereign states, connected through a dense network of relations, both ad hoc and institutionalized. Individuals and groups are regarded as legitimate actors in international relations (albeit with limited roles).
2 Certain peoples oppressed by colonial powers, racist regimes or foreign occupying forces are assigned rights of recognition and a determinate role in articulating their future and interests. The principle of self-determination is legitimized.
3 There is a gradual acceptance of standards and values which call into question the principle of effective state power; accordingly, major violations of given international rules are not in theory to be regarded as legitimate. Restrictions are placed on the resort to force, including the unwarranted use of economic force.
4 New rules, procedures and institutions are designed to aid law-making and law enforcement in international affairs.
5 Legal principles delimiting the form and scope of the conduct of all members of the international community, and providing a set of guidelines for the structuring of international rules, are adopted.
6 Fundamental concern is expressed for the rights of individuals, and a corpus of international rules is created seeking to constrain states to observe certain standards in the treatment of all, including their own citizens.
7 The preservation of peace, the advancement of human rights and the establishment of greater social justice are the stated collective priorities; "public affairs" include the whole of the international community. With respect to certain values – peace, the prohibition of genocide – international rules provide in principle for the personal responsibility of state officials and the attribution of criminal acts to states.
8 Systematic inequalities among peoples and states are recognized and new rules – including the concept of "the common heritage of mankind"* – are established to create ways of governing the distribution, appropriation and exploitation of territory, property and natural resources.

*First propounded in the late 1960s, the concept of "the common heritage of mankind" was proposed as a device to exclude a state or private right of appropriation over certain resources and to permit the development of those resources, where appropriate for the benefit of all, with due regard paid to environmental protection.

Source: Extract from Held 1995: 86, adapted from Cassese 1986: 398–400.

the unity began to give way to underlying ideological and geopolitical tensions that would shape the Cold War for almost 50 years. These tensions stemmed from political, economic, and military conflict between the Soviet Union and the United States, each bolstered by their respective allies. The world power structure became bipolar, continuously manifested through the threat and exercise of hard power. This standoff facilitated, somewhat paradoxically, a deepening of interdependence among world powers. The interdependence of states does not mean here a peaceful and institutionalized order; rather it connotes the recognition and governance of intertwined fates. It is difficult to imagine a more immediate form of interdependence than Mutually Assured Destruction. Once the world reached a point at which a small group of decision-makers could release weapons that could, literally, obliterate the rest of the world, it created a new recognition of shared vulnerability. This awareness demanded greater coordination among world powers. Thus, the nuclear standoff of the Cold War drew world powers closer together as a way to mitigate the threat and ensure that military posturing did not escalate into all-out nuclear confrontation.

The position of the United States throughout this era was established very early. In 1947 the Deputy Chief of Mission at the US embassy in Moscow, George Kennan, wrote a lengthy dispatch to Washington that argued that the Soviet system was inherently unstable. If communism could be prevented from spreading, the so-called "Long Telegram" argued, it would eventually collapse under the weight of its own weaknesses. This thesis was later given a different emphasis by the Eisenhower administration. In both private and public meetings, President Eisenhower propounded a "falling domino" theory of communism and containment (1954: 382). The logic of this theory held communism akin to some kind of contagion that, if allowed, would spread uncontrollably across the globe. This belief directly informed US foreign policy and was used to justify a number of major conflicts and "proxy wars" – a rough and ready distinction that captures a range of interventions from clandestine missions to large-scale wars such as Korea and Vietnam. Even though the world order was institutionalizing a new regulatory regime through multilateral agreements, organized violence remained a dominant feature of the second half of the twentieth century. Table 2.1 documents selected major conflicts from 1945 to present, whether they were mandated by the UN or not, and the scale of conflict-related deaths.

The Cold War included many military interventions other than those listed in the table. These involved wars and operations focused

Table 2.1 Selected major wars, UN mandates, and conflict-related deaths

War	Primary state actors	Battle and conflict deaths	UN legalized	Notes/Outcomes
Arab–Israeli, 1948	Israel Egypt	3,000 2,000	No	
Korean, 1950–3	China North Korea South Korea United States	422,612 316,579 113,248 54,487	Yes	UN Security Council approved military support while USSR boycotted the Council and thus could not issue its veto
Sinai, 1956	Israel Egypt	189 3,000	No	
Taiwan Straits, 1958	China (PRC) Taiwan (ROC)	300 1,500	No	
Vietnam, 1965–75	United States South Vietnam Vietnam	58,153 254,257 700,000	No	
Six Day, 1967	Israel Egypt Jordan Syria	1,000 10,000 6,100 2,500	No	
Sino-Vietnamese, 1979	China Vietnam	13,000 8,000	No	
Iran–Iraq, 1980–8	Iran Iraq	750,000 500,000	No	
Gulf War, 1990–1	United States Kuwait Iraq	376 1,000 40,000	Yes	
Yugoslav, 1991–5	Former Yugoslavia Croatia Bosnia and Herzegovina Kosovo	140,000	No	

Table 2.1 *(Continued)*

War	Primary state actors	Battle and conflict deaths	UN legalized	Notes/Outcomes
Invasion of Afghanistan, 2001–present	United States and Coalition Afghanistan	3,236 12,793 civilians since 2006	Yes	Violence has escalated significantly since 2010, particularly against civilians
Invasion of Iraq	United States and Coalition Iraq	4,795 100,000	No	US forces officially concluded "combat" operations; however, thousands of troops and private contractors remain
Libyan intervention	NATO and rebels Gaddafi loyalists	30,000, including combatants and civilians on both sides	Yes	Russia and China have expressed deep misgivings about the implementation of the R2P mandate and have objected to further application of it (Syria); Brazil has argued for a new concept of "responsibility while protecting"

Source: Most figures adapted from Sarkees and Wayman 2010; New COW War Data, 1816–2007 (v4.0) (www.correlatesofwar.org); UNAMA 2012; other figures from ICTJ 2009; icasualties.org 2012a, 2012b. Libyan figures are still contested: figure is from AP 2011, citing the new Minister of Health.

on containing the larger threat perceived from the Soviet Union and spread of communism, and took place across the global South. Reaching around the world, US interventions included, but were not limited to, Latin America (Guatemala and Panama), sub-Saharan Africa (DRC), Middle East (Iran, Lebanon), and Asia (Laos, Philippines, Indonesia, etc.) (see Westad 2006). The Cold War persisted in a paradoxical manner: on the one hand, the US and USSR were positioning for potential nuclear war against one another and significant violence was waged around the world; on the other hand, both states were participating in and thus legitimizing the postwar settlement and the security communities that evolved within it. That both countries held permanent seats on the Security Council shows how closely linked these two forces were. They sat in an institutional setting that emphasized rule-based relations and international law, while at the same time they prepared for the worst of possible conflicts. In many ways, whatever potential the UN's Security Council had was muted by this arrangement, as each side held counterbalancing vetoes that could be cast at any time if it suited their respective agendas. The most notable exception to this is perhaps the Korean War. In 1950, the USSR was boycotting the Security Council in protest at the exclusion of the People's Republic of China, and therefore was not present to cast its veto when the Council passed a resolution (S/RES/84) condemning North Korean actions and authorizing member states to "furnish" military assistance to the Republic of Korea (South) (UN Security Council 1950). But, broadly speaking, the result of the veto balance meant that the decision-making structure became "locked in" to its original form, as any zero-sum outcome or development in the Council could be blocked by any party that might lose standing as a result. Accordingly, there has been little evolution overall of the Security Council and related bodies.

The Cold War and its aftermath saw the development of various "zones of peace" that were codified throughout the world at various levels (see Kupchan 2010). Establishing zones of peace was the direct result of efforts made by state actors in pursuit of their continued security, and it necessarily accelerated their interconnectedness through establishing common means and ends. These efforts included a gradient process that can best be understood in stages: (1) initial rapprochement, (2) the formation of security communities, and (3) the creation of a security union (Kupchan 2010). Indeed, for many states the beginning of this process predates the onset of the world wars (e.g. the Anglo-American rapprochement in the late nineteenth century). The development of stages in this process can occur at

Box 2.2 NATO members

Year	*Membership additions*
1949 (founding)	Belgium, Canada, Denmark, France, Iceland, Italy, Luxembourg, Netherlands, Norway, Portugal, United Kingdom, United States
1952	Greece and Turkey
1955	Germany
1982	Spain
1999	Czech Republic, Hungary, Poland
2004	Bulgaria, Estonia, Latvia, Lithuania, Romania, Slovakia, Slovenia
2009	Albania and Croatia

Of the 12 states that have joined since the end of the Cold War, only the three Baltic states were formerly part of the Soviet Union (Estonia, Latvia, and Lithuania).
Source: NATO 2011.

various levels of the global order: bilateral, as was the case with the Anglo-American rapprochement, or more regionally, ASEAN and the European Union being two important examples (Kupchan 2010). As security relationships moved from rapprochement to security communities there was an increase in regional security arrangements; among which the Warsaw Pact and NATO (see box 2.2) are perhaps the two most noteworthy. The diversity of security communities that evolved over time illustrate further the deepening of interdependence in the governance of global security.

A security community, as defined by Kupchan, is the formation of states that have benign interests in relation to one another, formulated by rules and institutions for "managing their relations, resolving disputes peacefully, and preventing power inequalities from threatening group cohesion" (2010: 31). The Warsaw Pact was meant to counterbalance NATO power, founded as it was by the Soviet Union, and included eight communist countries. It was disbanded in 1991 shortly before the collapse of the Soviet Union. NATO grew slowly through the Cold War years, and accelerated after the fall of the Soviet Union, with post–Cold War membership growth accounting for 42 percent of the current total.

The earliest security community formed after World War II was the Organization of American States (OAS). Formed in 1948 (operationalized in 1951) it is a political, juridical and social governmental forum intended to maintain peace and security between the Americas.[1] In many ways the OAS was a precursor for many contemporary security communities. Its membership now includes all 35 independent states of the Americas, with 67 observer states (plus the EU) (OAS 2012). Elsewhere, and later, other security communities were forged and codified. The Association of Southeast Asian Nations, which formed in 1967, is an example. Despite serious political differences, "ASEAN evolved into an effective forum for resolving political and territorial disputes among its members and for addressing common security threats" (Kupchan 2010: 217). The transition out of the Cold War was the backdrop for further regional integration that reinforces communities of states. Mercosur, founded in 1991, is a political and economic agreement that has facilitated such integration among certain South American states (Argentina, Brazil, Paraguay, and Uruguay as the founding and principal members).[2] If the development of peace is perceived as a possible linear progression – through rapprochement, security community, then union – the furthest along this spectrum is, of course, the European Community, via the European Union. Formally established by the Maastricht Treaty (1992/1993), the creation of the EU illustrates the clearest example of a group of states deliberately and institutionally pooling their sovereignty into a collective whole. In terms of security, the European Political Community of the 1970s was the previous mechanism designed to synchronize foreign policy and security. This was replaced by the Common Foreign and Security Policy of the Maastricht Treaty. However, when it comes to security concerns, the CFSP has yet to effectually pool the respective and diverse sovereignty of the EU states. Kupchan observes: "the EU's member states are still jealously guarding this last redoubt of sovereignty" (2010: 213–14). And yet, stable peace has been established in the region and, in many ways, the EU model fulfills the criteria set forth for a "security union" per se; a designation that includes the subordination of state sovereignty to a supranational system of governance and in so doing minimizes the "geopolitical significance of their territorial borders" (Kupchan 2010: 31). This aspect of a security union is reminiscent of the notion of a Kantian *pacific federation*, which speaks of a "supreme legislative power" to which states must yield in pursuit of perpetual peace (Kant 2007: 85). Hence, the EU can be described as making a decisive shift from Hobbes to Kant.

The global institutional network of security governance remained intact with the end of the Cold War. In fact, the shift of authority from the Soviet Union to the Russian Federation reorganized global security interests in such a way that they would become more aligned. Indeed, in the post–Cold War era both Russian and Chinese security interests have been congruent in some significant respects with the American security agenda. Ikenberry argues that Russian security interests are no longer diametrically opposed to the West, while China has toned down anti-US rhetoric and worked with the US on fighting terrorism and acting as a diplomatic voice in engagement with North Korea (Ikenberry 2004: 89–90).

While there was further development and codification of global security communities after the Cold War, this does not reveal the whole picture. For the post–Cold War transition also ushered in a new era of unipolar American hegemony. The power of the United States was no longer checked by the counterbalancing Soviet Union. In some ways, this development distorted the logic of the multilateral order that had been created in the postwar settlement. The United States, while still an active participant in the multilateral system, was now in the position to "go it alone" if it was deemed necessary (Risse 2004: 218). The US retained superior military capacity – the greatest military force assembled in world history – but was emancipated from the constraints of the Cold War. When Bill Clinton assumed the US Presidency in 1993 he inherited a virtually unchecked American power in the global order. He was heir to "a world freed of the US–Soviet rivalry and bursting with new interest in UN-led efforts to bring peace" (Holt and Mackinnon 2008: 19). However, the military capacity of the US, fashioned with an advanced knowledge of interstate warfare, did not sit easily with many of the new security challenges that would emerge subsequently. Before examining these, we turn to an account of the institutional achievements and innovations that the Cold War era sustained.

Institutional Developments and Successes

The second half of the twentieth century saw many significant developments in the global governance of security, as evidenced by the growing treaties, organizations, and other trappings of multilateral governance. For example, one can clearly see the continued growth of interdependence when considering global efforts toward disarmament and arms control. Table 2.2 documents key developments to that

Table 2.2 Key developments in arms control and disarmament post–World War II

United Nations, 1945	Established after World War II in order to maintain peace and security, facilitate amicable international relations and improve global living conditions and human rights
International Atomic Energy Agency (IAEA), 1957	Core of the nonproliferation regime responsible for nuclear safety, verification, and peaceful transfer/application; technically independent of UN but reports to General Assembly and Security Council by mandate
Treaty on the Non-Proliferation of Nuclear Weapons (NPT), 1970	Multilateral treaty to prevent and reduce horizontal and vertical nuclear proliferation; regulation of peaceful nuclear (energy) applications
Strategic Arms Limitation Talks (SALT-I), 1972	Bilateral agreement (US and former USSR) limiting strategic offensive arms; expired 1977
Anti-Ballistic Missile Treaty (ABM), 1972	Bilateral agreement (US and former USSR) designed to codify deterrence, limiting missile defenses; US withdrew in 2002
Strategic Arms Limitation Talks (SALT-II), 1979	Followed the expiration of SALT-I; consideration was withdrawn from US Senate on the Soviet invasion of Afghanistan
Strategic Arms Reduction Treaty (START-I), July 1991	Bilateral agreement (US and former USSR) reducing long-range nuclear weapons on both sides
Strategic Arms Reduction Treaty (START-II), 1993	Bilateral agreement (US and Russia) reducing intercontinental ballistic missiles (ICBMs), respectively
Comprehensive Test Ban Treaty (Organization) (CTBT(O)), adopted 1996	Adopted by the UN General Assembly the CTBT is not yet in effect; 41 countries have yet to ratify the treaty, most notably the US and China
Strategic Arms Reduction Treaty (New START/III), 2010	Bilateral agreement (US and Russia) with commitment to halve nuclear warheads, further reduce ICBMs and related capabilities, and submit to site inspections by each other's weapons experts

Table 2.2 *(Continued)*

Biological Weapons Convention (BWC), 1975	International convention prohibiting the development/production, stockpiling, attainment, and preservation of biological weapons
Conference on Disarmament (CD), 1979	The single multilateral disarmament negotiating forum of the international community; headquartered at the UN in Geneva, though not technically a UN body
Wassenaar Arrangement on Export Controls for Conventional Arms and Dual-Use Goods and Technologies (WA), 1996	(Amended in 2001.) Complements existing arms control regimes pertaining to weapons of mass destruction (WMDs); specific use of export controls to prevent terrorism. The nonparticipating permanent member of the Security Council is China
Chemical Weapons Convention (CWC), 1997	Multilateral convention banning all chemical weapons (the first of its kind). Has an implementing secretariat (unlike the NPT and BWC) that provides for verification and site inspections, as well as peaceful conversions of existing chemical capabilities
Mine Ban Treaty (Ottawa Convention), 1997	Multilateral treaty prohibiting use of antipersonnel landmines and requiring the clearing/destruction of existing capacity. Of the five permanent members of the Security Council, the US, China, and Russia are not signatories
Geneva International Center for Humanitarian Demining (GICHD), 1998	Houses the Implementation Support Unit established by states party to the ICBL; independent of the UN
Convention on Cluster Munitions (CCM), 2010	Multilateral agreement prohibiting the use, stockpiling, production, and transfer of cluster munitions. It only has 61 states party to the Convention; of five permanent members of the Security Council, the US, China, and Russia are not party states

In general, dates provided are for when the agreement went into effect or otherwise became binding; the CTBT has yet to go into effect.

Source: Adapted from Clarke 2010; Weiss and Thakur 2010.

end, with key agreements and treaties pertaining to nuclear proliferation grouped together, followed by additional developments for other arms. Set atop the foundation of the United Nations itself, an overarching theme of these developments is the creation of a world order where a state's power is, in principle, delimited, subject to regulation, and the object of sanction when noncompliant. While particular state powers were tempered by this liberal construction, it also facilitated the entrenchment of leading powers by guaranteeing positions of privileged influence in the system. This trend can be clearly seen in the examination of three key elements in the global governance of security: the United Nations itself, management of weapons of mass destruction, and the regulation of small arms. An understanding of the overall impact must include both their successes as well as their limitations.

As a starting point it can be argued that the collective security system codified in the United Nations has been a success in certain key respects. Most simply, through the establishment of a liberal multilateral order the great powers were able to prevent another war among themselves. There is of course a considerable debate on the cause of geopolitical stability in second half of the twentieth century. Many observers hold that the UN was in fact not responsible for the stability achieved among the great powers, and would posit nuclear deterrence – understood as mutually assured destruction, reinforced by the recent memory of how catastrophic a nuclear attack could be – as the essential cause (Sokolski 2004; Lieber and Press 2006). This is an important element in understanding the relative peace throughout the Cold War; however, it should not detract from the overall significance of the UN system and subsequent security arrangements. For the operations and functions of the UN were instrumental in the institutionalization and legalization of regulatory regimes in the world military order.

This institutionalization has facilitated greater, self-reinforcing, interdependence, in part because the creation of the UN established a lasting institutional infrastructure for postwar international relations. Its mandate concerning the maintenance of global peace and security has led to significant growth of the UN system as a whole, with greater numbers of subsidiary, advisory, and related bodies, all contributing in some way to the governance of global security. Even when the implementation of security arrangements involves bodies formally independent of the UN (e.g. the Chemical Weapons Convention/Organization for the Prohibition of Chemical Weapons, CWC/OPCW, and, to some extent, the International Atomic Energy

Agency, IAEA, and the Comprehensive Test Ban Treaty, CTBT), there is still a very strong link to the UN system. This can take the form of the UN being used as the forum to initiate a security arrangement, such as the disarmament mechanism set forth by the preparatory commission for the CTBT; or it can be that external agencies report to the UN by mandate, as with the OPCW and IAEA. This link, *inter alia*, has positioned the UN as the primary provider of security as a global public good.

Secondly, a major focus in the governance of global security has been the management of weapons of mass destruction, most obviously the proliferation of nuclear weapons. As the US and USSR scrambled to build their nuclear arsenals in the wake of World War II the world entered the nuclear era. The need to prevent proliferation was acute and immediate such that "*all* governments – nonnuclear and nuclear as well as allies, adversaries, and neutral parties – became stakeholders in peace and demanded a voice in the governance of the nuclear order" (Weiss and Thakur 2010: 94). As early as 1946, the UN General Assembly called for a UN Atomic Energy Commission to prevent proliferation, but it would not be until 1957 that Western allies would submit a proposal to the UN advocating a halt to nuclear testing and stockpiling (2010: 94–5). As table 2.2 illustrates, these multilateral efforts were complemented with bilateral negotiations that took place between the US and USSR. While those talks continued, the multilateral Treaty on the Non-Proliferation of Nuclear Weapons gained momentum in the 1960s. The NPT is one of the major components of the non-proliferation regime, which is comprised of multilateral treaties and organizations, bilateral agreements, and informal arrangements geared towards managing and, ultimately, eradicating nuclear weapons.

The NPT "entered into force in March 1970, [and] has been considered to be one of the great success stories of arms control with some 190 states party to the treaty at the last NPT Review Conference" (M. Clarke 2010: 101). The postwar nuclear non-proliferation regime, largely through the NPT, sought first to prevent horizontal proliferation, but also address (at some point in the future) vertical proliferation. The former refers to the transfer of nuclear weapons from a state with nuclear weapons to those without, while the latter refers to the eventual disarmament of those states possessing nuclear weapons (M. Clarke 2010). Currently there are five recognized nuclear weapons states under the NPT (the N-5): United States, Russia, China, United Kingdom, and France. Apart from the N-5, the states that possess nuclear weapons include Israel, India, and Pakistan, recognized as "non-NPT nuclear weapons states," and lastly the Democratic People's Republic of Korea, which recently withdrew from the NPT (M. Clarke 2010: 101). Given the limited number of states that possess nuclear weapons, as well as the absence of nuclear conflict, one can see how the NPT has been relatively successful in important respects in achieving its mandate of preventing horizontal proliferation.

Additional achievements in the management of weapons of mass destruction can be seen in arrangements that are responsible for governing chemical and biological weapons. The Chemical Weapons Convention, which went into effect in 1997, has been recognized as a particularly effective arrangement. Unlike most arms control agreements, the CWC provides a relatively strong supervisory body – the Organization for the Prohibition of Chemical Weapons. The OPCW is the implementing secretariat of the CWC, a feature that is unique to this class of weapons; neither the NPT nor the Biological Weapons Convention can make this claim (though the IAEA provides some equivalent functions for the NPT). The OPCW reports to the UN General Assembly and possesses a unique challenge inspection feature wherein "States Parties have committed themselves to the principle of 'any time, anywhere' inspections with no right of refusal" (OPCW 2012). Any state party to the Convention can request on-site inspections of others under this regulatory scheme. The Biological Weapons Convention of 1975 is another example of such agreements, though it does not have nearly the same enforcement capability. Without an implementing secretariat (or equivalent) it lacks regulatory strength; and does not have the advanced technology for detection and verification that exists for its CWC counterpart. Global efforts to address the trinity of WMDs (nuclear, chemical, and biological) present a picture of extensive international cooperation and collaboration. They illustrate the intertwined fates of a global community with significant shared interests surrounding the governance of security.

The trinity of WMDs are the most easily referenced weapons of mass destruction, though it is important not to disregard the extensive violence caused by smaller arms. The UN has played a central role in small arms disarmament initiatives, including the UN Conference on the Illicit Trade in Small Arms and Light Weapons in All Its Aspects, in 2001, as well as the General Assembly's adoption of the Protocol against the Illicit Manufacturing of and Trafficking in Firearms, Their Parts and Components and Ammunition, of 2005. Additional significant developments surrounding small arms control include the Wassenaar Arrangement – operational since 1996 – which sets out to prevent acts of terrorism through export controls on weapons, dual-use goods/technologies and, more recently, the Convention on Cluster Munitions of 2010. At the regional level a significant development in the governance of small arms can be seen in the 1990 Treaty on Conventional Armed Forces in Europe, which "sets ceilings on five categories of treaty-limited equipment – tanks, armoured combat vehicles (ACV), artillery of at least 100-mm calibre, combat aircraft, and attack helicopters" (SIPRI 2010: 497). Within these distinctions, the treaty has been quite successful in reducing state holdings of treaty-limited equipment; decreases across the five categories from 1990 to 2010 are, respectively: –37,303 (tanks), –38,803 (ACVs), –22,896 (artillery), –8,201 (combat aircraft), and –1,687 (helicopters) (SIPRI 2010: 426).

An important element within the small arms category deserving greater focus is the issue of landmines. There are few issues with as much agreement internationally as that pertaining to abolishing their use. This issue not only speaks to the core of security in everyday life, but also demonstrates the changing security landscape which now includes nonstate actors at the negotiating table. Civil society advocacy surrounding the Mine Ban Treaty (commonly referred to as the Ottawa Treaty/Convention) of 1997 brought the issue to the fore of international political awareness. However, decisive action on the issue of landmines and, more specifically, on the Mine Ban Treaty was difficult to achieve in the established negotiating framework – the Conference on Disarmament. Established in 1979, "[t]he CD is in the paradoxical position of being the UN's sole disarmament legislative forum while not being a true UN body" (Weiss and Thakur 2010: 112). To complicate this relationship further, the CD operates under very different rules of governance than the UN. Under the CD Rules of Procedure (Article VI), it states clearly that all decisions are to be conducted through consensus. A combination of the nuclear weapons states plus 60 others has proven a difficult group of states to move toward consensus decisions. With frustration mounting regarding the lack of progress made within the CD on the issue of landmines, various civil society organizations as well as interested state parties have sought to remove the issue from the CD framework. Rather than relying solely on a state-centric model for negotiation, they created a process whereby states, nongovernmental organizations, and international organizations could work in concert rather than in competition, successfully culminating in the Mine Ban Treaty signed by 133 countries in 1997. The Geneva International Centre for Humanitarian Demining of 1998 houses the Implementation Support Unit established by state parties to the Ottawa Treaty. Even though this process was external to the CD and UN, the state parties have relied on the UN for "treaty review, reporting, and depository processes" (Weiss and Thakur 2010: 110).

One can, thus, see the enormous effort that has been going into small arms disarmament. This ranges from UN and multilateral arrangements to more regional agreements, and also to more contemporary conventions such as the Ottawa Treaty that breaks the traditional mold of state-based treaty negotiations. On the one hand, these developments, it can be argued, represent serious institutional responses to global security concerns. On the other, it has to be acknowledged that the system faces complex challenges, including a lack of participation by dominant powers and an absence of enforcement capacity. Add to this the fact that small weapons of many types are still widely available and that severe casualties can be inflicted from only a small number of arms, and it becomes apparent that ostensible progress in this arena should not be exaggerated.

While the second half of the twentieth century saw many major developments in the governance of global security which facilitated greater interdependence, one can clearly see a constant and problematic trend. Across the entire security landscape each step forward toward greater collaboration has been underwritten with disproportionate privilege afforded to the leading world powers. This type of embedded privilege has deep historical roots, dating at least as far back as the Congress of Vienna, but now stands out as a highly problematic feature of the liberal world order faced with new challenges. Some of the elements that made for the systematic and institutionalized success of the multilateral system now risk eroding its legitimacy and relevance in an altered global landscape. Before exploring this theme further, changing aspects of international law need examining.

Shifting Principles of Global Order

Very few developments in the postwar period highlight so clearly the complex interplay between states and more universal claims of law as does the evolution of the international law regime itself. Pioneering changes have established new meanings of sovereignty and, linked to this, a new meaning of security. In the early decades of the postwar period the geopolitical position of the 1945 victors was protected and nurtured through the UN system itself, which entrenched their power while it claimed to represent all states on an equal basis. Against the backdrop of the Cold War, the multilateral order was mediated by the clashing interests of its protagonists and their linked hierarchies of power. Yet, within this affirmation of state power, sovereignty and interests, the seeds were also laid for a new meaning of security and a reframed interstate order. The laws of war were increasingly complemented by the conventions on human rights that, in principle, recast the meaning of sovereignty itself. Sovereignty was reshaped and reconceived, no longer as effective power, but as rightful authority; that is, authority that upholds fundamental democratic values and human rights standards (Held 2004). The law of war and the human rights regime combined to reform the meaning of power and violence in the postwar order, delimiting in principle not only the behavior of states during times of war, but of all state and nonstate actors at all times. Thus, the beginnings were established to rethink the meaning of security. In this context, security no longer means the protection of state interests and bounded territories in the interest of settled power relations. Rather, security comes to mean the protection and nurturing of each and every person's interest in self-determination, human rights, and fundamental freedoms. Accordingly, the history of security since 1945 is the history of the development of new conceptions which sought to unsettle the understanding of security as state security, and refocus it on the security of each and every person – on human security. Needless to say, these developments have not gone unchallenged as states have sought to protect their positions.

The formation of the rules of warfare was based on the presupposition that, while war cannot be abolished, some of its most appalling consequences, for soldiers and citizens alike, should be made illegal. The major multilateral conventions governing war date back to the Declaration of Paris in 1856, pertaining to war at sea and the prohibition of privateering. Over the course of 150 years this system of rules and regulations has continued to grow, even though enforcement remains problematic. Table 2.3 includes the major milestones in the codification of the law of war. The Declaration of Paris, Geneva Conventions, and Hague Conferences aimed to forbid conduct during war that fell below minimum standards of civilized behavior which should be upheld by all parties to an armed conflict. To be sure, the rules of war are often violated but they have served to "put a brake on some of the more indiscriminate acts of state violence" (Held 2004: 120).

From the middle of the twentieth century the rules of war became more institutionalized through the creation of the International Court of Justice (ICJ), the prosecutions at the Nuremberg/Tokyo tribunals, as well as the tribunals for the former Yugoslavia and Rwanda.

Table 2.3 Selected developments in the law of war

Convention/Agreement	Purpose
Declaration of Paris, 1856	Sought to limit sea warfare by prohibiting privateering and to specify legality of blockades, determined by effectiveness
Geneva Conventions (4)	*1864*: Pertaining to the treatment of the wounded in the field *1906*: Enhanced measures for the wounded, and added protection for those wounded at sea *1929*: Rules governing the treatment of prisoners of war *1949*: Protection of neutral persons and civilians
Hague Conferences (2)	*1899*: Pertaining to rules of war; declarations included the prohibition of launching weapons from balloons, the employment of noxious gas weapons, and the use of dum-dum (expanding) bullets *1907*: Revision of the first; greater emphasis on war at sea
International Court of Justice (ICJ), 1945	Dual jurisdiction, to settle legal disputes submitted to it by states and to give advisory opinions on legal questions referred to it by authorized United Nations organs and specialized agencies
Nuremberg and Tokyo tribunals, 1945–6	Prosecution of war crimes committed during World War II
International Criminal Tribunal for the former Yugoslavia (ICTY), 1993	Initiated by the UN pertaining to war crimes committed in Bosnia and Kosovo
International Criminal Tribunal for Rwanda (ICTR), 1994	Initiated by the UN pertaining to the Rwandan genocide of 1994
The Rome Statue: International Criminal Court (ICC), 1998	A permanent court established in The Hague to prosecute genocide, crimes against humanity, war crimes, and crimes of aggression

Source: Adapted from Scott 1909; Held 2004; ICC 2012.

This shift, with specific regard to the tribunals, brought with it an emphasis on the primacy of individual responsibility; it set the precedent that when state laws are contrary to international humanitarian standards, individuals are obliged to comply with the latter and the state cannot be used as legal justification for acts deemed criminal by the international community (Cassese 1988: 132; Dinstein 1993: 968). While enforcement has led only to limited prosecutions, the operation of such tribunals has reduced the credibility gap between the standards of an emerging international legal system and their application. The implementation of justice-by-tribunal was constrained by the fact that it was administered with temporary institutional capacity, resulting in limited spatial and temporal jurisdiction. The creation of the International Criminal Court (ICC), via the Rome Statute, has sought to establish a permanent court that is designed to close this credibility gap in the longer term. There are 117 states parties to the ICC. However, three of the five permanent members of the UN Security Council are not included among them. Russia and the United States both became signatories to the Rome Statute, but have failed to ratify it, while China is not a signatory. Even so, the ICC marks a watershed in the institutionalization of international law because of its permanence as well as the different ways a case can be initiated. Proceedings at the ICC can be initiated in three ways: through a state referral, through the prosecutor's office, or by a UN Security Council referral (ICC 2012). The creation of the court has further emphasized changes in the meaning of sovereignty, from that of "effective power" to what has been called "liberal international sovereignty – the extension to the international sphere of the liberal concern with delimited political power and limited government" (Held 2004: 123).

The shifting notions of sovereignty and the codification of the law of war cannot be understood apart from the human rights regime – consisting of overlapping global, regional, and national conventions and institutions (see Donnelly 1998; Evans 1997), see table 2.4. This link is particularly significant because increasingly the purview of international law demonstrates that the mitigation of aggression and violent malfeasance must be pursued through both the control of war and the prevention of human rights abuses; for the distinctions between war and peace, and between aggression and repression, are eroded by changing patterns of violence (Kaldor 1998a, 1998b). The conflicts of the 1990s have the unfortunate record of massive civilian deaths (e.g. Rwanda, the former Yugoslavia). As the lines between war and more general human rights abuses have been blurred, they can

Table 2.4 Selected human rights agreements

June 1945	Charter of the United Nations
June 1946	UN Commission on Human Rights
Dec. 1948	Genocide Convention; Universal Declaration of Human Rights
Nov. 1950	European Convention on Human Rights
July 1951	Convention Relating to the Status of Refugees
Dec. 1952	Convention on the Political Rights of Women
Sept. 1954	Convention on the Status of Stateless Persons
Sept. 1956	Convention Abolishing Slavery
June 1957	ILO's Convention on the Abolition of Forced Labour
Nov. 1962	Convention on Consent to Marriage
Dec. 1965	Convention on the Elimination of Racial Discrimination
Dec. 1966	International Covenants on Economic, Social and Cultural Rights/Civil and Political Rights; Optional Protocol
Nov. 1973	Convention on the Suppression of Apartheid
June 1977	Two additional protocols to the Geneva Conventions
Dec. 1979	Convention on the Elimination of all Forms of Discrimination against Women
Dec. 1984	Convention against Torture
Nov. 1989	Convention on the Rights of the Child
May 1993	International Criminal Tribunal for the Former Yugoslavia
Nov. 1994	International Criminal Tribunal for Rwanda
July 1998	UN conference agrees to a treaty for a permanent International Criminal Court
July 1998	The Rome Statute is adopted establishing the ICC, going into effect in 2002

Source: Economist 1998, in Held 2004: 126.

be viewed as two sides of the same coin. Conflict prevention and the reduction of systematic violence now entail much more than preventing traditional patterns of war. In this way, the rules of war and human rights law must be understood as complementary (Kaldor 1998a, 1998b; refer to table 2.4).

All in all, the development of the law of war and the human rights regime constitutes an increasingly complex framework of international regulation. And it is this framework that has been the foundation of a further paradigmatic shift in the international community. Impetus for this shift lies in the changing nature and form of conflict. A variety of scholars have interpreted patterns of post–Cold War conflict as "new wars" – whereby civil war, and more specifically internationalized civil war, has become increasingly significant compared to

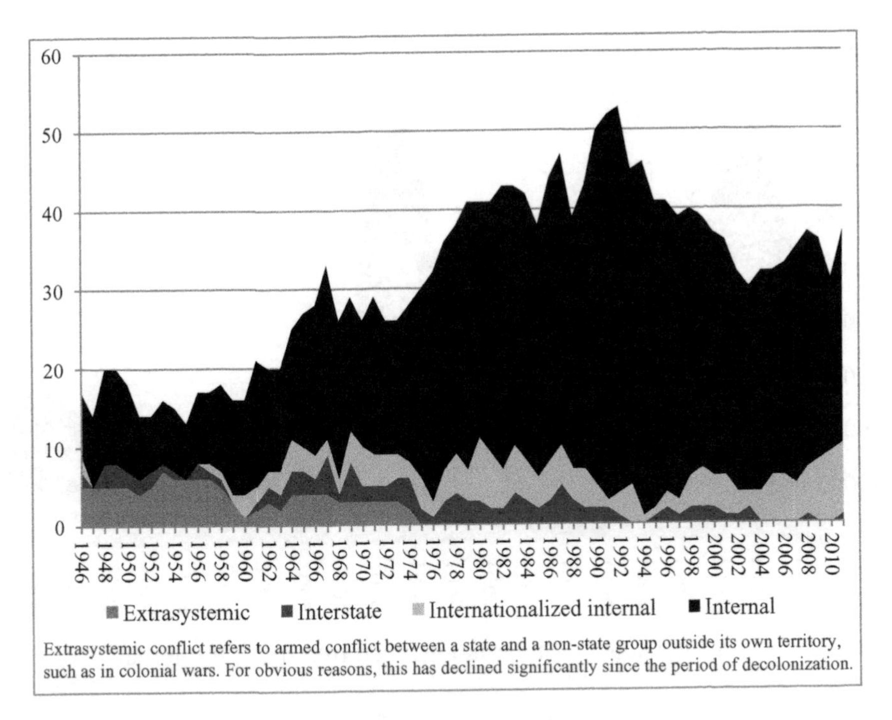

Figure 2.1 Number and type of armed conflicts, 1946–2011

Source: Data from UCDP/PRIO Armed Conflict Dataset v.4-2012, collapsed by year by the authors; see also Gleditsch et al. 2002; Lacina and Gleditsch 2005.

interstate war (see Enzenberger 1993; Kaplan 1994; Duffield 1998, 2001; Kaldor 1998a). Figure 2.1 plots the number and type of armed conflicts in the world since 1945. Interstate conflict occurs between two or more states, and this has generally decreased. Internal conflict refers to what most people understand by civil wars: armed conflict between the government of a state and one or more internal opposition groups, and this expanded significantly. Internationalized internal conflict refers to the same situation, but with outside intervention from other states.[3]

This argument faces challenges. For example, if the scope of war is to be accounted for through casualties, then one can see a very different picture in terms of battle deaths.[4] As Figure 2.2 illustrates, the conflicts accounting for the greatest number of battle deaths since 1945 have alternated over time between interstate and civil warfare. One can break down the number of battle deaths by types of warfare with particular accuracy since the end of the Cold War when more reliable data became available. Figure 2.2 shows that the number of

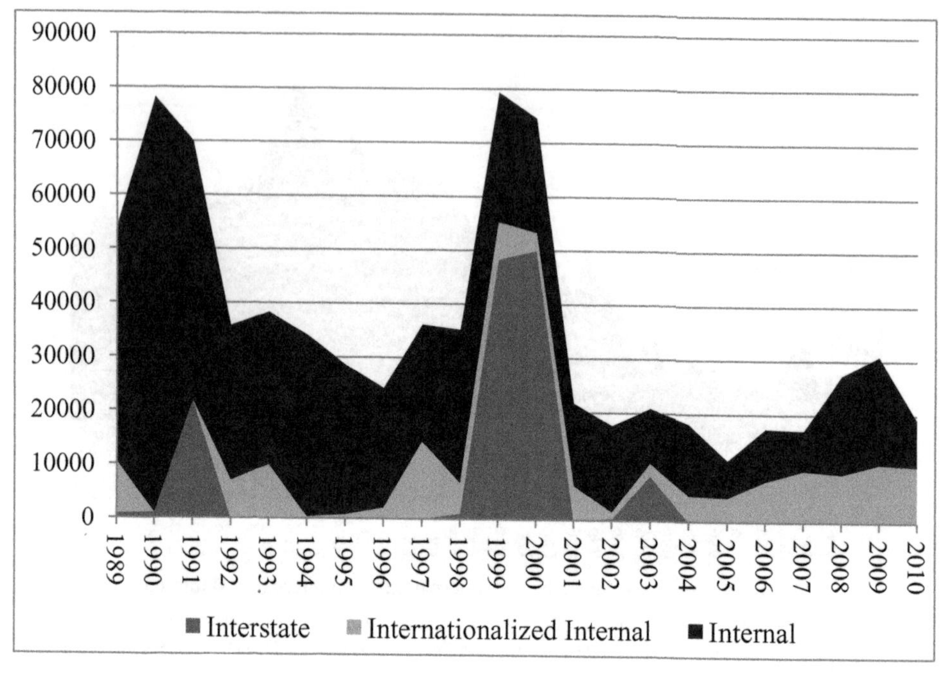

Figure 2.2 Battle deaths by category, 1989–2010

Source: Data from UCDP Battle-Related Deaths Dataset v.5-2011, collapsed by year by the authors, and based on the "best estimates" category.

battle deaths since the end of the Cold War has consistently been greater for civil (i.e. internal) wars throughout this period.[5]

While the question of whether there has been a shift to a new type of conflict remains debated (see Kalyvas 2001; Mundy 2011), recent conflicts have undoubtedly had a significant impact on the international community. Since the end of the Cold War, the international community has gradually refocused on the conflict-affected populations of civil wars. When this focus leads to intervention, the form and duration of a conflict can change (see Lockyer 2011). As figure 2.2 illustrates, internationalized civil wars now represent a significant proportion of recent armed conflict deaths. The plight of local populations in these conflicts has become a leading concern of international audiences. At the same time, the transformation in modern warfare has put pressures on the structure of international law that has been built up since the postwar period. As Bassiouni (2008) points out, the relative rise of nonstate actors in armed conflict has important consequences for the way that conflict interrelates with the existing system of international law, specifically the law of war. Nonstate actors fall largely outside of this framework, posing numerous challenges to security governance; and the fact of increasing numbers of "internationalized" civil wars only compounds this dynamic.

Another way in which the transformation of warfare has affected security governance more generally has been in the relative ineffectiveness of traditional military capacity to address the new character and composition of recent armed conflict. The Yugoslav wars of the early to mid 1990s, previously referred to, stand out as a striking example in this regard. The nature of these conflicts was ever more complex: ethnic divisions, weak states, and the lack of a legitimate monopoly of violence combined to make resolution of these conflicts a daunting task. The Yugoslav wars signaled a resurgence of genocidal violence, a pattern that would come to characterize other emerging conflicts. Yet, despite the focus on such conflicts, security provision in the 1990s was very much a "stop-and-go" affair – with international forces or outside states intervening in some conflicts and not in others, and sometimes entering the conflict very late after it had already escalated seriously. The questionable performance in the Yugoslav wars and the much publicized failure of US intervention in Somalia at the Battle of Mogadishu in 1993 tempered interventionist leanings (Beebe and Kaldor 2010: 48–9). This dampened the international community's willingness to intervene in conflicts which required decisive military action. Most notably, the Rwandan Genocide in 1994 demonstrated the complete and utter failure of the UN, and the international system at large, to prevent the worst of the atrocities – as approximately 800,000 ethnically Tutsi people were systematically slaughtered in only a few months. To say that the UN operation on the ground in Rwanda was insufficient is an understatement of drastic proportions (see Dallaire 2004). Throughout these violent civil and ethnic conflicts, it became apparent that many states, far from being the source of security and protection, were becoming fragmented, broken, and the source of terror against their citizens. In the early 1990s Francis Deng, then special representative to the UN Secretary General on Internal Displacement, began espousing the notion of "sovereignty as responsibility" (R. Cohen, 2010). This notion emphasized that states had a responsibility to protect their citizens and that their citizens had an elemental right to expect protection. As this idea made its way around various spheres of the international community, its usage became increasingly widespread. In 1999 UN Secretary General Kofi Annan spoke of two sovereignties: that of states and that of individuals, and a changing reality since World War II whereby individual rights progressively took precedent over, and came to trump, state sovereignty (Annan 1999b). This notable emphasis has been interpreted by some, especially in global civil society organizations, as generating a new basis for thinking about security. If sovereign authority is no longer linked just to states, then security shifts its meaning too; it must be understood no longer just as state-based action, but anchored in human rights and the sanctity of individual life.

This notion was taken further by the Canadian-led International Commission on Intervention and State Sovereignty (ICISS). In 2001 it produced a report entitled "The Responsibility to Protect" (R2P) which articulated criteria, linked to developments in international human rights law, that states must be able to meet for their citizens if they are to remain sovereign. It outlines a state's responsibility as threefold: the responsibility to "prevent" harm and illegitimate violence against its citizens; the responsibility to "react" when their citizens are threatened or at risk; and the responsibility to "rebuild" when conflict comes to an end (see Thakur 2010). A state's failure to comply with these criteria, according to the R2P doctrine, means that their sovereignty may be subject to forfeiture to the international community.

This development is significant for many reasons. Perhaps most important is that the "duty" of states and state actors is no longer framed in a negative sense – in terms of what behavior is prohibited – but, rather, it is framed in positive terms; it lays out the grounds for intervention when certain human rights standards are not met by the state in question. At the 2005 UN World Summit, the R2P doctrine was unanimously adopted by states through Resolution 1674 on the Protection of Civilians in Armed Conflict. The Resolution argues that states have a formal responsibility to protect their populations from genocide, war crimes, ethnic cleansing, and crimes against humanity. Furthermore, UN members not only have a duty to assist states in fulfilling these responsibilities but when a state manifestly fails on these grounds external actors may take "timely and decisive" actions to intervene to protect populations in a manner consistent with the UN Charter (see Ban Ki-moon 2009). The R2P doctrine has since been reaffirmed unanimously by the UN Security Council, in 2009 (Resolution 1819).

Parallel to the development of R2P has been the emergence of the notion of human security – which remains an evolving principle of global governance. The principle of human security was first introduced by the UNDP *Human Development Report* in 1994, but has been amended and refined since its inception.[6] At its core, it sets out a security agenda concerned to protect the basic prerequisites of human life (see Paris 2001; Alkire 2003; Owen 2004; UNOCHA 2012). It is currently defined by the Commission on Human Security as the "protection of the vital core of all human lives in ways that enhance human freedoms and fulfilment . . . protecting fundamental freedoms [and] people from critical and pervasive threats and situations" (UNOCHA 2012). Alkire points out that "it does not cover all necessary, important, and profound aspects of human living. Rather, it identifies and protects a limited vital core of human activities and abilities"; namely, the ability to sustain life within a framework of the rule of law and according to human rights standards (2003: 3). This emerging paradigm has served, in principle, to further subordinate state sovereignty in relation to human security concerns, whereby the vital interests of human beings are given priority over those of the state itself. Accordingly, the role and power of states are recast to ensure that they meet a set of common standards – those set down in the new international law. How far they actually meet these standards is, of course, another question. A question brought into sharp relief by the end of the Cold War and 9/11.

The very notion of state sovereignty and, thus, security, has undergone major transformations. However, there remains a considerable gap between what has been accomplished in principle, and what practices manifest on the ground. While the world community seemed to be moving in a human security direction, the realities of world politics were not far off. This was never more apparent than when the world was overcome by the terrorist attacks of 9/11 and the responses to it. The events of 9/11 and its aftermath have drastically reshaped the development of global security governance. The world's leading superpower was attacked, on its own soil, exposing layers of vulnerability rarely considered at all. Almost in an instant, the emerging human security project was halted and redirected toward more conventional terms of state-centric security. For this reason, it is an event, and indeed an era, that deserves closer examination.

Post-9/11 Global Security

The global security order was drastically altered after 9/11, weakening, in some crucial respects, the architecture of the postwar period. The terrorist attacks on the World Trade Center and the Pentagon, as well as the downed hijacked plane in Pennsylvania, were not the first terrorist attack on the United States, but they were the most significant. The American lives lost on 9/11 were greater in number than at Pearl Harbor, and the attack ultimately catalyzed a resurgence of American unilateralism under the Bush administration. The National Security Strategy set out by the Bush administration in 2002 explicitly committed the US to unilateralism "when our interests and unique responsibilities require" (White House 2002: 31; Risse 2004: 229). The initial response to 9/11 – the decision to invade Afghanistan – had overwhelming international support and was legally sanctioned by UN Resolution 1386 that established the International Security Assistance Force (ISAF) (UN Security Council 2001), which would later be handed over to NATO control in 2003. After a decade of war in Afghanistan, however, the situation is far from what was envisaged. By mid-2011, ISAF had swollen to more than 130,000 troops and suffered nearly 2,800 fatalities, with each year since 2003 bloodier than before (icasualties 2012a). Indeed, the International Crisis Group summarizes: "security has deteriorated across the country, with the highest civilian casualty rates since 2001, and the insurgency is spreading to areas previously considered relatively safe, including the provinces around the capital Kabul" (ICG 2011). The ICG pessimistically concluded that there was virtually no prospect of stabilizing the country before the end of the planned US and NATO withdrawal and the handover of security duties to the Afghan government by 2014. This pessimism is not without reason, as 2011 was in fact the most deadly year for civilians in Afghanistan. There were 3,021 civilians killed in Afghanistan in 2011; 2,332 were caused by "antigovernment" elements (77 percent), while another 410 were caused by pro-government forces (14 percent).[7]

The stoning to death of a woman and her daughter, in November of 2011, just 300 meters from the governor's office in Ghazni city, Afghanistan, provided a grisly example of the extreme limitations of functioning authority after ten years of Western intervention. This intervention, apart from triggering the enduring war in Afghanistan, was the beginning of the "War on Terror," which marked the start of a protracted conflict that included many complex and diffuse operations, and which has stretched far across the globe: from the Middle East to the Philippines, and from the Mediterranean to the Horn of Africa. This war's expansive reach is measured not just in physical terms, however, as it is also a "war" on the ideologies and politics of terrorism.

The US invasion of Iraq in 2003, even though couched in terms of terrorism and the threat of WMDs, was something altogether different than the war in Afghanistan. The Bush administration felt obliged to seek UN legitimization, largely due to the insistence of Secretary of State Colin Powell, but when it did not receive it, unilateral action was taken anyway. The successful invasion that toppled Saddam Hussein in less than three weeks quickly soured. Initial plans for a short occupation and rapid transition were naive at best, and the situation quickly deteriorated with the beginnings of an insurgency against what was turning into a tough and prolonged occupation. The results for the Iraqi people have been catastrophic. Civilian deaths remain a matter of dispute because of the official lack of interest in keeping figures, reflecting the infamous attitude expressed by General Tommy Franks, who declared "We don't do body counts" (BBC 2005). Thus, estimates on Iraqi deaths vary greatly. They range from an Iraq Body Count figure of 115,373 civilian deaths by January 2012 to a contentious survey published in *The Lancet* that suggested a much higher number of 654,965 excess deaths by June 2006 alone (Burnham et al. 2006). These measures of human insecurity were magnified by the displacement of more than 4 million Iraqis as a result of ethnic and sectarian cleansing.

Although levels of violence have dropped substantially since the sectarian slaughter peaked between 2005 and 2007, Iraq remains today one of the most dangerous countries in the world. The initial drive behind this conflict deserves highlighting – unilateral US action in flagrant breach of international law. However, it was not just unilateral action on the ground that the US exercised, but also unilateral power in determining the agenda and acceptable coercive measures that could be employed. Ikenberry points out that "unipolarity is prone toward rule of power rather than the rule of law" (2004: 86), and the US-directed policy directly reflected this fact. This resurgence of US unilateralism was bolstered by some European support, notably the UK's.

This development in the global security order was characterized by substantially different approaches in the international community. At one level, 9/11 triggered a divergence between the American-led security agenda and the rule-based human rights and development agenda (the agenda of the new international law), largely supported by European powers. Within Europe itself there was also disagreement about how to check American power. Britain in particular positioned itself very close to the United States, and attempted to shape policy as a primary member of the US-led coalition. France, on the other hand, distanced itself from the American foreign policy and attempted to build an opposing coalition (Ikenberry 2004: 92–3). These divergences, in many respects, have come to characterize the post-9/11 global order, wherein US interests are both supported and affected by key allies, while other powers seek to counterbalance the dominant US position through more direct opposition.

Other developments have been triggered by executive transitions in key states – the transition from Bush to Obama being the most notable with regard to the ongoing wars in Afghanistan and Iraq, and, more generally, the War on Terror. On August 31, 2010 the US government announced that it had ceased combat operations in Iraq, and in October 2011 Obama announced that he would withdraw US troops by the end of the year (Lander 2011). While this is significant, it should not be overstated. The US still has considerable forces in the region, and the War on Terror – centered around the Afghanistan invasion – has proven to be protracted, and increasingly complex.

As conflicts unfold and continue to be waged, it becomes clear that the world is increasingly characterized by a crisis of governance – wherein the magnitude of global insecurity and violent challenges creates a need for far greater cooperation and coordination than that envisaged by architects of the postwar settlement. This is the demand increasingly placed on the international community. The supply offered, however, is far from sufficient, as the rest of this chapter highlights. Progress on the most pressing issues facing world security is being inhibited by four pathways to gridlock – institutional inertia, emerging multipolarity, harder problems, and fragmentation.

GRIDLOCK: DYNAMICS OF INSTITUTIONAL DEFICIT AND MALFUNCTION

When one views the governance of security from a historical perspective, it becomes clear that as the geopolitical landscape changes the governance structures designed in one era do not necessarily fit the next. Thus, it is not entirely a surprise to discover that the global governance structures designed to address security threats in the postwar period currently face a class of barriers that inhibit progress on many pressing issues. Importantly, these second-order cooperation problems have their roots in the very successes of the postwar settlement. First, we examine how the deliberate entrenchment of dominant powers in the UN system and the disarmament regime, though necessary to foster participation, has created over time a state of institutional inertia resistant to the enfranchisement of emerging world powers. The result has been that global governance bodies have become ineffectual in some of the most important areas of security governance. Second, we consider how the new kinds of complex issues that have emerged over the last decades defy multilateral solutions. As interstate war has grown less common, in part due to the postwar order, these new challenges have proven less amenable to solution via multilateral cooperation. And finally, we note the incomplete shift toward a more humanistic view of sovereignty and security. The postwar order has done much to push this vision forward, but has proven unable to create the institutional changes necessary to realize it.

The UN Security Council and the Disarmament Regime

At the core of the postwar multilateral security order lay the UN Security Council and the various disarmament regimes. They fundamentally reflect the postwar balance of power, which is simultaneously a source of their historical effectiveness and an impediment to the emergent security realities we now face. Bound by institutional inertia but facing the reality of growing multipolarity, these formal intergovernmental bulwarks for peace between nation-states show increasing cracks. Each is explored in turn below.

The United Nations Security Council

The "architecture" of the UN was originally drawn up to accommodate the global power structure as it was understood in 1945. The division of the globe into powerful nation-states, with distinctive sets of geopolitical interests, was built into the Charter. Being a permanent member of the UN Security Council stands out as one of the most privileged positions of influence a state can hold in the governance of global security. The need to foster inclusion of the great powers at the end of World War II, and thus ensure the effectiveness of the UN system, led to the "grand bargain" of 1945 wherein China, France, Russia, the UK, and the US were given permanent positions with veto power (the P-5), as set forth by Chapter V of the UN Charter. However, the People's Republic of China (PRC) was systematically excluded from the UN system when the Communist Party came to power in mainland China in 1949 – isolating the previously ruling Republic of China government to Taiwan – and this changed only in 1971, when the US government and other Western allies accepted the PRC, through

Table 2.5 UN Security Council P-5 vetoes, 1945–2011

Country	Vetoes	Comments
USSR/Russia	122	79 vetoes used in the first 10 years of the UN. Recently used 3 vetoes to prevent intervention in Syria
United States	80	Largely used to block resolutions criticizing Israel
United Kingdom	32	UK's only solo-vetoes (7) pertained to Rhodesia/Zimbabwe
France	17	13 have been on resolutions also vetoed by US and UK
China	10	1972, Bangladeshi membership, and Middle East; 1997, Guatemala; 1999, Macedonia. Recently joined Russia in using 3 vetoes to prevent intervention in Syria

Source: Adapted and updated from UN 2004, 2012.

General Assembly Resolution 2758, as the only legitimate representative of China in the UN (see UN 1971).

On the whole, the design of the UN Security Council in the postwar years reflected the distribution of power in the global order. Yet the privileged status of the P-5 added authority and legitimacy to the position of each of the major powers: although they were barred in principle from the use of force on terms contrary to the Charter, they were protected against censure and sanction in the event of unilateral action by the power of their veto. The historical use of the veto reflects this privilege (see table 2.5). This history reveals a shifting series of great power interests: the Soviet Union used the veto 79 times in the first ten years of the UN; the US has used its veto numerous times to block resolutions on Israel and the Palestinian question; and the UK, France, and China have strategically deployed their veto in line with their foreign policy priorities. More recently, Russia and China invoked their veto against Security Council resolutions concerning the Syrian state's violent attacks on its civilians, the Sudanese government's violence against groups in Darfur, and in other similar cases. Russia and China have insisted on using their vetoes in these cases to prevent what they consider transgressions of state sovereignty. Thus, the entrenchment of privilege for leading states, which was once necessary to foster participation and legitimacy, now stands in the way of Security Council action on matters of life and death.

It is also important to reflect on the deterring effect the veto option carries with regard to actions taken by permanent members. Even when problems of counterfactuals are acknowledged, it is useful to consider the likely effect a country's potential veto has on the formulation of the Security Council agenda. Take, for instance, China's controversial operations in Tibet throughout the latter half of the twentieth century, Russia's highly debated tactics employed in the region of Chechnya, or the US and its allies' invasion of Iraq in 2003 and the subsequent bloodshed there. In all of these instances there would, in principle, be grounds for UN Security Council action; however, this has been almost entirely out of the question given their respective permanent memberships in the Security Council and veto capabilities. The threat and use of a Security Council veto has transformed that body into a typical state of inertia wherein very little progress is made on many pressing issues, and when change or progress does occur, it is both infrequent and often arbitrary.

The permanent five members of the Security Council have managed the growth of the UN system, and major political shifts among the P-5, all while maintaining their privileged participation in global governance bodies. In effect, the Security Council has become locked into this hierarchy of power. The potential veto serves as a shelter for the P-5 from international condemnation or sanction and thus has institutionalized a degree of impunity for the world's leading powers. Furthermore, it allows leading powers to use the UN system in pursuit of their particular interests – for example, the use of the US veto to block resolutions critical of Israel, or the efforts of the Russians and Chinese to block Western sanctions on Iran or Syria.

The UN Charter also gave renewed credence (through Article 51) to unilateral action if it was necessary in "self-defense," since there was no clear delimitation of the meaning of this phrase. In addition, while the Charter placed new obligations on states to settle disputes peacefully, and laid down certain procedures for passing judgment on alleged acts of self-defense, these procedures have rarely been used and there has been no insistence on compliance with them.

Aside from their veto power, an additional privilege of the P-5 members concerns the administration of international justice. One of the three ways in which proceedings at the ICC can be initiated is, as noted earlier, through a Security Council referral; not only could a P-5 member block a referral but also three of the five members are not even member states of the ICC (US, China, and Russia) and thus can side-step it. Even though the international legal regime has grown and changed over time, the privileges of dominance have allowed the most powerful states to manipulate these structures toward their own ends or at least in their favor. They also enjoy a supervisory role in the UN, as select bodies report to the Security Council – for example, the IAEA when matters require. This grants P-5 states clear discretionary authority over reporting bodies, as well as IAEA actions. Thus, while the UN system has contributed greatly to the institutionalization of global security, it has entrenched the position of the victors of 1945 in such a way as to guarantee aspects of their dominance, with the result that many parties affected by Security Council decisions have considerably less voice in the decision-making process, or none at all. Moreover, the P-5 system appears increasingly outmoded as power relations have evolved and other countries have risen to prominence (e.g. Japan, Germany, India, Brazil, South Africa, etc.). The lack of equitable representation and influence for rising world powers illustrates the links between problems of institutional inertia and emerging multipolarity. As new powers become more prominent in the world system, the state of institutional inertia that besets governance bodies inhibits their voice and equal enfranchisement – resulting in a P-5 structure that is anachronistic, reflecting the world order of 1945.

The debate over the role of the P-5 has been longstanding. Dating back to 1979 there are records of discussions within the UN (through General Assembly resolutions) on amending the Security Council structure. These were not taken up seriously until 1993 when the General Assembly commissioned the Open-Ended Working Group on the Question of Equitable Representation On and Increase in the Membership of the Security Council and Other Matters related to the Security Council. Their work was divided into two streams: the first addressed Security Council membership and associated issues (including debate surrounding the number of permanent members as well as the use of the veto), and the second stream addressed the Security Council's working methods (i.e. transparency, working with nonmember states, etc.) (UN 2004). However, reform has remained elusive. The little progress that has been made is in the category of Security Council working methods (UN 2004), while the Security Council members themselves have stalled on more structural reform that would expand the Council membership and extend permanent or, in some cases, temporary privileges. The unwillingness or inability to adopt reform demonstrates the lack of accommodation made by the dominant powers to any shift in their position of power, highlighting the ways in which institutional inertia and emerging multipolarity can interact to create gridlock. Leading powers have deliberately become "stuck" in current institutional arrangements, frequently opposing those "coming up the ranks," or indeed, those who have already arrived. It is the argument here that this lack of accommodation is in fact a weakness of the UN system, casting doubt on its legitimacy as a whole in an increasingly multipolar world.

Disarmament regimes

Further significant institutional difficulties can be uncovered in relation to the issue of WMDs. To be sure, progress has been made; however, the embedded privileges of the postwar era have now led to the onset of other problems. As with the UN system, the most powerful states participate in the governance of WMDs, successfully weaving their interests into the global agenda. With regard to nuclear weapons this is illustrated by the gap between horizontal and vertical proliferation. The leading nuclear powers have worked to prevent new countries from acquiring nuclear weapons while preserving their own standing. In most cases it can be argued that dominant powers have ridden roughshod over wider responsibilities to rid themselves, at some point in the future, of nuclear arms; in so doing, it should be pointed out, they have not violated the letter of the NPT agreement, but rather the norms and expectations created and engendered by it. Reciprocity and equality are central to international regimes, and nuclear weapons states have promised "to end their 'vertical' proliferation in return for a commitment to prevent 'horizontal proliferation' from the nonnuclear weapons states" (M. Clarke 2010: 102). However, this responsibility has largely been ignored by those states possessing nuclear weapons. Moreover, under the George W. Bush administration the US announced that it would create a new generation of tactical bunker-busting nuclear missiles, and so introduced new levels of uncertainty about nuclear risks. This highlights the added difficulty of maintaining continuity of disarmament talks and commitment throughout the executive transitions of the US (and other states); the disregard of the Bush administration (2000–8) for international commitments being a case in point.

The nuclear arena is further complicated by the propensity for state actors to forgo multilateral institutions in favor of bilateral agreements, or unilateral actions, such as those between the US and USSR/Russia: SALT-I and II, START-I, II, and "New START" (III), as well as the efforts to secure warheads after the USSR collapsed. Such negotiations can certainly be effective. Frequent temporary arrangements can be an important part of the construction of a stable peace, characterizing the foundation of security communities in the global order (Kupchan 2010).[8] But while these agreements can augment progress toward disarmament, there is no guarantee that the staggered progress of the cycle of great power negotiations will ever result in the oft-stated goal of living in a world free of nuclear weapons. To date this remains a very elusive ideal. Since 1945, there have been 2,055 recorded nuclear explosions – most recently conducted by North Korea in 2009 (SIPRI 2010; IAEA 2013). As the latter case illustrates, nuclear disaster can potentially occur from a state not party to bilateral negotiations and international agreements. After all, it only takes a single nuclear bomb to cause global devastation. While SALT/START has been an effective system for managing vertical proliferation between the US and Russia, the North Korean example highlights that the nuclear threat has not been eradicated, but rather, at best, managed and contained.

The Conference on Disarmament was established with high hopes, but it has not performed successfully on issues of huge significance, a prominent example being the question of a Fissile Materials Cutoff Treaty. The FMCT was born from a General Assembly resolution in the early 1990s, reflecting the growing demand that states pursue disarmament sincerely as well as in a cooperative and collective fashion. The CD operates under rules of consensus. This is a quality of many multilateral organizations, and with core interests at stake it is not a surprise that consensus is difficult to reach. Divergent interests among states in the CD have resulted in an effective stalemate on the FMCT. For example, China included security arrangements governing the pacific use of outer space as one of their top priorities in an address to the CD in 2002 (Hu Xiaodi 2002). A broad range of issues are on the negotiating table, reflecting the diverse priorities that must be confronted by the CD. The institutional structure of the CD makes this a particular problem, as it gives all countries equal power unilaterally to dictate the terms of debate. Accordingly, progress on measures like the FMCT have been slow, and results minimal.

Furthermore, the disarmament discussion now includes new nuclear powers – India, Pakistan, Israel, and North Korea – and states suspected of pursuing nuclear weapons (Iran), highlighting problems of emerging multipolarity. Even though the US and Russia stand far atop other states in terms of nuclear capabilities, the institutionalization of the NPT regime has created space for emerging powers to exercise voice and agency. One consequence of this is that the NPT has proven vulnerable to manipulation by rogue regimes which argue for autonomy in developing energy-related nuclear capacity, that can later be weaponized. In the case of North Korea, it upgraded its nuclear capabilities through Article IV of the NPT that allows for the pacific development of nuclear capabilities.[9] However, once they reached sufficient enrichment levels, North Korea exercised a clause in Article X of the treaty to withdraw completely. Article X, paragraph I, of the NPT clearly states: "Each Party shall in exercising its national sovereignty have the right to withdraw from the Treaty if it decides that extraordinary events, related to the subject matter of this Treaty, have jeopardized the supreme interests of its country" (UN 2005). At the 2005 NPT conference review, Article X was amended so that paragraph II extended the NPT indefinitely, but the exit mechanism remained intact, making the possibility of another nuclear weapon state a greater risk.[10]

North Korea falls outside conventional norms of behavior on many fronts, but it is important to recall that Israel, India, and Pakistan are also non-NPT nuclear weapons states. They have never signed the NPT and have subsequently developed and maintained nuclear arsenals. And there is, of course, growing concern over Iran's nuclear ambitions. While the official Iranian position maintains that its nuclear program is for peaceful purposes, the West continues to believe that this is not the case. The US and EU have pursued a strategy of economic sanctions which has in turn prompted Iran to return threats of disruption to oil shipping routes in the region. In February 2012 Iran announced it would no longer export crude to UK and French firms, and intensifying Western-led sanctions have brought economic hardship to the population (the spillover effects of this security dilemma into the global economy are marked). Iran's nuclear ambitions precisely demonstrate the tensions now afflicting the core of the security regime. The postwar order codified nuclear weapons as the privilege of the powerful. But as the Iranian case shows (like the North Korean case), they are now sought as "weapons of the weak." The existing dominant powers resist such changes, but the institutionalized bargains of the postwar era seem increasingly frayed under these tensions.

Disarmament negotiations and agreements have also run into difficulties in other areas. When the US deployed white phosphorus in the civilian-populated area of Fallujah in Iraq in 2004, it highlighted weaknesses in the 1993 Chemical Weapons Convention (Beebe and Kaldor 2010: 65; Held 2010: 159–60). White phosphorus is surprisingly not included in the schedule of banned chemical weapons, but arguably it ought to be – as an incendiary device that can cause horrific burns on the victims it touches. It is also alleged that white phosphorus has been deployed by NATO forces in Afghanistan (Goose and Docherty 2012). A lack of clear and consistent standards in matters related to weapons of mass destruction is evidenced by this example. Alongside the unwillingness to disarm nuclear stockpiles, cases such as this demonstrate the kind of double standard that allows dominant powers not only to make the rules according to their interests, but to create and maintain exceptions when it suits them. Lastly, the (non) proliferation problematic is compounded by nonstate actors playing greater roles in this arena. The best example of this was the revelation of a significant clandestine network of nuclear transfer from Dr A. Q. Khan of Pakistan to rogue nations, including, but not limited to, Libya and Iran (Fenn 2004). In the 2011 NATO-led intervention in Libya, the disorder and fragmentation in the country renewed concerns about the likelihood of nonstate terrorist networks obtaining the requisite supplies (i.e. fissile materials) to develop dirty bombs (Reuters 2011).

Arrangements governing the control of small arms are also plagued by a huge problem – the lack of participation from major world powers. Despite the optimistic pledges made by world leaders, powerful state actors inhibit the progress of small arms disarmament by often not participating and thus denying them legitimacy. For example, while significant success can be attributed to the 1990 Treaty on Conventional Armed Forces in Europe, its effectiveness was placed in question when Russia unilaterally "suspended" its participation in the treaty in 2007 (SIPRI 2010: 425). The issue of landmines illustrates this participation problem particularly well, as international consensus supports the Ottawa Treaty in principle yet it is not binding on three of the P-5 countries. Thus, the enforcement capability of the Ottawa Treaty is greatly hindered by the absence of the US, China, and Russia in the convention. The Ottawa Treaty illustrates how security arrangements can be initiated in a more flexible and inclusive process (with civil society participation), but at the same time it highlights the paradigm dependency that so often prevails, whereby the vital interests of the state take precedent over emerging norms and basic human security needs. The Ottawa Treaty was only pursued outside of the Conference on Disarmament because the CD proved itself to be inadequate in achieving progress in the first place.

Taken together, the halting progress of the CD and the lack of participation in the Ottawa Treaty further demonstrate the continuing preeminence of state-centric sovereign interests – even if it is only in the protection of sovereignty as a valued principle. This is in contrast to the emerging new legal regulatory regime and the human security paradigm, where state sovereignty is conditional on the protection of vital human interests. The notion of sovereignty, especially the closer it gets to the core of state power (particularly in the leading states), appears all too often to be more important than multilateral cooperation and coordination in solving many of today's most pressing global security issues.

Apart from the immense problem of landmines, other small arms and light weapons (SALW) remain readily available throughout the world, further exacerbating global insecurity – especially in zones already vulnerable to conflict. The UN estimates that some 875 million SALW are in circulation globally, and that on average over 250,000 deaths a year are the result of small arms use (Gillis 2009).[11] Moreover, the use of SALW accounts for more violent and conflict-related deaths than any other category of weapon – such as those designated as WMDs. This industry remains subject to only limited regulation and is an enormous source of profit for the companies involved. The top five arms producers in the world are the US, Russia, Germany, China, and the UK (SIPRI 2010). It appears, thus, that leading power interests remain opposed to collective and decisive action on small arms control. While an arms trade treaty has been recently passed by the UN General Assembly (2013), it stands little chance of securing ratification from the US, China, or Russia, major arms exporters and P-5 members.

Whether with regard to the UN system, or to the various levels of the disarmament regimes, significant progress in many areas appears outside the reach of the current governance arrangements. The embedded privileges afforded to the 1945 victors have led to obstacles that are hard to overcome and can be characterized as stasis or inertia. Progress has become so infrequent that it has plateaued in many respects. This has been compounded by the emerging multipolarity of the world order, where countries like Britain and France are increasingly clinging to their privileged UN positions despite the rise and accelerated development of other states.

Complex Intermestic Issues

Global integration has brought with it diverse threats of a transnational and intermestic character. Threats such as terrorism, cyber insecurity, and piracy are not confined to territorial boundaries, nor do they simply involve confrontation between conventional military structures. Rather, they penetrate more deeply into society to threaten the vital core of everyday life. They are diffused laterally across territorial boundaries as well as vertically into society, and are thus "harder problems" (see chapter 1). The following deals with several of these that fall high on the global agenda. In some cases the issues have emerged on the agenda because of their pressing impact; in other cases, they have become central in light of changing political and public awareness. In the latter case, a problem that may have existed for some time and was low on the horizon of policy-makers can quickly move up the scale of significance.

Terrorism

Globalization has given rise to nonstate transborder networks of organized violence. These networks operate, at different times and in different contexts, below, alongside, or through a state and exercise illegitimate coercion, often as a means to further some kind of ideological end. Many terrorist networks are enhanced by global infrastructures and have been able to exploit them by operating in shadow economies. In this way, contemporary terrorism has been engendered by growing interdependence in the postwar years. Terrorist groups often propagandize and recruit on the internet, raise funds around the world, and have even turned the very vehicles that facilitate global linkages – such as airplanes – into lethal weapons. Moreover, a great deal of contemporary terrorism represents a departure from quintessential state-centric violence. As terrorism targets civilians, it can be conceived of as a human security threat, even though the goal of its perpetrators is often to punish nation-states. Increasingly, the concern about terrorist threats is central to international political debate, renewed dramatically by 9/11. While the attacks of 9/11 stand out, and are the common referent for terrorism, an overview of the incidents of terrorism reveal a different trend (figure 2.3). Incidents of terrorism declined right after 9/11, though they increased after 2003, coinciding with the US invasion of Iraq. This is consistent with the fact that Iraq is ranked second in the world in the incident count of terrorist attacks by country (behind only Colombia) (START 2011).[12] This is, of course, an ironic trend given that Iraq was the centerpiece for Bush's War on Terror.

Terrorism by its nature subverts traditional conceptions of sovereignty. Interestingly, so has the response to terrorism. As the War on Terror has been pursued increasingly across borders, the US has shown a similar willingness to disregard traditional rights of sovereignty in

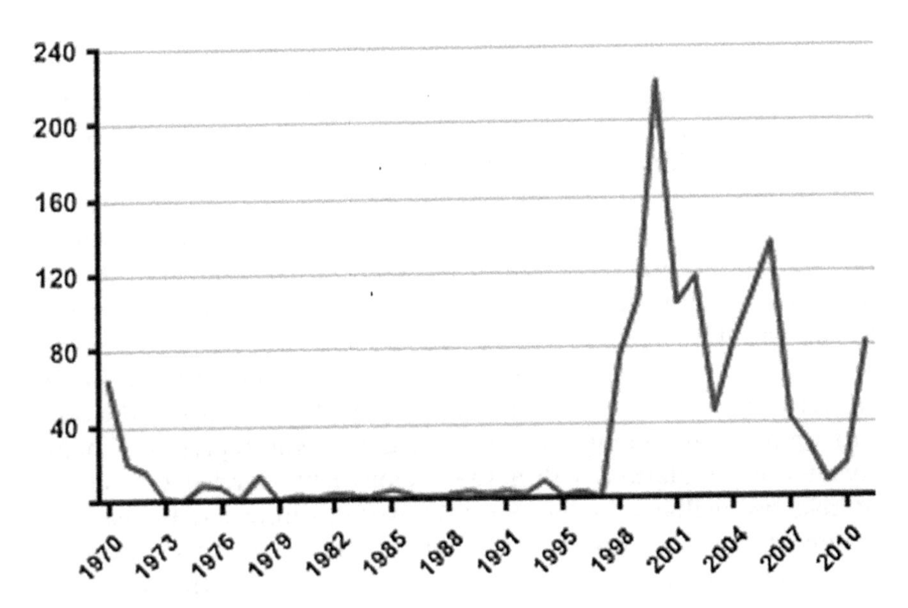

Figure 2.3 Incidents of terrorism, 1970–2010

Source: National Consortium for Terrorism, University of Maryland Global Terrorism Database, 2011.

its pursuit of identified threats. The 2011 operation that killed Osama bin Laden, and the ostensible lack of Pakistan's knowledge or participation, illustrates this point in dramatic fashion. But perhaps more significantly, the US has increasingly pursued a strategy of unmanned drone attacks to carry out what are intended to be more surgical military operations across borders (Beebe and Kaldor 2010: 13). The questionable legality of such use of drones was extended even further when, in September 2011, the US government used an unmanned drone attack to kill the American citizen and al-Qaeda operative Anwar al-Awlaki in Yemen. This established an extreme precedent of not only breaching international sovereignty, but also disregarding rights of traditional due process afforded by the US constitution to its citizens. Even more striking was the less publicized US drone attack two weeks later that killed Awlaki's 16-year-old son Abdulrahman al-Awlaki, who was also a US-born citizen. The US government has argued that this tactic is appropriate because it limits the scale of civilian casualties in its antiterrorism operations. However, the full scale of civilian casualties is extremely difficult to objectively gauge; in 2012 it was revealed that the Obama administration counts any and all "military-aged males" in the vicinity of a drone attack as potential terrorists (or "enemy combatants") and thus does not count or report such deaths as civilian (Becker and Shane 2012). While these deaths are justified by the US government as part of its ever growing antiterrorist operations, they risk placing US security operations above the rule of law, national and international.

It is important to recognize that terrorism takes place in many forms and in many different places. While 9/11 altered the world's perception of terrorism in significant ways, it has influenced the formation of antiterrorism policies that are entirely unrelated to al-Qaeda or 9/11 at all. For example, ever since the fall of the Soviet Union, China has experienced a growth in violent attacks in the western region of Xinjiang. There, the extreme elements of the separatist movement among the Muslim Uighurs, who represent a majority of the population within the region, have carried out several attacks on civilians. In the post-9/11 world, China has increasingly framed these incidents as acts of terror, which has driven a convergence between China's security interests and those of the West. "The term 'terror' began to be used intensively in its declarations; its diplomatic agenda included international cooperation against terror; and it undertook a variety of related actions on a multilateral, regional, and bilateral level" (Evron 2007). Similarly, Russia's persisting clashes with Chechen rebels have increasingly been framed by the Russian state as a form of antiterrorism policy. Yet it is clear that the diverse forms of "terror" make it very difficult to find a single or comprehensive policy that can be shared by all countries in a collective framework. What one country deems appropriate and legitimate antiterrorism policy might be viewed by others as egregious human rights abuse or violations of international law. Thus, we are left with competing and contradictory governance of terrorism as a whole.

Multilateral efforts to deal with terrorism have been multifaceted, but limited in effect. Perhaps the greatest success has occurred in the tracking and freezing of terrorists' finances. These efforts have been facilitated by transnational financial governance institutions, such as the Financial Action Task Force and the Basel Committee on Banking Supervision, both discussed in chapter 3 (see Taylor 2007; Tsingou 2010; Joint Forum 2003, 2005). While such efforts reflect the flexibility and innovative potential existing in an increasingly dense network of transnational institutions, they are very limited in their capacity to take effective action. And despite the salience of the problem of international terrorism since 9/11, multilateral bodies which have more substantive capacities have suffered from problems of diverging interests and institutional fragmentation.

The UN Global Counter-Terrorism Strategy, for example, has two different bureaucracies: a Counter-Terrorism Committee, which exists within the Security Council, and the "Ad Hoc 6th Committee," which operates within the General Assembly to focus on legal issues. While the UN has been able to agree on specific conventions aimed at particular problems – the International Convention for the Suppression of Terrorist Bombings (1997), the International Convention for the Suppression of the Financing of Terrorism (1999), and the International Convention for the Suppression of Acts of Nuclear Terrorism (2005) – it still cannot agree on a basic definition of terrorism. This has meant that the ambitious Comprehensive Convention on International Terrorism, crucial for development of a coherent and systematic approach at the global level, has been deadlocked since its inception in 1996.

Thus, while there have been major steps forward in collaboration between leading states in matters concerning, for example, intelligence sharing, information about illicit financial flows, and the coordination of law enforcement, these have rarely amounted to a coherent multilateral effort. The efforts of Western powers have succeeded in stifling al-Qaeda and similar networks in their own countries, but this cannot be said about countries in which they are broadly engaged. Afghanistan, Iraq, and Libya all remain mired in cycles of endemic violence and regional fragmentation. Each country is highly volatile and subject to widespread and frequent terrorist attacks. In many cases, the effects of these attacks spread to neighboring countries such as Pakistan, Jordan, and Mali. Accordingly, claims to success in the War on Terror are implicitly linked with security for only a limited number of, primarily Western, states – terrorism overall and across diverse countries shows little sign of abating.

Failed states

The idea of a failed state is relatively new, and its place on the agenda of the international community even more so. In addition to being a complex issue, the way the international community deals with failed states also highlights problems of fragmentation. The concept of a failed state did not exist until the postwar era, and more specifically until the end of European colonial rule in sub-Saharan Africa and South Asia (Weiss and Thakur 2010: 75). Thus, it is a designation that has mostly been used to refer to states in these regions which have struggled to establish effective rule throughout their early and ongoing independence. State-building remains a very difficult task and nowhere is this more evident than in postcolonial and conflict-affected countries.

The concept of a failed state refers to a state that is no longer able to function as a guarantor of protection for its citizenry, often giving way to armed contest over control of the state apparatus. This presents a fundamental problem of the erosion of the monopoly of violence. Patterns of state failure became more pronounced at the end of the Cold War, and thus it is in the 1990s that we can observe failed states becoming a priority for the international community (Wyler 2008). The international engagement with failed states at the time was mostly located on the spectrum of humanitarian action; ranging from NGO provision of assistance, to UN, NATO, or Western military intervention. Terrorism, and the widespread response to it, in the post-9/11 era shifted the way in which the international community prioritized the problem of failed states, from an initial ostensibly altruistic project to a self-serving one based on concerns of state security. Failed states are increasingly seen as incubators for global "bads" because they lack adequate capacity to resolve issues such as terrorism, trafficking, and disease. More specifically, failed states are taken to exacerbate threats of international terrorism, international crime, nuclear proliferation, and regional instability (Wyler 2008).

Responding to this potential for violence, the international community, and Western states in particular, have made it a priority to try to accelerate economic development in these countries in the belief that development engenders stability. State-based development agencies such as the UK's Department for International Development and the US Agency for International Development (USAID) have explicitly refocused their governance initiatives to address these issues (see Di John, 2010). These efforts have often been harnessed to the postwar reconstruction efforts in Iraq and Afghanistan. In Afghanistan, for example, huge efforts have been made to put the country on a development track and to ensure that the basis is set for a well-functioning state. However, endemic conflict remains and state-building has proved immensely difficult. After billions of dollars, and thousands of lost lives, little progress can be claimed.

The question of failed states has spread to the agendas of a wide range of international agencies. Notably, the World Bank's *World Development Report* for 2011 was subtitled *Conflict, Security and Development*, and explicitly connected notions of "citizen security" to the tasks of international development agencies (2011: 28–9). In some ways, this approach may act to help close the divergence between American-led

Western foreign policy and the international development and welfare agenda. Security-specific concerns have traditionally been outside the mandate of the World Bank – a fact that highlights just how significant this link is. This expansion of the Bank's mandate was directly alluded to by the Bank and justified as "a reflection of a growing international policy consensus that addressing violent conflict and promoting economic development both require a deeper understanding of the close relationship between politics, security, and development" (World Bank 2011). However, the value of this shift has yet to produce the desired results; that is, effectively shoring up acute state weaknesses.

This intersection of traditional security structures and development agencies highlights the complex nature of dealing with failed states. The diversity of actors (NGOs, IGOs, state security structures, etc.) currently engaged in failed states presents potential problems of fragmentation. The recent overlap of mandates between agencies such as the World Bank and traditional military structures discloses how these agencies have all too often operated in competition with, and disjointed from, each other. The efforts to bring together the forces of development and security, whether state led or NGO led, is only at its earliest stage of articulation, never mind its translation into effective policy on the ground; thus, the problem remains far from resolved.

Piracy

Recent years have seen a significant rise in concern for acts of piracy, illustrating a new frontier of maritime security threats that the international community must address. Piracy is a further example of a security threat closely linked to the notion of a failed state, as pirate networks operating in and out of Somalia account for a large share of recent attacks. Moreover, this issue has strong links with the international development agenda, as maritime insecurity in developing countries adversely affects a country's ability to pursue economic growth through fishing and related activities. Established in 1984 at a convention in Geneva, the International Maritime Organization (since 1982; previously the International Maritime Consultative Organization) is the specialized agency of the United Nations with responsibility for the safety and security of shipping and the prevention of marine pollution by ships. Originally focused on environmental and safety concerns, the IMO has developed an increasing concentration on security as piracy has grown. Despite bolstered policing powers provided by leading states, the threat piracy poses to human security has grown; see, for example, the growing numbers of crew who have been kidnapped or otherwise taken hostage, as shown in table 2.6.

In February 2011, while speaking at the launch of the IMO's action plan "Piracy: Orchestrating the Response," UN Secretary General Ban Ki-moon commented on the urgent need facing the international community to address Somali piracy, calling the growing problem "completely unacceptable," and one that requires a collective response. The International Maritime Bureau (a division of the International Chamber of Commerce) reported that in 2011 "596 seafarers of various nationalities [were] being held for ransom on board 28 ships. A total of 97 attacks were recorded off Somalia in the first quarter, up from 35" in 2010 (IMO 2011a, 2011b). A host of international bodies are now actively engaged in addressing this threat; ranging from state-specific arrangements such as the US and Combined Maritime Forces (CMF) to regional security communities like the EU and NATO, to international bodies such as the IMO and IMB. Despite the proliferation of agencies involved, the growth of global coordination between them, and some success in the matter, the persistence of pirate attacks demonstrates just how difficult it has become to solve this problem. Complex layers of governance and jurisdiction, and the mix of national and international forces, makes an effective collective response to piracy challenging. Having said this, this problem is perhaps the best example of an emerging, harder problem where the international community has succeeded in blunting the worst effects. In particular, there has been success in reducing the number of lives lost in pirate attacks, even though incidence overall and kidnappings remain high.

Cyber security

The importance of cyber security has emerged as another complex intermestic issue on the agendas of states, as well as corporate (private) actors and international organizations. Emerging cyber threats illustrate the transformative effects of technology on global governance concerns. Cyber attacks take place on a virtual platform, but can have very material consequences in society, constituting a threat to national security. In June 2011, amid his transition from the CIA to US Secretary of Defense, Leon Panetta testified before a US Senate hearing that "[t]he next Pearl Harbor we confront could very well be a cyber attack that cripples our power systems, our grid, our security systems, our financial systems, [and] our governmental systems" (Crimaldi 2011).

Table 2.6 Incidents of pirate attacks, 2002–2009

Year	Number of acts	Lives lost	Wounded crew	Missing crew	Crew hostage/ kidnapped	Crew assaulted	Ships hijacked	Ships missing
2002	383	6	38	99	125	86	16	5
2003	452	12	75	32	113	35	14	6
2004	330	29	60	44	147	145	8	1
2005	267	0	29	11	367	67	18	0
2006	254	17	23	0	224	225	10	0
2007	310	22	75	57	223	39	18	0
2008	330	6	22	38	773	21	47	1
2009	406	8	57	9	746	2	56	2

Source: IMO 2011a.

Acknowledging this fact, states have quickly developed infrastructures to mitigate cyber threats. However, this remains a new vulnerability for states which some have exploited.

The widely publicized "Stuxnet" worm discovered in 2010 is popularly though unofficially recognized as having been developed by Israel and/or the United States, and was designed to target specific Siemens software platforms used in Iranian nuclear enrichment technology. Unspecified damage was done to the Natanz nuclear plant in Iran; it was an elaborately orchestrated event that represents one element in the new frontier of security relations (BBC 2010). In May 2012 another highly advanced virus was detected, called the Flame virus, which most reports indicate was malware designed to target the computers of Iranian officials. Again, there has been no official recognition of who is responsible for the virus, though it is largely suspected to be a product of the growing cyber arsenal of the US (Perlroth 2012). The nature of cyber threats remains clandestine, difficult to predict, and on the cutting edge of technology; these threats are therefore difficult to accommodate simply within the prevailing logic of armed conflict relations between states. Yet this has not prevented knee-jerk reactions anchored in perceptions of conventional conflict; as an unnamed US military official in 2011 is reported to have stated: "If you shut down our power grid, maybe we will put a missile down one of your smokestacks" (Gorman and Barnes 2011). While there has yet to be a cyber attack of significance on leading powers, recent events do illustrate the vulnerability that exists; in September 2011 a virus was detected in single platform software of US drone facilities in Nevada (Lawrence 2011). This has since been described as conventional malware that did not affect any vital security functions, but it serves to demonstrate the complexity of emerging security risks which can be generated by state or nonstate actors. Even more troubling, it seems wise to assume that we can now only see the first layers of security vulnerabilities that come from an increasingly wired world. As more of our lives move online, we will likely become increasingly at risk of such problems.

The Budapest Convention on Cybercrime (or simply the Budapest Convention) was the first multilateral mechanism designed to address the growing cyber threats that have emerged with the growth of the internet. It was initiated by the Council of Europe, opened for signature in 2001, and went into force in 2004 (UNESCO 2004). The Convention is intended to foster and enhance international cooperation on cybercrime issues by harmonizing national laws into an international framework. It has been praised as a positive step forward, especially since the US ratified and enacted it in 2007. However, there is also some doubt about some of the consequences it could have. For example, it broadens jurisdiction of policing powers to cross virtual-national borders – allowing police forces to "access servers in other countries without the permission of the authorities, as long as the system owners sanction the access" – and gives technologically advanced countries a marked advantage in the global system (*Computer Weekly* 2010). Russia, in particular, was concerned with these implications and in 2010 attempted to initiate a treaty in the UN on cyber-crime that would help to address them. The Russian proposal had some support from China; however the US and European powers blocked its progress (*Computer Weekly* 2010). There may be room for a UN process in the future, but for now the Budapest Convention remains the sole multilateral governance mechanism on this issue.

Pandemics

Pandemics stand out as a further example of threats that have resulted from increased globalization and interdependence, though it must be recognized that pandemics (such as the Black Death) are certainly not new to the world. Rather, it is their capacity to spread unpredictably, rapidly, and globally that constitutes the contemporary pandemic security threat. Basic mechanisms of globalization, such as increased migration and trade, accelerate human interactions. These interactions have, throughout history, led to increased exposure to contagions, resulting in crises as diverse as the Spanish Flu in the early twentieth century, HIV-AIDS, and more recently, SARS and the H1N1 influenza. As the world becomes increasingly interconnected, the threat of a future pandemic persistently looms on the horizon while scientists and public health officials fight to prevent its manifestation.

Understanding pandemics as a security threat stems from an expanded notion of security itself. More specifically, the threat was formally incorporated into the global security regime through the international focus on the HIV-AIDS crisis at the turn of the century (Rubin 2011). Just six years after the publication of the 1994 UNDP report that largely introduced human security to the world, the UN Security Council passed Resolution 1308 on maintaining international peace and security, which put HIV/AIDS "squarely in the crosshairs of the security debate" (Rubin 2011: 4). While this might at the time have been an indication of a paradigm shift toward more human-centric security, any shift to that end was dramatically altered a year later when 9/11 refocused world attention on state security and terrorist violence. And yet, the subtle inclusion of pandemics in the security debate can still be observed. In 2011 President Obama, in an address to the United Nations, urged the world community to "come together to prevent, and detect, and fight every kind of biological danger – whether it's a pandemic like H1N1, or a terrorist threat, or a treatable disease" (Obama 2011; Rubin 2011).

Brief investigation of pandemics as a security threat is valuable for the further reason that it illuminates a controversial aspect of the human security project. In the 2011 OECD report on pandemics as a future global shock (Rubin 2011), it was pointed out that their inclusion in "human security" could lead to a transfer of decision-making authority over a public health crisis to security experts (i.e. military officers), rather than scientists or healthcare professionals. This example illustrates how controversial a paradigm shift toward human security could be under some circumstances. On the one hand, its primary interest in the protection of individual human lives directly challenges the primacy of state-centric interests. On the other hand, it demonstrates how humanitarian causes might be jeopardized by the transfer of such authority to traditional security structures – which up to the present persist along the nation-state military model. As this debate edges forward in policy discussions and think-tank publications, the pace of global integration continues to gain speed, exacerbating the risk of rapidly spreading diseases across the globe, from SARS to influenzas. Accordingly, a pandemic could become a major global security threat in the years ahead.

This potential pandemic threat – whether it be viral, from influenza, or from another source – is managed in a fragmented fashion. Individual countries, especially those which are more technologically and scientifically advanced, have national programs devoted to public health surveillance, geared to picking up significant outbreaks of illness. There are also growing regional efforts on this issue, initiated by bodies like the EU, ASEAN, and the African Union. Globally, public health is largely coordinated by the World Health Organization. The WHO provides, among other services, surveillance capacity for monitoring global public health risks. These are often linked to national and regional bodies and institutions that provide vital information. The WHO is, however, dependent on the willingness and ability of countries to participate in this system, and has a history of difficulties in this regard (for instance, with countries withholding information in order to protect economic interests) (see Kaufman 2008). Moreover, it has little or no power of enforcement when it comes to ensuring adequate information gathering and national compliance with its recommendations. Accordingly, global health governance is marked by problems of fragmentation. A recent report on global health governance and preparedness published by the Council on Foreign Relations (2012) in the US says that while there has been an increase in both funding of and focus on global health, the system remains anarchic and undercoordinated as a whole. Add to this the diversity of actors, public and private, operating in this field and the difficulties of producing coherent and effective global health governance are clearly illustrated (see Hale and Held 2011: 166–75).

Paradigm Shift or Realist Status Quo?

The global governance of security involves a vast institutional network of state, regional, and global actors. As noted previously, this arena also includes various nonstate actors. The exponential growth of these governance mechanisms has been made possible, at least in part, by the stability that was achieved by the postwar settlement – specifically pertaining to the enduring UN system. These mechanisms have been marked by an international division of labor wherein different organizations, agencies, and actors specialize in specific security concerns. This institutional division is not necessarily problematic in and of itself. Rather, one can observe a problem of fragmentation only when the result is weak and inadequate coordination, or overlapping and competing jurisdictions. In these circumstances, a deep-seated challenge can emerge to the current state of global security governance. The state, viewed in Weberian terms, is a consolidated monopoly of legitimate violence (Weber 1964). Yet when this monopoly is under pressure, as it is today, a number of problems develop. These can be observed in diverse situations, from so-called "new wars" and clandestine networks that operate in shadow (war) economies, to private military companies that operate in an emerging market for violence (Held and McGrew 2002: 56–7).

Erosion of the monopoly on violence

Private actors have become major actors in the security arena. As military operations are often conducted with and/or by private companies there has been a commercialization and globalization of organized violence. Private firms now take on many critical functions of security provision, everything from basic administrative functions and logistics to combat operations (Leander 2005, 2009). An example of this trend is the estimated 20,000 private security personnel from 60 different international firms that operated in Iraq in 2004 (Held and McGrew 2007: 57). Such a trend reflects a challenging development from the perspective of global governance. As Percy points out, the rise of private security forces represents an instance of "strong norms but weak laws" (2007). On the one side, the state's ability to legitimize violence is checked by the international community (for example, the contested 2003 invasion of Iraq), and on the other side there is a functional redistribution of the monopoly on legitimate violence – varying by context (Held and McGrew 2002). In the case of industrialized and developed states that maintain a stable regulatory regime, this may in fact mean that a state has a monopoly on the ability to *legitimize* violence, but not *monopolize* it (Deudney in I. Clarke 1999: 119). In a fragile state context, the state may in principle have the ability to legitimize and monopolize violence, though in practice this is a volatile hold on power that is vulnerable to both domestic and external threats.

Those groups that are contracted and provide private security functions differ, of course, in nature and form from those competing groups that use violence to challenge the state apparatus: the former, in principle, do not aim to replace the state, whereas the latter contest its control directly. In either case, a unifying theme is the erosion of the state's monopoly on violence. This erosion, as well as the evolving notion of state sovereignty and the emergence of the human security paradigm, calls for greater collaboration and control over the forces of violence. The problems that develop – difficulties of controlling armed forces, the fragmentation of forces of violence, new forms of terrorism, failed states, etc. – are beyond the scope of a single nation-state to address; they are transborder problems. Moreover, the existing division of protective labor, that is, security forces, designed originally for interstate conflict, is poorly matched to meet the demands of new security challenges, and to ensure the protection and maintenance of individual sovereignty, such as upholding human rights and democratic standards. The result is a capacity gap between existing military capacities and those required by the demands placed upon them.

Humanitarian crises

Humanitarian crises also provide illustrations of the erosion of the state's (claims to a monopoly on the) legitimate use of force and the problematic nature of military capacity today. These types of crises are common in the new forms of conflict that have emerged. This is perhaps most clearly observed in the regions of sub-Saharan Africa. Conflicts in countries such as Sudan, Uganda, Somalia, and the DRC have produced humanitarian crises of epic proportions. Efforts to provide assistance to affected populations in humanitarian disasters come from a range of actors: states, regional security communities, multilateral forces, nongovernmental organizations, etc. Humanitarian principles are grounded in a moral imperative that has been woven into international regimes and organizations. They rest on the basic and simple compulsion to provide assistance to those most in need. The basic principles recognized as definitively humanitarian are the universality of humanity, neutrality and impartiality with regard to the protection of vulnerable populations (see OCHA 2012). This is reflected in the language employed by preeminent humanitarian agencies. Established in 1863, there is no better example than that of the International Committee of the Red Cross; its mission statement clearly describes it as "an impartial, neutral and independent organization whose exclusively humanitarian mission is to protect the lives and dignity of victims of armed conflict and other situations of violence and to provide them with assistance" (ICRC 2010). While this presents a very apolitical picture of humanitarianism, reality proves to be much more complex.

Alongside the changing forms of conflict we have seen a significant rise in specifically humanitarian *intervention*, involving the use of force to provide basic protections. It is within this category of "intervention" that one can observe fundamental problems of jurisdiction and mandate. As global calls for humanitarian action increase, so too has the call for coordination between humanitarian actors and traditional military structures. This trend began to take form in the 1990s when humanitarian agencies pressed the United Nations for military intervention in places like Bosnia, Somalia, and Rwanda, among others (de Waal 1994). At the most fundamental level, this presents questions over who or which groups have the legitimate mandate to initiate the use of force and violence. Contemporary conflicts have led nonstate actors both to advocate the use of force and to coordinate with its implementation. Without the benefit of hindsight or, more precisely, knowing how different alternatives would impact the situation, such endeavors are largely guided by a moral imperative to assist vulnerable populations. However, it has been recognized that such a decision can in fact lead to suboptimal results, when analyzed through an, *ex post*, utilitarian view. Although the Ethiopian famine of 1985–6 did not involve military intervention, Alex de Waal, a noted critic of humanitarianism in all its guises, points out that it "is now no longer seriously disputed that the massive inflow of aid following Band-Aid contributed more to the survival of the Ethiopian government, whose army was the main reason for the famine, than the famine-stricken peasantry" (1994: 1). If this can be said with respect to humanitarian assistance, it can certainly be extended to intervention, as highlighted in the section that follows on R2P. Such observations are unlikely to deter the impetus for either humanitarian assistance or intervention, and even de Waal has recently said that he would be disappointed if his critical views were to result in fewer humanitarian missions (2011). However, the larger point that emerges from this debate is over what constitutes the legitimate and effective use of force, and which groups can claim this mantle as part of their institutional mission.

The increasing focus on humanitarian intervention in the 1990s went hand in hand with the development of the R2P doctrine, described above. This development began as a debate in the UN on evolving notions of sovereignty, and in particular on sovereignty as responsibility, as a way to focus on the plights of vulnerable populations located within their own state boundaries (internally displaced persons more specifically). However, the R2P concept has been significantly transformed since its inception. Its articulation by the ICISS in the late 1990s and early 2000s broadened the focus to basic criteria for humanitarian intervention, and its adoption by the UN was celebrated as a further step toward its institutionalization. This also meant that it became vulnerable to capture by the privileged powers in the UN system.

Applying the responsibility to protect

September 14, 2009 was a significant day for the formal incorporation of R2P principles into the UN system, when the General Assembly adopted its resolution (A/RES/63/308) pertaining to the principles (UN 2009). Since then, R2P has been refined and recently implemented by the international community. In March 2011, the R2P principles were invoked in UN Security Council Resolution 1973, focused on Libya: "*Reiterating* the responsibility of the Libyan authorities to protect the Libyan population and *reaffirming* that parties to armed conflicts bear the primary responsibility to take all feasible steps to ensure the protection of civilians," the international community authorized the creation of a no-fly zone, and whatever means necessary to ensure it

(UN 2011). Resolution 1973 passed with five abstentions in the Security Council – Germany, Brazil, India, Russia, and China. These reflected, in part, deep misgivings at the haste with which advocates of the resolution were making the case for intervention on the basis of what were considered unproven and unclear allegations, as well as doubts that military intervention would prove effective. For some countries, Russia and China in particular, the abstentions also represented longstanding support for the norm of untrammeled state sovereignty over humanitarian intervention or the responsibility to protect.

When the Gaddafi regime in Libya collapsed, the primary goal of the National Transitional Council along with its NATO allies was to establish a newly formed state capable of maintaining law and order, and reconsolidating the state's monopoly on the legitimate use of violence. However, the current state's accomplishments in this regard have been weak and tenuous at best as substate actors, particularly militias, refuse to give up arms and the country continues to be divided into multiple armed factions, tribes, and regions. In January 2012, the humanitarian group Médecins sans Frontières officially suspended its operations in Libya because of the violence and torture that was occurring in detention centers throughout the country. Christopher Stokes, General Director of MSF, described how detainees were brought to MSF humanitarian workers mid-interrogation, to be treated, and then subjected to further torture (MSF 2012). As the new Libyan state struggles to rein in violence, the lines of authority are blurred. The international community played a major role in supporting forces armed against the state, and now experiences profound challenges from militias that operate outside of effective state control.

It is hard to resist the conclusion that the initial UN mandate for a no-fly zone, with its limited justification for the use of force to protect the civilian population in Benghazi, was far exceeded by NATO. As Richard Falk, the UN Special Rapporteur on Palestinian human rights, wrote, the limited mandate from the UN was disregarded almost from the outset, and "NATO forces were obviously far less committed to their supposed protective role than to ensuring that the balance of forces in Libya would be tipped in the direction of insurrectionary challenge" (Falk 2011). For China and Russia these events have eroded their willingness to support, even if only tacitly, the implementation of the R2P doctrine. Thus, the practical consequences may be far-reaching if concepts such as R2P become discredited or associated with a militaristic agenda. The impunity with which certain NATO members stretched the UN mandate will likely make it more difficult to organize international consensus for humanitarian intervention in the future – evident already by the lack of UN consensus surrounding the violence in Syria, and the vetoes exercised by Russia and China.

The discretionary implementation of the R2P doctrine in Libya is symptomatic of a deeper problem. When these principles are administered in such a contested way, the whole doctrine risks being called into question. Advancement of the doctrine of sovereignty as responsibility and the human security agenda could be very beneficial in managing new threats to global security. However, the problem remains of who decides when they apply and under which criteria and evidence. A solution to this problem needs to be found that is not imposed by a select few, but rather arises from a legitimate process which has a reasonable chance of winning global political legitimacy. At issue would be the creation of new rules and procedures which would help weigh evidence in a manner that peoples around the world could find compelling and acceptable – ways independent of the particular interests and concerns of any one nation-state, whether powerful or humble. The Security Council as the center of such deliberations could not be the Security Council that prevails today, for this one is constituted by the geopolitical settlement of 1945, with embedded privileges and select interests built into its very structure (the P-5 vetoes). Thus, the problems of institutional inertia highlighted above serve to illuminate this problem, as does the emerging multipolarity in the world system.

The problem of military capacity

Existing military capacities remain drawn along state lines despite the growing need for multilateral forces more appropriately designed to address contemporary security demands. Table 2.7 illustrates the scale of state-based military efforts by comparing the respective military expenditures of the P-5 countries. The military expenditure of the US has been increasing consistently over the last decade; its spending remains vast and dwarfs the allocations made by other leading states. While France and the UK have contained their military allocations (made possible in part by expansive US military capacity), aggregate expenditure levels remain substantial. These figures are in stark contrast to the resources allocated to collective forces, where total global spending on multilateral operations, such as peacekeeping, was recently recorded at just $8.2 billion, or 0.56 percent of total military

Table 2.7 Military expenditure by country (P-5) (US$ millions)

Country	1990	1995	2000	2005	2010
China	17,200	20,000	32,100	62,100	114,300
France	67,930	62,566	59,508	62,724	61,285
Russia	232,546	29,427	25,977	38,669	52,586
UK	57,874	48,447	45,549	52,579	57,424
US	502,749	392,601	375,893	552,966	687,105

Source: SIPRI Military Expenditure Database, 2011; figures are at constant 2009 prices and exchange rates.

expenditure (SIPRI in Held 2010: 197). This paints an overall picture of the basic incongruence between the existing security capacities in the world, and the emerging demands placed upon it. Changing forms of conflict, as well as changing notions of security, require an updated capacity that is designed for context-specific concerns; however, the international community has yet to implement the kinds of innovations that this would entail. The result has been the persistence and indeed expansive growth of nation-state militaries in lieu of effective investment in collective forces.

The mismatch between existing capacity for addressing security and the demands placed before it is a daunting challenge by itself; but this is further compounded by the increasing ambiguity over who controls the legitimate use of violence. States' interests remain aligned along sovereign lines delineating their control and autonomy. Thus, attempting to build consensus around practical reforms and alternative capacities has been too difficult a task for the international community. This is a problem highlighted by the confrontation of state-centric interests with the prevailing universal human rights order, focused on the protection of individual sovereignty. The contemporary management of security is at a considerable distance from being appropriately designed to uphold both the laws of war and human right regimes. While elements of a universal constitutional framework exist, military capacity is neither appropriately designed nor operationalized to uphold them adequately. Hence, while the emergence of the human security paradigm and the R2P doctrine represents a major paradigmatic transformation, they have remained all too often shifts of principle. The situation on the ground often falls short of what has been proclaimed as a new universal mission. The realities of security are far more complex; a commitment to protect individuals from pervasive illegitimate violence, pushing state security into a position subordinate to individual security, has yet to be fulfilled in any systematic and impartial way.

The question of state-centric versus collective military or human security capacity highlights a key tension of global security governance. Against the backdrop of a dynamic and rapidly developing world order – which has included profound transformations of the notions of sovereignty and security – the primary mechanisms of security enforcement have remained fixed in form: state interests prevail and in turn produce a fragmented and increasingly ineffective division of protective labor.

Conclusion

The postwar era, as noted throughout this chapter, was hugely successful in many respects. The international system was able to prevent a third world war, and the previous institutional failures, such as the League of Nations, were supplanted by the creation of a more permanent United Nations. Upon this a dense and complex network of international and transnational institutions was subsequently built. Thus, security governance was increasingly managed by a multilevel and multi-actor framework that came to include nonstate actors as legitimate and influential participants. As the postwar system developed and expanded, so too did global interconnectedness. A process of self-reinforcing interdependence has come to characterize the world order. However, this process has also led to many consequences, some unintended and others not, as well as new challenges. The result has been gridlock. Institutional inertia and emerging multipolarity are both significant mechanisms of gridlock in security governance, with the Security Council frozen on virtually all issues that affect P-5 interests, and resistant to the emergence and influence of new powers. Elsewhere, the challenge of new transborder issues, from terrorism to cyber security, have stretched and tested the capacities of global governance arrangements to their limits. The fragmentation of the global security order further inhibits resolution of pressing security concerns. An enhanced and substantially reformed collective security system is required and yet it is difficult to see how it will be developed on current performance. This conclusion is reinforced by the dilemmas and weakness of global economic governance, explored in the chapter that follows.

3
Economy

Introduction

We began chapter 1 with Lorenzetti's insight that good government is essential for a stable and prosperous society. The same idea can be found in Plato (428–348 BCE), Confucius (551–479 BCE), or, indeed, Adam Smith (1723–90), but it took the modern field of economics a bit longer to arrive at the same conclusion. For most of the twentieth century, and especially the postwar period, much of the profession focused on highlighting the ways in which the state could undermine market efficiency. The Nobel Prize laureate Ronald Coase wrote an article in 1960 entitled "The Problem of Social Cost" that put the issue in a particularly vivid way. In a perfect market, Coase argued, there would be little role for laws or governments beyond the basic protection of property rights, because individuals could just bargain with each other until an efficient allocation of resources, rights, and responsibilities was reached. Of course, in the real world such bargains entail transaction costs; it would be impossibly time-consuming to negotiate a deal with every person whose actions affected you, and whom you in turn affected. Therefore the law and the state were needed to reduce this aggregate "social cost," even if they led to less optimal outcomes than a hypothetical world of near infinite, costless negotiations between individuals. In other words, we have the state for the same reason we buy readymade clothes instead of tailoring them ourselves; the former don't fit as well, but the latter are too bothersome.

This transactional view of the state does not suggest a strong role for government, but it turns out that "the problem of social cost" is enormous. Libertarian-minded economists thought that unfettered markets were the key drivers of prosperity; they overlooked the institutional assumptions built into their theories. Several scholars have since pointed out this oversight. For example, Huntington (1968) noted that economic modernization did not always lead to peace and prosperity, but, where it tore apart traditional social fabrics and was not replaced with a strong state, led to social upheaval. North (1981, 1990) argued that the miracle of European prosperity lay not in culture or technology, but in sound social and political institutions. For him, "the creation of the state in the millennia following the first economic revolution was the necessary condition for all subsequent economic development" (1981: 24). Outside the West, Wade (1990) showed how the state's capacity to govern the market played the central role in allowing the "East Asian Tigers" to grow, and historically minded scholars applied the idea to explain the success of medieval traders and Renaissance city-states (Greif 2006) – such as Lorenzetti's Siena. The artist's thesis now finds articulation not in paint but in a raft of regression results and formal mathematical models.

By the mid-1990s, these views had become sufficiently mainstream to find their way into the policies of the World Bank, the International Monetary Fund, and most of the providers of overseas development aid. These organizations began insisting that the recipients of their funding exemplify "good governance" – the rule of law, transparency, etc. This shift was an important, albeit belated, recognition of the importance of political institutions to economic development, but also highlights the difficulty of the challenge. It is phenomenally difficult to build the kind of strong, dynamic and accountable state that facilitates economic prosperity. The process is often long and violent (Kohli 2004). Success is rare. As Acemoglu and Robinson (2012) demonstrate in their wide-ranging study on the subject, the best available evidence tells us that man-made institutions are at the root of economic success or the lack thereof (see also Acemoglu et al. 2005). But this finding begs a question. If the quality of the state is essential to growth, how is it possible to sustain a global economy in a world divided between nearly 200 sovereign states? Just as the hypothetical individuals in Coase's world of infinite bargains affect one another, so too the economic decisions made in one country affect the prosperity of distant peoples. This suggests that the "problem of social cost" – and, correspondingly, the need for governance – at the global scale is vast indeed.

In the introduction we noted how theorists of international institutions have explained the conditions under which states can cooperate to fill this need. This chapter explains how these efforts have fared since World War II, and why the central "solution," multilateral cooperation, has now grown less efficacious relative to the collective challenges it faces. The development of global economic governance is the story of both remarkable success and increasing stagnation, with an evident undersupply of global public policy solutions to pressing problems. Efforts over the past 70 years have produced a plethora of novel governance arrangements to tackle a wide diversity of economic governance challenges. This system has enabled economic activity to become "global" on a scale never seen before. Yet many achievements in global economic governance have either stalled, or are characterized by so much institutional fragmentation that they are barely capable of tackling well-recognized problems. Despite the acknowledged importance of a well-ordered and predictable system of international trade rules and the fact that large and powerful administrative structures have been generated to facilitate it, a multilateral trade agreement has not been completed since 1994. Diverse global financial governance institutions have developed that made important achievements in specific technical areas. And countries were able to come together to make sure that the 2008–2009 financial crisis did not precipitate another Great Depression. But they neither predicted nor prevented the worst financial crisis since 1929, and subsequent developments show that reform is likely to proceed in an ad hoc and modest fashion, rather than in a clear and structured manner.

In short, we face gridlock in global economic governance. A rule-based, dynamic global economy has been institutionalized, but its governance structures fail in many respects. Institutional fragmentation is rife; institutional inertia makes many international organizations slow to change; harder problems have emerged, for which governance capacity is at best weak and often ad hoc; and perhaps most dramatically, the number of countries with a decisive impact on the world economy has expanded beyond the West. As in the domains of security and environmental governance, the need for decisive change is increasingly evident, but the institutional solutions to these problems have not been forthcoming. Paradoxically, it is our very success in governing global economic life that has given rise to these new challenges, for which existing institutions are poorly adapted.

The analysis which follows is divided into two parts. First, we lay out a brief history of global economic governance, and point to the successes achieved thus far. Two kinds of international cooperation are emphasized which have emerged in the postwar order: large "multilateral" institutions, on the one hand, and smaller, more specialized "transnational" institutions, on the other. We show how these institutional formations have been remarkably successful at not only addressing first-order coordination problems among states, but also tackling a number of public policy issues as they have emerged in the world economy, a process that has enabled global economic integration on a scale that is historically unprecedented.

In the second part of the chapter we evaluate recent developments in global economic governance. The analysis explores three different sets of attempts to govern the global economy in the face of recent pressures and developments. The first involves efforts to construct new global trade rules appropriate for an evolving global economy. In illustrating the haphazard history of the Doha Development Round and its successive stallings, we show a number of gridlock mechanisms at play. Second, we assess the global financial crisis of 2008–9, with a focus on the global governance mechanisms in place before and after the crisis. We argue that the record of global economic governance surrounding these events is a more complex one than complete failure, and that what the financial crisis revealed is both the resilience of global economic governance as well as its demonstrable inadequacies.

THE EVOLUTION OF GLOBAL ECONOMIC GOVERNANCE

The Imperial System and Its Demise

The governance of international economic affairs dates from the first trades made between different communities of human beings. In Europe, up through the medieval era and beyond, a plurality of social customs, compacts, and private institutions like merchant guilds provided most of the governance functions on which transborder transactions relied. But with the emergence of the modern state, governments began intervening in larger and larger swathes of the economy, bringing an increasingly statist character to global economic governance. The most visible manifestation of this trend was the economic empires of Spain, France, Britain, Holland, Portugal, and a few other European maritime powers in the early modern era. Under these systems, the rules of economic exchange were imposed by the metropoles on to their colonies, which served both as sources of natural resources like gold or tobacco, and as captive markets for the metropole's exports. Economic interdependence reached a new peak, with parts of the world that had previously been tangentially connected to the world economy suddenly bound together with distant Europeans. But as trade between the various empires was typically forbidden, this so-called mercantilist system represented a kind of globalization by bloc. Integration was largely contained within each European power's sphere of influence.

The shift in political economy spurred by the Industrial Revolution changed this system, laying the basis for the modern system of interstate economic relations we recognize today. Britain industrialized first. As it did, British capitalists and urban workers gained the upper hand in domestic politics over landowners and farmers.[1] These latter groups benefited enormously from the mercantilist system, which kept out foreign agricultural products. Factory owners and workers, in contrast, needed new consumers outside of the domestic market to buy the expanding range of manufactured goods they were churning out ever more efficiently. Because no other country came close to matching British industrial prowess, its factories had little to fear from an open global market, and much to gain. Once industrial interests gained control of government, they pushed a free-trade policy championed by the liberal economic thinkers of the time. This shift led to the repeal, in the 1840s to 1850s, of many of the laws that kept trade within the British Empire.

More importantly for our purposes, the shift to laissez-faire international economic policies prompted a spate of institution-building. In 1860 Britain and France signed the Cobden-Chevalier treaty, the first modern trade agreement, which lowered tariff barriers between them. Other nations decided they could not be left out of this profitable exchange, and over the next 15 years European nations negotiated some 56 similar treaties (Lampe 2011), creating a "spaghetti bowl" of bilateral tariff reductions across Europe (with the exception of the United States, most of the other economically significant countries remained under de jure or de facto colonial domination during this period). Because most of these treaties contained the confusingly named "most favored nation" clause – which meant the parties would have to give the same tariff concessions to each other that they gave to third parties – they created a broad zone of liberalized trade.

But merchants require more than an absence of trade barriers in order to develop commerce with other nations. Another crucial function is exchange rate stability, that is, the knowledge that investments or contracts valued in foreign currencies will maintain a predictable value. During the eighteenth and nineteenth centuries, the European powers established a system of mutually agreed rules to ensure exchange rate stability by linking international payments to gold – a system known as the "Gold Standard." This system also facilitated the management of different states' accounts with one another through the use of a common means of international payment – gold bullion (see Helleiner 2008). Though agreed between countries, the system was essentially underwritten by the British hegemon. Britain pledged to maintain the value of its currency, and this pledge was credible because of the Empire's extraordinary wealth (it accounted for over a third of global GDP in 1870). Other countries were thus able to peg their currencies to sterling, believing it was as good as gold. Britain's economic might also allowed it to play several other key roles in the global economy, acting as a lender of last resort to bankrupt countries and seeking to maintain the stability of the system as a whole.

The results were an unprecedented era of global economic integration. Flows of international commercial activity would only be matched toward the end of the twentieth century. As we discussed in chapter 1, this provision of public goods was decidedly self-interested. Britain benefited first and foremost from the system it built, and was willing and capable of imposing it on other states, either by shutting them out of its markets or utilizing "gunboat" diplomacy to coerce states into a common system. However, this liberal international order was not purely intentional and "designed." Rules and institutions also "evolved" as international commercial activity expanded and more governance was needed. Important rules, such as the international standardization of weights and measures to be used in international commerce, developed through a much more informal system of agreements and conventions, among states, among trading port cities, and among business elites of the time. Similarly, transborder commercial dispute resolution was performed by a variety of institutions ranging from public courts to private arbitral tribunals, many associated with the various trade associations that arose in the nineteenth century. However, it would be wrong to say that this liberal international economic order did not have sources of formal authority underlying it. Enforcing such a system was not difficult while it lasted, as the majority of the world's population was subjugated under colonial rule of some kind, and among the European powers, Great Britain acted as the central power broker throughout the nineteenth century.

Still, Britain could not prevent nations like Germany and the United States, which benefited from the stable, liberal order British hegemony provided, from rising to rival it in economic and, ultimately, military clout. World War I decisively broke the imperial system of global economic governance, giving way to a veritable free-for-all in economic policy during the 1920s. Tariffs rates began creeping up across Europe and the United States. Several countries ceased to abide by the gold standard system, leading to a wide fluctuation in currencies that both aggravated and was spurred on by rampant inflation in countries like Germany. Efforts to engage in international monetary cooperation, or to bail out countries that were defaulting on their payments, when they were attempted, failed utterly (see Eichengreen and Uzan 1990).

At the same time, though, the economy was growing rapidly in places like the United States, which experienced a "Roaring Twenties." Tragically, much of this exuberance was irrational (Shiller 2005). Financial markets had become complacent during the postwar boom, believing that stocks would continue to rise in value indefinitely. Dubious practices such as investing with borrowed money and margin trading proliferated, unburdened by regulation under the laissez-faire ethos that dominated policy circles. When the bubble burst on Black Thursday, October 24, 1929, it took decades for the world economy to recover.

As the liberal international order fell apart, it began to give way to self-defeating acts of policy adjustment. In order to compete against each other during the Great Depression, states decided to take actions they hoped would increase their countries' competitiveness on world markets, such as depreciating their currencies (which made their exports more competitive) and erecting high tariffs at their border (which protected domestic producers from foreign competition). While individually rational to a point, such policies are a collective folly. The fact that many states took these actions simultaneously led to a well-documented decline in overall economic activity, sinking entire economies even further into an even harsher set of conditions than before. International trade activity suffered, currencies competed for harsh devaluations, and the global economy sank deeper into depression (Carr 1946).

These difficulties might have been addressed through the creation of new institutions. At their very best, such institutions can not only avoid collective bads but also generate valuable collective goods which benefit the development of the global economy as a whole (as occurred in the postwar period). But during the 1930s such solutions proved elusive. As we discussed in chapter 1, the United States bears much of the blame for the failure of global economic governance during this period. Instead of using its new economic heft to maintain open global markets, create monetary stability, provide liquidity where needed, and coordinate macroeconomic policies across countries, it turned inward (Kindleberger 1973). But it is also interesting to note that the fledgling League of Nations also failed to deliver effective multilateral economic governance at this time. The League's Charter made no reference to economic management. But in 1920, at the suggestion of bureaucrats in the League secretariat, it created a Joint Provisional Economic and Financial Committee. In 1923 this body was divided into an Economic Committee and a Financial Committee, and these were made permanent. Internationalists had pushed for these committees to be fully intergovernmental in nature, as the UN's Economic and Social Council is now. But countries were unwilling to delegate sovereignty over economic issues to an intergovernmental process. Instead, the committees were made up of private individuals, nominally independent, but selected by the League Council. Representatives to the committees were often senior civil servants from the most economically important countries, and so national interests were never far from the bargaining table (Clavin and Wessels 2005). However, a number of private businessmen and representatives of groups like the International Chamber of Commerce, newly formed to represent the world's business interests, were also involved.[2] The Economic and Financial Committees thus represented "a fascinating and early mix of state, intergovernmental, and private authority, in many ways presaging the transgovernmental and hybrid networks that currently play a major role in global economic governance" (Hale 2012: 95).

Though they lacked the authority to create formal international law, the Economic and Financial committees had the ability to negotiate and draft suggestions that could be placed before the League's membership. In practice, this agenda-setting power was often so great that the committees possessed substantial de facto power (Clavin and Wessels 2005). On issues like standard-setting, keeping statistics, payment systems, commercial dispute resolution, and other basic functions of the global economy they generated vital rules. But the committees were largely unable to affect policy for issues like protectionism, monetary cooperation, or financial assistance. Technocracy alone was not sufficient to save the global economy.

Bretton Woods and the Creation of Multilateral Economic Institutions

As World War II began to draw to a close, the victors sought to establish a system of multilateral cooperation to coordinate economic recovery. In 1944 world leaders, including representatives from the

Soviet Union, met in Bretton Woods, New Hampshire for what was to be named the United Nations Conference on Monetary and Financial Affairs. Over 700 delegates from all of the 44 Allied powers met at the Mount Washington Hotel, which sits under the shadow of the tallest mountain in the eastern United States, named for the hero of the American Revolution. Delegates understood clearly which country would weigh most in the negotiations. While the United Kingdom played a very active role in the discussions, the undisputed leaders of the conference were the hosts.

Three intertwined concerns dominated the American agenda. First, though the US was officially allied to the USSR against the Axis powers, it was already clear that a struggle between East and West, and between market-based and planned economies, would play a central role in postwar geopolitics. A strong, market-based global economy was, in the US view, the best defense against communism, as well as the radical ideologies that had fueled World War II. The governance of the global economy was thus intimately linked to a more encompassing vision of international security. As US President Franklin D. Roosevelt exclaimed in his introductory remarks to the conference, "the economic health of every country is a proper matter of concern to all its neighbors, near and far" (cited in Sundaram and Rodriguez 2011: 98).

Second, the United States had learned from the failure of global governance during the 1920s and 1930s. The United Nations did not formally exist until a year later, through the creation of a UN Charter in San Francisco. Yet by calling Bretton Woods a United Nations conference, Roosevelt sought both to underline the failure of the earlier League of Nations and to emphasize the importance of a new, more robust multilateral effort to reshape and redesign the global economy (see Sundaram and Rodriguez 2011: 99). The enthusiasm for internationalism and formal rules that would undergird economic management reflected the widespread recognition that multilateral economic cooperation was superior to the kind of interstate disorder and regressive nationalism characterized by the interwar period.

Third, at the center of the Bretton Woods conference was not only a multilateralist sentiment, but a particular intellectual climate regarding economic governance – a set of ideas whose time had come. Before the war, in response to the Great Depression, Roosevelt had led a vast expansion of the American government into economic life. Under his New Deal, the economy was regulated (e.g. the financial practices that had sparked the 1929 crash were curtailed), and the federal government took on direct responsibility for employment, pensions, food, housing, and other social needs. These changes were first and foremost a response to the Depression, but were also seen as necessary in order to stave off more radical political movements such as socialism and Communism. In short, in the postwar hegemon, as in a number of other European states, a compromise was struck between free markets and social protection (Polanyi 1944). This grand bargain, which John Ruggie has termed "embedded liberalism" – that is, a classic liberal economic system that is bound within a social compact – would have a decisive impact on the nature of the postwar order.

Parallel changes were taking place in the field of economics, and at their center was the charismatic figure of John Maynard Keynes. The British economist had turned the profession on its head in the 1920s and 1930s, and now served as the central intellectual figure at the Bretton Woods conference. Prior to the war, in the midst of the Great Depression the dominant belief among economists and most policy-makers was that markets worked best when left to their own devices. Thus, the thinking went, even during times of economic depression governments would serve the public best by interfering only minimally and letting economic activity naturally pick up again. Keynes delivered a devastating critique of this idea, arguing that left to their own devices during a depression even the most developed capitalist markets would fail to regenerate economic activity, leaving the society in the pitfalls of "underemployment equilibrium" (Keynes 1936). He realized that capitalists could often be their own worst enemies, and thus needed intervention from outside the market to reinvigorate their "animal spirits" and to get the public consuming and investing once again. Achieving a return to prosperity required not the invisible hand of the markets but the very visible hand of government, in the form of strategic and intelligent use of monetary and fiscal policies to restimulate the economy. By the time the war was drawing to a close, "Keynesianism" not only had become accepted doctrine among the economics profession, but also had widespread buy-in from policy-makers eager to secure the conditions for postwar prosperity.

Keynesian ideas helped to justify not only active government intervention, but also an "internationalist" stance toward economic policy. For national economies to thrive, governments needed to be able to utilize a wide variety of economic policy tools so that they could manage the economy effectively. To properly manage central concerns such as unemployment and growth, for example, governments would be best served if they could easily control interest rates and engage in ambitious deficit spending when necessary. Yet the use of such policy tools was conditional on the way that the global economy was organized.[3] Lowering interest rates to stimulate growth and employment, for example, might lead financiers to take their money abroad, and national economic experimentation might only encourage things like international financial speculation. Thus in order to have successful national economic development, countries needed an international economic system that facilitated, rather than constrained, government policy options.

It is hardly surprising then that Keynes was a pivotal voice within the Bretton Woods conference (see Bordo 1993: 34).[4] While some of his ambitious ideas (such as to have an International Clearing Union which settled governments' national accounts with one another and issued a global currency) fell flat (amidst US opposition), the central thrust of his ideas was enshrined in the entire Bretton Woods endeavor. This was the notion that global economic governance should promote trade, but that international financial flows should be highly constrained and regulated. After the devastating consequences of the Great Depression, for which speculative financial markets were, in no small part, blamed, the postwar architects of the Bretton Woods system were highly critical of international finance. Even the US Treasury Secretary at the time, Henry Morgenthau, told the Bretton Woods conference that its goal was to "drive the usurious moneylenders from the temple of international finance" (Helleiner 1994b: 4).

Thus the states present at the Bretton Woods conference agreed on a set of terms to coordinate macroeconomic policy, to stabilize economic flows among each other. What came to be known as the "Bretton Woods system" established a system of formal coordination of national exchange rates by tying currency values around the world to the US dollar, which was itself pegged to gold. Doing so provided a tangible "anchor" to the global economy, thus reducing global monetary imbalances, and also provided a system of exchange rate stability, facilitating international trade. International financial flows were highly restricted. As Keynes remarked at the time:

> Not merely as a feature of this transition, but as a permanent arrangement, the plan accords to every member government the explicit right to control all capital movements. What used to be heresy is now endorsed as orthodoxy . . . our right to control the domestic capital market is secured on firmer foundations than ever before, and is formally accepted as a proper part of agreed international arrangements. (Keynes in 1944, in Moggridge 1980: 17)

Thus while the Bretton Woods system sought to create a liberal international regime for trade, its approach to international finance was a nonliberal one (see Helleiner 1994b: 3–5). As Ruggie (1982) has put it, the postwar architects sought to create not a new liberal international order, but a system of embedded liberalism in which the domestic policy autonomy of the new Keynesian interventionist state was endorsed and supported.

Both the ideas behind Bretton Woods and the multilateral institutions that emerged from it found fertile ground in the international political environment of the time. The will and capacity to create and fund new multilateral institutions for global economic management that would address this vision was facilitated in no insignificant part by the unquestioned dominance of the United States (see Ruggie 1982). As Rupert has argued, the new international hegemony of the United States was undergirded by "a great deal more than a convergence of interests and attitudes among international elites" (1995: 43). The American postwar vision was one of social harmony through productivity, growth, and prosperity – not just at home but abroad. Thus the postwar domestic project was fundamentally internationalist. And as noted above, this vision was not accidental – it was strategic. The socioeconomic structure of the entire non-Soviet world at the time was volatile: new and seemingly growing demands from working classes returning from war, and the threat of resurgent communist and socialist tendencies not only in Europe but throughout the developing world. Thus "American economic powers would be used to construct a stable, multilateral world economy," harnessing Germany to the West and containing the Soviet bloc (Rupert 1995: 43–4).

Achieving a prosperous and stable global economy meant not just adherence to a specific policy program, but also the generation of new multilateral institutions. Out of the Bretton Woods agreements two new institutions were born: the International Bank for Reconstruction and Development (which would later become the World Bank) and the International Monetary Fund. By pooling resources and ensuring a relatively centralized means of administering project coordination, these institutions' chief mission, in a nutshell, was to generate global public goods such as greater international monetary stability, and the conditions for managed, continual growth of the global economy. The IBRD/World Bank was charged with establishing a system of loans and assistance to war-ravaged Europe and then, predominantly, the developing world. Its aim was to make long-term capital available where it was urgently needed, and in so doing supplant purely private sector mechanisms on a global scale. The IMF would not only coordinate exchange rate adjustments during the Bretton Woods period, but also would provide emergency economic assistance to its members. While the distribution of voting power within the IMF was established to favor the major Western powers, it was set up to operate in a similar way to a gigantic multinational "co-op" to finance short-term imbalances in international payments in order to prevent the breakdown of international economic flows that had occurred between the two world wars.

Two other outcomes of the Bretton Woods conference would play critical roles in shaping postwar global economic governance. First, there was a plan, supported in particular by the United States and Norwegian delegations, to dissolve an earlier interwar multilateral institution, the Bank for International Settlements, located in Basel, Switzerland (see Seabrooke 2006). The BIS was founded in 1930 to organize German war reparations, and yet during World War II it was alleged to have played a role in helping Germany loot financial assets from other countries. The Bretton Woods conference recommended the liquidation of the BIS, a highly politicized institution during that time given its purported role in facilitating Nazi gold transfers, but the British delegation consistently opposed such plans, eventually winning out. In the postwar period, the BIS would remain as a kind of international "club and clearing house" for central banks. While its role remained relatively obscure, the importance of the BIS would skyrocket from the 1970s onward, as we discuss below.

Second, despite the ostensible commitment to free trade, the postwar international system did not include a formal international trade organization. The Bretton Woods conference proposed plans for an International Trade Organization, but the institution never came into being. While the ITO Charter was formally agreed at a later UN Conference on Trade and Employment in 1948 in Havana, Cuba, ratification of the charter in national legislatures proved impossible. The most serious opposition was, ironically, from the country that was best positioned in the global economy at the time: the US. After the US Senate refused to ratify the ITO charter on the grounds that would cede too much authority beyond US control, the US announced that it would not seek further Congressional ratification, effectively killing the ITO. Despite the absence of a formal ITO, efforts to generate a coherent set of multilateral agreements among states for mutual tariff reductions were nevertheless instituted. Beginning in 1948, the General Agreement on Tariffs and Trade instituted tariff reductions in a series of six successive global "rounds," in which thousands of mutual trade concessions were given, and billions of dollars of tariffs were reduced. In the spirit of the Keynesian underpinnings of Bretton Woods, arrangements were also made to allow developing countries exceptions to the scale and scope of trade liberalization in order to facilitate their development. While the GATT during this period promoted the liberalization of trade, developing countries were still left to do what they saw fit in terms of tariffs and other trade policy measures, and their domestic policy options were not severely restricted. While not constituting a formal international organization, the GATT achieved a series of major multilateral agreements. Table 3.1 lists the post–World War II multilateral meetings, from the beginning of the GATT in 1996 until the present.

Outcomes of the Bretton Woods system

The new global experiment with multilateral economic institutions was in many ways a success. Macroeconomic growth was not only higher than during other periods, it was also more evenly distributed (see Bordo 1993: 47). International trade expanded considerably under the new system of multilateral governance. Financial crises were relatively rare (see below). For the first time, global economic arrangements were governed through a system of multilateral cooperation and coordination. While there were clear geopolitical power imbalances during this period, the stable system of global economic governance was a great enabling condition for countries both in the advanced capitalist economies and in the developing world. Not all states prospered under this system, but it did generate a level of regularity and stability which allowed considerable experimentation in the ways national economies integrated themselves into the global economy.

Europe, whose industrial base had been literally destroyed by the war, grew rapidly under the new arrangements, buttressed by an inflow of American capital under the Marshall Plan and the potential that had lain dormant in the interwar period. Between 1948 and 1952 the European economies grew at an annual rate of over 10 percent, and by 1951 production was 55 percent greater than four years earlier (Eichengreen 1995: 3). The sources of this recovery were of course multiple, but a stable global system ranks high among them. Similarly, Japan had rapidly regained its prewar economic status by the early 1950s.

The truly impressive results came afterward, however, as countries used the new global economic system to grow as never before. In West

Table 3.1 Major multilateral trade meetings, 1946–present

Year(s)	Name of meeting/ round	Countries involved	Subjects covered	Significant outcomes
1946–7	Geneva	23	Tariffs	Signing of GATT; 15,000 tariff concessions
1948	Havana	23	Creation of an International Trade Organization (ITO)	Agreement on a charter for an ITO, but later ratification proved impossible
1949	Annecy	33	Tariffs	5,000 tariff concessions; 9 accessions under the GATT
1950	Torquay	34	Tariffs	8,700 tariff concessions; 4 accessions
1956	Geneva	22	Tariffs	Modest reductions
1960–1	Dillon	45	Tariffs, motivated in part by need to rebalance concessions following creation of the European Economic Community	4,400 concessions exchanged; EEC proposal for a 20 percent linear cut in manufactures tariffs rejected
1964–7	"Kennedy Round"	48	Tariffs, antidumping, customs valuation	Average tariffs reduced by 35 percent; some 33,000 tariff lines bound (limits on tariffs); agreements on customs valuation and antidumping

Table 3.1 *(Continued)*

Year(s)	Name of meeting/ round	Countries involved	Subjects covered	Significant outcomes
1973–9	"Tokyo Round"	99	Tariffs, "framework agreements," nontariff measures: antidumping, customs valuation, subsidies and countervailing measures, government procurement, import licensing, product standards, safeguards, special and differential treatment of developing countries	Average tariffs reduced by one-third to 6 percent for OECD manufactures imports; voluntary codes of conduct agreed for all nontariff issues except safeguards
1986–94	"Uruguay Round"	123	Tariffs, nontariff measures, intellectual property, textiles, agriculture, trade-related investment measures, dispute settlement, transparency and surveillance of trade policies	Creation of the World Trade Organization (WTO); average tariffs again reduced by one-third on average; agriculture and textiles and clothing subjected to rules; new agreements on services and TRIPs; majority of Tokyo Round codes extended to all WTO members
2001–present	"Doha Round"	141	Tariffs, nontariff measures, agriculture, labor standards, environment, competition, investment, intellectual property, trade facilitation, rules, services, environment	Some "framework agreements," but little actually achieved

Source: Adapted from WTO 2007: 198.

Germany a *Wirtschaftswunder*, an "economic miracle," fueled by high investment and a skilled workforce solidified the country's place as the economic center of Europe. Smaller economies prospered as well, however, such as Italy under "La Boom" of the 1950s and 1960s, which transformed what was still largely a rural, agrarian society into an urban, industrial one (Crafts and Toniolo 1996). In Japan, strategic government policies galvanized growth of around 10 percent per year between 1951 and 1970, allowing Japan to overtake Germany as the world's second largest economy (C. Johnson 1982). And in the United States, growth was slower (but building from a much higher starting point), closer to 5 percent per year during the 1950s and 1960s, but fast by historical standards, and stable and widespread.

Even states that had been less than central players in the global economy, such as South Korea and Taiwan, were able to combine the right mixture of strategic government intervention and openness to international economic flows. As such, they were tremendously successful and began a process of developmental "catch up" on a scale never seen before (Wade 1990). Even in Latin America, the postwar years saw a burst in prosperity. Many Latin American nations had pursued a policy of protectionist industrialization in which tariffs kept out foreign manufactures, giving domestic industries the space they needed to grow and become competitive. Ultimately this strategy would founder – the industries grew, but never became competitive – but in the immediate postwar era it led to broad growth in countries like Argentina, Mexico, and Brazil. Strong global demand for Latin American commodities gave the countries favorable terms of trade, augmented government revenues, and allowed states to invest in industrialization (Randall 1997).

The postwar era also saw a new approach toward the world's least developed regions, with the advent of the modern field of development. Global poverty was seen as a geopolitical threat to the West (poor countries might be tempted to side with the Soviet Union), and so the United States and, later, European governments began offering poor regions technical advice and financial resources with the goal of building "modern" societies around the world. So-called "modernization theory" predicted that growth, political development, and social change would all go hand in hand, provided countries established the right formal structures and received adequate capital (Lipset 1959). Of course, this view proved naive (Huntington 1968; Przeworski and Limongi 1997; Easterly 2006), and arguably exacerbated the dismal performance of some LDCs (least developed countries) over the following decades as inflows of aid and capital exacerbated existing dysfunctions in poor countries' economies.[5] In the 1950s, however, it seemed that underdevelopment was a solvable, technical problem, and one that the modern global economy would soon eliminate.

Self-Reinforcing Interdependence and the End of Bretton Woods

Though phenomenally successful, the postwar economic order contained some elements that proved unsustainable, the gold standard chief among them. There were serious problems in the way the system was constructed and how it functioned in practice (see Garber 1993). While the IFIs themselves operated well, the Bretton Woods system was effectively underwritten by the US (see Kindleberger 1973; Keohane 1980), which facilitated a system of fixed exchange rates worldwide by anchoring the value of the US dollar to gold (sometimes called "dollar–gold convertibility").[6] As with the imperial system of the nineteenth century, hegemony proved an unsustainable basis for monetary stability. Pressures from the costs of the Vietnam War and its own domestic economic issues meant that this arrangement proved overly costly to the US, and in 1971 President Nixon broke dollar–gold convertibility, spelling the end of the Bretton Woods era (see Odell 1979). This put enormous pressure on most countries' ability to ensure exchange rate stability while pursuing other desirable goals such as domestic monetary policy autonomy, which effectively forced a liberalization of international capital flows all over the world (see Goodman and Pauly 1993; Best 2008). While the US had benefited from the Bretton Woods arrangements, it would benefit even more from a more market-driven system of international exchanges – in particular in the area of financial services, in which it had numerous advantages (Gowan 1999). In the words of Gourinchas and Rey, the US went from being the world's banker to being the world's venture capitalist (2005: 3).

While the monetary and financial policies of the Bretton Woods order did not endure, its general commitment to liberalism did, as well as the multilateral institutions that underpinned it. Indeed, their roles, as well as that of the GATT, evolved in dramatic ways, and a variety of new transnational institutions arose to supplement their revised agenda (described below). The result was a progressive undoing of the "embeddedness" of the global economy. Under the Bretton Woods system the international financial institutions had facilitated trade and integration, but also allowed countries significant domestic policy space. Financial flows were restricted and monetary policy was coordinated via fixed exchange rates. But in the post–Bretton Woods system the IFIs worked to remove restrictions on capital flows, and the major currencies traded freely. In other words, the liberal elements of the postwar order (e.g. trade) deepened and institutionalized, while the less laissez-faire elements (e.g. the currency regime) broke down and gave way to what would come to be called neoliberal policies. The effect of both these shifts was a profound deepening of economic integration.

To understand these developments, it is necessary to understand the international economic environment that characterized the post–Bretton Woods period. Only then is it possible to make sense of the institutional developments that followed, which are important precursors to gridlock in global economic governance. We argue that a cycle of self-reinforcing interdependence was at work. On the one hand, the globalization of economic activity that the postwar order had facilitated led to deeper levels of interdependence, and thus to new challenges. On the other hand, a series of corresponding institutional developments allowed for even more integration. Even the breakdown of the Bretton Woods monetary system meant that international finance accelerated at a rapid pace, leading to far deeper levels of interdependence (see Helleiner 1994b).

The rise of the multinational corporation and global production

The acceleration of international commerce was manifest not just in freer flows of international trade and investment per se, but in particular in the flourishing of large multinational corporations, which became a central part of the globalized economy as never before. Production became globalized in many respects, with products assembled across the world in transborder value chains. This mode of corporate organization entailed not only a speeding up of the international transportation of goods and services, but also the development of a highly advanced international division of labor. It also created a powerful new set of actors in world politics.

In chapter 1 we mentioned how the predictable and stable opening of global markets gave firms incentives to structure their operations across national borders and reinforced political support for liberalization (Milner 1987). American multinational corporations (MNCs), in particular, benefited from the rapid growth of Europe and Japan in the postwar period, starting, as they did, from a much sounder foundation than their foreign rivals. Affiliates of American firms in Europe more than tripled in size between 1950 and 1966, and grew by a factor of four in Japan (UN DESA 1973: 7). But European and Japanese companies did not lag far behind. By the late 1960s some 7,000 MNCs could be identified across the developed world, only about one-third of them American (UN DESA 1973), though the United States continued to dominate in terms of economic heft (with eight of the ten biggest MNCs based in the US).

The growth of MNCs in the 1950s and 1960s created a new governance problem in the 1970s, driven by concern from both developed and developing countries. Regarding the latter, many African and Asian nations had only recently won independence from colonial rulers, and they now feared they would suffer a similar economic fate at the hands of private corporations based in the North. In Latin America, where MNCs tended to dominate the commodity sectors, the companies were often thought to constitute a direct threat to the indigenous industrialization programs that had brought relative prosperity in the postwar years. Many of these ideas were grouped together under the rubric of "dependency theory," which became popular in the South during the 1970s. This idea argued that the structure of the global economy locked poor countries into low-value economic activities (such as natural resource exploitation); instead of providing them with opportunities for growth, it actually held them back (Dos Santos 1970; Valenzuela and Valenzuela 1978). The concentration of economic power in northern MNCs was seen as one of the chief mechanisms behind this structural blockage to development.

The resulting policy implication for many developing countries was to nationalize foreign businesses, asserting national control over the capital foreign investors had sent them. A spate of such nationalizations occurred in the 1960s and 1970s. This, in turn, created an interdependence problem for rich countries: how to ensure stability and predictability for foreign direct investment? As in other areas of global economic governance, the conflict was decided in favor of the North, although not without significant contestation. The economic difficulties of the early 1970s provided a platform for the Southern agenda. Following the 1973 Yom Kippur War and the retaliatory oil embargo against the West, the global South, sensing its rising heft in the global economy, made a bold push to bring about what was called a New International Economic Order (UN Doc. A/RES/S-6/3201). Had it succeeded, NIEO would have represented a substantial shift away from the liberal postwar economic order and toward a more organized world economy in which, for example, commodity prices would be regulated to suit the needs of producers in the South. It also would have imposed a series of regulations on MNCs that would have made them more constrained by host governments (UN DESA 1973). Like the rest of the NIEO, however, these ideas failed in the face of stiff opposition from the North and, equally importantly, a schism within the southern coalition advocating reform (the oil producers proved more loyal to their northern customers than to their southern neighbors).

At the same time, however, the needs of foreign investors received increasing protection. Though discussed both in the OECD and in the more recent trade rounds, protections for foreign investors have proven too controversial to agree at the multilateral level. But since the 1970s an increasing number of bilateral investment treaties and regional agreements (e.g. the North American Free Trade Agreement) have given private investors the right to sue sovereign states if they believe their property has been unfairly expropriated. The first of these agreements was signed in 1959, but their numbers exploded in the 1970s and 1990s, and now some 2,700 exist (UNDP 2010). Many of these treaties allow private investors to bring their host governments before domestic courts or an international tribunal (most commonly the International Centre for the Settlement of Investment Disputes, an IGO affiliated with the World Bank), which can award damages.

The result of these policy battles has been a relatively unfettered environment for transnational corporations (TNCs) to grow, and in the subsequent four decades they have increased over tenfold. Today there are over 82,000 TNCs around the world, which together possess some 810,000 foreign affiliates. About a third of global exports are sold by these companies, and they employed, in 2008, 77 million people (UNCTAD 2009), equivalent to half the US labor force. While corporations have grown increasingly transnational, with an increasing share of their assets distributed globally, and despite the growth of global South, the northern bias has largely persisted. Over 70 percent of global MNCs are headquartered in the North, and over half are based in Europe (see table 3.2). This discrepancy is even larger if we look at the size of corporations. Only seven companies based in the developing world figure among the 100 largest nonfinancial TNCs globally (UNCTAD 2009), although this still represents growth; as recently as 1993 the figure was zero. By comparison, the US has 17, the UK 15, France 14, Germany 13, and Japan 9.

The transnationalization of production is visible not just in the quantitative spread of MNCs, but also in the qualitative shift in their production techniques. Almost any moderately sophisticated manufacturing process now takes place across several countries, with different companies engaged in the provision of materials, parts,

Table 3.2 Distribution of MNCs by location of parent company, 2009

Group	MNCs	%
World	82,053	100
Asia	17,146	20.9
China	3,429	4.2
Japan	4,663	5.7
India	815	1.0
Latin America	3,533	4.3
Brazil	226	0.3
Africa	746	0.9
Europe	47,765	58.2
United States	2,418	2.9
Developed	58,783	71.6
Developing	21,425	26.1

Source: UNCTAD 2009.

assembly, transport, and retail of a product (Gereffi and Lee 2012). Information technology has enabled companies to develop extraordinarily sophisticated supply chains that transmit data from retailers to manufacturers, suppliers, and shippers in real time, allowing for "just in time" production techniques that enhance efficiency and push down prices. The result has been a steady surge of cheap consumer products that have fed the consumption of the growing global middle classes.

The expansion of trade

As production internationalized, it created new demands on the international trading system, placing strain on the GATT system (P. Gallagher 2005). Having eliminated most of the onerous tariffs on industrial products in the 1950s and 1960s, in the 1970s developed states became increasingly concerned with trade barriers other than tariffs. The Tokyo Round of GATT negotiations (1973–9) was the first to address these so-called "nontariff barriers," but because of the more complex and intrusive nature of nontariff barriers, they were not accepted by the full GATT membership, and thus could only take the form of "plurilateral" agreements among some members – a departure from the larger multilateral trading rounds of the postwar period.

These pressures in the new system led to new demands for the transformation of multilateral trade governance. In 1982 a GATT

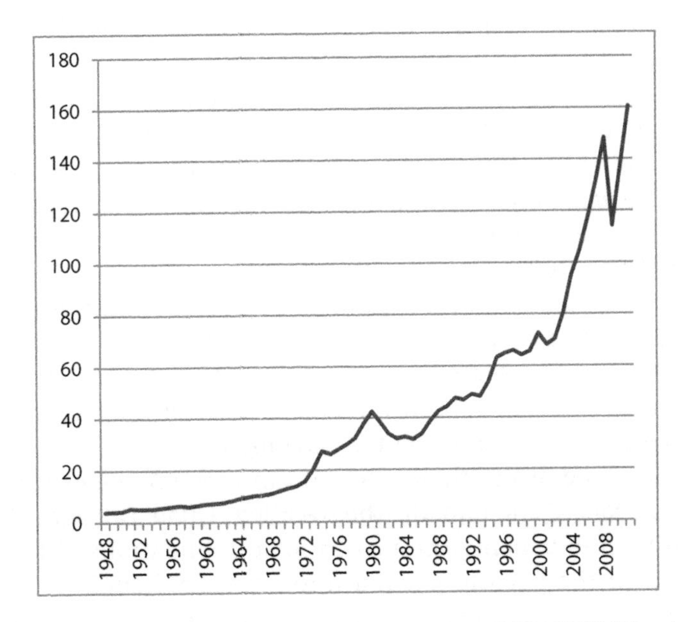

Figure 3.1 Increased volume of world trade, 1948–2011 (2005 US$ billions)

Source: WTO dataset, Total Merchandise Exports, World. Figures originally expressed in current US$ then converted to 2005 US$ using US Bureau of Economic Analysis implicit price deflators for GDP.

Ministerial Declaration stated that the existing system needed to be fundamentally overhauled, because of the changing nature and composition of international commercial activity. The volume of international trade flows was expanding at a considerable pace, as depicted in figure 3.1. As the volume of international trade increased and its structural importance to economic development became more and more central to development strategies, the idea of revisiting the notion of an ITO thus came back onto the agenda. These transformations led to the Uruguay Round of GATT negotiations, which began in 1986 and ended in 1994. The major outcome of the Uruguay Round was the creation of a formal organization in the guise of the earlier idea of an ITO. On this basis, in 1995 the World Trade Organization was created. The WTO's expansion to issues "beyond trade," such as the areas of intellectual property, services, health and sanitation standards, and environmental regulations came in response to the more advanced form of global capitalism that self-reinforcing interdependence helped to generate (Picciotto 2011: 308–13).

In addition to continuing with the expansion of nontariff based issues, the creation of the WTO also saw the creation of new mechanisms which sought to govern international trade in a more centralized and formal way than had been done under the GATT. In particular, the WTO featured a dispute resolution mechanism, whereby a state could formally institute grievance procedures if it believed another state had violated a given international trade agreement. In this way, states agreed that the violation of multilateral agreements was best resolved through a multilateral framework of settling disputes, rather than by states taking action on a unilateral basis (see Bown 2009).

Given the gridlock that has now enveloped the trade regime, and the failed attempt to negotiate an ITO in the 1940s, it is important to explain what made this momentous institutional development possible. Indeed, it was in several ways an absence of the factors that we relate to gridlock that allowed for agreement.

First, the issue of multipolarity was not a pressing constraint. The US, Europe, Japan, and Canada (the so-called "Quad") all agreed on the desirability of enhancing the institutional foundations of the GATT, as well as on the need to expand into nontariff issues. At this time these regions accounted for the vast majority of global trade, and collectively represented a make-or-break export market for poor countries. Though GATT negotiations were formally a consensus process, suggesting that even a weak country could wield a veto, in practice the balance of power significantly favored rich over poor. Moreover, some of the key actors that might have offered more opposition to the rich countries (e.g. Russia and China) were not yet members of the GATT, and so did not participate in the negotiations.

Taking advantage of their favorable position, the Quad included a "single undertaking clause" in the draft text, which meant that countries would have to accept the entirety of the new arrangements, or be left outside the "club" of free trade. This in effect made the Uruguay Round an "all or nothing" deal. It was an offer the developing world could not refuse: join the new WTO and accept the heightened controls on nontariff barriers and the binding dispute settlement system, or stay outside and lose access to the most valuable export markets available (Baldwin 2010).

The explosion of global finance

Importantly, it was not just commerce that flourished in the "post-Bretton Woods" period, but in particular commerce associated with international financial flows. Released from the constraints of the Bretton Woods system, international banking became a critical instru-

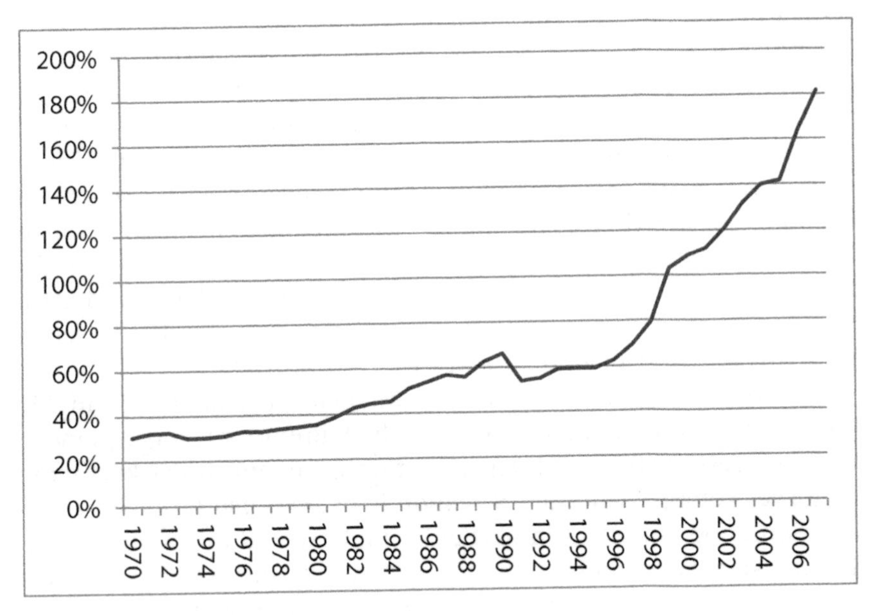

Figure 3.2 International financial integration, 1970–2007

Source: Calculations based on summation of all countries' foreign assets plus foreign liabilities, divided by GDP. Updated and extended version of the External Wealth of Nations Mark II database developed by Lane and Milesi-Ferretti 2007.

ment in the commercial development of both developed and developing states. While the Bretton Woods system had restricted international financial flows, the post–Bretton Woods system featured a growing pool of international monetary flows, with powerful financial institutions organizing these flows, and states seeking to attract such capital into their borders to finance domestic spending. Thus just as global trade was expanding and evolving in new ways after the decline of the Bretton Woods system in the 1970s, global financial market integration was also taking off. Figure 3.2 calculates global financial integration over time by measuring the sum of foreign assets and liabilities and dividing this figure by these countries' GDP, for all countries where data is available.[7] While the United States was the unquestioned leader in international financial affairs, many other countries – such as in Latin America for example – also saw important benefits in the post–Bretton Woods system. The free flow of international finance meant that developing countries could attract capital at potentially cheaper rates than they could domestically.

The dynamic flow of international finance became increasingly prominent over the course of the 1970s, after OPEC succeeded in generating a formal international oil cartel. While the OPEC countries succeeded in dramatically raising energy costs for the rich developed countries, the OPEC countries themselves reaped windfall economic profits, which they invested – somewhat ironically – in US banks. Awash with new capital, US banks saw much more opportunity in structuring loans to developing country governments ("sovereign lending"), rather than investing in rich developed countries, which were suffering from both oil price-induced recession and rapid inflation at the time. Developing country governments in Africa and Latin America sought to take advantage of these new opportunities by securing loans for infrastructure and a variety of projects.

The dominance of the US as the financial hegemon in a highly liberal international financial order had important consequences. With the rest of the world dependent on US financial markets more than ever before, domestic US economic policies had powerful reverberations, and one event in particular underscored this dramatically. To deal with the pressures of national inflation, the US Federal Reserve Chairman Paul Volcker executed a radical plan in which US interest rates rose dramatically to over 20 percent in 1979 and 1980.[8] The effect on those who had taken out loans in the developing world was crushing. Not only did the event trigger recessions across the developed world (thus stifling demand for developing country products), but developing countries' borrowing schedules were dramatically interrupted. Latin America suffered particularly acutely, and beginning in 1982 it became evident that a number of countries were at risk of defaulting on their loans from US banks. The rest of the 1980s became known as the "lost decade" for Latin America, as its economic progress was stifled on a huge scale. This meant mass unemployment, dramatic cutbacks to public services (often enforced by international institutions such as the World Bank and the IMF), and a dramatic stagnation of living standards. The world of opportunity offered by the freer movement of international finance was showing its dark side. The Latin American debt crisis revealed that rather than enhancing the prospects of developing countries in the global economic system, post-Bretton Woods economic conditions could also make them worse.

From embedded liberalism to neoliberalism

The post-Bretton Woods order saw a more active and interventionist role for both the World Bank and the IMF. Both institutions expanded their activities to deal with the new international economic environment, and engaged in what some scholars have since referred to as "mission creep" on a global scale (see Babb and Buira 2005). Both institutions intervened in the domestic political economy of countries on a much more extensive scale than previously, and in particular the IMF took on roles such as promoting capital account liberalization, not part of its prior remit.

Many of the transformations in the global economy after the decline of the Bretton Woods system were undergirded by a particular ideological factor; that is, the rise of neoliberalism. In many ways, the reorientation of states' economic policies toward world markets, and the confidence in free markets, represented a historic reversal of global proportions, a kind of return to the classical liberal international order (see above). A crucial difference, however, was the fact that now multilateral institutions sought to promote and enforce deregulation and more liberal market integration. After the 1970s, many economists and policy-makers experienced a general crisis of confidence in the notion that the economy can be effectively managed by government intervention and sought to replace this idea with the notion of an untrammeled market. The Keynesian vision established at Bretton Woods was now turned on its head.

Many have emphasized the ideational aspects of the rise of neoliberal thinking (see e.g. Leeson 2003; Chwieroth 2010), with key neoliberal intellectuals mobilizing to capture policy-making debates in influential economic institutions. However, the rise of neoliberalism has also been driven by political interests, as its core ideas helped to buttress the arguments of powerful forces critical of certain forms of government intervention. The central ideas of neoliberalism offered economic elites a hospitable policy environment to accumulate greater wealth (Harvey 2005), international financial institutions a consistent policy paradigm that they could work with (Babb 2012), and the increasingly powerful multinational corporations an ideology that was supportive of their globalizing ambitions (Crouch 2012).

Particular historical events also provided grist to the neoliberal mill. In particular, the "stagflation" crises of the 1970s, in which countries like the United States experienced both high inflation and high unemployment simultaneously (previously the two were considered a trade-off), allowed free-market liberals to push their agenda more aggressively not only within the economics profession, but within public policy debates. They also contributed directly to the election of laissez-faire politicians in the major economies in the early 1980s (e.g. Thatcher in Britain; Reagan in the US), providing top-level political support for anti-Keynesian policies. Major international events also facilitated a turn to a more neoliberal set of multilateral institutions. In particular, the Latin American debt crisis and its subsequent consequences in the 1980s provided further grounds for those seeking to argue that state intervention in the economy should be severely restricted. Both the World Bank and the IMF began imposing strict conditions on their lending and assistance to developing countries. Emblematic in this regard was the abandonment of earlier support programs in favor of wholesale "structural adjustment policies" which demanded strict deregulatory and contractionary macroeconomic policies as conditions for financial assistance and support.

Strong ideological commitment to the "Washington Consensus" set of policies (see Williamson 1990), which included a commitment to open financial flows, elimination of subsidies, privatization of formerly state-owned enterprises, and deregulation, became a central focus of the IMF and the World Bank in this period. In effect, the Washington Consensus meant that existing multilateral institutions sought to orient developing countries' policies toward the world market, rather than toward the inward-oriented articulation of their own national development strategies. Between 1991 and 2001, for example, 94 percent of all national regulations concerning foreign direct investment were modified to facilitate FDI, rather than restrict it (UNCTAD 2002: 7, in Fritsch 2008: 2). Developing countries were encouraged to attract foreign investment, to sell state assets, and in general to liberalize their approach to trade and finance, as summarized in the initial "Washington Consensus" column of table 3.3.

Washington Consensus policies also reflected the new international financial environment which came to fruition after the fall of Bretton Woods. The dramatic expansion of international financial markets meant that certain national economic policies were severely affected. A dramatic example of this involved Francois Mitterrand, the French President in the early 1980s. While his Socialist government had no desire to liberalize the French economy to assist international financial flows, Mitterrand found that not doing so meant that rich French citizens and businesses simply managed to move their money out of the country regardless. Thus, his reluctance to liberalize capital flows produced negative consequences that were borne disproportionately by the poor and the working class. Responding to this, Mitterrand's government decided to liberalize its own country's engagement with international financial flows, and also promote financial openness worldwide, through organizations like the OECD (see Abdelal 2007). The fact that it was a Socialist President who promoted the financial

Table 3.3 Central features of the Washington Consensus and augmented Washington Consensus

	Washington Consensus *c.* 1980s and 1990s	"Augmented" Washington Consensus *c.* late 1990s–2008
National macroeconomic policies	Contractionary fiscal and monetary policies Tax reform to lower rates Liberalization of interest rates	Independent central banks and inflation targeting Targeted poverty reduction Use of financial codes and standards
Form of international integration	Competitive exchange rate Trade liberalization Liberalization of foreign direct investment (FDI) Capital account liberalization	Financial deregulation Some allowances for selective and temporary restrictions
Political institutions	Deregulation Property rights	Corporate governance and anticorruption Addressing barriers to property rights

liberalization of France is a telling example of the new constraints that even rich developed states were under in the post-Bretton Woods international economic environment.

These institutional developments since the collapse of the "embedded liberalism" elements of the Bretton Woods system both responded to and helped accelerate economic globalization. The transformation of the IMF and World Bank, and new multilateral institutions such as the WTO enhanced these trends as well. Figure 3.3 illustrates the average level of economic restrictiveness for all countries included in a standardized international index of economic globalization, the KOF index (Dreher 2006; Dreher et al. 2008). This indicator is a composite measure of the level of restrictiveness/openness of national economies in general to international economic flows, and includes not only tariff rates but also hidden import barriers, taxes on international trade, and capital account restrictions.

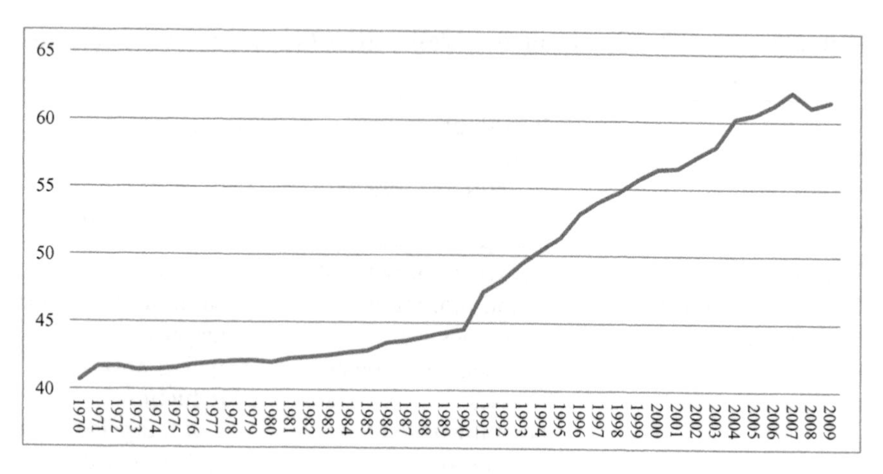

Figure 3.3 KOF index of economic liberalization, 1970–2009 (average of all countries)

Source: KOF Index of Globalization, Economic Globalization Indicator aii (restrictiveness); see Dreher 2006; Dreher et al. 2008. Because this indicator measures higher restrictiveness with lower values and lower restrictiveness with higher values, we have used it here as a measure of general economic liberalization over time.

Figure 3.3 illustrates the dramatic increase in economic openness across the world since the collapse of the Bretton Woods system. From the early 1970s to the 1990s the world witnessed a significant shift away from the use of capital controls, which were a fundamental part of the Bretton Woods system (see Helleiner 1994a). As Goodman and Pauly observed in the midst of this dramatic transformation: "In country after country, governments have abolished controls and dismantled the bureaucratic machinery to administer them. And in rare instances where governments have fallen back on controls, their temporary nature has usually been emphasized" (1993: 50). Such trends would only accelerate further over the 1990s and into the 2000s. Figure 3.4 illustrates the significant rise of states' openness to financial flows, as measured by the liberalization of national economies' "capital accounts" – effectively the willingness or otherwise of national governments to allow flows of finance across their borders.

Figure 3.4 collapses all available data for all countries for illustrative purposes into rich developed countries and developing countries. The trends are striking, especially given the fact that managed restrictions to financial flows were a central feature of the Bretton Woods period and a key theme in the decisions to limit the volatility associated with global financial markets that so mauled many national economies in

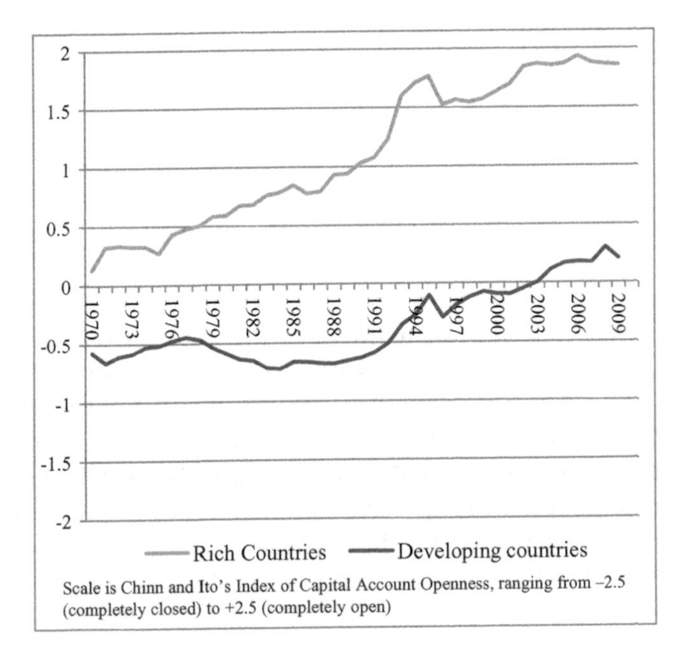

Figure 3.4 Average levels of capital account openness, rich countries and developing countries, 1970–2009. Date are not weighted by country size

Source: Calculations by authors, based on dataset from Chinn and Ito 2008.

the period before World War II. These figures underline the neoliberal orientation underlying the Washington Consensus and the enthusiasm of many international organizations such as the World Bank, the IMF, and the OECD – especially in the 1990s – for the aggressive liberalization of international finance. Yet as Abdelal (2007) has pointed out, the link between capital account liberalization and growth is far from clear. Two findings emerge. First, the benefits of capital account liberalization are not always clear and are highly conditional on the quality of the institutional environment. Specifically, the positive effects of capital account liberalization have been found to be systematically limited to countries with a relatively well-developed financial system, good accounting standards, strong creditor rights, and the rule of law (e.g. Eichengreen et al. 2011). The second robust finding is that even where there have been benefits from capital account liberalization, these benefits evaporate during financial crises. It is this particularly strong acceleration of international financial activity in the post-Bretton Woods environment that has had a number of important consequences. As we detail below, the post-Bretton Woods internationalization of financial markets was not a smooth ride. New problems emerged which demanded new institutions and new responses.

Patching up the cracks in the new system: transnational financial institutions

The post–Bretton Woods international economic system generated pressures that could not be handled by the IMF and World Bank, nor by rich developed country governments working alone. While large multilateral institutions constitute critical institutions of global economic governance, they are not the only institutions that govern economic affairs. Since the collapse of the Bretton Woods system, new "transnational" institutions have emerged to tackle new economic governance problems as they have developed. These institutions are distinct from the large multilaterals in that they are highly informal, often driven by people other than heads of state, and highly specialized (see Hale and Held 2011).[9]

After the fall of the Bretton Woods system in the 1970s, the acceleration of international financial flows began to introduce new problems for national financial regulators. Such problems included the threat of collapse among banks operating in several different states at once, which raised questions regarding who was responsible for resolving these types of crisis. Meanwhile, intensifying international competition among banks led to a perilous "race to the bottom" among many national bank regulators in terms of what they would allow their banks to do. Specifically, national banking regulators began to allow their banks to have lower and lower levels of capital adequacy – extra funds kept in reserve in the event of unexpected bank losses. In response to such problems, financial regulators from the major financial powers at the time began meeting to address some of the new collective problems they faced, and established the Basel Committee on Banking Supervision (BCBS) (see Young 2011b; Young 2012), a transnational institution often regarded as highly successful in its flexibility and informal governance structure (see Kapstein 1992; Slaughter 2004a).

Another example of a new transnational financial governance institution relates to the problem of illicit finance. In this regard, the reemergence of global financial flows allowed criminal drug and terrorist activity to essentially free-ride on nonillicit financial transactions (Taylor 2007; Tsingou 2010). In response to this new challenge, finance ministers from the G7 in 1989 produced a series of international recommendations and agreed-upon standards for monitoring and enforcement in relation to terrorist finance and money laundering. The Financial Action Task Force has since generated many international recommendations and facilitated policy to tackle illicit finance around the world. Further examples could be given of such innovative responses by transnationally organized economic institutions, in particular when it comes to facilitating the diffusion of international standards and best practice in areas such as taxation, accounting (see Nölke 2011; Botzem 2012), financial conglomerates (see Young 2011b), and insurance (see Masciandaro 2011). Some transnational financial governance institutions emerged to tackle larger, systemic issues. For example, the Financial Stability Forum was established in 1999 after widespread concerns over the contagion of financial instability following the East Asian financial crises (see Germain 2001). While it included central bankers, finance ministers, and representatives from other issue-specific transnational economic governance institutions, its role was mainly confined to research and the dissemination of standards.

These diverse, smaller "transnational" institutions have also been instrumental in establishing a system of collective standards and cooperation. In terms of facilitating both formal and informal communication between and among national and subnational regulatory regimes, this system has been tremendously successful. Through the establishment of transnational institutions, the competitive pressures of private institutions and markets on national governments have been countered or mitigated by a kind of "regulatory globalization," wherein new international standards have been established (Macey 2003). Table 3.4 offers a list of some of these transnational financial governance institutions and the areas of finance that they seek to govern. These institutions have played an important role in the "augmented" Washington Consensus summarized in table 3.3, as they have generated the international standards and codes that have been used by national governments and other international organizations, such as the IMF (Ponte et al. 2011). As a network of institutions often working on highly technical issues, they have provided the communicative infrastructure that has established norms and frameworks with which financial regulatory and monetary policies have been organized around the world.

The development of these various transnational financial governance institutions has given rise to a highly decentered system. While the global trade regime is organized around one large multilateral

Table 3.4 Selected transnational financial governance institutions

Name	Year formed	Composition	Area of activity	Main function
Bank for International Settlements (BIS)	1930	National central banks	Monetary policy and central banking	Coordination among central banks; serves as a hub for the BCBS, IOSCO, Joint Forum (see below), and CPSS
Basel Committee on Banking Supervision (BCBS)	1974	Regulators from central banks and national financial regulatory agencies	Banking regulation and supervision	Generation of international standards and codes
International Organization of Securities Commissions (IOSCO)	1983	National and subnational securities and exchange regulatory bodies	Securities and stock markets	Exchange of information and the generation of best practice standards
International Association of Insurance Supervisors (IAIS)	1984	National insurance regulators	Insurance	Monitoring and generation of international standards
Financial Action Task Force (FATF)	1989	Ministries of Finance	Money laundering	Generates recommendations to national governments
Committee on Payment and Settlement Systems (CPSS)	1990	Central banks	Financial system payments and processing	Sets standards, conducts research
Joint Forum on Financial Conglomerates	1995	Other transnational bodies: BCBS, IOSCO, IAIS	Financial conglomerates covering banking, insurance, and securities	Develops guidance and principles, identifies best practice

institution, the WTO, a parallel has not existed for global financial governance. Although the IMF has played an important role in coordinating emergency financing in exchange for structural and institutional reform of national economies, the task of regulating private financial markets in the post–Bretton Woods period has been largely governed by a network of transnational institutions. Rather than the IMF, it has been the BIS that has operated at the center of this network, although only in a very modest way in offering many of these transnational institutions some organizational resources. Institutions like the BCBS and the Financial Stability Forum (now the Financial Stability *Board* – see below), for example, were given headquarters there, though their respective secretariats and resources were kept at a bare minimum.

Self-reinforcing interdependence at work

A plethora of institutions has been developed to "govern" the global economy in the postwar period. These institutions have evolved as the global economy has grown larger and more interdependent, yet they have not been just a response to emerging economic needs. Rather, the system of global economic governance has given rise to higher levels of global economic integration than otherwise would have been the case.

Despite the many shortcomings of this system, which will be discussed in the next section, its ability to execute global policy initiatives is a considerable achievement, especially when viewed historically. The emergence of a complex system of institutions, international covenants, processes and other legal mechanisms has prevented a return to the beggar-thy-neighbor chaos of the interwar period, or to the nineteenth-century style of imperial domination. Multilateral institutions such as the IMF, World Bank, and WTO play important roles in the way the global economy functions, in particular facilitating the dramatic liberal integration of the global economy. Transnational economic institutions have arisen to respond to new problems as they have emerged, thereby demonstrating that global economic governance can be flexible and adaptive. The level of global economic integration has accelerated over the course of the postwar order, with some of the most striking increases occurring around the time of the WTO's creation. Figure 3.5 shows the ratio of total global exports, measured in terms of total merchandise exports, to global economic output.

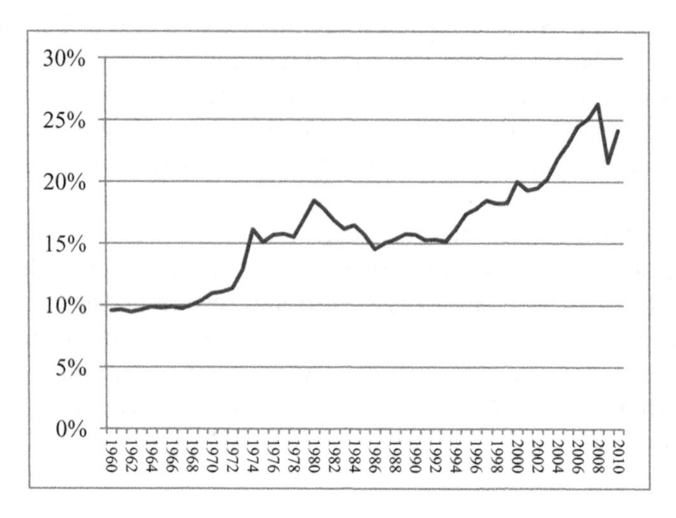

Figure 3.5 Ratio of total global exports to global GDP, 1960–2010

Source: WTO dataset (World Merchandise Exports, in current US$ terms), World Development Indicators (World GDP in current US$ terms).

Table 3.5 Exports to GDP ratios, selected years, 1870–2008

	1870	1913	1929	1950	1973	1998	2008
France	4.9	7.8	8.6	7.6	14.0	21.8	21.8
Germany	9.5	16.1	12.8	6.2	17.5	25.0	39.9
Japan	0.2	2.4	3.5	2.2	8.8	10.1	16.0
UK	12.2	17.5	13.3	11.3	16.2	18.8	17.3
USA	2.5	3.7	3.6	3.0	5.2	7.8	9.0
Brazil	12.2	9.8	6.9	3.9	7.8	6.1	12.0
Russia						27.6	28.4
India	2.6	4.6	4.7	2.9	3.4	8.0	16.0
China	0.7	1.7	1.8	2.6	4.3	18.0	31.6
World	4.6	7.9	9.0	5.5	12.9	18.3	26.3

Source: Maddison 2001: 363 for pre-1973 data; subsequent data calculated by authors, based on the following: GDP in current US$ (World Development Indicators), total merchandise exports in current US$, all deflated to constant 1990 US$ using US Bureau of Economic Analysis GDP deflator figures.

Table 3.5 shows similar data but over a longer historical period, using selected years and countries where data is available from 1870 until 2008. This table illustrates two important features of the development of the global economy. First, the importance of trade in the global economy has increased dramatically, especially since the end of the Bretton Woods era in 1973. At the same time, the level of integration in the global trading system has been highly variegated across countries. Most notable in this regard is the rapid increase in recent years of the integration of Brazil, India, and even more dramatically, China.

These figures illustrate a striking fact – that global governance institutions have helped to make the global economy more open, integrated, and densely interconnected. Yet in the post-Bretton Woods era, this push for integration has often been seen not just as a means to prosperity, but as an end in, and of, itself (Rodrik and Subramanian 2009; Rodrik 2006a; Abdelal 2007). Indeed, the causal connection between many forms of policy liberalization and growth is at best tenuous and conditional. Successful models of development "catch up" – such as Korea and Taiwan and Singapore – have not generally been forthcoming in the post-Bretton Woods period, and inequality has increased in some of the fastest growing countries, such as China. The relative success stories that we do have – countries such as India, China, and Brazil, which reflect the growing multipolarity in the world today – are not countries that have engaged in rapid and rough-shod liberalization, but rather have developed their own models of strategic engagement with the global economy. These have emphasized practices of strategic intervention in markets, whereby the government selectively intervenes in the process of industrial development to emphasize not only export promotion, but also diversification of production (see Rodrik 2010; Wade 2010). These lessons have yet to be seriously institutionalized within existing multilateral institutions, and thus rather than learning from successful development experiences, the "augmented" Washington Consensus has often emphasized poverty alleviation much more than developmental catch-up (see Wade 2003a).

Indeed, the transformation to the "augmented" Washington Consensus might be interpreted in some ways as an institutional reaction to policy failures, and the politicization of those failures. Many Washington Consensus policies pursued were seen to limit the "policy space" of developing countries, for example prohibiting forms of industrial policy which were seen to "distort" markets (as opposed to the more positive view which sees them as creating markets in the longer term) (see Rodrik 2006a). The aggressive role of the IMF in restructuring economies has been particularly problematic. This led, in many cases, to developing countries insulating themselves from the institution as much as possible. As Babb points out (2012: 16), many medium-income countries have insulated themselves from IMF conditionality by accumulating large currency reserves (see below). In Latin

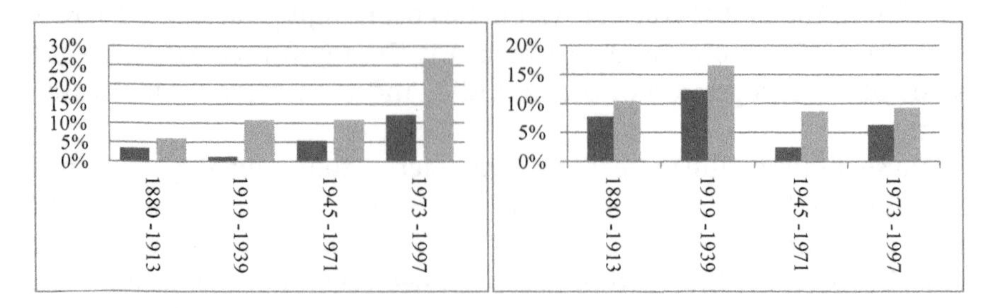

Figure 3.6 Dimensions of financial crises, periods compared between 1880 and 1997

Source: Data derived from Bordo et al. 2001.

America there has been no IMF conditionality package in over a decade, and there have been regional efforts to provide an alternative to the Bretton Woods institutions through institutions such as the Bank of the South, the Latin American Reserve Fund, and the Andean Development Corporation (Babb 2012: 16). Middle-income countries have become "increasingly selective about the areas in which they invite bank engagement" (Babb 2012: 16).

While development policies have evolved somewhat in the post-Bretton Woods period, international financial flows increased in their importance in the global economy. One important manifestation of the liberalization of financial flows has been an international environment in which financial crises are more frequent. Despite the manifold institutions that exist to govern global finance, the long-term trend suggests that things have gotten worse rather than better.[10] Figure 3.6 shows the situation up until the 1997–8 East Asian financial crisis. The left-hand graph measures the number of financial crises in each time period, and includes currency and banking crises. Crisis depth, on the right, measures the percentage of GDP estimated to have decreased as a result of financial crises in each period. As these data reveal, while the depth of crises has decreased since 1945 compared to earlier periods (no doubt due to better institutions, both national and intergovernmental), the Bretton Woods period (1945–70) was superior to the Washington Consensus period (1973–97).

Looking beyond the East Asia crisis, and focusing on banking crises, the trend continues to worsen. Figure 3.7 counts the number of banking crises in a given year from the end of the Bretton Woods period to the outbreak of the financial crisis of 2008 (quality yearly data outside these ranges is unfortunately not available).

As these data illustrate, there was a secular decline in the frequency of financial crises after the late 1990s. Were it not for the events of

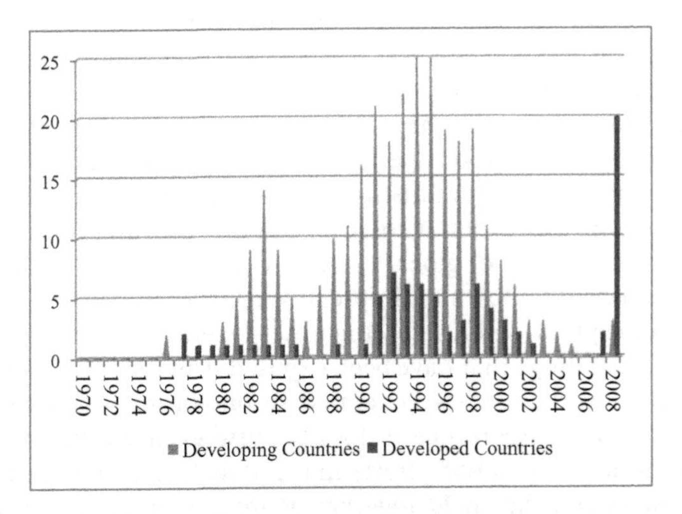

Figure 3.7 Number of banking crises occurring in a given year, 1970–2008

Source: Authors' calculation from data in Laeven and Valencia 2010.

the global financial crisis of 2008, one might be tempted to think that the existing structure of global financial governance had successfully secured a modicum of international financial stability. What is distinct about the global financial crisis of 2008 – sometimes referred to as the North Atlantic Crisis – is the way in which it centered quite squarely on the rich developed countries, the "core" economies of the global financial system such as the United States and the United Kingdom.

How can we understand these failings? One prominent way is through a critique of the particular content of the dominant economic ideology prevailing over most of this period, that of neoliberalism (see Harvey 2005). Another, sometimes related view, is that poor global economic performance can be traced to deep structural problems within global capitalism itself and its inherent and cyclical tendencies to generate massive economic crises that simply shift the balance of power around geopolitically without achieving fundamental system-changing reform (cf. Arrighi 2007; Arrighi and Moore 2001; Brenner 2002). Yet another view is that governance of global economic problems are difficult simply because it is extremely difficult to have states agree with each other. Each of these views may have some merits. However, they cannot explain many features of contemporary global economic governance. Neoliberalism has been an important animating ideology of economic reform, but it has not been a unilateral driver of problems. Structural change of the global economy has of course occurred, but the emergence of institutions to manage particular governance problems has shown that challenges can be addressed in a number of cases to manage this change. Multilateral cooperation has of course been difficult, but the international system in the post–Bretton woods period has seen the emergence of a wide variety of new governance institutions, and the continued utilization of old ones. At least when it comes to specific coordination problems, the historical record of global economic governance over the last 30 years has actually shown an impressive record.

The concept of self-reinforcing interdependence helps us make sense of the failings that have been exposed. The very success of global economic governance has generated second-order problems. Global finance has the importance it does because earlier multilateral and transnational cooperative efforts made global financial markets possible. The system has held together as long as it has because it has been a governed system. Yet, paradoxically, the governance structures that have evolved alongside the global economy cannot adequately address the forces that they have helped to unleash.

Making sense of global economic governance challenges requires that we make sense of the fundamentally *partial* nature of governance success – the fact that we have been paradoxically both too good and too bad at global economic governance at the same time. Global financial flows have been made possible through a network of multilateral and transnational institutions which facilitate such flows; yet the transmission of crises is also now more rapid and rapacious than ever. Large, well-financed global bodies such as the IMF now exist to assist with crises once they occur – yet our ability to prevent crises in the first place through these institutions is not particularly good. International trade integration has reached incredible heights, also thanks to the institutions we have put in place which avert the worst forms of protectionism. Yet global trade deals have stalled, and are plagued by incredibly difficult problems that are the very result of such earlier successes. The next section argues the case for seeing such gridlock in contemporary global economic governance, pointing out the multilayered manifestations of the problem.

GRIDLOCK IN GLOBAL ECONOMIC GOVERNANCE

The postwar economic order and its subsequent evolution have made a world today that would have been unrecognizable to the architects of Bretton Woods. First, the globalization of economic relations has surpassed all historical benchmarks. The 2008–9 financial crisis, discussed below, was only the most recent manifestation of this reality. Second, the years since World War II have seen the largest increase in aggregate human welfare in history. The lifespan of the average human being increased from 47 years in 1950–5 to 68 for 2005–10 (UNDP 2010). GDP per capita increased by about 400 percent between 1950 and 2000, even as the world's population more than doubled (US Census Bureau 2012). Third, there has been a massive shift eastward in the world's economic center of gravity, as Asia returns to its historical position as the world's largest economic region. The extraordinary growth of Japan, Korea, Taiwan, Singapore, and Southeast Asia during the postwar period has shown that some states can use integration with the global economy to radically improve the lives of their citizens. And China has shown how transformative that process can be, lifting more than 600 million people out of poverty over the last three decades (World Bank 2012).

The success we have achieved has given way to new problems and dilemmas that, following the logic of gridlock, have outstripped the existing institutional infrastructure. The development of global economic governance has enabled, but not kept pace with the evolution of the global economy. In this section we describe some of the manifestations of gridlock in global economic governance. As in our earlier chapters, gridlock mechanisms are examined with our view directed at both the operation of governance institutions and toward emergent problems. We begin by detailing the difficulty in completing the current global WTO trade round known as the Doha Development Round. We argue that despite significant institutionalization of trade governance, harder problems at the frontier of global trade governance – problems only possible because of earlier achievements – have significantly stalled a new multilateral trade agreement. We then move to the global governance of finance. While the world proved able to coordinate macroeconomic policies to head off the worst of the crisis, principally through flexible mechanisms like the G20, institutional safeguards also failed to predict or prevent the crisis. More worryingly, countries have not been able to put in place the reforms needed to prevent the next crisis. While much blame certainly goes to bad policy choices in financial centers, we argue that gridlock explains why it has been so difficult to make institutional reforms. We follow this discussion with an analysis of three emergent problems associated with the current global economic order: the problem of systemic risk, the problem of "global imbalances," and the issue of global corporate accountability.

Gridlock in Multilateral Trade Negotiations

The completion of the Uruguay Round in 1994, culminating in the formation of the WTO in 1995, was a major event in the world of multilateral governance. Yet, in the following years many developing countries declared themselves to be somewhat suspicious of another trade round, given the way they had fared in the Uruguay Round vis-à-vis developed countries (Scott and Wilkinson 2011: 617). A major ministerial conference was held in Seattle, Washington in 1999. Developing countries articulated their reservations forcefully. The Indian Minister of Commerce and Industry summed up the sentiment of many developing countries at the time by beginning the conference by noting systemic "asymmetries and inequities" in WTO agreements and that the special and differential treatment clauses that developing countries were promised "remained virtually inoperative."[11] Furthermore, the Seattle Ministerial became politicized even within the rich developed world, as thousands of protesting citizens and over 1,200 nongovernmental organizations, from labor unions to human rights groups to environmental groups, sought to raise issues of inequity concerning the negotiations. In the end the Seattle Ministerial achieved very little, and was widely regarded as a failure – stemming in large part from developed country intransigence and developing country resistance (Schott 2000). The fact that this first major multilateral trade negotiation failed did not bode well for the new WTO; and yet this was just a sign of things to come.

Given the social fury over international trade negotiations in Seattle, the countries decided to hold the next meeting on the Qatari island of Doha, far from protesters in Western democratic countries. Named the Doha "Development" Round, it promised to put greater priority on developing country issues. But in addition to negotiations over agricultural and manufacturing markets, the Doha Round also featured efforts to liberalize trade in services (through the General Agreement on Trade in Services, GATS) and to generate a robust system of protection for intellectual property rights (through the Agreement on Trade-Related Aspects of Intellectual Property Rights, TRIPS). The latter issues were seen as critically important for rich countries, which sought to protect their established interests in leading sectors such as financial services, pharmaceuticals, and computer science and technology markets through deeper integration of the world economy. Yet issues related to agriculture were critical to developing countries, which continued to lose substantial market

Table 3.6 Selected major events in the Doha Development Round negotiations

Year(s)	Main location of negotiation	Central outcomes and developments
1997–2000	Various locations, culminating in Seattle, USA	Talks begin for a new round of multilateral trade negotiations
2001	Ministerial Conference in Doha, Qatar	Doha Development Agenda launched
2003	Cancún Ministerial and Mid-Term Review	No agreement; ended in deadlock
2003–4	Geneva	Culmination in the "July 2004" package: only some "framework" issues agreed on
2005	Hong Kong Ministerial Conference	Some further minor agreements achieved
2008	Geneva	The "July 2008" package attempted to break deadlock, some differences narrowed, but multilateral negotiations collapsed
2009–	Several locations	There have been various attempts to get the Doha Round negotiations up and running again; all thus far have failed

share because of agricultural protectionism in rich countries, where farmers enjoyed significant political power. While each side had something the other wanted, negotiation was extremely difficult from the beginning. The negotiation deadlocks in international trade are now a highly theorized subject within the academic literature (Narlikar 2010; Odell 2009).

Table 3.6 lays out the major multilateral trade meetings associated with the Doha Round. In each set of negotiations, countries have failed to resolve the major items. Just as the Doha Round got off the ground, at the Cancún Ministerial in 2003, significant problems began. One blockage was the joint EU and US refusal to reform the Common Agricultural Policy and the US Farm Bill, respectively. Domestic agricultural interest groups trumped the multilateral agenda (S. Cho

2010: 573). Yet the key factor was the "Singapore issues," so named because of the issues put on the agenda at the Singapore meeting in 1996. These included trade-related issues associated with "deep integration" such as investment, competition, government procurement, and trade facilitation. At Cancún the EU pushed these issues hard, and was effectively backed by the US. Yet a reticent bloc of developing countries forged a "Group of 22" to resist these proposals. Reflecting the complex nature of multilateral negotiations of late, most NGOs from the developed world sought to support such efforts (see S. Cho 2004: 235). Unlike during the Uruguay Round, the G22 now had sufficient heft to block the EU and US, and the Cancún Ministerial collapsed without any results.

After the Cancún Ministerial, the contentious "Singapore" issues gave way to an increased focus on agriculture. Agriculture was itself highly controversial, and many developing countries hoped that undelivered promises in the Uruguay Round could be rectified through Doha negotiations (Scott and Wilkinson 2011: 616–17). The US and EU put what appeared to be substantial offers on the table, but as Scott and Wilkinson point out (2011: 617–18), these amounted to relatively modest concessions from current practices, and were designed to give the US and the EU considerable flexibility.

Successive attempts to reinvigorate trade talks have failed at every turn. The lack of movement in the Doha Round prompted the WTO's General Council to adopt a "tiered approach" known as the July Package, whereby developing countries' demands would be treated in relation to the respective level of trade distortion they experienced. This did not succeed. Another attempt was made in 2005 at the Hong Kong Ministerial, in which a schedule was proposed to dismantle various agricultural subsidies in the rich countries along with the provision of special terms of access for developing countries for 97 percent of the goods they exported by 2013. This sounded good, but it turned out the remaining 3 percent of good excluded from this deal covered approximately 98 percent of the goods that developing countries exported in terms of value (Laborde 2008: 9). In 2006 two "mini-ministerials" of January and July 2006 failed to achieve anything of substance (Das 2008: 295). WTO Director-General Pascal Lamy gathered members of the G6 (comprised of Australia, Brazil, the EU, India, Japan, and the US) to meet in a plurilateral consultative meeting in London for two long days in March 2006, but this also failed to bridge crucial differences in positions on modalities of agricultural subsidies and industrial tariffs (Das 2008: 295). On July 24, 2006, Lamy formally suspended negotiations because of insurmountable differences –

the first time this had been done in the life of the GATT/WTO (WTO 2006). After a later attempt to negotiate with a smaller group of countries (involving the EU, US, India, and Brazil) in Potsdam fell apart in 2007, Lamy launched a "package of elements" proposal in 2008, an attempted compromise (WTO 2008; ICTSD 2008: 593; Ismail 2009). This too failed, principally because of disagreement between the US, India, and China over issues such as cotton, despite agreement on 18 out of 20 areas.

At the July 2008 Doha Ministerial, the US offered to make serious compromises on the subsidies it provides to its agricultural industry. Yet it also openly criticized and sought reform of the agricultural policies of India and China. This entreaty proved a nonstarter with India, in particular, where over two-thirds of the population works in the agricultural sector, many at, or near, the subsistence level. In such a context, the Indian trade minister declared: "I'm not risking the livelihood of millions of farmers" (Dickson 2008).

More recently, there has been a proposal for a "Doha light" which differentiates "three lanes": a fast lane for developing country topics; a middle lane for consensus topics; and a slow lane for the difficult issues such as agriculture and the Singapore issues, to be tackled at a later date (WTO 2011a). As Lamy has noted, the problem is not a technical one, but one which is fundamentally political at its core (Pennay et al. 2010). Growing multipolarity plays an important role in every successive attempt to deal with the Doha agenda. The poorest countries in Africa, Asia, and the Caribbean have forged a "Group of 90" group, which has different preferences and priorities from the US and the EU, which themselves are faced with an increasingly assertive group of developing countries often led by emerging powers such as Brazil. General stalemates of positions and a dragging out of the negotiations has led to a form of what Pascal Lamy has referred to as "negotiation exhaustion" (Reuters interview in 2010).

A wide variety of solutions were proposed, everything from specific recommendations to states as to how they should negotiate, to establishing a "knowledge platform" for services to educate the developing world on the potential gains of liberalization and to increase their leverage through South–South liberalization (S. Cho 2010: 589; Scott and Wilkinson 2011: 149; Hoekman and Matoo 2011: 14). After considerable difficulties, Lamy made proposals to focus the WTO's negotiation progress around a smaller set of questions with the objective of reaching a mini-agreement during a ministerial conference in December 2011.

The dynamic of rising multipolarity plays a critical role in the stalling of Doha, because the stalling of this trade round is in many ways a result of North–South differences. The institutional innovation of the WTO, that of creating a "single undertaking" rule, means that WTO agreements are not only more important, but they give important weight to active dissent. The "single undertaking" format of WTO agreements requires that for a trade round to close, WTO members must agree on all elements of the package: there is no space for picking and choosing. As discussed above, this rule, and its consequences, are the product of previous successes and self-reinforcing interdependence processes in the multilateral order. Greater interdependence led to the enfranchisement of developing countries in the WTO framework. However, confronted by the intransigence of leading states (i.e. the US and EU), this enfranchisement, combined with the single undertaking rule, has led to a stalemate on trade agreements. This was not a problem in the Uruguay Round of trade negotiations, as developed countries were still able to muster a "power play" over developing countries (Steinberg 2002), securing agreement on a variety of "deep integration" issues (not related to tariffs) seen as critical to rich developed countries. At that time, the single undertaking arrangement arguably facilitated cooperation, because it allowed the rich world to tell poorer countries: take it or leave it. Global trade negotiation successes of the past were often built on the fact that substantial agreement could always be reached between the US and Europe, but the rise of Brazil, India, and China has challenged this (Guerrieri 2006: 97–8). Developing countries in general have been more assertive both in their stance toward the agricultural protectionism of the developed countries, which rich countries try to keep off the agenda, and in their stance on "deep integration" issues such as intellectual property protection and trade in services, which rich countries try to put at the top of the agenda. Brazil and India increasingly have acted as representatives for the rest of the global South. As Efstathopoulos (2012) argues, both countries are well positioned to exercise leadership on issues of concern to the South. Subordinate states have also deployed resistance strategies themselves. Lee (2012) documents how African states have utilized the discourse of "development" at the heart of the Doha Round to leverage their disapproval of the negotiations. It is also useful to point out that even *among* reemergent global powers there is often disagreement: the BRICs (Brazil, Russia, India, China) do not necessarily agree among themselves in many instances. Over the course of Doha Round the developmental content of the negotiations has decreased, and the relative importance of agriculture increased.

While agricultural market access is important and consequential to many developing countries, this transformation (some would say deflation of ambition) of the content of Doha has been marked. Thus from one developmentalist perspective, the focus on agricultural market access, which yields little and risks locking developing countries into an agriculture-based development strategy, weakens the attractiveness of concluding the round at all (Scott and Wilkinson 2011: 617).

While agricultural liberalization in the rich world would be a boon for developing countries, as Kevin Gallagher (2008) argues, the actual deal on offer within the Doha Round has questionable benefits for developing countries, at least when viewed in the aggregate. Economists at the World Bank estimated the potential global welfare gains to be as great as US$300 billion per year (Anderson and Martin 2005). Such estimates were for a scenario of "full" global trade liberalization, that is, assuming that all tariffs and nontariff barriers were completely eliminated – a highly unlikely scenario (see K. Gallagher 2008: 78). Thus, the World Bank reestimated projections for a "likely Doha scenario," which assumed that while trade liberalization would still be ambitious, it would be more restricted. These new estimates help to understand the resistance that many developing countries had to the Doha Round. For developed countries, the expected aggregate gains from a Doha agreement were considerable, with the economic modeling estimates measured at approximately US$80 billion, compared to the loss of tariff revenue from nonagricultural market access items at US$38 billion. The situation for developing countries was quite the reverse. The combined estimates for all developing countries were that Doha would yield benefits of approximately US$16 billion. This simply pales in comparison to the expected losses from tariff revenue, of approximately US$63 billion (see K. Gallagher 2008: 80–1, using Anderson and Martin 2005; De Cordoba and Vanzetti 2005).

Gridlock in Doha is also a manifestation of the emergence of harder transborder problems. As the WTO itself acknowledges, the vast majority of global trade rules were designed for a simpler world in which trade barriers took the form of tariff barriers and easily identifiable actions by states (see WTO 2012: 203–5). As noted earlier, the intensification of economic globalization has meant increasing pressure to address not just tariff-based but nontariff barriers as well. This can be understood through the prism of the "intensity" dimension of harder problems, explicated in chapter 1. As the global economy has developed and international competition intensified, securing the privileges of highly profitable industries has become a critical component of the diplomatic strategies of rich developed countries. In particular, the sustained profitability and market share of the information/communications/technology industry, the entertainment industry, and the pharmaceutical industry all depend on such "deep integration" issues, and important "intellectual property" industry coalitions have lobbied hard for such issues to become a priority (see Dobusch and Quack 2012; Sell and Prakash 2004). The increasing global economic importance of countries such as China, India, and Brazil means that such issues remain critical at the very same time that these countries are able to either resist such developments or use them as bargaining chips for other demands of relative greater importance to them.

At the same time, the increasing integration of developing countries into the world economy makes the system of agricultural protections and subsidies all the more important, as it is in those areas that LDCs stand to gain the most from trade. But agricultural liberalization reaches deep into domestic politics. In Europe, Japan, and the United States, rural interests represent a crucial constituency that politicians cross at their peril. The role farmers play in domestic politics makes them far more difficult to bargain with than industrial firms. Though many manufacturing firms in rich countries of course lost out on various trade deals, these were in part balanced by corresponding gains for other industries. For subsidized farmers, for whom agriculture represents not just a job but often a heritage, the outlook is far more bleak.

There is no question that international negotiations are often challenging, but the gridlock at play in the Doha Round reflects deeper challenges than simply cooperation problems among self-interested states. The reason why the Doha Round has been plagued by difficulties is not simply because international cooperation is difficult to achieve per se; rather, the challenges associated with the Doha Round also reflect the difficulty associated with regulating the extensity and intensity of global economic integration. Furthermore, as we have seen, emergent powers such as China, India, and Brazil, which represent the world's growing multipolarity, have played an increasingly important role, often together with other developing countries, in acting as an opposing force to some of the demands and dictates of the rich developed countries.

The challenges of the Doha Round are also challenges associated with fragmentation. While the WTO represents the model of what an overarching, centralized authority on global governance might look

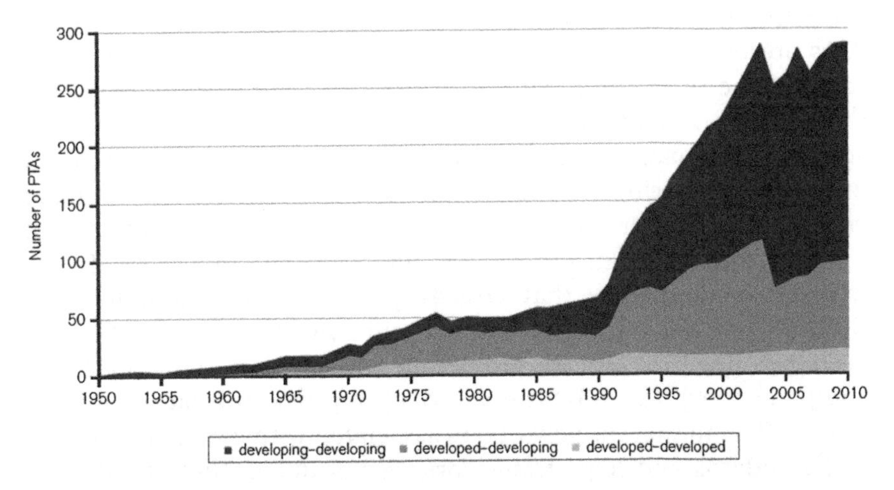

Figure 3.8 Cumulative number of preferential trade agreements in force, 1950–2010, notified and nonnotified, between country groups

Source: WTO 2011b.

like (at least in one area), it is nevertheless not "the only game in town" when it comes to conducting trade deals. In particular, preferential trade agreements (PTAs), such as regional or (even more common) bilateral trade deals, have emerged as an institutional competitor to multilateral, WTO-level trade negotiations. As Lee (2012) points out, the less effective the WTO is at actually executing multilateral trade governance, the more its member states simply ignore the WTO's efforts and seek bilateral and regional alternatives to secure market opening. There are numerous indications that regional and bilateral trade agreements have risen in just this way (see figure 3.8 – see also Shadlen 2008; Jaleel 2008; Wesley 2008). The effects of the recent PTA explosion are perverse, whether global free trade is seen as an unequivocal good thing or not. The economic benefits from PTAs tend to be small given the low level of tariffs that prevail in most parts of the world after years of prior trade liberalization. Countries are typically unwilling to liberalize "sensitive" sectors and as such the mutual economic gains tend to be small (Dee 2008; Ravenhill 2008). The continued development of PTAs does not mean a global increase in free trade simply by regional and bilateral means (Andriamananjara 2002). Moreover, as Ravenhill (2008) points out, PTAs have a strategic consequence: the demands coming from "pro-liberalization" coalitions within countries tend to soften as PTAs increase. If such an effect continues, PTAs might further weaken prospects in the longer term for multilateral trade cooperation.

For those who do not see global free trade as an unequivocal goal, PTAs present a number of troubling issues. Despite whatever shortcomings the WTO might have, PTAs are seen to be even more restrictive on governments' developmental "policy space" than are WTO agreements (Shadlen 2005, 2008). At the same time, PTAs have an inherently redistributive component to them – one that favors large powers over smaller ones. Bilateral PTAs in particular often involve a highly uneven balance of power among negotiation participants, with the consequence that already powerful economies, like the United States and the EU, and reemergent powers, such as China, have been pursuing PTAs over the last decade with great vigor (see Ravenhill and Jiang 2009). The WTO is not perfect. Yet as a multilateral institution it offers numerous advantages associated with common multilateral standards and legal framework. For example, the formal WTO dispute settlement procedures offer developing countries a means to negotiate the reduction of trade barriers against the products that they currently export, offering them more bargaining leverage than they would otherwise have (see Bown 2009. As Davis puts it, the use of legal adjudication "allows developing countries to gain better outcomes in negotiations with their powerful trade partners than they could in a bilateral negotiation" outside of this formal, multilateral setting (see Davis 2006: 220). Having a formal multilateral institution means that developing countries have a right to negotiate with more powerful states, instead of only bargaining bilaterally; moreover the formal and centralized character of WTO negotiations means that developing countries have opportunities to forge coalitions (even though this might not always be successful – see Narlikar and Odell 2006).[12]

Gridlock in Global Financial Governance

As in trade, global financial institutions have been successful enough to reinforce interdependence, but less able to confront the second-order problems that constitute gridlock. Institutions have undergirded both the globalization of finance and the financialization of the world economy over the past 30 years. These processes have made even the world's most powerful states vulnerable to financial crises in a way that would have been difficult to imagine under the original Bretton Woods system. But unlike the global trade regime, which is organized around a central formal institution, global financial institutions have developed in a largely ad hoc fashion. While the IMF continues to play a critical role, financial governance is characterized by a web of diverse institutions, including a number of highly specialized transgovernmental bodies.

This fragmented system is not without its virtues. In the face of the worst financial crisis since 1929, institutions like the G20 helped facilitate a coordinated Keynesian stimulus, providing assurance against beggar-thy-neighbors and therefore helping keep the world out of another Great Depression. But, following the logic of self-reinforcing interdependence, this partial success breeds second-order problems. As we explain below, financial institutionalization has made us more interdependent, but not given us the ability to reduce the associated risks. Nor have countries proven able to achieve cooperation on the deeper questions raised by financial interdependence, such as macroprudential oversight and global imbalances.

Before assessing the role of gridlock in hampering financial governance, it is important to understand how powerful and potentially dangerous financial interdependence has become. The 2008–9 crisis was a stark illustration of this reality. What was initially perceived as a series of surprising difficulties in the US housing market evolved in a matter of months from a problem in the markets for obscure financial instruments to a general, global financial crisis – the worst the world had seen since the beginning of the Great Depression (see Crotty 2009). Financial market liquidity turned, figuratively speaking, from an ocean to a desert in a matter of days. International capital flows, which had been expanding since the breakdown of Bretton Woods at an accelerating pace, experienced a dramatic decline (see Milesi-Ferretti and Tille 2011; see also figure 3.9).

The close relationship between global economic activity and financial flows that had developed over the previous 30 years meant that the consequences of the global financial crisis were severe, to say the least. As figure 3.10 illustrates, the effect of the financial crisis was a sudden and marked decline in global economic activity. The average annual world economic growth rate in the five years before 2009 was 4.56 percent; in 2009 it was –0.06 percent.[13] The financial crisis not only lowered levels of world output, but also adversely affected trade flows. This is not only because of the decline in demand that follows economic crisis in rich countries, but also because international trade flows depend on secure and highly liquid international financial markets in order to operate effectively. As figure 3.10 demonstrates, trade volume plummeted much more rapidly and severely

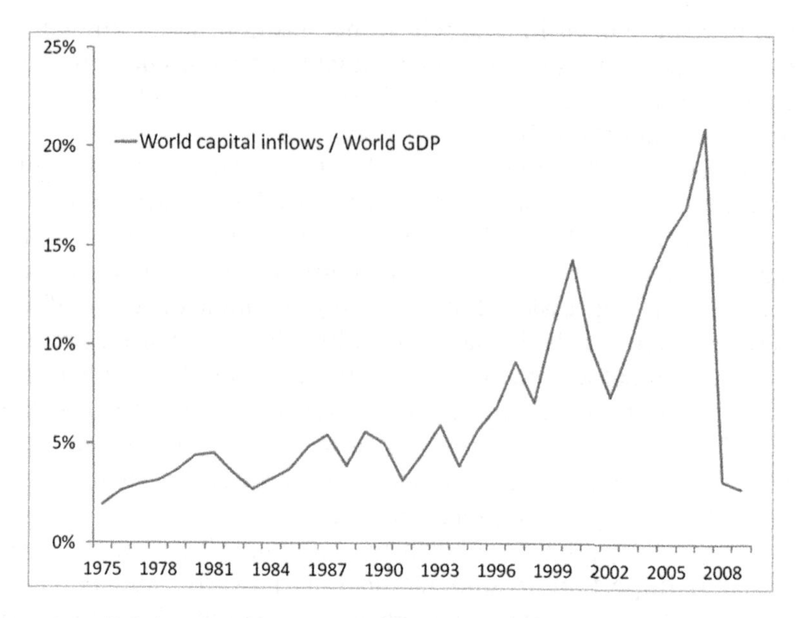

Figure 3.9 Global capital flows, 1975–2009

Source: External Wealth of Nations Mark II database developed by Lane and Milesi-Ferretti 2007; IMF balance of payments statistics. Data are sum of gross capital inflows across the world's countries, as a ratio of world GDP.

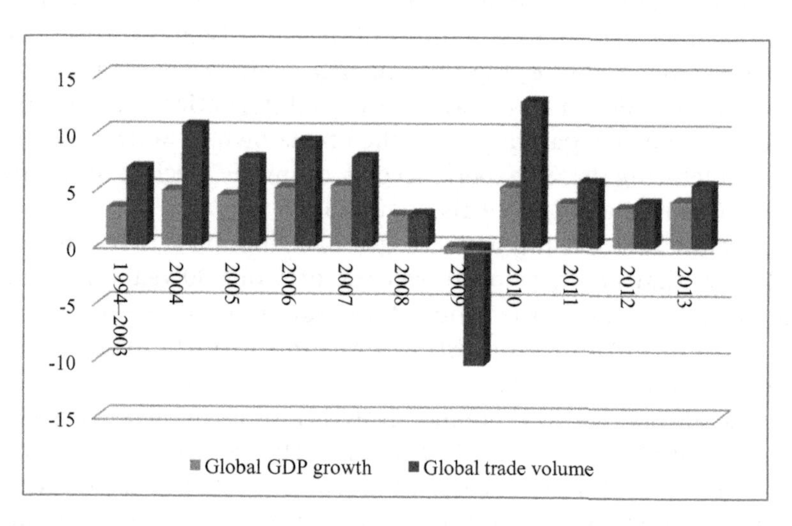

Figure 3.10 Percent annual change in global GDP and trade volume, 1994–2013 (projection)

Source: IMF 2012: 190 (table A1), 205 (table A9). Trade data are annual percentage change for trade in goods and services at global level, measured by volume; global GDP data is annual percentage change in world output, measured in real GDP terms.

than global output, contracting by over 10 percent. Global commodity markets also suffered from lack of financing and demand (Nissanke 2012).

Despite these various transmission mechanisms, the largest impact was of course in financial markets. It is well appreciated that international stock markets are intimately linked – but when fear and uncertainty spread internationally, particularly pernicious contagion effects set in which generate global-level spillover effects (see Cheung et al. 2010). These effects can only exist in the context of a highly integrated global financial system. The particular enthusiasm for liberalized capital flows has exacerbated such trends. As Jeong and Kim (2010: 4–5) point out, as financial firms in the US began to deleverage and credit conditions deteriorated, the subsequent "flight to quality" led investors to seek financial assets in the rich developed world. The magnitude of this global "swing effect" was colossal: in 2009 net private capital inflow to developing countries of $600 billion quickly turned to an outflow of $180 billion, representing a global swing of $780 billion.

The financial crisis had differential effects on different regions of the world. Global growth suffered severely, but some regions suffered more than others. In particular, developed and EU economies experienced the sharpest declines in growth, with the most dramatic declines occurring in Central and Eastern Europe. Many Asian economies were less affected by the early stages of the financial crisis but subsequent knock-on effects of the recession in the Western economies translated into sharp declines in growth (see Das 2012). Table 3.7 illustrates annual growth rates for selected regions and country groupings.

As these figures illustrate on a regional scale, the adverse effects of the global financial crisis have been redistributive, whereby the least culpable countries and regions often suffer considerably. The financial crisis was initially greeted with expansionary monetary policies designed to prevent the economy from sharply contracting, although, it must be noted, the vast majority of new spending went directly to the banking sector (see ILO and World Bank 2012), leading some to deploy the term "Wall Street Keynesianism" (ILO 2012: xviii). After these initial expansionary fiscal policies, which sought to shore up confidence in global capital markets, many countries engaged in fiscal austerity (see ILO 2012: 10–12). Such austerity has weakened global demand (ILO 2012: 17–18), putting further downward pressure on the global economic recovery. Just as importantly, it has affected many vulnerable populations – which disproportionately depend more on public services than those already well off.

Table 3.7 Annual real GDP growth rates, by region and country groups, 2007–2016 (projected)

	2007	2008	2009	2010	2011	2012	2013	2014	2015	2016
World	5.4	2.8	−0.7	5.1	4.0	4.5	4.4	4.6	4.8	4.9
Developed and EU	2.7	0.1	−3.9	2.6	1.4	1.1	2.0	2.4	2.5	2.5
Central and Southeastern Europe (non-EU) and CIS	7.8	4.3	−5.9	5.3	4.9	3.7	4.0	4.1	4.0	4.0
East Asia	12.1	7.8	7.1	9.8	8.7	7.7	8.8	8.4	8.6	8.8
Southeast Asia and Pacific	6.7	4.5	1.6	7.6	5.1	5.2	5.8	6.0	6.0	6.0
South Asia	9.4	5.9	6.2	9.2	7.0	6.6	7.6	7.9	7.7	7.9
Latin America and Caribbean	5.8	4.3	−1.7	6.1	4.4	3.7	4.0	4.0	4.0	4.2
Middle East	7.1	4.4	2.2	4.4	5.0	3.7	4.1	4.4	4.5	4.5
North Africa	5.8	5.1	3.5	4.4	2.1	3.1	4.3	5.0	6.0	6.3
Sub-Saharan Africa	7.1	5.6	2.8	5.4	5.1	5.6	5.5	5.4	5.2	5.3

Source: ILO and World Bank 2012: 2 (table 1). Data from ILO calculations 2012 based on ILO 2011; IMF 2011b. Figures for 2011–16 are econometric projections based on available data.

Changes in the trajectory of average economic growth is only one dimension of the fallout of the global financial crisis: global growth in real average wages was reduced by half in 2008 and 2009 compared to earlier years. Global unemployment increased significantly, with 29 million more people unemployed in 2009 than in the previous two years.[14] While most unemployment has occurred in the developed countries, the impact of the crisis in low and middle-income countries has been marked by a shift toward more insecure forms of employment (ILO 2010: xv). Indeed, it has been estimated that by 2015, 20 million more people in sub-Saharan Africa, and 53 million more people globally, will be in extreme poverty (World Bank 2010c). In addition, 1.2 million more children under the age of five are expected to die between 2009 and 2015 as an indirect result of the crisis, and 35,000 more students will not complete primary education by 2015 (World Bank 2010b; see also Panitchpakdi 2008).

As these developments illustrate, the global financial crisis has had negative consequences that extend far beyond financial markets themselves. In many ways this reflects the increased centrality of global financial markets and the self-reinforcing interdependence dynamics described in the first part of this chapter.

Despite the profound damage caused by the crisis, we argue that the macro-response to the crisis should be regarded as a partial institutional success.[15] As we explain blow, loose networks like the G20 managed to facilitate some degree of coordination between monetary and fiscal policymakers in the key economies. Finance ministers met on several occasions to discuss the timing and magnitude of fiscal stimuli, and central banks worked together to provide financing after the commercial markets ground to a halt. Competitive currency devaluations were largely avoided. The strength of the trade regime also provided a bulwark against beggar-thy-neighbor policies, largely dissuading countries from raising tariffs as they had done, for example following the 1929 crash (see Drezner 2012 for an optimistic view). There were, of course, some exceptions; in October 2008, the EU reintroduced tariffs on cereal that had been eliminated in January of that year. These and other forms of “murky protectionism” (Berensmann and Brandi 2011: 3) are more difficult for the WTO to dissuade than more blatant forms of non-compliance.

Still, as figure 3.10 points out, global GDP and trade have both rebounded to a certain extent since the crisis – thanks in particular to growth in East Asia. Standing on the brink of an imminent global economic collapse, states were able to pull themselves back from disaster even through weak and ad hoc institutions like the G20. These actions were temporary (aside from the WTO commitments), but they prevented the crisis from becoming even worse. As even the harshest critics will acknowledge (e.g. see Wade 2009: 547; Pinto et al. 2011), existing governance during the crisis was much more of a success than the World Economic Conference of 1993 in the midst of the Great depression, which achieved nothing.

And yet, this every success highlights the "second-order" nature of global economic governance challenges today. The problem of fragmentation is evident when one attempts to map what the institutions of global financial governance are and what regulatory domains they cover. Put simply, the emerging system of global financial governance over the last 20 years has been, for most intents and purposes, weak and highly fractured. The institutions that govern banking are very separate institutions from those that govern accounting, which are different from those that govern deposit insurance, which are different still from those that govern securities markets. Just as importantly, central coordination and steering mechanisms have been lacking, as cooperation in finance has been highly informal (see Germain 2004; Davies and Green 2008). Some institutions mentioned in the first part above, such as the BIS and the Financial Stability Forum, have existed to a certain extent as overarching institutions which seek to monitor and conduct research on global financial risks and disseminate ideas. However, their ability to guide the existing constellations of institutions has been weak at best. For example, one of the most significant efforts to institutionalize cooperation across sectors of finance has been through the Joint Forum, which has brought together regulators in the insurance, securities, and banking industries across countries to coordinate a common approach to the risks posed by large financial conglomerates. But the output of the Joint Forum has been limited generally to making recommendations to other transnational financial institutions, which themselves can only integrate this into their own particular rules and standards (see Young 2011b).

All the hallmarks of institutional fragmentation were on display in the response to the financial crisis: there was a wide but often inefficient division of labor, in a diversity of institutions which allowed existing institutions such as the G20 to direct their attention in different areas when this was expedient. Moreover, the fact that responsibility was diffuse (among a variety of different institutions) rather than specific (centralized in one or at least a few critical institutions) meant that political focus and will were diffused. This let financial governance institutions off the hook and weakened the potential to improve them.

A clear manifestation of fragmentation was the ad hoc way in which the attempt to manage the crisis actually took place. When the crisis was still considered relatively localized to the financial markets of the United States and the United Kingdom in 2007 and early 2008, there was ad hoc coordination among central banks of the rich developed countries, through a group called the Committee on the Global Financial System, in an attempt to contain what was seen as a potential liquidity crisis from looming further (see CGFS 2008: 6–8). This did little to prevent what would occur only months later in September 2008, when all hell broke loose with the US Federal Reserve's decision not to bail out the huge investment bank Lehman Brothers. In the midst of what became a virtual global panic, two things happened. Through their transnational networks of communication, central bankers and financial regulators communicated with each other. Monetary policy adjustment to the crisis was facilitated by such networks, as were attempts to extend deposit insurance schemes, for example. The crisis also featured national governments making use of international coordination structures that had been built up successfully in previous decades through the network-type governance that the existing system described in the first part of this chapter helped to generate. For example, immediately after the crash of Lehman Brothers, on October 8, 2008, the central banks of Canada, UK, US, Sweden, and Switzerland, together with the European Central Bank, jointly announced interest rate adjustments to compensate for the liquidity shock then occurring in financial markets. This was followed by interest rate cuts in Asia, in particular in China, and in Australia, and represented a relatively well-coordinated policy response that probably weakened the severity of the recession in important ways. Following the crisis all of the transnational financial governance institutions discussed in the first part of the chapter began working on new standards – some of which (such as in the area of financial accounting) had to be addressed at once. At the same time, however, the lack of any proper multilateral forum to address the big global governance questions of the day meant that a new institution, barely known and barely relevant before this moment, emerged to set the agenda: the Group of 20.

The G20 was actually a relatively ad hoc construction in the first place, developed in the aftermath of the East Asian financial crisis of 1997–8 (see Germain 2001). As its name suggests, the G20 represents a larger share of countries than the G8, as it includes not only these powers but also developing and emerging countries such as Brazil, China, India, and Mexico. The problem with the G20 taking the steering role for global financial governance was that it lacked the kind of administrative structure needed to execute and enforce its marching orders.[16] Rather than being an enforcement power or a functional bureaucracy, most of its institutional design was established to facilitate high-profile communiques among politicians directed at the public and financial markets. The broad calls for reform that the G20 produced from September 2008 until October 2010 were taken up by the existing international standard setting bodies, and not coordinated by a centralized institution with a substantive administrative bureaucracy with which to carry them out. Initial signs of ambition dropped off relatively quickly as public attention to reform waned (see Helleiner and Pagliari 2009b; Griesgraber 2009). Thus financial regulatory reform, even across the G20, has been highly variegated, with some countries instituting strong reforms, others none at all (see Young and Park 2013). While unified approaches to the reform of banking regulation, for example, have been thought about at the global level, different national governments (and the EU) have begun to cherry-pick which of these standards they will implement and which not – undermining the idea of a global minimum floor of regulation in the first place.

Despite the weakness of the G20 as a governance body, its rise can be explained by a number of factors related to the historical conjuncture of the global financial crisis. First, the G20 played a very minor governance role before the global financial crisis, and this allowed it to emerge in the context of the crisis as a high-profile institution without being seen as already illegitimate, as might have been the case with more technocratic transnational institutions or the IMF. Second, the relatively greater balance of developing countries in the G20 gave the institution more buy-in from key emerging economies. As Li and Chen have documented (2010: 19–23), China has seen the G20 as a much more balanced and fruitful organ of multilateral governance than many other bodies, because it has a more representative fit between emerging and developed economies. Third, countries such as the United States and the United Kingdom have preferred the G20 as a high-level coordinating mechanism because of what it potentially replaces. As Wade (2012) has argued, the crisis saw considerable efforts within the UN General Assembly to offer high-level coordination, analysis, and recommendations on global financial reform, yet high-level diplomatic efforts by the United States and the United Kingdom have often sought to undercut these efforts.

In sum, the management of the financial crisis – though a success compared to previous global financial disasters – was hampered by gridlock as well. The globalization of financial markets, facilitated by existing global cooperation, has integrated the global economy in unprecedented ways. Yet the rules and institutions that monitor and regulate financial market activity have not kept pace. This problem of "catch-up" has long been recognized by scholars of international political economy, but it has been brought into even sharper relief by the global financial crisis (Strange 1988; Cerny 1994). Obviously a more centralized institutional architecture is not, on its own, sufficient to mitigate financial risk. After all, even strong national regulators like those that existed in the US and the UK were unable to foresee or prevent the crisis, even though they possessed significant capacity to do so. But this was to a large extent a problem of making bad policy choices, not a problem of institutional design. Other national regulators, like in Canada, imposed more conservative financial regulations and therefore saved their countries from the most direct effects of the crisis. Nonetheless, it is important to note that, in a globalized world, prudent national policies are only partial safeguards against financial risk. Despite Canada's sound banking practices, the US recession had profound effects on its northern neighbor.

Global Financial Governance Reform

If the global financial crisis represents a partial success in global economic governance, then the efforts to reform this system since the crisis speak even louder to the contemporary dynamics of gridlock. This is not to say that some of the reforms that have taken place have not been significant. The IMF received a trebling of resources, as well as a general increase in Special Drawing Rights (Woods 2010), although its capacity for either generating or enforcing global standards has not changed, and nor have its central features as a crisis fire-fighter and a lender of last resort (rather than, for example, becoming more of a global manager). The G20 also demanded that existing transnational financial standard setting bodies review their memberships. This change was long overdue, and had led to massive asymmetries in country representation (Held and Young 2011; Carvalho and Kregel 2007). In the months that followed, institutions such as the Basel Committee, the International Organization of Securities Commissions (IOSCO), and several other groups significantly reformed their transnational memberships, with many including developing country representatives for the first time.

Despite these significant reforms to country membership, there was no real creation of new institutional capacities. The Financial Stability *Forum* was renamed the Financial Stability *Board* (FSB), and the new institution also expanded its institutional capacities modestly through a small secretariat, a full-time secretary general, a steering committee, and three standing committees (Germain 2011). This more permanent administrative structure means that the FSB is more robust than its predecessor, but the extent of its powers is still quite limited, as it is left to engage in monitoring activities and to make broad recommendations (Helleiner 2010: 284). There are significant doubts about how robust the FSB can be in coordinating global financial governance over the longer term (see Moschella 2012).

These changes are not trivial. But they are marginal in comparison to the colossal problems that have become increasingly evident since the crisis. Because the existing systems of financial standards and codes have effectively constituted "soft law" arrangements (Abbott and Snidal 2000), financial governance has relied on the collaboration of national governments to implement them, and on financial markets to use these standards and codes as signals of credibility and soundness.[17] This lack of supranational enforcement power certainly results from the refusal to cede regulatory authority to a supranational agency (Kahler and Lake 2008). However, another part of the problem likely stems from fragmentation within the existing system of global financial governance. Incremental policy responses to governance weaknesses are channeled through existing institutions, rather than through the generation of new ones that limit the governance weaknesses in the first place or address its underlying causes.

For all the institutional innovation present within the system of global financial governance, the fragmentation problem has nevertheless persisted. New transnational institutions have emerged to tackle particular problems, such as the Over the Counter Derivatives Regulators' Forum, but their roles vis-à-vis other governance bodies are not formally institutionalized. Fragmentation also interacts with the dynamic of emerging multipolarity in a way which compounds existing governance challenges. On many issues of financial regulation, such as bank capital adequacy standards and accounting standards, there is a great divide between developed and developing countries. Not only do different stages of development mean different national regulatory capacities and cultures, but years of marginalization and/or exclusion from the international financial governance bodies have left developing countries ill-equipped to integrate their activities into those of global financial regulatory forums. Following the financial crisis, for example, China has increasingly posed countervailing positions to those of Anglo-American countries, whose legitimacy has been put into question (see Sohn 2013).

Another example of the fragmentation problem at work has been the way in which global financial governance and global trade governance have related to one another. Reflecting the extensity and intensity of global economic interdependence, a great deal of the decline in global trade volume was due to financing problems: when the global financial system seized up, so did global trade financing. Yet instead of helping this situation, the response of some global governance institutions was to (unintentionally) make it worse. In an effort to shore up regulatory standards at banks, the Basel Committee put strong restrictions on the ability of banks to support flows of credit for trade financing purposes. This problem was recognized: not by the financial regulators sitting on the Basel Committee, but by other groups far away in their own institutional silos. It took an extensive lobbying campaign by the International Chamber of Commerce, aided by the World Bank and the WTO, to secure a change in new global financial regulations to address this problem; and it was not until 2011 that the new global banking rules were altered. While it is certainly a good thing that they were changed, this example helps to highlight the costs of fragmentation in global economic governance.

A further example of fragmentation in the governance of finance has to do with the recent reform efforts associated with the regulation of derivatives – complex financial instruments based on the price of other assets. New multilateral institutions such as the FSB have sought to steward a unified reform process across the world, yet have been extremely constrained in terms of their lack of regulatory authority. Countries which dominate the derivatives markets, such as the United States and Britain, have had their own regulatory reforms, which differ to significant degrees. The regional reform efforts under way at the European Union are strikingly different from the efforts in the United States. There is of course nothing wrong with countries or regions deciding their own reform paths that might be appropriate. However, regulatory reform would likely be better served if global stewardship of the standards of reform was itself actually unified. Unfortunately, the institutional fragmentation at the subglobal level has simply replicated itself at the global level. Derivatives are used by a wide variety of public and private institutions, and the international standards for their use have been developed by different global governance institutions, and at different times. The rules for banks' exposures to derivatives clearing institutions have been organized by the Basel Committee, yet the standards for oversight of financial market infrastructures have been organized by the Committee on Payment and Settlement Systems (CPSS) and IOSCO. Furthermore, in keeping with the historical tradition outlined in the first part of this chapter, the Over the Counter Derivatives Regulators' Forum has also arisen in this context. While each of these institutions may play valuable roles in their own right, it is not at all clear how they formally relate to one another – a daunting prospect for the future as financial markets continue to evolve.

The postcrisis world of financial regulation has actually seen dynamics of multipolarity and fragmentation interact in particularly negative ways. Emerging powers act as stewards of regional reform efforts and weaken demand for more comprehensive institutional reform at the multilateral level. A glaring example of this can be seen in the reform efforts directed at East Asian financial integration since the global financial crisis. Financial regulators, central bankers, and finance ministries in East Asia have strengthened their own regional networks and formal agreements in the region since the crisis. In 2008, Finance Ministries in the ASEAN+3 countries, through the Asian Bond Markets Initiative, have generated a roadmap which creates taskforces for the promotion of local financial markets and all-around regulatory improvements. In 2009, governments in the region established the Credit Guarantee and Investment Mechanism to support the issuance of corporate bonds denominated in local currency to further develop Asian bond markets with the aim of protecting the region from various vulnerabilities, such as its dependence on the banking sector (Sohn 2012: 5; Nanto 2009: 65). There have also been proposals for an Asian Financial Stability Dialogue, envisaged for the moment to be a complement, not a competitor to the "global" FSB (though this has yet to be realized). The most substantial in East Asian financial regionalism has been the recent transformation of the Chiang Mai Initiative into a well-financed regional framework. The Chiang Mai Initiative was a set of proposals which, under the leadership of Japan following the East Asian financial crisis of 1997–8, sought initially to form a "regional" alternative to the IMF. Shut down at the time (in no small part due to the activism of the US Treasury), the Chiang Mai Initiative survived as an informal system of currency swap arrangements, whereby countries provide mutual assistance to each other in times of financial liquidity stress. Since the recent global financial crisis, efforts have advanced considerably. The Chiang Mai Initiative Multilateralization (CMIM) now is formalized, with agreements on financial surveillance, reserve eligibility, and a budget recently increased from $80 billion to $120 billion.[18] China and Japan are the largest contributors, but voting rules (a two-thirds majority required for key decisions) have been set high enough that neither of these countries can block decisions on its own.

Despite these new institutional developments, the legacy of institutional inertias from multilateral institutions persists. After the global financial crisis hit Korea in 2008 and the country experienced an attack on its currency, the government refused to use the IMF for help, because of its poor institutional legacy in the country after its controversial restructuring of the Korean economy after the financial crisis of 1997–8. Yet the Korean government also refused to utilize even the new Chiang Mai Initiative swap line, because doing so requires that CMI member countries drawing more than 20 percent of their respective swap lines engage in an agreement with the IMF (see Sohn 2012: 5). Instead the Korean central bank signed a $30 billion swap arrangement with the US Federal Reserve Board, and simply expanded its bilateral swap arrangements with Japan and China (see Jeong and Kim 2010: 5–7).

As Sohn points out (2012: 17), the accelerated development of an East Asian regional financial architecture has potential implications for the future of global financial governance. Most significantly, it may contribute to the decentralizing tendency.[19] Such fragmentation may simply result in "cooperative decentralization" (Helleiner and Pagliari 2011: 192), whereby governance diversity allows institutional learning and governance forums to better reflect local circumstances, rather than a "one size fits all" approach (see Rodrik 2007). From this perspective, fragmentation leads to coexistence and competition among multiple regimes, and should even be encouraged (see Sohn 2012: 18). While this is a possibility, there is no reason why fragmentation in global financial governance will take this "liberal positive-sum" form, rather than the form of perversely competing financial regions.

Many have pointed to the lackluster extent of financial regulatory reform since the crisis (e.g. see Nesvetailova and Palan 2009; Wade 2009; Crotty 2009; Moschella and Tsingou, forthcoming), often citing the effects of institutional inertia on existing global economic governance arrangements. They are right to do so. However increasing multipolarity also plays an important role in generating gridlock as well. The financial crisis emboldened those that had already sought to differentiate themselves in terms of their developmental and regulatory approaches, such as China (see Breslin 2012, Young 2011a). Because of the membership reform that has taken place in many financial standard setting bodies (described above) and the increased importance of the G20, coherent and bold policy proposals have been more difficult than in the past, when much more homogeneous groupings like the G8 sought to steer the global economy (see Breslin 2012; Wade 2011). This is likely to get more intense as multipolarity increases. Confidence in existing multilateral governance institutions, such as the World Bank and the IMF, may wane in this context, since these institutions still have highly unrepresentative membership structures, even after some minor governance reforms following the crisis.[20]

Conceptual shifts and harder problems in financial governance

One of the consequences of the recent financial crisis has been the fact that a new host of harder problems have come into sharp relief reflecting second-order problems characteristic of gridlock. In particular, the challenge associated with regulating financial markets and institutions has been revealed to be more difficult than before, as manifested in what might be called the "macroprudential challenge," described below. In the section following, we highlight an even more dramatic harder problem, the issue of global imbalances.

One significant harder problem which has developed in global financial governance involves dealing with an important conceptual innovation that has emerged since the crisis. There has been an increased recognition that financial crisis and financial regulation should be understood through the prism of "macroprudentialism" (see Baker 2013). What this means is that rather than seeking to regulate the activities of a single financial institution, the best way to regulate finance is to understand the banking system as a coherent, changing whole. These notions started to take hold within technocratic circles and represent a recognition of systemic risk in financial markets (see Cooper 2011: 371–2).

The rise of macroprudentialism represents the recognition of a harder problem in that it is technically more difficult and requires much more coordination than before among different areas of finance and different national jurisdictions. Regulating a single bank is challenging enough, in particular when the bank is large and engages in complex transactions in many different countries. But regulating the banking system as a whole is even more challenging, because it means taking stock of banks' interrelationships with the economy as a whole and seeing the "emergent-level" processes at work in the complex adaptive system that is the financial order (see Haldane and May 2011; Baker 2013). The underlying basis of such thinking is not based on traditional ways of conceiving the economy, but rather is rooted in complex systems theory (Cooper 2011). The new "macroprudential challenge" befalling financial regulators cannot be tackled exclusively at the national level, because of the extreme interconnectivity of financial activity worldwide. Thus the concept naturally puts stress on the global dimension. One step that has been taken related to these conceptual developments has been the introduction of special new capital requirements for "Systemically Important Financial Institutions" (SIFIs) – essentially the largest and most interconnected financial institutions. This represents an important step. Yet tackling financial regulation in a macroprudential way on an ongoing basis will require a high degree of global-level monitoring, regulation, and enforcement that is very challenging under a highly fragmented global financial governance system which features only very weak enforcement capacity.

The problem of global imbalances

A second "harder problem" is the problematic nature of global imbalances in world savings and demand. Global imbalances refer to the disjointed pattern of current account deficits and surpluses which have built up in the global economy in the last decade and a half. It reflects a disjuncture between the high consumption and demand of countries like the US and the low level of consumption in East Asia, as depicted in figure 3.11. As one commentator put it, "China exports and saves, Europe consumes and the United States prints money and consumes."[21] Such a systemic, global-level problem has been widely recognized as "one of the main challenges facing the global economy and world community" (Trichet, quoted in Reuters 2011; see also Blanchard and Milesi-Ferretti 2009). It is almost universally recognized that the solution to this problem must be multilateral in nature. Yet very little has happened in terms of dealing with global imbalances. Attempts have been made to address the problem through the IMF (see IMF 2005 for an early explication of the problem). In 2006 and 2007, major governments agreed to implement wide-ranging policies to redistribute the pattern of global demand to moderate these risks (IMF 2007). But as the IMF itself has reported, many observers took a relatively sanguine view of the problem of structural imbalances, arguing that as long as the structural conditions of the global economy did not change too quickly, structural imbalances were sustainable (IMF 2009a: 34). The events of the financial crisis shattered this view.

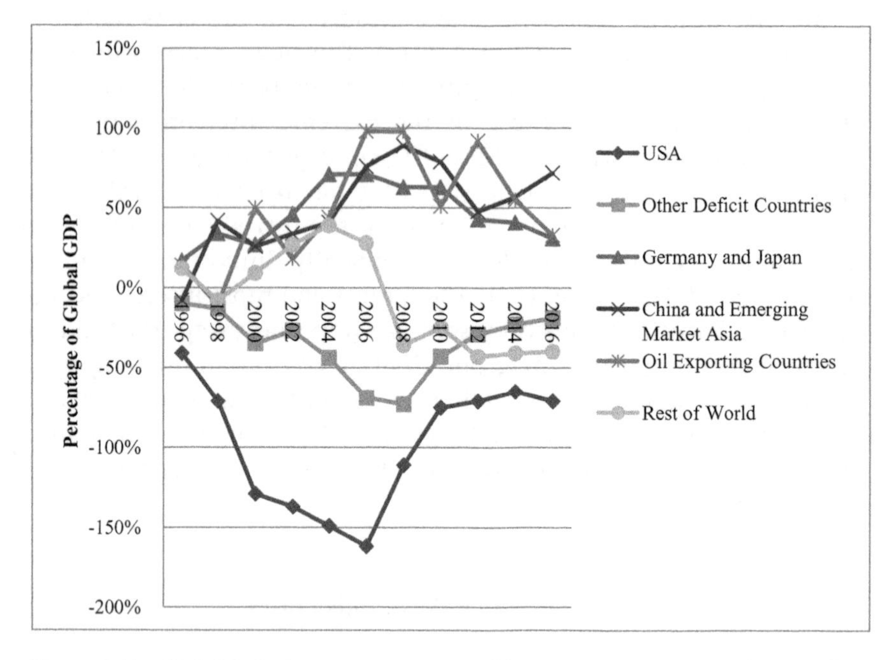

Figure 3.11 Global imbalances, as represented by current account surpluses and deficits, 1996–2012, with projections to 2016

Source: IMF 2012, using the source data from chart 1.11.

Since the financial crisis, structural imbalances have been at the forefront of policy debates, with many arguing that these imbalances contributed in a significant way to the financial crisis itself, as deficit countries were able to fuel their credit booms thanks to high-saving surplus flows from East Asia (see Lin et al. 2010; Borio and Disyatat 2011; Yeah 2010). As the global economic recovery has proceeded since 2010, the extent of global imbalances has become less severe than before the crisis, thanks to slower global economic growth and weakened credit conditions in the United States and Europe. Yet as Eichengreen (2006) stated years before the crisis, "the longer the current global imbalances persist, the less agreement there is about how they ultimately will be resolved." One hope was that the increased salience of the problem since the crisis would have led to a successful resolution. As Stiglitz put it, this "is a multilateral problem within a system in disequilibrium."[22] However, multilateral solutions have been wanting, to say the least.

The existing architecture of global financial governance offers only partial help. Transnational financial governance institutions such as the BIS and the FSB increasingly generate knowledge about how perverse the problem is, but there is a distinct lack of capacity to deal with the problem itself (see BIS 2011). A variety of policy-makers from the IMF, the BIS, the FSB and leading states have all concluded that the global imbalances situation is extremely serious, and that "left unresolved, these problems could even sow the seeds of the next crisis." (Strauss-Kahn, quoted in *IFC Review* 2011).

The cornerstone of what has been achieved is known as the "mutual assessment process" (MAP), which the G20 agreed to at the 2009 summit in Pittsburgh. The MAP is a process in which public debt, fiscal deficits and private debt are monitored through a series of warning indicators (see IMF 2011a).[23] Through multilateral guidance, each country is supposed to monitor each other's progress and to eventually find agreement on new rules that will allow deficit and surplus countries to share the burden of adjustment required in addressing global imbalances. The G20 initially tasked the IMF with initial technical analysis and indicator development. This in itself was not challenging. Getting the finance ministries to agree on what these indicators should be, on the other hand, was.

In 2011, the G20 finance ministers agreed on a set of indicators that would be used to detect "possibly destabilizing" global imbalances. Both the G20 and the IMF painted a rosy picture of the negotiated agreement but in reality there was considerable consternation from one G20 member, China. The Chinese finance ministry objected to both the use of current account imbalances and exchange rate indicators in the new global set of indicators for assessing global imbalances (Atkins and Peel 2011). It took the diplomacy of German negotiators – a country, like China, with large current account surpluses – to get China to agree on a final package, which carefully avoided the language of specific exchange rate indicators. Since then, addressing the global imbalances problem has been confined largely to working on solutions for how to successfully "grow out" of the problem. Accordingly, the G20 set up a Working Group on Sustainable and Balanced Growth, cochaired by Canada and India. As Chinn (2011) points out, for most developing countries the central imbalance in the global economy reflects a *developmental* imbalance – the gap between the rich North and the poor South. Yet, perversely, while the G20 does concern itself with development issues, these discussions are hived off into a separate working group (the G20 "Development Working Group"). This and the fact that these efforts are not directly channeled through the IMF and the World Bank are examples of fragmentation.

The global imbalances problem is a second-order cooperation problem. It arises from previous international cooperation, and is characterized by increasing multipolarity, harder problems and institutional inertia. Because the problem configures itself as an East–West (read: China–US) issue, it allows national policy-makers who might otherwise have an interest in collective action the opportunity to engage in geopolitical blame-shifting. Waning US geopolitical power is coming head to head with the rising importance of China on the world stage, creating diplomatic frictions that leave the problem further from being addressed than is actually warranted. Many place a great deal of responsibility on the US, in particular for its insatiable capacity to generate debt and the Dollar-Wall-Street regime which sustains it. Yet others (including many within the US) have been keen to point the blame at China, specifically at the undervaluation of its currency. Chinese policy-makers disagree; arguing that the problem is more one of the global economic structure.[24] Yet focusing attention on China and demanding an appreciation of the yuan will not correct US–Chinese trade imbalances as the real problem is a global one (see D. Hale and Hale 2008). Dealing with structural imbalances cannot be tackled in a piecemeal fashion, as the scale is both large and the problem fundamentally global in scope: indeed, there is a surprising consensus that global imbalances cannot be addressed by short-run measures, and that they require long-term structural reform (Lin et al. 2010).

Even before the rise in importance of the G20, structural imbalances were a difficult issue to deal with. As Walter (forthcoming) points out, multilateralism in the form of the G7 and the IMF alone was largely unable to deal with the problem even before China's resurgence in the global economy. The most significant attempt by far was in 1985, in the form of the "Plaza Accord" – so named after the meeting place of the G5 Ministers of Finance and central bank governors, the Plaza Hotel in New York City. The group mutually agreed to intervene in foreign exchange markets to appreciate the US dollar relative to other countries, in particular Japan. Despite the significant adjustment costs and challenges with coordination, a rapidly rising Japan at the time was nevertheless willing to appreciate its currency rapidly against the US dollar.

Though the fix was only temporary and partial at the time, this historical precedent has led some to suggest that what the world needs now is simply a "Plaza Accord II." Yet conditions in the contemporary global economy are very different. In 1985 the position of the United States was much more dominant than it is presently. The extent of global imbalances themselves, even when ranked as a percentage of world GDP, was also smaller then than now. More importantly, the recent global imbalances reflect a deeper, more complex set of political-economic conditions within the countries at the core of the problem, such as both China's and America's debt and consumption relationships. Addressing global imbalances necessitates, more than ever, dealing with the constitution of domestic economic conditions. As Lin et al. (2010) argue, China's domestic income inequality causes domestic consumption to remain a very small share of the country's GDP, leaving a giant glut of domestic savings (much of it corporate savings). US current account deficits, on the other hand, can be attributable to its own domestic political economy: housing and financial sector bubbles have contributed to a build-up of debt (see Montgomerie 2009; Schwartz 2009). The level of global economic integration achieved through earlier institutional successes has allowed Chinese savings to be "matched" with the US demand for more and more debt. Such a situation simply would not be possible without the vast institutional infrastructure underlying the contemporary global economic system. Yet spending, taxation, and consumption issues in China and the United States are very politically sensitive issues within national political processes; and negotiating such issues at the multilateral level is yet more difficult (see Walter, forthcoming; Huang 2010). Accordingly, the problem of structural imbalances is not simply a matter of international coordination; like the harder problems discussed in the previous chapter, it is a fundamentally "intermestic" issue.

This "harder problem" aspect of the global imbalances issue is yet further compounded by a pernicious institutional inertia mechanism at work. There is a near universal consensus that global imbalances require the intervention of multilateral institutions. Yet the very institution with the present capability to facilitate this process, the IMF, is not regarded as impartial or legitimate enough to carry out such multilateral coordination. Because of its legacy in many parts of the world, the IMF is not seen as sufficiently responsive to the concerns of emerging countries, weakening its potential role. This and the fact of continued volatility within a global financial system which is still dominated by Western financial institutions has led central banks in East Asia, in particular, to accumulate foreign exchange reserves, a trend which began to accelerate after the 1997–8 East Asian financial crisis. The trend is seen by some to be a perverse one, as it represents wealth that is not productively invested (see Rodrik 2006b). Figure 3.12 reflects the important trend of international reserve holdings in today's global economy. As this figure demonstrates, developing countries' share of international reserves has increased dramatically in the last decade. The vast majority of this historic rise in international

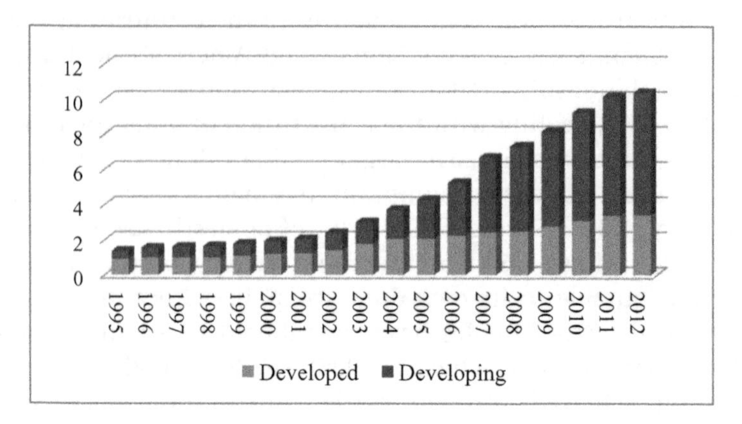

Figure 3.12 International reserve holdings, 1995–2012 (US$ trillions)

Source: IMF Currency Composition of Official Foreign Exchange Reserves (COFER) database, updated June 29, 2012; figures converted from millions to trillions of US$. Several countries joined the sample in 1996 and 1997, but this does not likely affect the early time series here. Figure for 2012 reflects the first quarter of the year only.

reserves is due to China. Having said this, the relationship is a symmetrical one, in the sense that it reflects the continued importance of the US dollar: the majority of these reserves, both in China and elsewhere, are denominated in US dollars. This allows the US to continue its privileged position in the global financial system, and allows further debt-based consumption in the US (see Wade 2003b). This situation is self-reinforcing, since a significant amount of the global imbalances are driven by the accumulation of foreign exchange reserves (IMF 2012; Gagnon 2012).

Conclusion: A Reembedded Global Market?

The above discussion shows how far we have come from the vision of embedded liberalism that underpinned the agreement at Bretton Woods. The postwar economic order led to extraordinary globalization, but it quickly lost sight of the original goal of ensuring that global market forces served, and did not impede, social welfare. Indeed, the economic changes the postwar order enabled eventually outstripped the capacity of global institutions to "embed" them, following a process of self-reinforcing interdependence.[25] Financial and trade flows have knit the world ever more tightly together. But they have also increased multipolarity, generated new and harder problems, rendered existing institutional structures dysfunctional, and led to a proliferation of fragmented responses. It is now more difficult for countries to collectively manage our global economy, and thus to ensure the kind of broad, sustainable growth seen in the postwar years. This has raised the question of whether the system of global economic governance can evolve to generate a new "Great Transformation" (Polanyi 1944; Ruggie 1982), one in which regulatory authority in some form can reembed the global economy in meaningful social values while still realizing the value of global markets (see Cerny 1994).

Again, the question only arises following previous successes. Though the system has been partially "disembedded" since the 1970s, it has nonetheless produced enormous gains in human welfare. In 1981, 52 percent of the world lived in extreme poverty (on less than US$1.25 per day), and over 75 percent fell below the $2 line. Today those numbers are 22 percent and 43 percent, respectively, even though the world population has grown by a third (World Bank 2012). But the bar has also been raised. On the most direct level, global poverty interacts with transnational problems ranging from disease, to conflict, to migration. As interdependence grows, extreme poverty around the world becomes increasingly dangerous to all of us. There is also, we would argue, growing "moral interdependence," or deepening concern for the welfare of distant people (see chapter 2). Our expectations for human betterment are, rightly so, commensurate with our material capabilities. Today 1.3 billion people live in extreme poverty, and 2.5 billion make do on less than US$2 per day (World Bank 2012). It in no way diminishes the gains to recognize the ongoing moral catastrophe of global poverty.

Moreover, in many cases recent growth has not been equitable (Stiglitz 2012). While countries have converged in GDP per capita – that is, rich countries are not, on average, as far ahead of poor countries as they used to be – inequality has grown within some of the fastest growing countries like India and, especially, China, whose Gini coefficient (a measure of inequality) has increased 50 percent since 1981.[26] The gap between rich and poor has also grown in some of the world's wealthiest countries (OECD 2011), and especially the United States, where the top 1 percent of households increased their real, after-tax income by 278 percent from 1979 to 2007, compared to just 40 percent for the middle 60 percent of households. As Krueger (2012) put it, "these are mind-boggling figures . . . Put another way, the increase in the share of income going to the top 1 percent over this period exceeds the total amount of income that the entire bottom 40 percent of households receives." The US figures are the most striking, but they reflect trends that reach across countries, as a greater share of economic wealth accrues to owners of capital relative to labor (Ellis and Smith 2007). Inequality is on the rise in many ways, and while its pernicious social effects are many, extreme inequality, as Stiglitz (2012) notes, also undermines the growth that gave rise to it by leading to systematic underinvestment in human capital and public services (see also Wilkinson and Pickett 2010). The recent global financial crisis and its aftermath continue to show in dramatic terms how systemic vulnerabilities can not only go undetected, but exacerbate human hardship globally.

In many ways, the failures of global governance we attribute to gridlock make it more difficult for countries to sustain global markets, much less embed them within a social compact. Multilateral inability to negotiate a meaningful "development round" in the trade arena has left markets closed to poor countries' agricultural goods. Multilateral inability to limit financial risk means we will likely succumb again to a crisis in which disreputable practices impose massive costs on the real economy. And multilateral inability to manage global monetary imbalances is setting us up for a profound reckoning in the future. Expanding global trade and financial flows have been undergirded by an adaptive global institutional environment which has created a plethora of ad hoc institutional solutions. At the same time, this fragmented environment now impedes further progress in global economic governance. Under gridlock, the notion of a grand compromise between liberal flows of commerce and industry, on the one hand, and social needs, on the other, seems increasingly quixotic. The only political institution that has achieved a meaningful balance between social needs and market efficiency is the welfare state that emerged in the mid 20th century. Obviously no such solution is currently considered feasible at the global scale.

Given this constraint, activists and even the United Nations have tried a different approach, seeking to address the various externalities of the global economy by focusing not on states but on MNCs, of which over 80,000 now exist. In contrast to the 1970s efforts to regulate MNCs, mentioned above, contemporary attempts have not pushed formal intergovernmental regulation. Instead, they have largely turned to a variety of voluntary and market-based institutions. The originator of the phrase "embedded liberalism," John Ruggie, has been at the center of the UN's work in this area. In a highly interdependent world, the embedded liberalism envisioned in Bretton Woods is no longer possible, he argues. That view

> presupposed the existence of *national* economies, engaged in *external* transactions, conducted at *arms length*, which governments could mediate at the *border* by tariffs and exchange rates, among other tools. The globalization of financial markets and production chains, however, challenges each of these premises and threatens to leave behind merely national social bargains. (Ruggie 2003)

Speaking at the World Economic Forum in Davos, in 1999, UN Secretary General Kofi Annan noted this problem and declared that the solution would be "to devise a similar compact on the global scale, to underpin the new global economy. . . . Until we do the global economy will be fragile and vulnerable – vulnerable to backlash from all the 'isms' of our post-Cold War world: protectionism, populism, nationalism, ethnic chauvinism, fanaticism and terrorism" (Annan 1999a).

The solution was the UN Global Compact, a voluntary governance program that seeks to commit MNCs to pro-social policies regarding the environment, human rights, labor, and good governance.[27] The Global Compact was formally launched a year later, and featured the participation of a wide variety of UN agencies, but was not a formal UN program or resolution.[28] The Global Compact is not legally binding; nor is it a means of monitoring company behavior and enforcing compliance (Global Compact 2007). The Global Compact Office within the UN has neither the mandate nor the resources to monitor or measure corporate performance. It is essentially a voluntary initiative that seeks to advance universally accepted principles through engagement with corporations. As Ruggie points out, the Compact's focus is on "norm diffusion and the dissemination of practical know-how and tools" (2007: 820). When a firm joins the Compact, it declares its adherence to a set of human rights, labor, environmental, and anticorruption principles. These principles are themselves drawn from already agreed international declarations within the UN system, such as the UN Declaration of Human Rights, the ILO's Declaration on Fundamental Principles and Rights at Work, the Rio Declaration on Environment and Development, and the UN Convention against Corruption.

The costs of signing on to the Global Compact are thus very low. Moreover, even its strongest proponents attest that the "interests and commitments of participating companies vary considerably" (Ruggie 2004: 516; see also Fritsch 2008: 21–3). Nonetheless, there is some evidence that the Global Compact has an impact on firm behavior. Bernhagen and Mitchell (2010) have shown that firms recognize that their commitments to human rights, environmental and good governance standards have to be credible (see also Grant and Keohane 2005: 38; Potoski and Prakash 2005). Ruggie (2003) has argued that there are a variety of reasons why the Global Compact is the best route to accomplish the task of greater corporate accountability on a global level. On the one hand, the probability of the UN General Assembly adopting a formal code is very small, and the ability to monitor multinational activity in an attempt to impose a code would provoke resistance. But the main benefit of a code of practice for multinational corporations is not simply "do-ability"; it is also hoped that an accumulation of experience will initiate a race-to-the-top dynamic among firms (Ruggie 2001: 373).

There has been some success in firms joining the Global Compact. From 47 corporate members in 2000, the Global Compact had 8,700 by 2009 (Global Compact 2010). The Compact has also become more robust over time, with new initiatives to try to expand its scope. For example, firms have to publicly disclose their adherence to the Compact every year, with failure leading to a public delisting on the Global Compact webpage (Global Compact 2008). More recently, there have been new initiatives to encourage corporate sustainability and leadership. Yet while there is little doubt that the Global Compact is a positive step away from the status quo, it is not difficult to criticize its robustness. It is relatively easy to circumvent the rules without any significant consequences (Deva 2006; Tesner and Kell 2000; Sethi 2003). There is also a potentially significant adverse selection problem at work in joining something like the Global Compact, in that only those firms join who need a better image or reputation (Williams 2004: 762; Hagen 2008). There is a general lack of regulatory and institutional framework for effective screening and monitoring of participants (see Fall and Zahran 2010). Defenders of the Global Compact attest that it is simply meant to be a "yardstick for exchange of ideas, learning and discussion" and thus is not meant to be a benchmark or an enforcement mechanism (Rasche 2009: 523; Global Compact Office 2011). This is a perfectly fair point about the goals of the Compact. However, in relation to the largest corporate accountability initiative in the world, this fact is somewhat emblematic of the wider problems that are faced. The institution which is meant to be the "moral compass of firms" (Kell 2003: 47) can only point out the right direction, but cannot compel firms to act.[29]

The Global Compact is only one example of the hundreds if not thousands of voluntary regulations that have emerged to steer corporate behavior over the last decades (see Hale and Held 2011; Vogel 2008). Some, like the Compact, are merely hortatory. Others seek to use market power to pressure firms to comply with certain social goals, by persuading their customers or investors to demand certain changes before opening their wallets. This market power can be significant. In the United States alone, socially responsible investment funds had US$3 trillion under management in 2010, or one in every eight dollars invested in the country (US SIF 2011). In many cases these types of initiatives have had a powerful impact on firm behavior. Campaigns against companies doing business in South Africa under apartheid, companies using sweatshops to manufacture athletics gear, companies selling rainforest timber, and companies marketing "blood diamonds" all stand out as examples of successful voluntary regulation (see Vogel 2008). For many others, the results are mixed. Nonetheless, almost no major corporations today write annual reports without mentioning their corporate social responsibility (CSR) programs, and for many businesses these activities have led to real changes in how they affect the communities and environments where they operate.

In a related development, some are seeking to go beyond the "do no harm" philosophy of CSR, and build businesses that deliver both financial and social returns on investment (Mulgan et al. 2007). So-called "social enterprises" aim not only to comply with ethical principles, but to build social benefits directly into their business models. Examples run from restaurants that provide employment to disadvantaged youth to designers who work only with reclaimed materials. The number of these companies has grown enormously over the past 10–15 years, though the various definitions of "social enterprise" make it difficult to quantify. To take just one measure, though, in the UK the "SE100" – an index of top social enterprises – grew 79 percent in 2010, compared to the blue-chip FTSE100, which grew just 5 percent (Social Enterprise 2011).

Voluntary codes of conduct, market-based pressures, CSR, and social enterprise are all reshaping the modern corporation. In many cases they have led to tangible improvements for real people and places. Nonetheless, they represent at best only a very partial solution to the problem of reembedding the global economy. Nor are these transnational governance institutions immune from the challenges of gridlock. Consider multipolarity. As economic heft shifts to Asia, corporate codes have confronted less pluralistic and liberal economic systems, which have impeded the uptake of transnational corporate governance programs. China, where many of the most important corporations are state-owned, represents a particularly telling case. In the last few years Chinese companies have significantly increased their participation in the Global Compact. They are also large employers of the various ISO standards, as MNCs often require all elements of their supply chain to receive such certifications. But both of these standards are quite soft. The Global Compact requires only minimal reporting, and the ISO system requires companies to adopt certain management practices, not to actually raise their production standards. Other programs that require more substantial disclosure or behavioral changes from Chinese firms have received much less uptake (Hale and Roger 2011). The more controversial ones are actively discouraged by the government.

There is a broader problem, however. Even if firm-level changes were to become universally adopted, it is difficult to see how they would provide the same level of social security as the modern welfare state. And of course they offer no solution to the macroeconomic and international coordination challenges discussed above. Initiatives like the Global Compact, then, leave us with the same questions with which we began the chapter. We know "good governance" is the key to economic prosperity. But how can we ensure such governance in a world of hundreds of sovereign states when our tools of multilateral cooperation have become gridlocked?

4

Environment

Introduction: A Zanjera *for the Globe?*

The farmers of Ilocos Norte, a province spanning the northwestern tip of the Philippine island of Luzon, had a problem. They relied on the Bacarra-Zantar river to water their crops, but the river was unpredictable. When the Bacarra-Zantar was low and too many farmers diverted its flow to their wilting fields, water would fail to reach the furthest plots. When, in turn, there was too much water, the river would burst dams and canals, each of which required many men to repair. Either drought or flood could ruin a family, and no farmer could mitigate them by himself. In other words, the farmers' environment made them dependent on collective action.

Even at this micro-scale, collective action is hard to organize. Every farmer could ensure a better harvest for himself by sneaking a little extra water during droughts, or by working his plot while the others were digging a canal. But if everyone dodged the group responsibilities, all the farmers would be back at the mercy of the river. The farmers of Ilocos Norte faced a dilemma common to all human societies, "the tragedy of the commons."

This poetic phrase was coined by Garret Hardin in a 1968 *Science* article that extrapolated the kind of situation faced by the farmers of Ilocos Norte to the global scale. We all benefit from natural resources like fisheries, forests, water, and the atmosphere, but following the globalization of industrialization and mass consumerism, we have come up against their limits. Without a collective constraint against overexploitation, we, like the farmers, run the risk of using up common resources, to the detriment of all.

Typically we think of the state as ensuring the common good against selfish interests. After all, only coercive authority can compel individuals to give up that extra water or contribute to building a canal instead of working their own land, or so the thinking went. But at the global level, there is no central rule-maker and enforcer. Is overexploitation therefore inevitable?

The farmers of Ilocos Norte offer a different kind of solution. For much of their history, the Philippine state and its predecessors did not bother themselves with river governance, and public institutions were, at any rate, distant and weak. Instead, the people along the Bacarra-Zantar created a *zanjera*, an association through which the farmers themselves regulated the river by building canals and dams, and regulated the people who used the river by establishing rules about how much water could be used. Individuals who broke faith with their neighbors faced social ostracism, which proved to be a strong enforcement tool. The *zanjera* was a simple form of cooperation, but an effective one. It also showed that "top down" solutions are not always needed.

This insight won the Nobel Prize for the political scientist Elinor Ostrom in 2009. In her central work, *Governing the Commons* (1990), Ostrom held up the *zanjera* of Ilocos Norte as one of several cases of successful "bottom up" solutions to the tragedy of the commons. By explaining how communities managed common resources, Ostrom showed how people could organize themselves even without a central, hierarchical authority. Her work upended the conventional wisdom, particularly prominent in economics, which doubted the possibility of collaborative group action without some form of hierarchy (Olson 1965).

It's an insight we need on a far vaster scale today. Every country, and every person in every country, needs finite resources like water, air, energy, metals, and the products of plants, animals, and other forms of life. But no global government exists to limit their use. Instead, we have 190-odd countries – and 7 billion people across them, perhaps 10 billion by the end of the century – each of whom would like to consume a larger share of the global pie. Worse, in the latter half of the twentieth century the world has experienced a so-called "Great Acceleration" in which our collective consumption of natural resources has increased exponentially, putting multiple and complex strains on the natural world that we only partially understand (Steffen et al. 2004: 1078). Because the expansion and globalization of industrial production over the postwar period has been indirectly facilitated by the peaceful and liberal postwar order, we can think of the Great Acceleration as one of the unanticipated (partial) effects of postwar institution-building.

The stakes are far higher than wilted crops or burst dams. If the people of Ilocos Norte had failed to cooperate, they could have moved elsewhere. In a globalized, industrial world economy of billions, those exit options simply do not exist (barring rapid advances in interstellar travel). Ecologists have dubbed the present age the "Anthropocene," a period when the Earth's ecosystems are defined primarily by the actions of man. This is a powerful and entirely new form of interdependence, the expansion of the "shared community of fate" from the village level to, literally, the world as we know it.

It is therefore a question of *existence*, or at least existence as we know it, whether we can create a kind of global *zanjera* to prevent this unprecedented tragedy of the commons. As we show in the first part of this chapter, since the first waves of industrial globalization the world has attempted to create just such a solution through multilateral institutions. A watershed for modern efforts came in 1972, at the United Nations Conference on the Human Environment, in Stockholm. This event was intended as a "San Francisco" or a "Bretton Woods" moment (see chapters 2 and 3, respectively) for the natural world. But the international institution it gave birth to, the United Nations Environment Programme (UNEP), was given a mandate as broad and ambitious as its authority and resources were limited. Over the following decades, countries have negotiated a dizzying array of treaties and multilateral organizations to manage global environmental issues ranging from air pollution, to biodiversity, to desertification, to ozone, to the climate. Nearly 700 such treaties now exist, and some, like those that seek to control transboundary air pollution or ozone-depleting pollutants, have proven largely successful. These institutions resemble the community-based solutions that Ostrom's work has highlighted in that they facilitate cooperation between self-interested parties without a central authority (see Keohane and Ostrom 1995).

But Ostrom's work focused primarily on small groups and tight communities. The scale of global problems of course introduces complexities far beyond those that faced the farmers of Ilocos Norte. In 1992, some 20 years after the Stockholm summit, an unprecedented gathering of global leaders convened in Rio to "relaunch" global environmental governance. But two decades after this second "foundational moment," the Rio Earth Summit, the general panorama is one of institutional failure and gridlock. When leaders met again at "Rio+20" in 2012 they had essentially given up on negotiating a kind of multilateral *zanjera*, instead emphasizing the diverse – but ultimately fragmented – array of actions being taken by individual countries, cities, regions, NGOs, and private companies.

This failure of multilateralism is documented in the second part of the chapter, which shows how the gridlock mechanisms have frustrated cooperation across several key environmental issues. The growth of the emerging economies has come with a host of local and global externalities, and exacerbated the longstanding tension in environmental cooperation between rich and poor nations. New, harder problems like climate change – which researchers have dubbed a "super wicked" problem – require far deeper policy adjustments than previous issues. Meanwhile, the nature of the existing architecture for global environmental governance has in some ways impeded further cooperation. UNEP has always lacked authority and resources, and without a firm "anchor organization," countries have created a fragmented array of issue-specific agreements and organizations. Moreover, historical distinctions between rich and poor have continued to delineate the fault lines of global debates, even as economic conditions have changed, and the kinds of institutional tools that worked in the past have been blindly applied to problems for which they are ill-suited. In short, efforts to design a *zanjera* for our global commons have become gridlocked.

The consequences of this failure are also increasingly visible, as the people of Ilocos Norte, a region now considered to be at "extreme risk" from climate change, know well. Various indices rank the Philippines as one of the most climate-vulnerable countries in the world. With a coastline as long as the circumference of the Earth – home to 60 percent of the population – the Philippines will suffer significant damage from a rise in sea level and storm surges. It also lies directly in the path of the annual Pacific typhoons. According to the World Bank, category 4 and 5 storms were more than twice as common between 1999 and 2004 compared to the period from 1975 to 1989 (World Bank Group 2011). And with much of the rural population still dependent on agriculture, droughts and landslides threaten people and their food on a scale far beyond what the Bacarra-Zantar ever could.

The lesson of Ilocos Norte, however, also contains seeds of hope. In 2005 the provincial government commissioned a massive wind farm on Bangui Bay, the first of its kind in Southeast Asia. By 2010 the turbines were producing 25 MW of electricity, enough to meet almost half the province's electricity needs. With existing technology, the Philippines as a whole possesses some 76,600 MW of potential wind-power capacity, more than enough to power the nation. And the Philippines is already a world leader in geothermal energy, which provides 27 percent of the country's energy needs. These actions may be worthy, but unless the rest of the world follows suit, they will be just as futile as a single farmer trying to dam the river alone. Just as the *zanjera* can work together to share and manage the Bacarra-Zantar, we can, if we choose, manage our larger tragedy of the commons.

GLOBALIZATION OF THE COMMONS AND PARTIAL GLOBALIZATION OF THEIR MANAGEMENT

Human communities have always faced environmental challenges (see McCormick 1989: vii). What is distinctive about our present conundrum is the *extensity* and *intensity* (see chapter 1) of these threats. A dirty power plant in one city is a local environmental problem. A dirty power plant in every city is an entirely different challenge. As we explain below, the emergence of an industrial economy from the nineteenth century onward has been the main driver of environmental stress, and the globalization of that industrialization has been one of its chief catalysts. Of course, hypothetically, autarchic industrialization would have produced the same kind of environmental interdependence as globalized industrialization, had it reached the same scale. In practice, industrialization, particularly in the postwar period, has been nurtured by global flows of capital, and has often been aimed at producing goods to be traded across borders. To the extent that economic globalization has broadened the scope and depth of industrialization, it has contributed to environmental threats.[1]

Just as environmental problems have tracked industrial globalization, so have efforts to mitigate them. Most accounts of global environmental governance begin in the 1970s, following the emergence of the modern environmental movement. For our purposes, however, it is important to note previous efforts to manage global environmental interdependence as well. Attempts at international cooperation were made during the nineteenth century, the interwar period, and the 1940s. The first part of this chapter shows how industrialization, globalization, environmental impacts, and efforts to mitigate them, including internationally, all developed in tandem, and then reached an inflection point in the postwar era, as the Great Acceleration sped up.

Though the 1970s represented a new phase for global environmental governance – specifically, an increase in political salience, state involvement, and intergovernmental cooperation – several continuities run through the historical record. First, the technical nature of many environmental issues has always meant that scientists have played a leading role in defining problems and advocating for their solution. Scientific groups have long organized themselves transnationally, forming "epistemic communities" (Haas 1991) around certain issues. Second, citizens' groups – what we would today call environmental activists – have always been another chief force driving political action. Most of the greatest environmental achievements can be traced to individual campaigners and NGOs who have mobilized public outrage, as well as individual "norm entrepreneurs" at international organizations. This grassroots emphasis distinguishes the environmental realm from the governance of security or the economy, where top national-level policy-makers have often led change. Third, private groups have traditionally gone beyond mere advocacy to play a direct role in global environmental governance, often stepping in to compensate for the lackluster performance of states and the intergovernmental bodies they create.

Industrial Globalization and the Origins of Modern Environmental Governance

The modern environmental movement sprouted from the smokestacks of the Industrial Revolution. As people moved from countryside to city, from farm to factory, they began to realize the price of progress. Charles Dickens opened his novel *Bleak House*, published in 1852, with a dystopian vision of London:

> Fog everywhere. Fog up the river, where it flows among green aits[2] and meadows; fog down the river, where it rolls defiled among the tiers of shipping and the waterside pollutions of a great (and dirty) city. Fog on the Essex marshes, fog on the Kentish heights. Fog creeping into the cabooses of collier-brigs; fog lying out on the yards, and hovering in the rigging of great ships; fog drooping on the gunwales of barges and small boats. Fog in the eyes and throats of ancient Greenwich pensioners, wheezing by the firesides of their wards; fog in the stem and bowl of the afternoon pipe of the wrathful skipper, down in his close cabin; fog cruelly pinching the toes and fingers of his shivering little 'prentice boy on deck. Chance people on the bridges peeping over the parapets into a nether sky of fog, with fog all round them, as if they were up in a balloon, and hanging in the misty clouds.

Dickens wasn't speaking about fog as we understand the term today, but rather the particulate matter that spewed from the coal-burning chimneys across southern England, collected in the Thames Valley, and coated Victorian London in its infamous "pea-soupers."[3]

These conditions sparked protest and, ultimately, reform. A year after Dickens's description appeared, Parliament passed the Smoke Nuisance Abatement Act, one of the first modern pieces of pollution control legislation. Further measures soon followed. The 1863 Alkali Acts banned the hydrochloric acid given off by gases in smelting, the 1866 Sanitary Act declared black smoke a public health nuisance, and the 1872 River Pollution Control Act made it illegal to dump sewage into a river (Flick 1980). New nongovernmental organizations had formed to advocate for these reforms, and joined the growing public appreciation of nature exemplified by bird-watching societies, geographic societies, and animal protection societies, most of which date from this era (McCormick 1989).

As industrialization spread to Western Europe and North America under the nineteenth-century phase of globalization, so too did its effects on the natural world. Environmental movements and advocacy groups soon followed. In the New World the scale and majesty of the existing wilderness led proto-environmentalists to a more "conservationist" approach that sought to preserve the wild character of nature from the hand of man (Fox 1986). In the United States, the campaign that led to the creation of Yellowstone National Park in 1872, the first national park in the world, galvanized a broader movement that became institutionalized in groups like the Sierra Club (1892) and the Audubon Society (1905). In Germany, groups sprang up advocating everything from protecting birds to the humane treatment of animals. By the end of the nineteenth century, every industrialized country had seen an environmental movement arise to address the effects of spreading industrialization.

From the very beginning of the modern age, then, environmental problems and the political efforts to solve them were connected to the globalization of the industrial economy.[4] Just as significantly, the *interdependent* nature of environmental problems was recognized as well, and some first attempts at international cooperation were made (Boardman 1981). Appropriately, a major focus of early intergovernmental efforts was an environmental problem that, by its nature, could not be caged within national borders – birds. As a meeting of ornithologists in 1928 concluded,

> Although it is obvious that the protection of birds must largely be left to individual effort and unofficial action in the different countries, the fact that the vast majority of birds are migratory and, therefore,

> international in their habits, often crossing many different countries between their winter and summer homes, clearly demonstrates that international action is necessary if protection is to be really effective. (Quoted in Boardman 1981: 31)

Bird watching and appreciating societies were common across Europe and North America, and especially in Britain, in the late nineteenth and early twentieth centuries, giving efforts to protect birds a level of political salience that may seem strange today. In 1872 the Swiss Federal Council proposed a commission to draft an intergovernmental agreement on bird protection, but the suggestion was not taken up (Boardman 1981: 27). Private groups moved ahead, however. In 1884 the International Ornithological Congress, meeting in Vienna, created a committee to determine which species warranted protection. Based on these studies, the Convention for the Protection of Birds Useful to Agriculture was adopted in 1902, though it was not particularly effective, leading to few domestic policy changes and scarcely enforced (Boardman 1981), with only 13 European countries joining (Takahashi 2012). Similarly, the United States and Great Britain signed a treaty in 1916 that aimed to protect birds migrating between Canada and the United States.

A more ambitious idea, however, had emerged at the 1909 International Congress for the Protection of Nature, where environmental groups from across Europe gathered in Paris. Conservationists presented papers documenting environmental conditions in their different countries, and made the first ever call for the creation of an international environmental body (Boardman 1981; Falkner 2012). The idea was the brainchild of Paul Sarasin, a Swiss naturalist who had led efforts to establish a national park system in his country. Sarasin lobbied the Swiss government to invite other countries to discuss a potential intergovernmental body, and in 1913 some 17 European countries met in Berne to create the Consultative Commission for the International Protection of Nature. As the name suggests, the body was granted little authority or resources. Rather, its mandate was limited to "The collecting, classifying, and publishing of every item dealing with international protection of nature," and "Propaganda for the international protection of nature" (quoted in Boardman 1981: 29). This combination of broad mandate and limited authority would set the tone for many subsequent environmental IGOs.

As it turned out, world events effectively neutered even the minimal agenda-setting power granted to the Consultative Commission. A large conference was planned for August 1914 to discuss whaling, hunting, and the trade in certain species, among other topics, but the outbreak of World War I prevented it from convening. In fact, the world's first global environmental body never actually met at all (Boardman 1981).

Conservationists were not put off their efforts to create a global body, however. With the formation of the League of Nations in 1919, they saw a new body that could become an even stronger force for the protection of nature at the international level. Sarasin and a number of other environmental activists and groups lobbied the League to create an office that would take over the functions of the defunct Consultative Commission, and indeed, go beyond them. Initially, they found some success. Inazo Nitobe, the head of the League's International Bureau Section, took up the cause and began lobbying governments and other members of the League bureaucracy for support (Wöbse 2008). These activities reflected another pattern that would become an important part of environmental governance many decades later – NGOs directly lobbying IGOs, with both groups serving as norm entrepreneurs. But the campaign made little headway. Just as today countries seek to retain sovereignty over environmental matters, states were reluctant to expand the League's mandate to include the protection of nature.

In the meantime, the international community of scientists and activists concerned with natural protection grew. In 1922 the International Committee for Bird Protection was founded in London, serving as a transnational umbrella group for many of the North American and European bird advocacy groups. In 1923 a second International Congress on the Protection of Nature was held in Paris. And in 1925 the Netherlands Committee for International Nature Protection was founded, a private group backed by the Dutch government, with the explicit goal of providing, through an international network of similar organizations, the kind of international clearinghouse function that the League had failed to provide. This too proved elusive, however. The Dutch campaigners managed to enlist allies in France and Belgium, but not beyond. And in 1928 the International Union of Biological Sciences, a scientific body, created an Office International de Documentation et de Corrélation pour la Protection de la Nature. In 1934 this body became the International Office for the Protection of Nature (IOPN), finally creating a private version of Sarasin's original version (Boardman 1981).

These and related activities built the seeds of what would later become the modern international environmental movement, but they did not, largely, lead to significant policy changes at the domestic or international levels. The few treaties that were agreed aimed at protecting wildlife. Some, like the 1911 Fur Seals Treaty were effective. But most were not. In 1933 countries approved the London Convention for the Protection of the Fauna and Flora of Africa. In 1934, the UK government made a half-hearted attempt to secure an international agreement that would limit marine oil discharges, largely so it could appease domestic birding interests, but other countries refused to go along (Wöbse 2008). In 1936 the US and Canada extended their migratory bird treaty to Mexico. And in 1937 the International Agreement for the Regulation of Whaling was signed in London.

Postwar Internationalization

At the close of World War II, environmental issues figured hardly at all on policy-makers' agendas. It is therefore unsurprising that global environmental governance did not experience a foundational moment in the 1940s and 1950s as security and economic institutions did. Instead, the same conservation groups that had been active in the interwar period returned to their early ideas, and sought to build upon them.

Just as earlier efforts had chiefly targeted birds and sea life, postwar international cooperation first centered around a few issue areas that were particularly transnational in nature. In 1946 the whaling regime of the 1930s was replaced with the more ambitious International Convention for the Regulation of Whaling, which set stricter limits on hunting. In 1955 an International Air Pollution Conference was convened in New York, and another in London in 1961. While no international agreements emerged, these events served as precursors to the transboundary air pollution regime (see below).

But an issue-by-issue approach seemed increasingly piecemeal to conservationists. Jean-Paul Harroy, a Belgian official who would feature prominently in international conservation efforts during this time, noted the scant institutionalization that immediately followed the war:

> one must consider the conditions prevailing at that time. There were still very few countries where organisations devoted all their time to the conservation of nature. A few isolated individuals working in universities and museums were launching lonely battles, with little contact among them. There was no international centralised mechanism on which these individuals could rely to overcome their isolation. (Quoted in Boardman 1981: 104)

In fact, IOPN had survived the war, and resumed its information-sharing function in the mid-1940s. Meanwhile, the latent transnational community of scientific organizations and conservation groups began meeting again and considering how to move forward. As before, the Swiss conservationists were particularly active. At an international meeting of nature-protection groups in Basel in 1946, organized by Swiss groups, delegates declared: "it is desirable that there should be an active international organisation, widely international and representative in character, adequately financed and with adequate terms of reference" (quoted in Boardman 1981: 37). But there was substantial disagreement about what form this organization ought to take. Should it be private, like the existing IOPN? Or should it re-create the more governmental Consultative Commission that had laid dormant since before World War I?

Further complicating the picture, several of the new intergovernmental organs of the newly created United Nations were becoming involved with different aspects of environmental protection. Both the Food and Agriculture Organization (FAO) and the Economic and Social Committee (ECOSOC) concerned themselves with the management of natural resources, the latter following a strong push by the United States (McCormick 1989). It was the UN's Educational, Scientific, and Cultural Organization that played the most central role, however. UNESCO's first Director-General was Julian Huxley, a British biologist who had served as secretary of the Zoological Society of London and attended the 1946 Basel conference in that capacity. Just a few months later he was elected to lead UNESCO at the organization's first conference. Nowhere in the group's original mandate can an explicit focus on conservation be found. Rather, Huxley persuaded the organization that natural landscapes formed part of culture, and that the preservation of the Earth's species was integral to science (Boardman 1981). From the beginning of the postwar period, then, it was unclear where within the UN system environmental issues would be addressed.

Huxley also continued discussing the possibility of a specialized world environment organization – public or private, affiliated with UNESCO or not – with the groups that had met in Basel. These organizations continued to debate what form a global environmental organization might take, meeting a second time in Brunnen, Switzerland, in 1947. This conference benefited from a wider attendance than the Basel meeting, and included the representatives of 14 national governments (McCormick 1989: 33). The Swiss attendees continued to favor a specialized organization with governmental involvement, and used the Brunnen conference to declare a provisional International Union for the Protection of Nature (IUPN). The proposal was loosely modeled on the Consultative Committee, although in practice its membership was largely limited to Swiss nature organizations. Other groups, such as the New York Zoological Society, instead preferred a private structure, and would go on to create a Conservation Foundation to support the work of the already existing IOPN. UNESCO was more in concordance with this latter position, believing that governments would be reluctant to commit themselves to a formal international environmental organization.

In the end, UNESCO organized a conference at Fontainebleau, in 1948, at which both governmental representatives (invited by UNESCO and the French government) and private groups (invited by IUPN, i.e. the Swiss groups) were represented. This somewhat unusual event created a very unique organization. The IUPN (which in 1956 changed its name to the International Union for the Conservation of Nature, IUCN) became a hybrid international organization. Several categories of members were admitted: governments, agencies of governments, intergovernmental organizations, and international and domestic NGOs. All of these members voted in the organization's General Assembly, but the governmental delegates received two votes and the private groups only one. The result was an extraordinary network that combined what we would today identify as intergovernmental, transgovernmental, and transnational elements, orchestrated by UNESCO.[5] The new union was charged with the protection of nature, which "may be defined as the preservation of the entire world biotic community, or man's natural environment, which includes the Earth's renewable natural resources of which it is composed, and on which rests the foundation of human civilization." Its mandate was similarly broad, to "encourage and facilitate co-operation between governments and national and international organizations," to "promote and recommend national and international action," and to conduct and disseminate scientific research (IUCN 1948).

But as ample as this mission was, the delegates at Fontainebleau declined to offer the financial resources or decision-making authority IUCN would need to realize these lofty goals. Instead, the group served as a kind of general forum for environmental issues, a place where issues could be raised and discussed, but not acted upon. An explicit decision was made to avoid interfering in the internal affairs of countries (Boardman 1981). Today its main contributions to global environmental governance are largely on the scientific front and in relation to information sharing.

By the start of the 1950s, then, before the modern environmental movement emerged, there was already in place a loose, hybrid international organization. It differed in form from the strictly intergovernmental security or economic institutions negotiated at the same time. It lacked the top-level sponsorship of the major powers (though groups from the major countries participated), and was instead the creation of private groups and entrepreneurs in the new international bureaucracy. It also lacked the authority and resources of the UN or Bretton Woods institutions. Still, IUCN might have served as a focal point for the activism and policy shifts that would come in the 1960s and 1970s. This did not occur. Instead, the momentum of the growing environmental movement was directed into a proliferation of groups and campaigns, often "thinking globally" but "acting locally." As Boardman observed of the period, "While there is some virtue in proliferation – small, independent, specialised bodies can often tackle problems with greater vigour and freedom than the subunits of bigger institutions – the problems of co-ordination have also at times seemed insuperable" (1981: 45).

The Modern Environmental Movement

It was not until the 1960s and 1970s that the environment became a central element of global interdependence. This was not coincidental, but directly connected to the postwar burst of economic growth and the further diffusion of industrialization that the 1945 settlement facilitated. In many countries, industrial production had undergone a step-change during the war, and then rocketed even further ahead in the burst of reconstruction and economic expansion that characterized the postwar era under the Bretton Woods system described in chapter 3.

As in earlier periods, industrialization brought need impacts on human health and the natural environment. Now, however, a new science of ecology was emerging from advances in climatology, toxicology, epidemiology, biology, and geology. Scientists were gaining a new ability to understand the origins of environmental problems, and to make the link between industrial activities and human and environmental health. Moreover, this science-based approach was extended across the entire globe, facilitated in part by the new technical intergovernmental organizations like WHO, UNESCO, and IUCN (Held et al. 1999: 391).

But perhaps the most important shift was the change in social understandings and norms relating to the environment. Beginning in the 1950s, but especially in the 1960s and 1970s, environmental issues gained a new level of political salience in the industrialized world. Key events made the state of environmental damage increasingly visible to the public and galvanized unprecedented concern for what came to be called environmental problems (the modern usage of the term dates from this time).

In 1952, exactly 100 years after it was first published, Dickens' opening to *Bleak House* could once again have served to describe London, which was for four days coated in a thick haze. Now, however, the fog had a new name, a neologism made from "smoke" and "fog." The Great Smog of '52, as the event was called, killed a horrific number of people – 12,000 in less than a week (Bell and Davis 2001).[6] This was about half as many as were killed in the months-long bombing of the city in World War II. But because the smog mostly affected the old and sick, the public and the authorities did not recognize the extent of the toll until undertakers started reporting a shortage of coffins (Davis et al. 2002). The result was the 1956 Clean Air Act, which set stringent new limits on the kinds of fuel that could be burnt in urban areas.

Similar events galvanized concern around the world. In 1956 researchers discovered why the children of Minamata, a small city in southwestern Japan, were being born with extreme deformities and damage to their nervous systems. Mercury from a nearby chemical factory had flooded the Yatsushiro Sea over several decades, building up in the shellfish that filtered it out of the seawater and, traveling through the food chain, in the bodies of the people. In 1972, *Life* magazine published a deeply shocking photo of Tomoko Uemura that became a global symbol for the dangers of pollution. Cradled by her mother like a Renaissance Pietà, the girl's body is shrunken and gnarled by mercury. The scene was posed – the photographer knew he needed an iconic image to bring attention to the cause – but it captured an even more grim reality, with over 1,000 deaths directly attributable to the poisoning (Ministry of the Environment, Government of Japan 2002).

But perhaps nothing did more to raise awareness than naturalist Rachel Carson's *Silent Spring*, which was first serialized in the *New Yorker* in 1962 and went on to become an international bestseller (McCormick 1989). A detailed investigation of the effects of DDT (a chemical used to kill mosquitos) on birds and humans, the book highlighted the *political* nature of environmental problems. Carson reported on the way in which the companies that manufactured DDT had misinformed the public about its effects, and how politicians had bent to the industry's goals, despite rising information about the dangers DDT posed. While that story may sound all too familiar today, no one had ever put it in quite those terms before, leading some to declare *Silent Spring* the green movement's *Uncle Tom's Cabin*, the book that had so radically altered public views on slavery (Ivanova 2007: 340).

New advocacy groups arose to give direction to the outrage these and other events fueled: The Nature Conservancy in 1951, the World Wildlife Fund in 1961, the Environmental Defence League and Greenpeace in 1967, Friends of the Earth in 1969, and the Natural Resources Defence Council in 1970. Today these groups and others like them have grown to rank among the largest and most influential nonstate actors in world politics. Slightly later, beginning in the early 1970s, whole political parties dedicated to environmental protection originated in Northern Europe and other industrialized countries. Over the course of the next decade many of these groups would cohere into a transnational political party devoted to environmental protection, the Green Party, which operates today across some 90 countries (Rüdig 1991).

The combination of public awareness and organized advocacy produced what we now refer to as the environmental movement.[7] Whereas conservation had been, since the nineteenth century, the preserve of elites, naturalists, and scientists, it was now a subject of mass politics (McCormick 1989). The conditions were thus set for policy reform, and in the 1960s and 1970s a host of modern environmental legislation was passed across the industrialized countries. In the United States, California led the way by imposing emissions standards for automobiles in 1959 and a Clean Water Act in 1960. The federal government followed with its own landmark Clean Air Act (research began in 1963, regulation in 1970) and Clean Water Act (1972). In 1970 the United States created the Environmental Protection Agency to implement these laws and serve as a national environmental regulator. In Japan, an extraordinary legislative session was convened in 1970 to address the country's environmental challenges. The so-called "Pollution Diet" (the Diet is the name of the Japanese Parliament) passed 14 basic environmental laws, and established, in 1971, the country's Environment Agency (Mason 1999). In Europe all the major countries had adopted similar measures. By the 1970s the modern state had adopted a radically more proactive role in the preservation of the natural environment.

Given the growing severity of environmental threats, their increased political salience, and the more active role governments played in tackling them, conditions were ripe for deeper international cooperation in this area. Moreover, the environment was increasingly seen as a transnational issue. This was reflected in one of the chief slogans of the movement, "Think globally, act locally," which highlights both the commonality of the problem and the role of each community, and each individual, in its solution. But for many it was clear that local actions alone would not be able to confront the problem. Again, it was activists and entrepreneurs at intergovernmental organizations who initiated efforts to address the problems at a higher level. In 1967 the UN was preparing to organize a conference, its fourth, on the peaceful use of nuclear power. Several members of the Swedish delegation deeply opposed to nuclear power, peaceful or otherwise, instead suggested a conference "to facilitate co-ordination and to focus the interest of Member countries on the extremely complex problems related to the human environment" (quoted in Ivanova 2005: 3). This decision appears to have been taken by the delegates themselves, receiving official approval from Stockholm only afterward.

Remarkably, the suggestion took. At a later ECOSOC meeting the Swedish delegation circulated a more detailed memo to which environmental groups had contributed and that laid out various environmental challenges. Importantly, ECOSOC rules gave non-state actors more access to deliberations than most international organizations did. On December 15, 1969 the UN General Assembly voted to hold a conference on the "human environment" in Stockholm in 1972. The resolution approving the meeting stated that the event would

> serve as a practical means to encourage, and to provide guidelines for, action by Governments and international organizations designed to protect and improve the human environment and to remedy and prevent its impairment, by means of international cooperation, bearing in mind the particular importance of enabling the developing countries to forestall the occurrence of such problems. (UN Doc. A/RES/2581, XXIV)

Already, though, political cleavages were emerging, principally between the North and South. These are discussed in more detail below, but southern opposition to the "green imperialism conference" almost derailed the event before it could begin. Most observers give the lion's share of credit for preventing this potential stillbirth to Maurice Strong. Strong, a Canadian businessman and public servant, took leave from his position as head of the Canadian International Development Agency to serve as Secretary-General of the event in

1970. He immediately began crisscrossing the world to personally persuade recalcitrant governments, leader by leader, to send a delegation to Stockholm (Rowland 1973; Stone 1973).

But even if countries could be persuaded to attend the Stockholm conference, what might they do there? The Swedish ambassador, when proposing the conference originally, had assured the other member states that no new organization would result (Ivanova 2007: 345). But to many it seemed that the logical step would be to create some kind of world environment organization. Unlike IUCN, which was more of a forum for discussion, several proposals envisioned a strictly intergovernmental organization more along the lines of the specialized agencies of the United Nations. The argument was made by many, but by few more astutely than the American diplomat George Kennan. The author of the famous Long Telegram of 1946, which first laid out the West's policy of containment toward the Soviet Union (see chapter 2), Kennan was perhaps an unexpected advocate of global environmental institutions. A conservative Realist who was rarely seen around his offices in Foggy Bottom or the Institute of Advanced Study in Princeton without a three-piece suit, Kennan shared little with the foot soldiers of the environmental movement. Yet in *Foreign Affairs* in 1970 he wrote an article, "To Prevent a World Wasteland," that makes as strong a case for international cooperation to protect the environment as any protestor on the streets of Berkeley might have made.

For Kennan, the smattering of international organizations dedicated to environmental protection were inadequate "to prevent a further general deterioration in man's environment, a deterioration of such seriousness as to be in many respects irreparable." Instead, he argued, "there will have to be an international effort much more urgent in its timing, bolder and more comprehensive in its conception and more vigorous in its execution than anything created or planned to date." Kennan saw a need for four crucial functions. First, adequate facilities for the pooling of scientific knowledge were needed so that the contours of the problem could be understood. Second, the world needed a central clearing house for existing scientific and operational activities at the international level that would seek to reduce redundancies and highlight omissions. Third, and more ambitiously, Kennan saw a need for a body to establish international standards on environmental matters within states, and to offer governments advice and assistance in meeting them. Kennan did not believe that such a body could or should exert direct authority over governments, but rather saw global environmental governance as a matter "of establishing and explaining requirements, of pressing governments to accept and enforce standards, [and] of helping them to overcome domestic opposition." Last, and most radically, Kennan called for "the establishment and enforcement of suitable rules for all human activities" conducted in the global commons that fell beyond the reach of any one country: the high seas, the atmosphere, outer space, and the poles.

To achieve these goals Kennan proposed an International Environmental Agency. He imagined it would only involve the advanced countries (as they were, after all, those mainly responsible for environmental degradation), and argued that development issues should be dealt with elsewhere. He also believed that the institution would begin with only "soft" authority, but

> one could hope that eventually, as powers were accumulated and authority delegated under multilateral arrangements, the Agency could gradually take over many of the functions of enforcement for such international arrangements as might require enforcement . . . and in this way expand its function and designation from that of an advisory agency to that of the single commanding International Environmental Authority which the international community is bound, at some point, to require.

Two years later, these ideas would have a chance to become reality as 113 countries gathered in Stockholm for the United Nations Conference on the Human Environment. The event was envisioned as a kind of environmental Bretton Woods. Even Kennan permitted himself an audacious optimism:

> The great communist and Western powers, particularly, have need to replace the waning fixations of the cold war with interests which they can pursue in common and to everyone's benefit. For young people the world over, some new opening of hope and creativity is becoming an urgent spiritual necessity. Could there, one wonders, be any undertaking better designed to meet these needs, to relieve the great convulsions of anxiety and ingrained hostility that now rack international society, than a major international effort to restore the hope, the beauty, and the salubriousness of the natural environment in which man has his being?

An Environmental "Bretton Woods"? The Stockholm Compromise and UNEP

Despite the optimism and ambition that preceded it, in retrospect the Stockholm conference was unlikely to generate the effective global environmental governance that activists and intellectuals like George Kennan had hoped for. A weak international organization was created, the United Nations Environment Programme (UNEP), envisioned more as a coordinating body than as a regulator. This reduced version of the International Environment Agency was compromised by some of the trends we have classified under gridlock. Given the evolutionary nature of our argument, we should not be surprised to see such trends emerging here. The delegates in Stockholm were meeting in 1972, some three decades after the foundational moment of the postwar order. Moreover, they were discussing a type of interdependence problem, the global commons, that was quite different from security or the economy and, in some ways, a product of advances in the latter field.

Specifically, three of the gridlock mechanisms hampered cooperation at Stockholm; each is considered in more detail below. First, power in environmental affairs has always been more broadly distributed than in security or economic matters. Developing countries contain much of the natural beauty, the biodiversity, and the natural resources that are the object of environmental governance claims, and so insisted, rightly, in having a say in how these would be governed. Moreover, unlike in 1945, by 1972 most of the developing world was independent, and eager to assert its hard-won sovereignty. Second, environmental problems are "harder" problems, in the way described in chapter 1. Delegating authority over "local" matters like forests, fisheries, or factories to an international body represents a sharp sovereignty cost for states, one that few of the delegations at Stockholm were willing to pay. Third, several international organizations already existed with responsibility for areas of environmental governance, and they were reluctant to cede authority or resources to some new organization. Inertia thus built fragmentation into the global environmental regime from the beginning. Despite these limitations, Stockholm was a partial success, putting environmental issues on the agenda as never before. But, as with other issue areas, the early gains would give way to second-order problems.

Multipolarity: the North–South divide

The international system of 1972 was very different from that of 1945. Forty-four countries attended the Bretton Woods summit in 1944, 50 met in San Francisco to launch the United Nations in 1946, but in 1972 some 113 countries met in the Swedish capital. Almost all of the new participants were newly independent countries in the developing world. The large number of attendees is particularly remarkable given that none of the Eastern bloc countries attended. Because East Germany was not recognized in the United Nations system, it was not allowed to participate in the conference, and its allies decided to boycott in solidarity (at any rate, environmental concerns did not figure highly with communist leaders). This Cold War quirk perhaps made agreement at Stockholm more likely by removing a source of geopolitical friction, but the remaining countries still found plenty to disagree about, with a clear cleavage dividing wealthy and poor countries. Several factors fed this schism.

First, and most basically, at this point in history only developed countries – by definition – had experienced wide-scale industrialization. This meant that rich and poor countries faced very different kinds of environmental problems. The central issues of the mid-century environmental movement (e.g. water and air pollution, toxins, nuclear power, species depletion) were largely concerns of the wealthy world. Rich countries suffered the ill effects of these problems most directly, but were also by far the largest contributors to them. This was widely acknowledged, as the US delegate told the conference:

> As the world's most industrialized nation, we are the greatest polluter . . . with less than 6 percent of the world's population, we account for the use of more than one-third of the world's energy production . . . We have almost half of the automobiles in use in the world, and we consume about one-fourth of the world's phosphate, potash, and nitrogenous fertilizers, almost half of its newsprint and synthetic rubber, and more than a fourth of its steel . . . these few statistics are indicative of the relative global pollution burden that we in the United States are creating. (Quoted in Ivanova 2007: 353)

Developing countries, in turn, experienced environmental problems primarily in the form of disease from contaminated food and water, or disruptions to agriculture or subsistence activities. These were not problems of industrialization, but just the opposite – problems of underdevelopment. Northern countries' insistence on addressing the adverse effects of industrial development, and even of limiting such development, were therefore met with extreme suspicion. The Brazilian delegate Bernardo de Azevedo Brito argued, "I do not believe we are prepared to become new Robinson Crusoes . . . Each country must be free to evolve its own development plans, to exploit its own resources and to define its own environmental standards" (quoted in Ivanova 2007: 342). China, which had recently been recognized by the

UN, was even more opposed to global regulation. "Whenever Chinese delegates felt their position was being ignored, they took the floor to make strong statements attacking colonialism, imperialism, and capitalism, themes which would then be taken up by one or more developing countries" (Rowland 1973: 94). The Chinese delegate Tang Ke told the conference, "Each country has the right to determine its own environment standards and policies in the light of its own conditions, and no country whatsoever should undermine the interests of the developing countries under the pretext of protecting the environment" (quoted in McCormick 1989: 99).

Second, and related, public opinion also differed across North and South. At this time the modern environmental movement was largely limited to North America, Northern Europe, and Japan. Almost all the 400-odd NGOs represented at Stockholm came from the developed world (McCormick 1989: 100). The governments of poor countries therefore had few domestic political incentives to create strong environmental institutions. Indeed, limits on development would be seen unfavorably by strong domestic interest groups in developing countries, such as urban workers and local industrialists.

Third, even if there had been widespread environmental movements in poor countries at this time, it is unlikely they would have had much influence. Industrialized countries (at least those in the First World) almost all possessed democratic political institutions that gave policy-makers incentives to address environmental concerns. The developing world, however, had been swept by a wave of postcolonial coups, which had largely brought many authoritarian, developmentalist regimes to power. For such countries, national industrial development was not only a moral imperative to overcome poverty, it was key to protecting hard-won sovereignty from both foreign and domestic opponents. Military regimes in particular favored rapid industrialization as a source of material power. This was reflected in the basic bureaucratic structures of developing countries. In 1972 only 11 developing countries had environmental agencies (by 1980 nearly 102 would have such institutions) (McCormick 1989: 158).

Finally, the natural concentration of the Earth's most dynamic ecosystems in the warmest parts of the globe meant that developing countries possessed the majority of the biodiversity and natural resources that conservation groups in the North wanted to protect. Their cooperation was thus essential to any successful environmental agreement (see also discussion below). The nature of environmental problems thus gave developing countries significant "power" in the sense that rich countries depended on them to achieve their goals

(Keohane and Nye 1977). In other words, the environmental regime was characterized not only by a sharp divergence in interests across North and South, but countries on both sides of this divide held significant bargaining power.

The compromised ambitions of Stockholm can therefore be read in part as an early example of the role of multipolarity in generating gridlock. In contrast to the security or economic realms, global environmental politics never had a unipolar foundational moment akin to the 1940s, in which the victorious countries were able to devise a set of institutions under conditions that gave them an exceptionally free hand. Instead, the early 1970s were a period of tension between North and South as newly independent nations in Africa and Asia, especially, sought to reassert their recently restored sovereignty and place in the global order. Moreover, the nature of environmental issues meant that these countries could not simply be ignored. Kennan may have been right that the developed world was largely responsible for existing degradation, but it was clear to the delegates at Stockholm that the world's environmental issues could not be solved without the participation of developing countries rich in biodiversity, rainforests, and natural resources, and with impoverished, rapidly expanding populations. As we will see below, the spread of industrialization in subsequent decades would increase the multipolarity of environmental politics even further, but it is crucial to note that, unlike security or economic matters, it began from a high base.

Harder problems and sovereignty

Crucially, however, the failure to create a stronger environmental regulatory framework at Stockholm was not only because of the fact that some countries were more concerned with development than with its externalities. Even some of the most pro-environment countries were wary of creating a global institution with significant power over issues like health, safety, land use, energy, and other matters that went to the core of a nation's economic interests.

The United States was a key example. The fervor of the environmental movement in the US in the 1960s and 1970s had made the government eager to be seen as leading global progress on the issue, so the US was one of the key backers of the Stockholm conference. But at the same time US enthusiasm for the United Nations had waned significantly since the 1940s. The rising number of Third World countries had diluted US influence in the UN General Assembly. As delegations were meeting in Stockholm, the US Congress was taking steps to scale back its funding of various UN agencies, which it viewed as overly bureaucratic. There was thus a gap between countries' concern for the environment and their willingness to delegate sovereignty to multilateral institutions to address that concern (Ivanova 2007).

Instead of the quasi-regulatory agency outlined by Kennan, pro-environment countries envisioned a kind of watchdog for environmental issues within the UN system. The United States wanted a small, but high-level body that would act as an agenda-setter and catalyst. Strong himself echoed a similar view, stating, "what is needed to deal with the task of improving man's global environment is not a new specialized agency or operating body but a policy evaluation and review mechanism which can become the institutional 'center' or 'brain' of the environmental network" (quoted in Ivanova 2007: 349). Some environmentalists stated that creating a specialized agency for the environment would simply marginalize the issue, when the real need was to infuse all the UN's work with an environmental ethos. In sum, the issues were deemed so hard that no sovereignty pooling was even contemplated.

Fragmentation

Bretton Woods and San Francisco took place on as clean an institutional slate as can be found in world politics. Stockholm took place in a world shaped by the outcomes of those previous meetings, including the array of specialized agencies that had arisen to address, in part, aspects of the environmental problem. These included the World Meteorological Organization, the Food and Agriculture Organization, the World Health Organization, the International Atomic Energy Agency, UNESCO, the United Nations Conference on Trade and Development (UNCTAD), the United Nations Industrial Development Organization (UNIDO), parts of the World Bank group, and, of course, IUCN. The Environmental Studies Board, a group of experts convened by the US National Academy of Sciences, worried that "even if all organizations in this bewildering array were effective and well managed, they would provide far too fragmented a structure for the conduct of international environmental affairs" (quoted in Ivanova 2007: 346). As noted above, the delegates at Stockholm thus sought a "brain" or "center" to coordinate this work across the UN system.

Crucially, however, the existence of this fragmented structure created barriers to greater coherence. The Environmental Studies

Board noted a strong regulatory body would require taking authority and resources away from the existing agencies, which would "consolidate opposition among the agencies and their constituencies to any attempt to develop institutional machinery for international environmental affairs" (quoted in Ivanova 2007: 346). Indeed, the existing agencies made their case very clear. UN Secretary General U Thant's preparatory report warned that any new institution "that is expected to influence and co-ordinate the activities of other agencies should not itself have operational functions which in any way compete with the organizations over which it expects to exercise such influence" (quoted in McCormick 1989: 93). Another paper prepared by a list of existing agencies argued that "new responsibilities do not automatically require new institutions and mechanisms, but do mean an adaptation of existing arrangements" (quoted in McCormick 1989: 94). A strong, centralized environmental agency was thus never proposed, even by the UN itself.

The United Nations Environmental Programme

Given these impediments, the fact that the Stockholm conference generated any positive outcomes is a testament to the skills and dedication of Strong and his team, who managed to find cooperation where none might have seemed possible. The chief institutional result of the conference was the United Nations Environmental Programme, an organization whose broad mandate for global environmental protection stood – and continues to stand – in contrast to its lack of authority and resources. The UN General Assembly tasked UNEP to "keep under review the world environmental situation" and "to promote the contribution of the relevant scientific and other professional communities to the acquisition, assessment and exchange of environmental knowledge and information." These functions met two of Kennan's list. But no mandate for rule-making was bestowed, with the organization only being asked "to promote international co-operation in the field of the environment and to recommend, as appropriate, policies to this end" (UN Res. 2997, 1972). Enforcement, needless to say, was not mentioned.

Beyond its official mission, UNEP's weakness (compared, for example, to the Bretton Woods institutions in economic governance, described in chapter 3), can be seen in its funding, its legal status, and even the location of its headquarters. First, it was agreed that the organization's general funding (e.g. for its secretariat) would come from the UN budget, while program funds would instead be put into a special Environmental Fund, which UNEP would administer.[8] The Environmental Fund was the idea of the United States, which offered $100 million to kick-start its activities. In later years this arrangement would be criticized by environmentalists as it essentially left UNEP's funding dependent on voluntary contributions. But as Ivanova (2007) points out, developing countries were unwilling to join an organization with annually assessed funds (like the UN's specialized agencies) because it would put them in the position of paying for the problems of the rich world, even if the amount was negligibly small. The voluntary fund therefore represented the only politically feasible way to dedicate resources to environmental protection.

Interestingly, the United States proposed that contributions to the Environmental Fund be assessed on the amount of pollution a country contributed to the global environment, the so-called "polluter pays" principle. This would have made the United States liable for significant funds. But, in a move that in retrospect looks supremely short-sighted, the developing countries refused to accept this offer of a formula for allocating contributions to the fund. They feared that every dollar donated by rich countries to the Environmental Fund would be one less dollar available for development funding. In the end, then, contributions to the Environmental Fund were made strictly voluntary.

Second, an elaborate debate took place over what official status the environmental entity should possess. The most powerful units within the UN system are the specialized agencies, as these possess universal membership, receive regularly assessed funds from member states, and enjoy significant autonomy. Programs, in contrast, report to the General Assembly or its subcommittees. Because UNEP was not envisioned as playing an operational role, but rather as serving as a convener and catalyst, it was deemed inappropriate to make it a specialized agency. The question then arose of whether it should report to the General Assembly as a whole, or to the Economic and Social Council. Developing countries favored the latter option, as it would emphasize the economic considerations they thought should condition concerns with the natural environment. The United States, Sweden, and other developed countries thought that this was too narrow a mandate. In the end, a compromise was struck that only further complicated the institution's organizational structure. UNEP was created as a subordinate of both the General Assembly and ECOSOC, and reported to the General Assembly through ECOSOC (Ivanova 2007).

Finally, the location of UNEP's headquarters provoked a disproportionate amount of interest and political energy following the Stockholm conference. Again the key fissure lay between developed and developing countries. From an efficiency perspective, all agreed that locating the organization in New York or Geneva would make most sense, particularly for an organization intended to serve as a bridge and catalyst within the UN system on environmental issues. Indeed, so certain was the UN that the UNEP secretariat would be established in Geneva, that it only prepared cost estimates for that location (Ivanova 2007). Developing countries, and the Kenya delegation in particular, had other plans. Kenya had lost its 1967 bid to host UNIDO, and was determined to succeed this time. Without consulting the developed countries, it managed to persuade the other potential developing world hosts (Egypt, India, and Mexico) to support its bid. The Organization for African Unity then proposed a resolution declaring Nairobi the UNEP headquarters, bypassing the process that had been agreed at Geneva to review each of the alternative sites individually. The General Assembly's Second Committee approved the Kenyan proposal 93 to 1 (the United States opposing), with 30 abstentions; almost all developing countries voted in favor; and almost all developed countries abstained.

In sum, the environmental regulator that emerged from Stockholm fell far short of fulfilling the four functions Kennan had identified for his International Environmental Agency. While it was strongest as a clearinghouse of science and a channel for capacity building, it lacked any kind of rule-making authority (hard or soft), much less enforcement power. Even its ability to act as a "brain," in Strong's formulation, was limited by its lack of funding and physical distance from key decision-making centers. Still, Kennan had noted the evolutionary nature which was likely for any international environmental regulator. And, indeed, over the next decades, UNEP and other elements of the rapidly expanding global environmental regime accumulated a number of successes.

The Stockholm conference also achieved less tangible, but equally important successes. It served as a key inflection point for the globalization of environmental issues by bringing developing countries to the center of the environmental debate. This forced a rethinking of the conservation- and pollution-focused perspective of the northern NGOs, and focused attention on the concept that would become known as "sustainable development." At the same time, Stockholm and the related preparations and discussions brought a new awareness to environmental issues to the South. Many southern NGOs and policy reforms can trace their origins to the conference and related events. "By 1982, the ELC [Environmental Liaison Centre] estimated that there were 2,230 environmental NGOs in less developed countries, of which 60 percent had been formed since Stockholm, and 13,000 in more developed countries, of which 30 percent had been formed since Stockholm" (McCormick 1989: 101). Perhaps even more importantly, there were 11 environmental agencies in LDCs in 1972; by 1982 there were 102. These changes facilitated the most productive period of environmental treaty-making, to which we now turn, a period before gridlock became a dominant force.

Early Successes, Lingering Challenges

The Stockholm compromise set the tone for environmental governance in the decades that followed. In a number of key issue areas the ambition and activism of a small group of norm entrepreneurs and scientists – often grouped in networks centered around UNEP – were able to achieve at least partial successes in the face of powerful structural constraints. The result was that over the 1970s and 1980s a plethora of new treaties and institutions were dedicated to discrete environmental issues. This period, from just before the Stockholm conference until just after the 1992 Rio conference (next section), was the most productive era of global environmental governance (see figure 4.1). While most of these multilateral agreements can only be regarded as partial successes, a handful showed how, under the right conditions, global environmental governance could be strikingly effective. Some of the more successful regimes concerned transboundary air pollution (UNECE 2006), dumping waste in the high seas, whaling, and the governance of the Arctic and Antarctic. An exhaustive review of the various efforts, successful and not, is beyond the scope of the present study. But below we briefly review what was arguably the most successful case of global environmental governance – the regime to protect the Earth's ozone layer. As we will see, the regime's success can in large part be explained by the lack of the four gridlock mechanisms.

Ozone

Ozone is a molecule made up of three oxygen atoms, and occurs naturally in the upper stratosphere 10 to 50 kilometers above the Earth.

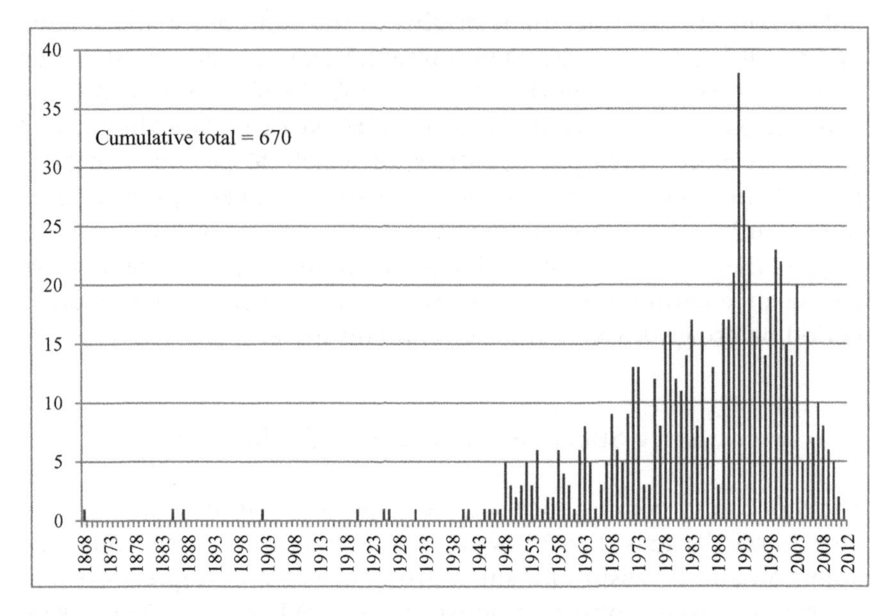

Figure 4.1 Environmental treaties created per year, 1868–2012

Source: UNEP 2012.

Its size and composition allows it to absorb much of the ultraviolet radiation from the sun that, in excess, can cause cancer in humans and other organisms. But ozone is not particularly stable. Certain man-made chemicals – most importantly chlorofluorocarbons (CFCs), which are useful in refrigeration, aerosol propellants, and electrical cleaning – rip apart the ozone molecules they encounter and inhibit their natural bonding, thus depleting the total amount of atmospheric ozone. Because these pollutants persist in the atmosphere for years, traveling around the Earth on air currents, pollutants released anywhere end up depleting ozone everywhere, though prevailing forces tend to concentrate depletion at the poles. This makes the ozone layer a paradigmatic global commons. While everyone can individually benefit from using CFCs and other ozone depleting substances (ODSs), their impact on the ozone layer raises everyone's risk of cancer. These conditions create a powerful and truly global form of interdependence, and thus a need for institutional solutions to safely manage human "use" of the ozone layer.

Between the late 1970s and the early 1990s, the international community built a series of progressively stronger agreements that have banned or sharply reduced the primary ODSs. By the end of 2009, the parties to these agreements had phased out fully 98 percent of the pollutants controlled by the treaties. It is now estimated that the concentration of ODSs in atmosphere will return to pre-1980 levels by the middle of this century. The United States government estimates that in that country alone, these changes will prevent 6.3 million deaths from skin cancer and save some $4.2 trillion in costs over the next century (UNEP 2009).

For these reasons, the ozone regime is widely regarded to be the most successful example of global environmental governance yet achieved. Below we explore what made this success possible, noting an absence of the gridlock mechanisms that have impeded other environmental agreements. The ozone regime's success has made it a template for subsequent attempts at multilateral environmental cooperation, the climate regime in particular. But though these two issues possess a broadly similar problem structure, the latter has succumbed to gridlock while the former has not. As we explain below, the key differences can be understood through the rubric of gridlock.

Ozone was first placed on the international agenda at the 1972 Stockholm conference, where it was proposed that the ozone layer be monitored. No more specific action was taken. Two years later, scientists working in the US developed a theory that CFCs could deplete the ozone layer and thus expose the Earth to harmful radiation. This was surprising and unwelcome news. CFCs had been invented in the 1920s by DuPont and General Motors (Parson 1993). Nontoxic, cheap, and versatile, they had found a host of consumer and industrial applications. Still, the implications of the study were sufficiently troubling that the newly created environmental regulators in the US government began investigating the problem.

The alleged link between CFCs and skin cancer also seized the American public's imagination, though it remained far less salient in Europe and elsewhere. Environmental groups like the Natural Resources Defense Council lobbied to ban CFCs, with industry groups responding that the science was overly speculative. But public fears were stoked, and in 1977 Congress eliminated CFCs from aerosol sprays (though not from other applications). This led to a 50 percent drop in US CFC production by the end of the 1970s, which represented a quarter of the world total. In the next few years, Norway, Sweden, and Canada also banned CFCs from consumer applications.

Having lost the domestic battle, US industry began seeking alternatives. DuPont, which accounted for half the US market, began investing heavily in CFC substitutes, although it stopped once the new Reagan administration, elected in 1980, signaled it would not further tighten regulation (Parson 1993).

Just a few months after Congress banned aerosol CFCs, UNEP sponsored an ozone-related meeting in Washington that 33 countries attended. The conference agreed a World Plan of Action on the Ozone Layer, which envisioned a wide array of monitoring and modeling activities aimed at better understanding changes in the ozone layer, under the leadership of a Coordinating Committee on the Ozone Layer. Though most of the work would be done by various national agencies, UNEP was positioned as the "brain" of this scientific network (Haas 1992).

Throughout the late 1970s and early 1980s, however, the science of ozone depletion remained uncertain. Ozone levels had been measured for some 30 years, but showed few signs of consistent depletion (Wettestad 2002: 156), with a range of studies coming to varying findings. Countries' positions on the issue remained similarly disparate, driven largely by their domestic industries. The United States still accounted for the largest share of world production, but US firms already faced domestic regulation, and so were by no means opposed to global efforts to put their European and Japanese competitors on a similar playing field. Other significant producers of ODSs could be found in the UK, France, Germany, Italy, the Netherlands, and Japan, and, on a smaller scale, in Spain, Greece, the USSR, and a smattering of developing countries. In other words, the participation of only a handful of countries was necessary to solve the problem.

Again, Sweden led global efforts to bring other countries into line with the policies of the more ambitious countries (which formed the so-called Toronto Group, advocating for CFC bans, in 1983). In 1981 Sweden persuaded UNEP's governing council to establish a working group to begin discussing a possible international convention on CFC usage. The group made little headway, however. Though US industry was not explicitly opposed to globalizing existing US regulation, the Reagan administration, which took power in 1981, was ideologically opposed to strengthening global environmental governance.[9] Meanwhile, producers in Europe (specifically, the UK, France, Spain, and Italy) and Japan were vehemently opposed to substantive limits. Repeated negotiations between 1982 and 1985 resulted in deadlock. In the meantime, the CFC problem was worsening. New applications for the useful chemicals were being found, and in 1984 both US and world production passed the pre-ban peaks of the 1970s (Parson 1993: 39).

In the end, the only way the Toronto Group was able to convince the laggards to sign an agreement was to remove any reference to specific reduction obligations. The result was the 1985 Vienna

Convention for the Protection of the Ozone Layer, signed by 28 countries. Substantively, there was very little in the Vienna Convention that had not already been agreed under the Action Plan agreed in Washington in 1977 (Parson 1993). Countries agreed to coordinate scientific activities and to take appropriate action, including, possibly, negotiating binding reductions, in the future. However, the treaty further solidified the international scientific infrastructure surrounding ozone research by creating a Meeting of Ozone Research Managers, composed of government climate scientists, which pooled information on ozone depletion and its effects and reported to the Conference of Parties on what actions might be taken. It also created a system for dispute resolution between the parties, which would turn out to be useful in the future. Still, it seemed that little progress at the global level had been made between the mid-1970s and the mid-1980s.

But scientific certainty around the ozone problem was increasing dramatically in the mid-1980s. In 1984 WMO and NASA created a research program, the Ozone Trends Panel, that brought together some 150 scientists from 11 countries (Wettestad 2002: 160). More dramatically, no sooner had the Vienna Convention been signed than new scientific studies emerged that built a powerful case for more aggressive action. In 1985, the British Antarctic Survey discovered an actual hole in the ozone layer over the South Pole. The team had observed the hole for several years, but had delayed publishing their findings because the amount of depletion seemed too large to be real. Similarly, a NASA satellite had tracked the ozone hole since the late 1970s, but had disregarded the low readings as instrument error. Together, the studies suggested that ozone depletion was not only real, but potentially far more severe than had been previously understood (Parson 1993).

This solidifying scientific certainty strengthened the hand of the ambitious countries, which began pushing for a more binding protocol with the Vienna framework. The United States, having resolved its internal policy divisions, now strongly supported a binding treaty and worked to convince Japan and the European Community to commit to cuts, or at least a freeze. Internal divisions were also fraying the EC opposition, as its intransigence was sharply criticized in the press both by foreign diplomats and environmental groups. This added domestic scrutiny to the external pressures the Toronto Group was placing on its position (Benedick 1998: 71). UNEP also played a key role. Mostafa Tolba of Egypt had succeeded Maurice Strong as director, and now took a personal interest in driving the ozone negotiations forward. Tolba brought both charisma and diplomatic savvy to the negotiations, and is widely credited with forging the growing consensus around ozone protection (Benedick 1998; Andersen and Sarma 2005).

After a series of preparatory meetings, delegates met in Montreal in September 1987 to see if an agreement might be reached. After an often emotional and dramatic negotiating session, the Montreal Protocol was agreed on September 16. The final text mandated a freeze in the production of the most common CFCs by 1989, a 20 percent reduction by 1993, and a 50 percent reduction by 1998. It also required a freeze in halon production, another ODS, by 1992. A decade after they were first demanded at the 1977 Washington meeting, hard targets for CFC reductions were finally enshrined in international law.

Equally important, however, were the institutional and procedural outcomes. The Protocol established a Multilateral Fund, financed by developed countries, to fund transitions in developing countries. The Fund is governed by a separate executive committee (controlled by donors) and has a separate secretariat in Montreal. The Protocol also built on the ozone regime's scientific infrastructure by creating three panels of experts, a Scientific Assessment Panel, a Technology and Economics Assessment Panel, and an Environmental Effects Panel (there have also been ad hoc groups on other matters as they arise). For Tolba, the Protocol showed "that the environment can be a bridge between the worlds of East and West, and of North and South . . . As a scientist, I salute you: for with this agreement the worlds of science and public affairs have taken a step closer together . . . a union which must guide the affairs of the world into the next century" (quoted in Benedick 1998: 76).

Just as science had leapt ahead following the Vienna Convention, new impetus to climate efforts came just after the adoption of the Montreal Protocol in 1987. The Ozone Trends Panel (the 1984 study led by NASA and WMO) found strong evidence of the impact of CFCs on ozone in a 16 country survey. Even a research team sponsored by CFC manufacturers, reanalyzing the data, confirmed the panel's conclusion that ozone depletion was real, and was driven by CFCs (Parson 1993). Technological solutions also moved sharply forward at this time. In the wake of Montreal an industry conference in Washington brought together hundreds of industry representatives to discuss alternative technologies. Crucially, cost-effective alternatives to CFCs were within reach. At the same time, the technology panels created by the Protocol began sharing this information across countries. The panel also concluded that more ambitious reductions would be both necessary to address the problem, and technically feasible.

There was thus a clear need for deeper cooperation, and technological solutions seemed within reach. The final ingredient for the more ambitious cuts agreed at London and beyond was political salience, which also spiked at this time. Ozone began the 1970s as a relatively technical issue, of interest primarily to atmospheric scientists, but it quickly became an issue of public concern. After a dip around 1980, the issue ended the decade as arguably the dominant environmental concern of the day, particularly after dramatized reports of a growing hole in the ozone layer over Antarctica.[10]

Feeding on public concern, the US now took a more activist position. DuPont announced it would phase out production of CFCs and halons by 1999. Shortly afterward, the United States called for a complete end to production globally by the same deadline. This now put increased pressure on France and the United Kingdom. The Thatcher government had hitherto resisted environmental concerns, but as the decade closed it began shifting its position on environmental issues, largely due to pressure in Parliament. At a March 1989 meeting in London dedicated to ozone protection, France found itself alone in opposition to a CFC phase-out, and gave in, allowing the EC to join the US in its call for a complete ban on CFCs by the end of the century (Wettestad 2002). With all developed countries now essentially supporting sharp reductions in ODSs, strong regulations followed, with progressively ambitious amendments to the Montreal Protocol agreed in 1990, 1992, 1995, 1996, and 1999 (see table 4.1).

The regime's success can in large part be attributed to the absence of gridlock mechanisms. First, and perhaps most importantly, the regime largely avoided the third rail of global environmental politics, the North–South schism. During the 1970s and 1980s developing countries were marginal producers of CFCs and other ODSs. In 1986 they produced just 5 percent of the global total. The US, the EC, and Japan accounted for over 80 percent of global production (see figure 4.2). These countries possessed similar political structures, similar domestic interest groups, and similar economic conditions. Each was affected relatively similarly by ozone depletion. Once the scientific case for action on ozone had solidified and cost-effective solutions were identified, interests converged across all these countries and political solutions followed relatively quickly. Moreover, the convergence of preferences was facilitated by the process of European integration. If every European country had been free to choose its own position, it is likely that the laggards would have held out longer, as

Table 4.1 Components of the ozone regime, 1977–1999

Agreement	Date	Reductions	Institutions/ processes
Coordinating Committee on the Ozone Layer (UNEP)	1977	–	• Scientific monitoring and information sharing
Vienna Convention	1985	–	• Pooled monitoring and research • Dispute resolution system
Montreal Protocol	1987	• Basic CFCs freeze by 1989, reduce 20% by 1993, 50% by 1998 • Freeze halons by 1992	• Scientific and technology transfer panels • Multilateral Fund
London Amendment	1990	• Eliminate basic CFCs and halons by 2000 • Eliminate 12 other ODSs by 2000	
Copenhagen Amendment	1992	• Eliminate basic CFCs and other ODSs by 1996 • Eliminate halons by 1994 • Freeze HCFCs by 1996, eliminate by 2020	
Vienna meeting	1995	• Lower baseline for HCFC reductions • Freeze methyl bromide and eliminate by 2010	
Montreal Amendment	1997	• Eliminate methyl bromide by 2005	
Beijing Amendment	1999	• Ban trade in HCFCs with countries that have not ratified the Copenhagen amendment • Eliminate bromochloromethane by 2002	

Developing countries generally have a 10-year grace period for reductions.
Source: Adapted from Wettestad 2002.

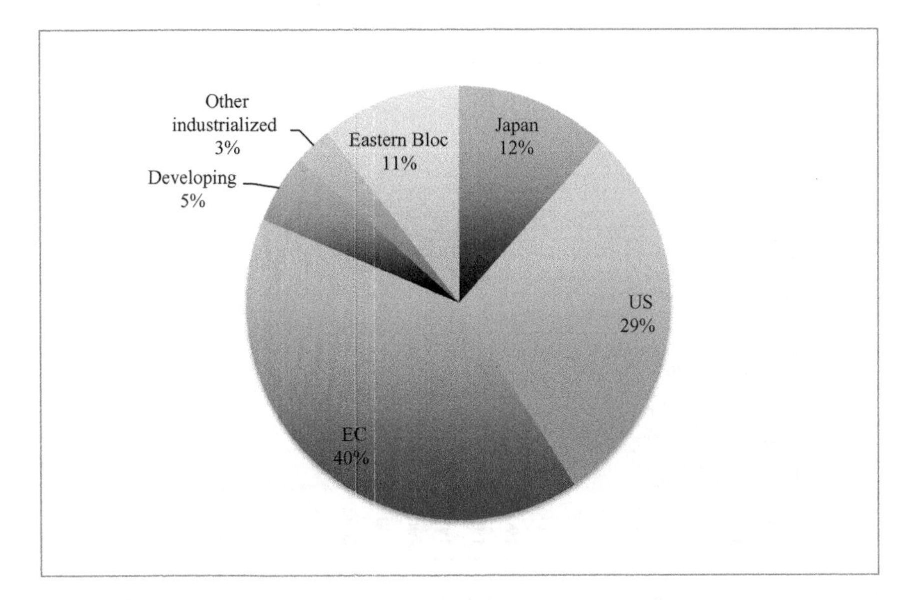

Figure 4.2 Production of ozone-depleting substances, by select countries and regions, 1986 (ODP tonnes)

Source: UN Environment Programme.

they would have faced nothing more than moral scolding from the ozone leaders. But as responsibility for ozone policy shifted to the European level, countries were forced to develop a common stance. Now ozone policy was linked to a host of other policy areas around which European governments were negotiating common positions. This linkage gave countries like Germany significant leverage over the European laggards. Absent such pressure from their European colleagues, it would have been far less costly for holdouts like France to remain outside the ozone regime.

However, in the 1980s and 1990s many developing countries were growing quickly, and anticipated greater ODS needs in the future. In the mid-1990s developing countries began producing more ODSs than the industrialized world (see figure 4.3). This did not represent noncompliance, as developing countries were given a grace period before introducing cuts. But it did create worries that the extraordinary cuts the industrialized countries had achieved would be undermined as the developing world grew increasingly industrialized. Fortunately, two developments prevented this scenario. One, the technologies the rich world had developed to replace ODSs diffused to the developing countries. This was not accidental, but rather explicitly organized by

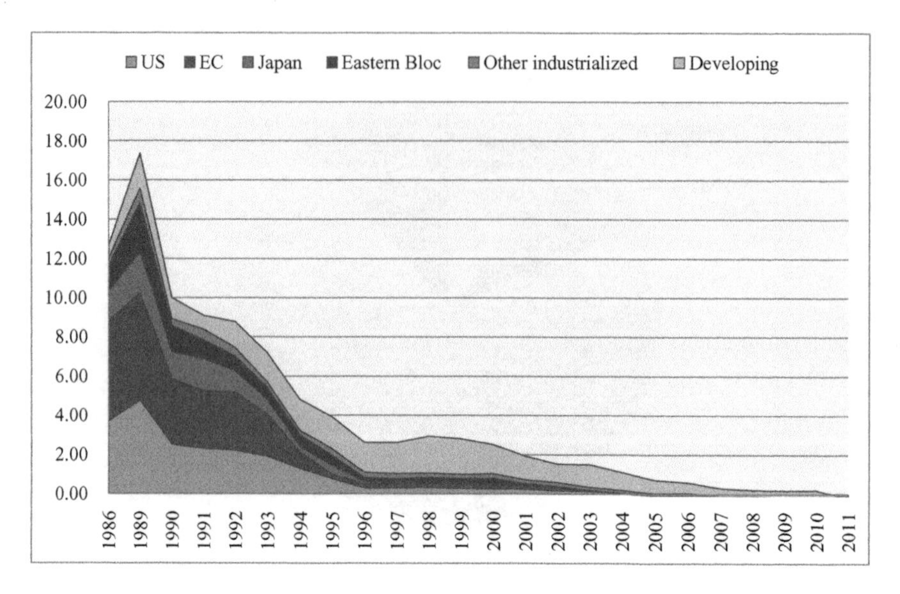

Figure 4.3 Production of ozone-depleting substances, by select countries and regions, 1986–2011

Source: UN Environment Programme.

the technical panels created by the Montreal Protocol. Two, the Multilateral Fund administered direct subsidies to the developing world to ease the cost of adopting the new technologies. Since 1991 the Fund has awarded $2.8 billion in grants to help developing countries eliminate ODSs, with funds contributed by 45 countries according to the standard UN assessment scale. These funds have financed 6,785 projects in 145 countries. Together, the Multilateral Fund and the technology transfer panels created by the Montreal Protocol essentially removed the cost developing countries would have had to pay to adhere to the regime. The developing world's production of ODSs peaked at the turn of the century, and is now below where it stood in the mid-1980s, even as those countries' share of global GDP has grown enormously (Multilateral Fund 2012).

In short, the ozone regime succeeded in large part because it only required a small number of quite similar industrialized countries to agree. Though developing countries required different targets, the cost of bringing them into the regime was fairly minimal, and readily paid by the richer nations. It is perhaps for this reason that the Montreal Protocol became the very first United Nations treaty to be ratified by every single member of the global body (UNEP 2009).

Second, ozone was set a harder problem. Though ozone depletion is vexingly global in scope and scientifically complex, solving it does not require particularly broad or deep domestic policy adjustments. Indeed, the largest producer, the United States, had enacted more ambitious regulation even before the global discussion of emissions cuts began. CFCs and other ODSs were very useful chemicals, but hardly essential to the economy. Feasible technological alternatives also lay within reach, and industry played a constructive role in developing them (though it resisted regulation throughout the 1970s and 1980s). As Wettestad notes, "After receiving the crucial international regulatory signals, market forces pretty much drove the implementation process" (2002: 153). The structure of the industry was important in this respect. A single corporation, DuPont, represented half the US market and a quarter of the global total. DuPont's size and expertise meant that it could adapt to changing regulatory patterns through innovation and economies of scale more easily than its competitors, making it less hostile to regulation than it might have been in a more competitive market. Moreover, CFCs represented just 2 percent of the massive corporation's revenues in the early 1980s (Parsons 1993: 29), meaning that regulation was hardly an issue of corporate survival. Once DuPont had begun developing effective alternatives, other firms had little choice but to adopt them as well.

More broadly, though estimates of the overall cost of eliminating ODSs are subject to significant degrees of uncertainty, every serious cost-benefit analysis shows that the gains in reduced health impacts far outweigh the adjustment costs. The most widely cited study by the Canadian government estimated the total global adjustment costs (for industry, governments, and consumers) at around $235 billion (in 1997 dollars), which is about 0.0004 percent of global GDP (Bornman and van der Luen 1998). In sum, this was not a particularly "hard" problem.

Finally, the ozone regime suffered from neither fragmentation nor institutional inertia. At the Vienna meeting that led to the 1985 Convention, WMO and UNEP competed to host the regime's secretariat. Scientists wanted the WMO to lead on the issue, reflecting that organization's apolitical nature and technical proficiency, while policy-makers favored UNEP (Wettestad 2002). However, once this minor issue was resolved, the political leadership of UNEP and the general cohesiveness of the international scientific community meant there were few conflicts or redundancies (Haas 1991). And because ozone depletion was a new issue, no existing institutional arrangements existed to impede efficient problem-solving.

A New Foundational Moment? From Compromise to Gridlock at Rio

In sum, the environmental regimes that succeeded in the 1970s and 1980s were those that largely avoided the mechanisms of gridlock. They were typically negotiated between relatively small groups of countries with similar interests, and the nature of the issues meant that there were relatively few "veto players" that had to be accommodated. The domestic policy adjustments required were relatively low, and were amenable to relatively cost-effective technological adjustments. The preexisting institutional landscape (e.g. UNEP, WMO) served as a useful focal point and springboard for new institutions, tending not to reinforce dysfunction or render cooperation more complex.

However, other environmental problems were tackled at the same time as these issues, and with mixed success, such as forests (see below). By the late 1980s, and particularly following the strong outcomes of the ozone regime, the international environmental movement had reached a new inflection point. Could the successful regimes of the 1970s and 1980s be consolidated and built upon? As the twentieth anniversary of the Stockholm summit drew near, environmentalists pushed for a new "foundational moment" in global environmental politics. The conceptual groundwork for a new "global deal" had been laid over the course of the 1980s. In 1983 the General Assembly passed a resolution establishing a World Commission on Environment and Development (WCED) to "propose long-term environmental strategies for achieving sustainable development to the year 2000 and beyond." These included concrete "ways in which concern for the environment may be translated into greater co-operation among . . . countries at different stages of economic and social development," and also the more conceptual goal of defining "shared perceptions of long-term environmental issues and of the appropriate efforts needed to deal successfully with the problems of protecting and enhancing the environment" (UN Doc. A/RES/38/161).

This Commission's most lasting impact was on this latter, more conceptual goal. The UN Secretary General asked Gro Harlem Brundtland, who had served as prime minister of Norway, to chair the new group of "eminent persons," which carried out three years of consultations around the world. In 1987 the Commission issued the so-called Brundtland Report, *Our Common Future*, which remains perhaps the most eloquent and powerful argument for "sustainable development" – a term WCED did not invent but did much to develop and place firmly in the public lexicon. *Our Common Future* argued that sustainable development should be conceived as three essential pillars: economic growth, environmental protection, and social equality. In the short run, it might be possible to achieve just one or two of these goals, the report argued. Indeed, economic growth could arguably be achieved more quickly by neglecting the other two. However, in the long run, society required all three in order to build a stable foundation for prosperity and well-being; otherwise efforts to meet the current needs of human beings would compromise the ability of future human beings to meet their own needs. Today this tripartite, intergenerational framing may seem obvious (if idealistic), but at the time it represented a significant conceptual change from the way many policy-makers, activists, and citizens thought about environmental issues.

The Commission also recommended more concrete policy changes in a range of issue areas. Despite some successes, the authors noted that "most of the institutions facing [environmental] challenges tend to be independent, fragmented, working to relatively narrow mandates with closed decision processes." Instead, a more holistic view was required. Though it stopped short of recommending a fully fledged global environment organization, the Commission did call for additional resources and authority to be bestowed upon UNEP. It also called on all international organizations to "ensure that their programmes encourage and support sustainable development, and they should greatly improve their coordination and cooperation."

The strongest institutional recommendation in the report, however, was the recognition that "the international legal framework must also be significantly strengthened in support of sustainable development."[11] This recommendation was adopted by the UN General Assembly in 1989. Resolution 44/228 called for a United Nations Conference on Environment and Development (UNCED) to be convened in Rio de Janeiro in June 1992, 20 years after the Stockholm meeting. It also established a series of Preparatory Committee meetings ("PrepComs") to negotiate on key points in advance of the conference itself. Maurice Strong, who had worked so hard and so effectively to coordinate the 1972 Stockholm conference, was brought back to organize the UNCED secretariat as the Secretary General of the conference.

The Rio Earth Summit of 1992 was the most ambitious effort to manage our global commons ever attempted. Larger than any diplomatic gathering that had taken place before, the Rio Summit brought together 167 countries, 150 of which were represented by their heads of state or government, including the major powers. This amounted to some 5,000 governmental delegates. But even this army of diplomats was vastly outnumbered by the 25,000 NGO representatives who filled the parallel forum meeting nearby. One UNEP official estimated the total cost of the process at half a billion dollars (Palmer 1992: 1009).

The scale of optimism and ambition surrounding the event was similarly unprecedented. Rio aimed to give practical meaning to the balance between development, social equality, and environmental protection that the Brundtland Report had laid out. In broad terms, this would require a kind of grand bargain in which developed countries would assist developing countries financially and technically in exchange for firm commitments from those countries to adopt pro-environment policies on issues like forests and the atmosphere. All countries would have to be willing to forgo some sovereignty in order to place joint limits on activities that harmed the natural world. Such a deal had been struck for ozone, but could it be reproduced on a far grander scale? As Strong noted in his opening speech, Rio would "define the state of political will to save our planet" (quoted in Palmer 1992: 1007).

Tragically but perhaps predictably, it turned out that the state of political will was insufficient to generate outcomes worthy of the conference's ambitions. Some important steps forward were made, but, as in Stockholm, these were more prospective than concrete. New agendas and targets were set, but it was not clear how to pursue them. Given the scope and complexity of the issues, agreement would have been difficult even if countries had basically wanted the same things. One observer described the proceedings as "a chaotic process more akin to a street brawl than a diplomatic meeting" (quoted in Palmer 1992: 1014). But the same issues that had prevented a strong agreement at Stockholm 20 years earlier were again on display at Rio, and in the four PrepComs that led up to it. Indeed, under the deepening logic of gridlock, they were stronger than ever.

The North–South divide

Though the concept of sustainable development was now universally accepted in the rhetoric of rich and poor alike, a fundamental barrier to a "global deal" at Rio remained the fact that for many issue areas wealthier countries prioritized the "sustainable" part while poorer nations insisted on the "development" part. In forests, for example, the G7 had called for a binding agreement on forest protection to be agreed at Rio. But developing states like India and Malaysia flatly refused (see below).

The heterogeneity of interests represented at Rio was exacerbated by the conference's adoption of a consensus-based process. Every country had to agree to every word, and this meant that any state was able to block international regulation of its pet issue. Oil-producing states blocked energy measures. The United States blocked calls to reduce consumption. Tropical states blocked efforts to limit the logging of rainforests. The Vatican and Islamic states blocked calls for family planning. As it turned out, the lowest common denominator of 167 countries is very low indeed.

Already in the preparatory meetings it was clear that countries had the ability to effectively kill most proposals that went against their interests, or at least to ensure that whatever they agreed would have little practical effect. By the end of the fourth PrepCom some 85 percent of the draft text had been negotiated, but very little of substance had been agreed. Many of the most important topics – forests, the atmosphere, and crucially, financing – remained to be worked out (S. Johnson 1993: 4). A global deal thus still seemed possible as delegates began to arrive in Rio.

Ultimately, however, the North–South split over financing prevented a stronger outcome. UNCED estimated that all of the recommendations the final conference document put forward would cost about $600 billion per year to implement, with a need for $125 billion of that to take the form of additional financial assistance from North to South (CSD 1992). The South took the position that all of this money would have to represent new commitments, and not be redirected from existing aid flows. Some wealthy countries in Europe, as well as Japan, did indeed offer substantial increases in their foreign aid. But the final figure on offer was less than $10 billion. For the developing world, this low bid was simply a nonstarter.

Sovereignty and environmental problems

The other fundamental barrier to success at Rio was the unwillingness of countries to delegate control over environmental issues to collective decision-making. Here the United States stood out as a major obstacle. Environmental interests at the conference, and European states in particular, had pushed delegates to adopt a firm stance on a relatively newly recognized problem known as global warming. Most of the OECD countries were willing to adopt a goal of limiting emissions to 1990 levels by the year 2000 (which would have represented a significantly more ambitious target than they later agreed to in the 1997 Kyoto Protocol, see below), but the United States, alone, refused. This disunity among the industrialized countries gave the developing countries few incentives to adopt reduction targets of their own, and no climate agreement appeared at Rio.

The failure of the United States to lead was a widespread problem. During the 1970s and even in the 1980s the United States had consistently been a relatively ambitious country. But the administration of George H. W. Bush took a more skeptical position toward the conference. In the end, only the fact that Rio was taking place just a few months before an election – and that environmental issues were publically popular in the US in the early 1990s – likely persuaded Bush to attend the conference. But such a minimal gesture was insufficient to drive a deal, as William Reilly, Bush's own Environmental Protection Agency director, made clear in a memo to EPA employees in the wake of the conference:

> Another key question, frankly, is why did the United States play such a low-key defensive game in preparing for Rio? We assigned a low priority to the negotiations of the biodiversity treaty, were slow to engage the climate issue, were last to commit our President to attend Rio. We put our delegation together late and we committed few resources. No doubt this contributed to the negative feelings toward the United States. (Quoted in Palmer 1992: 1006)

The results of Rio: exhortations and further negotiations

Given these barriers, it is thus not surprising that Rio did not give adequate institutional support to the vision of sustainable development outlined in *Our Common Future*. Instead, the largest diplomatic meeting ever convened generated an enormous number of suggestions, or "soft law." At best, it was a roadmap and a framework for future action. Several key outcomes can be identified.

First, the Rio Declaration affirmed the concept of sustainable development the Brundtland Report had outlined, and enshrined 27 principles as the official norms to which the 157 members of UNCED aspired. The declaration was symbolic, but important on that level, recalling the role the Universal Declaration of Human Rights had played in laying out a series of principles in that field. For example, the precautionary principle received a soft endorsement.

Second, and more concretely, the delegates at Rio adopted Agenda 21, a 40-chapter, 600-page action plan that made specific recommendations to governments and international bodies on almost every environmental and development-related issue. That so many issues were negotiated and agreed through a consensus-based process is a testament to the heroic negotiation efforts. But the purely hortatory nature of the recommendations reflects the deep barriers to agreement. Countries argued bitterly over Agenda 21, but in the end it imposed no binding commitments on them. As one observer noted, the document contains "quite a lot of mush" (Palmer 1992: 1019).

Third, Rio established a new institution through which progress on Agenda 21 would be evaluated and reported, and where new actions might be taken. Countries essentially agreed to make permanent the process they had spent the last three years participating in. A Commission on Sustainable Development was created, an intergovernmental body that meets annually, reporting to the General Assembly via ECOSOC. While CSD is more intergovernmental in nature, focused on its annual conferences, its mandate inevitably overlaps significantly with that of UNEP.

Fourth, and more concretely, Rio generated three agreements on specific issues: forests, biodiversity, and climate.[12] None of these created specific commitments for countries, but, like the 1985 Vienna Convention for the Protection of the Ozone Layer, created scientific processes and frameworks that, it was hoped, might lead to future agreements.

In sum, then, like Stockholm, Rio was no Bretton Woods. It did not commit countries to specific actions that would reduce overuse of the global commons. It did not create a "grand bargain" that would give meaning to the concept of sustainable development. And it did not create stronger intergovernmental institutions that would be able to coordinate policy in the future. Still, while few observers left Rio feeling that they had "saved the world," many hoped that the lofty principles in the Rio Declaration, the ambitious plan laid out in Agenda 21, and the more specific negotiations envisioned in the forest, biodiversity, and climate conventions would push the world toward greater cooperation in the future. As UNEP executive director Mostafa Tolba cautioned delegates, "Probably, it will take us several years before we ascertain that this meeting in Rio has entered that select pantheon of events which truly marked a turning point in the affairs of mankind" (quoted in S. Johnson 1993: 8).

Tragically, some two decades later, it is clear that the conference did not start the world on a path of deeper environmental cooperation. Though subsequent years would see a major increase in activity in international environmental policymaking, results were in short supply. Rio marked a new deepening of gridlock, initiating a period in which multilateral environmental governance has fallen further behind the growing need to manage the interdependence created by our unhealthy relationship with the natural world.

ENVIRONMENTAL GRIDLOCK

Self-Reinforcing Interdependence and the Global Environment

Today, many of the environmental problems that first inspired activists in the 1960s and 1970s have been remedied in the wealthy parts of the world. Dickens would not recognize London today. The presence of airborne toxins in the UK has fallen by 70 percent from the early 1980s (Medical News Today 2008). In the United States, pollutants like SO_x and NO_x have fallen by 60 percent since the introduction of the Clean Air Act, and the number of Americans with access to water that meets health standards improved from 79 percent in 1993 to 92 percent in 2008 (EPA 2012).

But the gains in the wealthy countries on some issues must be balanced against the sharp deterioration of the environment in many areas of the developing world. Today, it is not London that suffers from excessive "fog" but cities like Beijing, where, remarkably, the government continued to employ the same term used in *Bleak House* until public outrage, fueled by social media, forced it to accept the obvious. Now, however, the choice of language is a deliberate euphemism, as smog is politically sensitive, and for good reason. The WHO estimates that some 300,000–400,000 people die prematurely in China each year because of air pollution (Cohen et al. 2004). That is more than ten times the number of people killed in the wartime Blitz. Moreover, some studies suggest that up to a third of China's emissions are driven by exports (Weber et al. 2008), implying that some of the environmental successes in the rich countries have not derived from absolute improvements, but rather from transferring pollution, along with manufacturing, to the developing world. Still, the environmental crisis is now on such a scale that "outsourcing" pollution is decreasingly feasible for the wealthy. During some periods of the year, coal-related pollution from China drifts all the way across the Pacific Ocean, where it can form up to 20 percent of the air pollutants found on the West Coast of United States (Bradsher and Barboza 2006). This last point reveals the fundamental reality of environmental issues today. Regardless of how we add up the balance of improvement versus deterioration at the local or national level, the global trend is decidedly negative. The vast increase in human production and consumption over the postwar era has fundamentally changed the nature of environmental problems, rendering them ever more systemic.

How did we reach this point? As usual, the Brundtland Commission presciently and eloquently captured the growing interaction between the globalizing economy and the deepening reality of ecological interdependence in *Our Common Future*:

> These related changes have locked the global economy and global ecology together in new ways. We have in the past been concerned about the impacts of economic growth upon the environment. We are now forced to concern ourselves with the impacts of ecological stress – degradation of soils, water regimes, atmosphere, and forests – upon our economic prospects. We have in the more recent past been forced to face up to a sharp increase in economic interdependence among nations. We are now forced to accustom ourselves to an accelerating ecological interdependence among nations. Ecology and economy are becoming ever more interwoven locally, regionally, nationally, and globally into a seamless net of causes and effects. (WCED 1987)

The expansion of the industrial economy has now reached a point where pollution does not just affect one species, one watershed, or even one ecosystem – it alters the entire Earth system. Ecologists increasingly understand the "environment" as a single global system made up of numerous subsystems – the climate, the oceans, plant and animal life, etc. – that interact with each other in extremely complex ways. Many of these interactions are poorly understood, but what seems clear is that humankind's intervention across them is now the primary factor driving the system as a whole. As a leading group of ecologists explain:

> Half of Earth's land surface has been domesticated for direct human use. Most of the world's fisheries are fully or over-exploited. The composition of the atmosphere – greenhouse gases, reactive gases, aerosol particles – is now significantly different than it was a century ago. The Earth is now in the midst of its sixth great extinction event. The evidence that these changes are affecting the basic functioning of the Earth System, particularly the climate, grows stronger every year. The magnitude and rates of human-driven changes to the global environment are in many cases unprecedented for at least the last half-million years. (Steffen et al. 2004: 2)

Hence, the Anthropocene. Figure 4.4 captures just some of the changes in the natural world that humankind has wrought. While most trends show a rapid increase from the Industrial Revolution onward, note how many of the trends have undergone step-changes in the postwar period.

The primary driver of this crisis is unprecedented industrial production and consumption, the Great Acceleration of the postwar period. There are many indicators of this growth, but the consumption of oil and coal, the two chief power sources of the twentieth century, is perhaps the most telling. As figures 4.5 and 4.6 demonstrate, both the absolute expansion of industrialization and its diffusion around the world – principally to Asia – characterized the postwar period.

Of course, not all industrialization is driven by globalization, and not all globalization can be attributed to the peaceful, stable, and liberal postwar order. Rather, we can think of globalization and its institutional underpinnings as principal catalysts for the diffusion of industrialization, and thus for its ecological impacts. In other words, in some ways the present global environmental crisis, and the powerful interdependence it imposes on each inhabitant of the planet, is an unintended consequence of the postwar order. It is therefore unsurprising that many environmental issues from the 1970s onward show characteristics of gridlock.

Just as the problems themselves have undergone the Great Acceleration in the postwar years, since the Rio conference environmental gridlock has grown from a tendency into the defining trend. Environmental problems have grown more severe, but efforts to manage them have stalled (note the fall-off in environmental treaty-making in figure 4.1 above). Below we show how the gridlock mechanisms have come to stymie efforts to manage our global commons in two key issue areas: forests and climate. But before turning to those issues, consider some general manifestations of gridlock in current global environmental governance.

First, though the North–South divide has always plagued global environmental cooperation, the expanding economic power of developing countries – and the associated ecological impact – has exacerbated the problem severely. If the developed world is largely responsible for the damage to the environment thus far, it is the developing countries that are on course to finish it off. Moreover, globalization has pushed industrialization from countries with strong environmental protections (and the political institutions that underpin them, such as a strong rule of law, participatory political institutions, and an

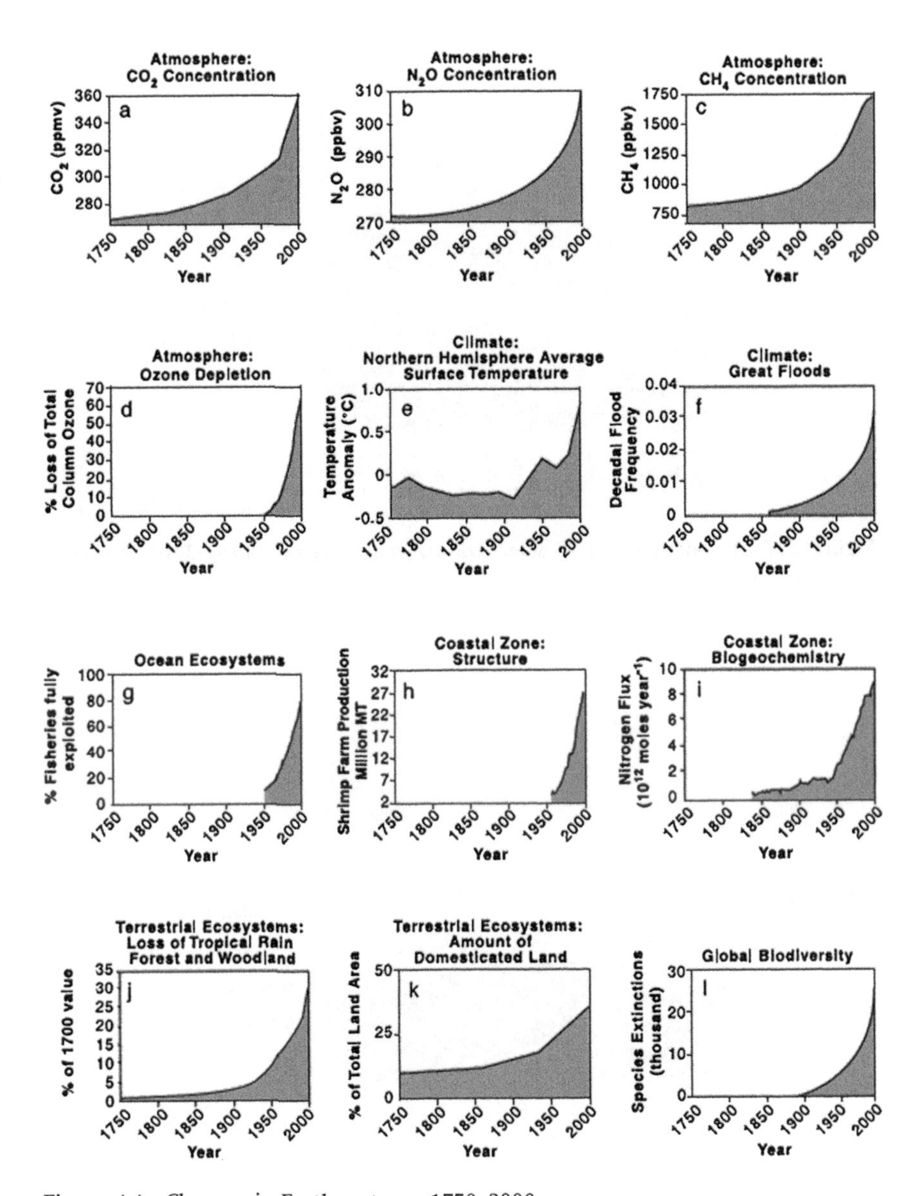

Figure 4.4 Changes in Earth systems, 1750–2000

Source: Steffen et al. 2011.

active civil society) to many countries that have historically lacked such protections.

Second, contemporary environmental problems also penetrate more deeply into domestic policy choices – and daily life – than

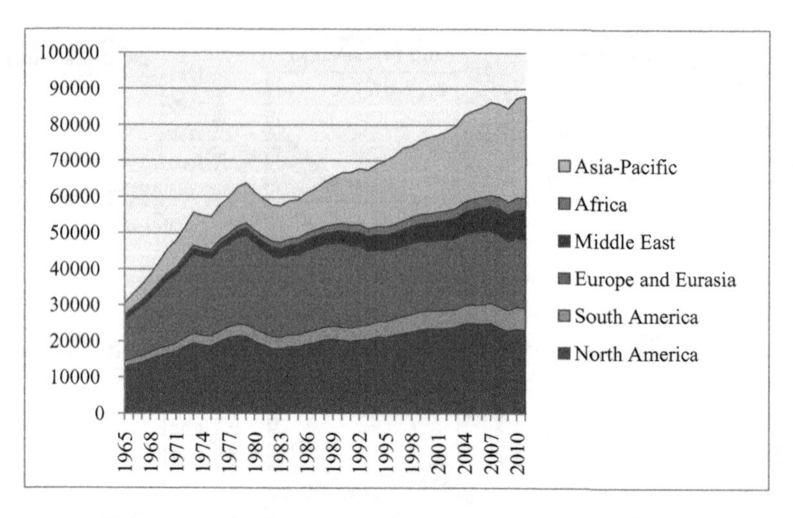

Figure 4.5 Oil consumption, by select countries and regions, 1965–2010 (thousand barrels per day)

Source: BP 2012.

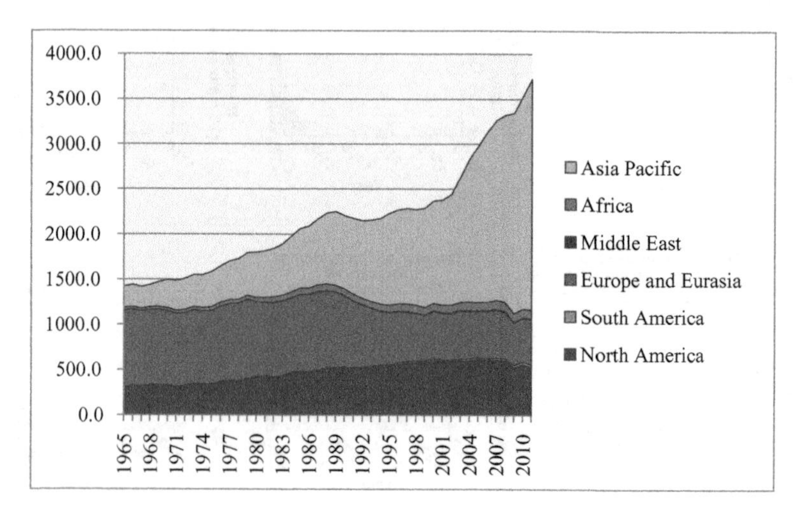

Figure 4.6 Coal consumption, by select countries and regions, 1965–2010 (million tons oil equivalent)

Source: BP 2012.

previous issues. As we discuss below, problems like climate change implicate almost every action we take every day in some way. But at the same time, perversely, it is more difficult to galvanize public sentiment around systemic issues, which seem remote compared to clean air, clean water, and the other tangible concerns that mobilized mass environmental politics in the twentieth century. Activists therefore find it more difficult to generate pressure on governments to address such problems.

Third, as the problems get worse, we find ourselves now hobbled by the weak, fragmented array of institutions created over the last 40 years. These institutions have both locked in dysfunctional decision-making procedures and increased the transaction costs of negotiating new deals.

Fourth, the successful examples of environmental cooperation have given policy-makers a set of templates that are ill-suited to problems like forests or climate change. The "convention and protocols" model, which worked so well for ozone and a number of other regimes, has been applied to issues like forests, biodiversity, and climate, with much worse results. This copying of successful examples is logical for policy-makers with limited resources (Ovodenko and Keohane 2012), but has proven insufficient to manage growing environmental challenges.

In sum, to the extent that the postwar order facilitated the globalization of industrialization – and it is certainly difficult to see how it would have reached such a scale without a stable, open, peaceful global economy – then the environmental problems that follow from it can be considered in some part endogenous to the process of cooperation itself. The expansion of the scale of environmental problems from the level of the Bacarra-Zantar to the globe therefore represents one of the strongest forms of endogenous interdependence, broadly understood.

Yet, since 1992, there has been *no* major environmental success at the multilateral level. Instead, gridlock has set in. Again, a comprehensive review is beyond the scope of the present book, but even a brief survey of some central issues reveals the difficulties of meeting the needs of second-generation interdependence problems through multilateral means. While any number of issues might have been selected, we focus on two issues that were given specific agreements at Rio: forests and climate.

Forests

Forests provide a mix of public and private goods to people both near and far. They can be cut down to provide fuel, farmland, or tradable commodities that benefit some local groups, multinational wood-product companies, and consumers in far-off lands. But left intact they provide homes and livelihoods for traditional communities, support industries ranging from nut production to ecotourism, and mitigate a host of local environmental threats such as erosion, water pollution, and desertification. At the global scale they are the Earth's most important repository of biodiversity, and the principal source of new medical compounds. Perhaps most importantly, they are the planet's lungs; the Amazon alone produces about 15 percent of the oxygen we breathe (Malhi et al. 2008). But despite these global effects, trees themselves, unlike ozone, whales, or migratory birds, remain firmly rooted in national territories, subject to local control and sovereignty. Moreover, not all forests are created equal. While the northern forests cover more land area, tropical forests, covering only 2 percent of the Earth's surface, are home to half its species of plants and animals (TNC 2012). Of the plants identified by the US National Cancer Institute as useful in the treatment of cancer, 70 percent occur only in rainforests, but only around 1 percent of rainforest species have been analyzed for their medicinal value (TNC 2012).

The precise rate of deforestation at the global level is difficult to calculate, although advances in satellite imaging technology are making it easier to measure remote regions. There is consensus, however, that humans have destroyed about half of all forests in the world since the Industrial Revolution, the vast majority in the last 50 to 60 years (TNC 2012). Tropical forests have faired even worse, with just 2.6 million of the original 6 million square miles still intact (TNC 2012). However, signs suggest that the rate of deforestation is slowing. The Food and Agriculture Organization estimates that the world lost 8.3 million hectares per year in the 1990s, and "only" 5.2 million hectares per year from 2000 to 2010. This is still, however, an annual loss equal to the size of Costa Rica (FAO 2010), and more than high enough to leave dozens of crucial forest ecosystems in danger of collapse.

The diverse array of functions that forests perform in both the economy and the ecosystem, locally and globally, makes them difficult to govern. It is significant, for an argument about "gridlock," that one of the leading studies of the international forest regime is entitled *Logjam: Deforestation and the Crisis in Global Governance* (Humphreys 2006). Since the Rio summit, countries have attempted to negotiate a global agreement on forest conservation, but have never succeeded. Instead, they have been forced to settle for a series of voluntary principles countries may choose to follow. At the same time, a number of private, market-based schemes have attempted to harness the power of green consumers to force changes, but these programs fall far short of the scale needed to address the problem. Below, we show how the gridlock mechanisms have prevented effective governance of this crucial ecosystem.

Development of the forest regime

International attention to forest conservation dates back as far as the creation, in 1892, of the International Union of Forest Research Organizations (Humphreys 1996: 22). Forestry also fell under the mandate of the UN's Food and Agriculture Organization, which set up a Forestry Committee in 1971, though this body was initially more dedicated to economic management than conservation. Modern attempts to protect forests at the international level began in the 1970s with large environmental organizations like WWF raising the issue in the IUCN, UNEP, and other fora (Keck and Sikkink 1998). In 1980 these three organizations issued a World Conservation Strategy that framed the problem of forest degradation as a global issue and laid out a list of actions that countries could take to protect forests.

However, the first intergovernmental agreement on forests originated not in the environmental sphere, but under the auspices of UNCTAD, created in the 1970s to increase the standing of developing countries in the global economy. Part of UNCTAD's work involved organizing the commodity trades on which so many developing countries depended, including the trade in forest products. Technical negotiations on this subject began under UN auspices in 1976.

Over the course of the 1980s and early 1990s forests gained new political salience, particularly in northern countries. Tropical forests in particular captured the public imagination, as activists exhorted people to "Save the Rainforest" (Keck and Sikkink 1998). The issue proved easy to communicate to the public at large, which embraced forest conservation as a tangible and visceral manifestation of environmental problems. A 1995 poll placed the issue slightly ahead of climate and ozone as a public concern in both developed and developing countries (Bloom 1995). This activism led northern countries to push for a more conservation-oriented agreement. In 1983 a bargain was struck between consumers in the North and producers in the South, the International Tropical Timber Agreement (ITTA). Producing countries agreed to develop and implement national plans to enhance sustainability, for which they would receive financial support and technical assistance from northern consumers. A new intergovernmental organization, the International Tropical Timber Organization (ITTO) was created in 1986 to monitor and facilitate this deal. Importantly, this somewhat unique cross between a trade-commodity organization and a conservation body does not impose limits on deforestation beyond what countries decide for themselves in their national forestry strategies. Nor has it been a vehicle for significant financial transfers from North to South. Though the ITTA has been updated twice (in 1994 and 2006), and includes the vast majority of both producers and consumers, it has done little to stem deforestation. Agreement has been possible, unlike in the CSD process (see below), but only because ambition has been low.

The 1980s also saw the adoption of the ill-fated Tropical Forestry Action Plan, under which the World Bank, FAO, UNDP, and the non-governmental World Resources Institute joined forces to develop a list of forest projects in participating countries – most of which never occurred – as well as a series of bilateral "debt for nature" swaps. However, by the end of the decade the focus of forest conservation efforts became the Rio Earth Summit. Rich countries were eager to negotiate a binding forest convention at the summit that would commit all countries – but especially those that controlled tropical forests – to mandatory conservation measures. A "grand bargain" was imagined in which developed countries would transfer resources and expertise to developing countries in exchange for binding commitments to halt deforestation.

However, advocates underestimated the opposition from timber-rich developing countries like Malaysia, which insisted that forests fell under national sovereignty, not the "common heritage of mankind." No forest treaty emerged from Rio, though delegates did agree to include an aspirational chapter on forests in the summit report (Chapter 11) and adopted a "Non-legally Binding Statement of Principles for a Global Consensus on the Management, Conservation and Sustainable Development of All Types of Forests" (the "Forest Principles").

Formal intergovernmental negotiations did not end after the failure at Rio, however. The newly created Commission on Sustainable Development was scheduled to address the issue at its 1995 meeting. In 1993 and 1994 Malaysia and Canada chaired a joint Intergovernmental Working Group on Forests that brought developed and developing countries together to discuss forestry issues. While not a negotiating forum, the group built trust and confidence on the issues, and revived some of the hopes that the contentious meetings at Rio had dashed. Still, when formal multilateral negotiations on forests resumed at the

1995 CSD meeting, no major decisions were made. Instead, delegates agreed to create a new group, the Intergovernmental Panel on Forests (IPF), which would serve as a subsidiary of the CSD (including 53 CSD members and any other states that wished to join). The IPF was tasked with five issues: implementing the Rio agenda, financial assistance and technology transfer, scientific research and assessment, trade and certification schemes, and institutional structures and agreements, including the possibility of adopting a binding forest treaty. At four meetings spread across two years, countries and a number of IGOs and NGOs struggled through this agenda. Instead of a "traditional" secretariat, the intergovernmental process was supported by an ad hoc group of several different international organizations called the Interagency Taskforce on Forests.[13]

As at Rio, northern and southern countries tried to strike a "grand bargain" under which developing countries would make firm commitments for forest protection in return for additional resources from the developed world. But the financing issue continued to block progress, with developed countries demanding that developing countries make more efficient use of existing resources, and developing countries insisting that existing aid flows were not sufficient (Humphreys 2006: 34). The wealthy countries sought to emphasize the possibility of private financial flows for forest conservation, but these were not specified. The developing world's calls for a global forests fund went unheeded.

Countries' positions on a possible forest treaty had evolved since Rio. The US, once one of the strongest supporters, was now opposed to a binding instrument (Humphreys 2006: 43). Meanwhile, a number of members of the G77 bloc of developing countries, mostly in Africa, had come to support a treaty. Even Malaysia, the most vocal opponent of an agreement at Rio, said it would support a convention that contained adequate financing provisions. NGOs, for their part, worried that any convention would serve more to enshrine weak management practices. In the end, the IPF left the decision of whether to open negotiations on a binding forest convention to the CSD.

The IPF thus had little progress to report when its mandate expired in 1997. But instead of beginning negotiations on a more binding instrument, or ending the discussions altogether, countries decided to keep talking. At the 1997 CSD meeting they created a follow-up body, the International Forum on Forests (IFF), to pursue a broadly similar agenda. The Interagency Taskforce for Forests was again retained to support this work. As before, progress proved elusive, with little agreement on financing or a legal convention. Countries became particularly bogged down in discussions of how a potential convention would treat so-called "traditional forest-related knowledge," the body of ideas and practices employed by people, including indigenous groups, who lived in and used forests. Developing countries wanted these practices to be defended under intellectual property laws, but multinationals argued that doing so would inhibit their ability to develop useful compounds, and especially medicines, from forests. It was by no means obvious what angle of the issue the forestry regime in particular might address, as parallel discussions were taking place under the WTO related to the TRIPS convention (see chapter 3), in the World Intellectual Property Organization, and in the Convention on Biological Diversity process.

When the IFF's mandate expired in 2000 it had little to show beyond an agreement, phrased in language contorted to match the underlying disagreement, to "consider with a view to recommending the parameters of a mandate for developing a legal framework on all types of forests" (quoted in Humphreys 2006: 89). However, the one thing delegates had managed to agree on was to continue the intergovernmental process in yet another successor body, this one designated the UN Forum on Forests (UNFF). This body continues as the chief intergovernmental forum dedicated solely to forest issues to this day.

Like its predecessors, UNFF is a subsidiary of ECOSOC but, unlike them, it boasts a universal membership, and thus represented a slight institutional strengthening. It has also featured events beyond intergovernmental meetings, including a series of ministerial meetings, stakeholder dialogues, and an expanded role for experts. And the body's "secretariat" has been expanded to include several more international institutions (and was renamed the Collaborative Partnership on Forests). However, just like its predecessors, UNFF has made little further progress on the issues discussed since before Rio. Indeed, it has indefinitely postponed the question of whether to begin negotiations on a forest treaty. Instead, it has created a voluntary set of principles, a so-called Codex Sylvus modeled on the Codex Alimentarius (a set of food safety standards developed by the FAO and WHO). However, critics have noted that these principles offer little beyond what was agreed in the original Forest Principles in 1992 (Humphreys 2006: 115). In other words, countries have debated forests for some two decades now, but have ended up just where they started.

Alongside the stalled UN process, NGOs and businesses have created a number of private governance schemes that seek to promote forest conservation – or, as some observers believe, retard it – via market-based certification. These programs ask forest managers, harvesters, and other companies in the value chain to adhere to certain standards. Companies that comply with these voluntary regulations, as certified by independent auditors, earn the right to label their products as sustainable. Consumers can then use this information to ensure their purchases support well-managed forestry. The first major such initiative began at the behest of WWF in 1991, and in 1993 it was launched as the Forest Stewardship Council (FSC). This innovative organization has members representing environmental, business, and social interests. Its principles, which are negotiated between stakeholders from all of these groups, thus seek to give practical meaning to the tripartite vision of sustainable development outlined in the Brundtland Report (Viana et al. 1996; Bartley 2003; Cashore et al. 2004; Pattberg 2005, 2011).

Though some businesses chose to work within the FSC, others found it too "environmental," and could not be persuaded to join either via moral suasion or market pressure. Nonetheless, these firms recognized that certification and labeling could increase or protect their market share, and so set out to create their own private governance schemes. Industry groups in Canada (Canadian Standards Association) and the United States (Sustainable Forestry Initiative) created competitor schemes to the FSC that most NGOs have criticized as insufficiently stringent. European producers in turn created their own competitor, the Pan-European Forest Certification scheme, which was similarly criticized by NGOs. More recently, these various industry groups have merged into the Programme for the Endorsement of Forest Certification (PEFC), a global, industry-led certification scheme. Instead of applying universal principles negotiated among the relevant stakeholders, the industry version simply asks companies to mutually recognize each other's certification standards.

States have recognized the role that private certification schemes can play in global forest governance since the mid-1990s. The IPF officially endorsed the development of voluntary forestry codes, largely at the insistence of NGOs, but refused to go beyond that. After nearly two decades of operation the private schemes have grown considerably. By Fall of 2012 the FSC had certified some 162 million hectares and the PEFC 240 million hectares. These are enormous swathes of land, but still account for just 4 and 6 percent of all the world's forests, respectively. Moreover, 80 percent of the FSC-certified forests are in Europe and North America, with Latin America accounting for just 7 percent of the FSC's certified forests, Africa 4 percent, Asia 3 percent, and Oceania 2 percent (FSC 2012). PEFC is even more concentrated in the North, with over 90 percent of its acreage in North America and Europe (FSC 2012; PEFC 2012).

Most recently, forest governance has become largely tied up with an even larger environmental problem, climate change. Deforestation likely accounts for 15–20 percent of greenhouse gases. The biomass of the Amazon alone holds as much carbon as humans emit globally over a decade, at current rates (WWF 2007). Forests thus represent a key opportunity to make progress on mitigating greenhouse gases. In 2008, countries created the United Nations Collaborative Programme on Reducing Emissions from Deforestation and Forest Degradation in Developing Countries (UN-REDD). This body seeks to help countries develop national plans to use forest-related measures to combat climate change, providing the technical and (some of) the financial resources for them to do so. UN-REDD, and the wider REDD+ initiative, have the potential to direct vast new resources to forest conservation. But they also place new demands on forest governance, along with a new institutional framework and a host of new stakeholders. As table 4.2 shows, the overall forest regime has grown remarkably complex.

Multipolarity

"Power" in negotiations over the forest convention is largely based on how much forest a nation controls. By this measure, the countries in the "Forest G20", which together account for 80 percent of the world's forests, are a very heterogeneous group (see table 4.3), ranging from wealthy, to middle income, to desperately poor. The group of countries that controls most of the world's tropical forests is less heterogeneous, but includes many of the poorest countries on Earth. Countries like Brazil or Indonesia could effectively veto global forest cooperation.

Given this distribution of power, to achieve the kind of "global deal" envisioned at Rio wealthy countries would have needed to offer significant financial incentives, or other kinds of carrots and sticks, in order to elicit the cooperation of poorer countries. But they did not. Although forests were politically salient, and governments in the North benefited politically from being seen to be active on the issue, the total amount of resources that could be devoted to forest protection, given political constraints, remained far below the demands of the developing world.

Table 4.2 Components of the forest regime

Regime component	Date	
FAO Committee on Forestry	1971	Committee at which heads of national forestry services could discuss issues of international concern
World Conservation Strategy	1980	Action plan for forest conservation
International Tropical Timber Organization/ Agreement	1983	National forestry plans in tropical countries, technical assistance from North
Tropical Forestry Action Plan	1985	Series of forest conservation projects promoted by northern NGOs and donors, limited impact
Chapter 11 of Agenda 21	1992	Nonbinding recommendations for forestry actions and policies
Forest Principles	1992	Nonbinding principles for forest management
Forest Stewardship Council	1993	Private, market-based labeling scheme for forest products (NGO oriented)
Canadian Standards Association (CSA)	1993	Private, market-based labeling scheme for forest products (firm oriented)
Sustainable Forestry Initiative (SFI)	1994	Private, market-based labeling scheme for forest products (firm oriented)
World Commission on Forests and Sustainable Development	1995–9	Panel of eminent persons to build consensus on governance of forests
Intergovernmental Panel on Forests (IPF)	1995–7	Subsidiary of CSD, intergovernmental negotiation on forest issues
International Forum on Forests (IFF)	1997–2000	Subsidiary of CSD, intergovernmental negotiation on forest issues, successor to IPF
Programme for the Endorsement of Forest Certification (PEFC) (SFI and CSA affiliated)	1999	Private, market-based labeling scheme for forest products (firm oriented)

Table 4.2 *(Continued)*

Regime component	Date	
UN Forum on Forests (UNFF)	2000	Subsidiary of CSD, intergovernmental negotiation on forest issues, successor to IFF
Voluntary agreement on forests, "Codex Sylvus"	2007	Nonbinding principles on forest management
UN-REDD	2008	Inclusion of forests as carbon sinks in the climate regime and various emissions trading schemes

If this grim political calculus made a deal at Rio extremely unlikely, it renders it all but impossible today, with consumption of forest products shifting from relatively green countries in North America, Europe, and Japan to emerging markets (figure 4.7). As noted above, private certification schemes like the FSC and PEFC show a similar disparity. These schemes have been able to use activist pressure to force retailers in large northern markets to adopt FSC-certified products. For example, after a concentrated activist campaign, Home Depot, the largest retailer of forest products in the United States, pledged to purchase FSC-certified wood. But the group faces great challenges in China, which is now the world's second largest market for timber, pulp, and paper, and where the FSC certifies only a tiny fraction of products (WWF 2012).

A harder problem

Forest conservation is a hard problem. In some ways, trees form part of the global commons: producing oxygen, sequestering carbon, providing medicines, and housing biodiversity. But they are also exploitable as private goods, both as internationally traded commodities like timber and paper and as local sources of fuel or, once destroyed, pasture and farmland. And they also provide local public goods ranging from water filtration, to erosion control, to natural beauty. For many indigenous people, forests are not only the only means available of making a living, but also the center of their cultural and spiritual life. Ironically, the broad utility of forests generates a welter

Table 4.3 The "Forest G20"

Country	Forests (mil ha)	% of world	Country	Tropical forests (mil ha)
Russia	809	20%	Brazil	481
Brazil	478	12%	Congo	177
Canada	310	8%	Indonesia	127
United States	303	8%	Peru	75
China	197	5%	Bolivia	65
Australia	164	4%	Angola	50
DR Congo	134	3%	Venezuela	50
Indonesia	88	2%	Mexico	49
Peru	69	2%	India	43
India	68	2%	Central African Republic	42
Sudan	68	2%	Myanmar	42
Mexico	64	2%	Papua NG	37
Colombia	61	2%	Mozambique	35
Angola	59	1%	Zambia	31
Bolivia	59	1%	Cameroon	30
Venezuela	48	1%	Paraguay	25
Zambia	42	1%	Malaysia	25
Tanzania	35	1%	Rep. of Congo	24
Argentina	33	1%	Gabon	22
Burma	32	1%	Guyana	18

Note that different studies were used to estimate total forests and tropical forests. As the methods for estimating forest coverage in remote regions are quite imprecise, there can be considerable discrepancy between the numbers reported for some countries.
Source: Food and Agriculture Organization.

of competing claims that renders their governance extremely complicated.

But though forests form, in part, a key element of the global commons, they are of course firmly rooted in the jurisdiction of nation-states. Indeed, the designation of forests as the "common heritage of mankind" has been rejected by local users and the forest-rich states. The sovereignty costs of submitting forests to global control are high, as deforestation cannot be solved by simply installing more green technology as with, say, air pollution. Rather, it requires the entire social and economic fabric of forest-dependent communities to

Fibreboard

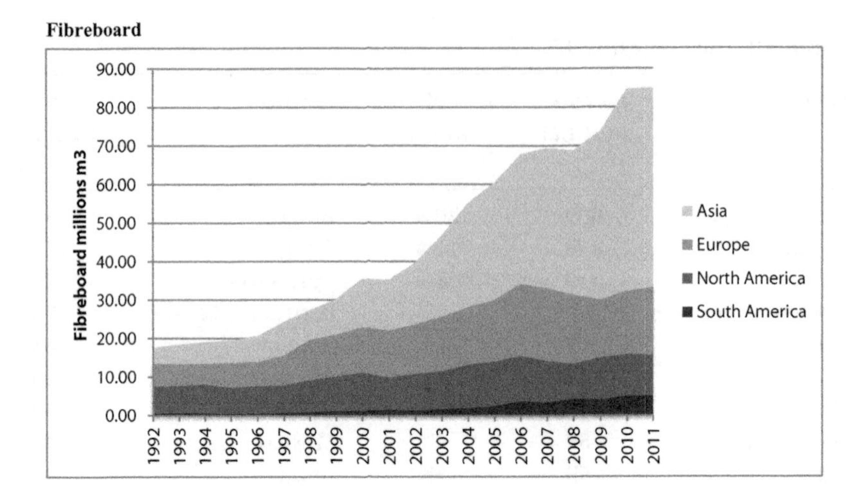

Paper

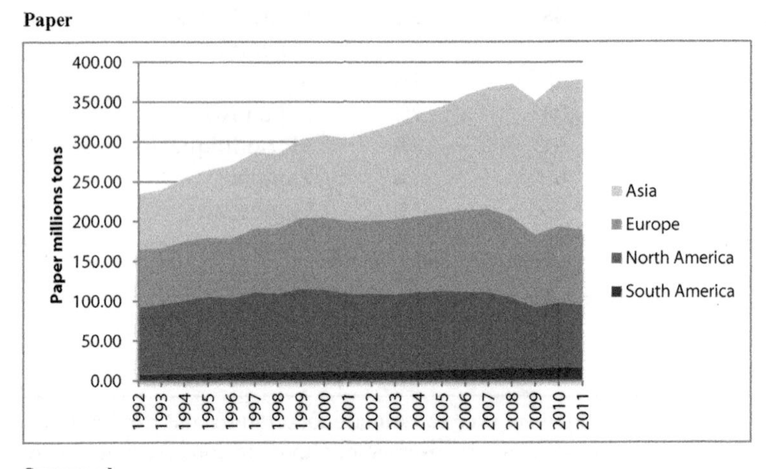

Sawnwood

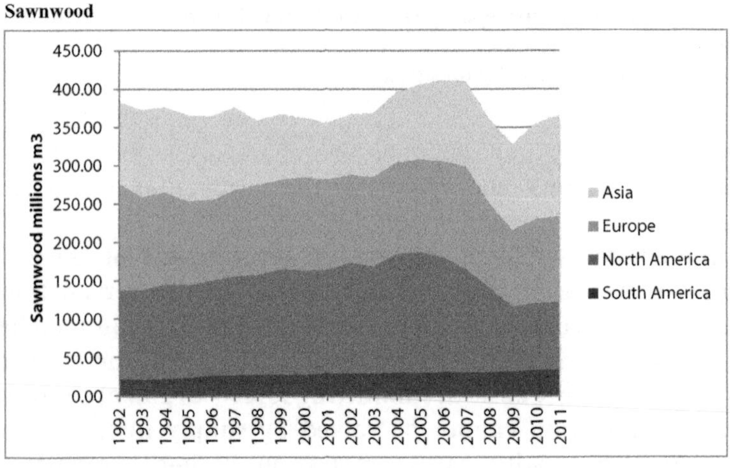

Figure 4.7 Consumption of selected forest products by region, 1992–2011

Source: Food and Agriculture Organization.

change. Alternative livelihoods must be created for loggers and farmers, and forest product companies, which often wield considerable political power, must be either incorporated in the solution or bought off.

Effecting these changes is difficult even in wealthy countries. But because so many forests, especially tropical forests, are located in lower-income and/or weak states, the problems are significantly more difficult. In many parts of the world the state, or agencies or local authorities within it, in fact owns forests, and profits directly from their exploitation (98 percent of African forests are owned by public entities, FAO 2012). Timber-rich countries are therefore loath to give up an important source of government revenue. And even when the state wants to manage forests sustainably, it often finds implementation difficult. The remoteness of many forests and the weakness of the states in which they grow have made illegal logging a major barrier to effective conservation. Interpol estimates the value of the illegal timber trade at $30 billion per year, or about a quarter the size of the legal trade (Melik 2012). Much of this trade operates through global criminal networks that exploit corrupt officials at the local level. NGOs estimate that more than half of deforestation in Brazil, Russia, and Indonesia can be attributed to illicit activities (Toyne et al. 2002). Even if there were a global agreement to limit deforestation, implementation would be extraordinarily difficult.

Fragmentation

In the forest regime, fragmentation has fueled gridlock, and gridlock has fueled fragmentation. Since before Rio, responsibility for forests has been dispersed across a wide range of institutional settings. At least four types of global institutions bear on forests. First, a number of technically oriented intergovernmental institutions, chiefly the FAO and ITTO, monitor global forests and the trade in their products. The 14 international organizations with some say on forest policy are grouped together as the Collaborative Partnership for Forests, the "secretariat" for the UNFF, but there is little coordination at the programming level. Each of these institutions is focused on a different aspect of forests. For example, the FAO secretariat, populated chiefly by forestry experts, is concerned with managing forests as a sustainable resource, UNEP, staffed with ecologists, focuses mainly on biodiversity and conservation, and the World Bank, charged with fighting poverty, aims to provide alternative livelihoods. These goals are not mutually exclusive, but they entail different trade-offs and allocations of scarce resources.

Second, there are the competing private certification schemes. While the FSC, at least, has had significant successes, these schemes remain far from a comprehensive solution to the problem. More controversial is the question of whether they divert political will from formal legal solutions, and if so, whether that effect is good or bad. We have no comparable case to measure against, of course, but given the other barriers to cooperation in this area, it seems unlikely that the marginal impact of the certification schemes is the key factor holding back agreement. But even if we can be relatively certain that the certification schemes are not preventing a global deal, the question remains whether they are distracting from other kinds of solutions, such as a "minilateral" treaty or, more ambitiously, more formal government-backed sanctions on trade in unsustainable wood products.

Third, there is a range of related international regimes that have major implications for forest governance. For example, global intellectual property rules affect how governments regulate the genetic resources in their forests. If strong patent protections are awarded to multinational pharmaceutical firms, for example, it may affect the ability of indigenous groups to use or profit from their traditional medicinal practices. Similarly, to the extent that the biodiversity regime guides governments' behavior, it may lead them to discount other aspects of forest governance. Finally, since the climate regime began accepting forestry related actions (preserving "carbon sinks," reforestation, etc.) as part of countries' carbon budgets, powerful new incentives have been put in place to preserve carbon in the form of trees. While this can be an opportunity for forests, it also represents an additional, partially competing claim on them.

And fourth, there is of course the CSD process and its latest incarnation, the UNFF. After 20 years of talks, countries have essentially "agreed to disagree," with no binding convention now being actively promoted. It is difficult to evaluate the impact of the Codex Sylvus, as it is purely hortatory, but its effects lie at the level of information-sharing and norm-building, not concrete policy change. Given that the only international body dedicated solely to forest issues, in their entirety, has reduced the scale of its ambitions to voluntary principles, a leadership vacuum has emerged in global forest governance that promotes *further* fragmentation. In contrast to regimes like ozone, where a strong series of agreements brought previously disparate actors together, forests have lacked a strong institutional focal point. Instead, other regimes and existing institutions, public and private, have filled the gap. As these processes have institutionalized, they now make future coherence even less likely.

In sum, forests have become gridlocked, or "logjammed," as Humphreys (2006) puts it. And the failure of global governance has itself become something of a self-reinforcing process. With agreement unlikely, activists have largely given up trying to coordinate at the global level. As one veteran of global debates on forests has noted,

> Throughout the 1980s and 1990s there was a groundswell of support for the idea that international political action was the key to success. Now, in the early years of the 21st century, people are tiring of endless meetings and negotiations that produce few, if any, visible outcomes. The groundswell is moving towards local action. Community management, devolution and decentralized governance are seen as the new beacons of hope. (Jeffery A. Sayer in Humphreys 2006: xi)

Climate Change

Certain atmospheric gases like methane, nitrous oxide, ozone, and, chiefly, carbon dioxide act as a blanket around the Earth, holding in the heat of the sun by preventing it from radiating back into space. These greenhouse gases (GHGs) occur naturally, but humans have increased them dramatically since the start of the Industrial Revolution, mostly by burning fossil fuels (see figure 4.8). GHGs released anywhere change the climate everywhere, making climate change perhaps the most perfect example of a deep form of interdependence at work. Because so many of our basic activities – heating, transportation, manufacturing, consumption, farming – affect the climate, every person's actions have an impact on every other person. Moreover, because GHGs can persist in the atmosphere for 100 years or more, we are also affected by the actions of past generations, just as future generations are dependent on the choices we make.

Of the few threats that could fundamentally alter life on Earth and, with it, human civilization – such as nuclear war, a superdisease, a meteor impact – climate change is among the most certain. There is no scientific disagreement that man-made gases are altering the composition of the Earth's atmosphere, with profound implications for the world's temperature, sea levels, weather patterns, and a host of

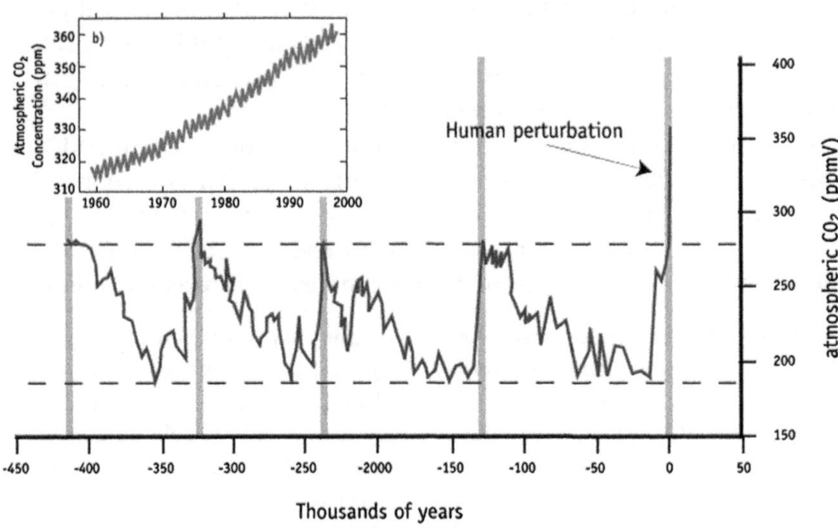

ppm = parts per million; ppmV = parts per million by volume

Figure 4.8 Atmospheric CO_2 concentration from the Vostok ice core record with recent human perturbation superimposed

Source: Steffen et al. 2004 (recent human perturbation measured by the Mauna Loa Observatory).

other natural systems. We are less certain, however, exactly what the nature of these disruptions will be. Even if we had frozen emissions at 2000 levels (which we did not do, see figure 4.14 later in the chapter), the Intergovernmental Panel on Climate Change (IPCC) predicts that average temperatures would still increase half a degree Celsius over the next century. A more likely outcome is a 1–6 degree average temperature change, depending on what actions we take (IPCC 2007). A 2 degree change, the ceiling countries have chosen to aim for, would still result in higher seas, a massive increase in species extinctions (including the devastation of the world's coral reefs), lower crop yields, increased disease, and less potable water (see figure 4.9). The impact of a 5 degree change is all but inconceivable. The choice is stark. If we decisively reduce the amount of carbon and GHGs we release into the atmosphere, we can reasonably expect to limit the impacts of a changing climate to difficult but ultimately solvable problems. But if we do not, the natural world and human civilization will change in ways we can scarcely imagine. Unfortunately, this quintessential collective action problem is also a quintessential case of gridlock in global governance.

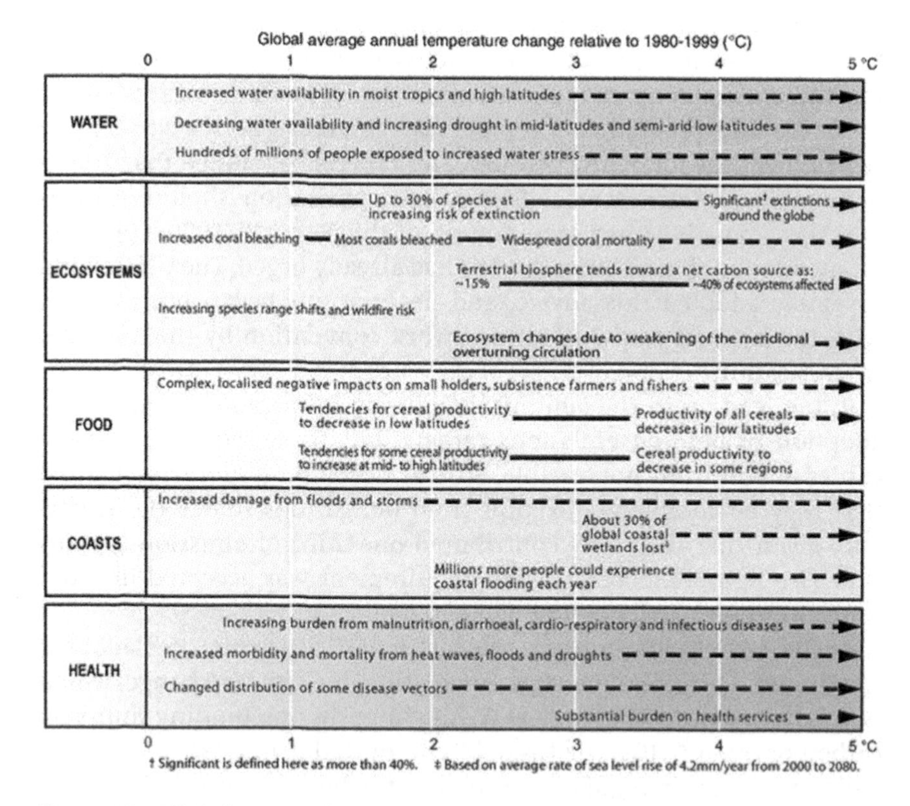

Figure 4.9 Likely impacts of climate change over the next century

Source: IPCC 2007.

Overview of the climate regime

International efforts to control anthropogenic climate change formally began in 1988 at a Toronto conference organized by UNEP and the WMO. With the Montreal Protocol (agreed the previous year) fresh in their minds, delegates called for a 20 percent cut in GHGs below 1988 levels by 2005 – a target based more on symbolism than science, as no one really understood what would be required to solve the problem (none of the governments making the pledge would come close to meeting it). That same year, the UN General Assembly voted to create the IPCC, a body of climate scientists from various countries mandated to assess the science of climate change and its impact on the world in order to provide a basis for policy-making. Perhaps alone within the climate regime, this body has achieved the task set out for it, coordinating climate research and giving the world a scientific gold standard on which to make policy decisions.

The IPCC released its first assessment report in 1990, declaring: "Emissions resulting from human activities are substantially increasing the atmospheric concentrations of the greenhouse gases" (IPCC 1990: 52) and predicting a temperature increase of 1.5–4.5 degrees Celsius over the following century. The experts concluded that "international negotiations on a framework convention should start as quickly as possible after presentation of this Report" (1990: 60), a recommendation that UNEP and WMO had already urged. The UN General Assembly adopted this advice, and negotiations began immediately with the hope of agreeing a framework convention by the 1992 Rio Earth Summit.

In the lead up to the summit, ambitious countries pushed for the adoption of binding emissions targets, but these were quickly discarded as politically not feasible. Instead, developing countries insisted that they be completely exempt from obligations under the treaty, and, given that they only contributed one-third of emissions at this time (see figure 4.15 below), this requirement was accepted in order to secure their participation.

At the 1992 Earth Summit, the vast majority of countries adopted the United Nations Framework Convention on Climate Change, which now boasts some 195 members. While imposing no binding limits on carbon or other GHGs, the UNFCCC committed countries to study the issue and to meet regularly to discuss further measures. The ozone regime, now bolstered by the 1990 London Amendment, was explicitly cited as a model. The idea was, first, to bring all countries together to study the issue, and to create a forum for sharing information and building trust, as the 1985 Vienna Convention for the Protection of the Ozone Layer had done. Then to begin to negotiate specific, binding commitments, beginning with small steps (the 1987 Montreal Protocol) and, with growing consensus and economic innovation, moving on to more ambitious measures (the London Amendment).

At first this model seemed to work well. Negotiations on a more binding climate agreement began in 1995, after the UNFCCC entered into force, and led, in 1997, to the Kyoto Protocol. Under this agreement industrialized countries – listed in the first appendix of the treaty, and therefore called the "Annex I" group – agreed an average 5.2 percent reduction in carbon emissions below 1990 levels. This was far less ambitious than was required to solve the problem, but seen as an important first step. Developing countries were not given national reduction targets, though they were encouraged to participate in the Clean Development Mechanism (CDM) and other so-called "flexibility measures." These schemes allow rich countries or their companies to undertake GHG reduction projects in developing countries, where reductions are technologically easier and more cost-effective, and use the saved carbon against their own quotas.

The ink was not even dry on the Kyoto treaty before problems began to emerge, however. First, it became clear that the world's largest emitter at the time, and a driving force behind a climate treaty, had made commitments at the international level that it was unable to keep. As the Kyoto negotiations were being finalized, the US Senate passed a resolution, 95–0, declaring that the United States would never ratify a treaty that did not contain specific requirements for all large emitters, including developing countries. The Clinton administration signed Kyoto anyway, but never attempted to push it through the Senate. Because the treaty required countries representing 55 percent of global emissions to ratify it before it came into effect, US rejection delayed the start of the Kyoto process until 2005, when Russia joined (because Russia's baseline target was fixed before the economic collapse that followed the end of the Soviet Union, compliance was essentially costless for Russia, which in fact benefited from selling carbon credits to Europe; see below).

Second, Kyoto reinforced the exemption of developing countries from reduction targets, and reaffirmed their "right" to development. In view of the historical responsibility of wealthy countries for emissions, as well as their higher per capita emissions, this type of bifurcation was clearly justified. The United States and Europe (27 members of the EU) each counted for about 30 percent of cumulative emissions, while China and India counted for just 5 percent and 1 percent, respectively (see figure 4.13 below). But, tragically, the rapid growth of emissions in the developing world meant that fairness was decreasingly compatible with a safe climate. Even if rich countries had reduced greenhouse gases to zero, the developing world alone would still be on course to radically alter the Earth's climate under a "business as usual" scenario (see figure 4.15 below).

Third, the one area of Kyoto in which developing countries did participate were the flexibility mechanisms, the Clean Development Mechanism and the joint implementation programs. Many of the negotiations immediately post-Kyoto focused on figuring out how these should be structured. But the CDM and other carbon markets have been plagued with implementation difficulties, in large part because they are extremely complicated to administer (Wara and Victor 2008). To be effective, carbon markets must allow buyers to pay countries and firms to take carbon-mitigating measures that they would not otherwise take. That is, they trade in counterfactuals, which are phenomenally difficult to certify and measure. It is therefore difficult to say whether the GHG reductions processed by the CDM (or other carbon markets) are "real" reductions, or only represent actions taken to meet market demand. China, which has provided over 60 percent of carbon credits under the CDM (UNFCCC 2012), demonstrates these difficulties. The country has invested significantly in renewable energy, and nearly every new wind farm, solar station, and other renewable power source in the country has applied for CDM credits. Individually, this makes sense, as these projects reduce reliance on coal. But taken together the implication is that not one of China's investments would have happened without CDM funding, a nonsensical result that belies the efficiency justification underpinning the market logic. Worse, the CDM has encouraged businesses that produce powerful greenhouse gases such as hydrochlorofluorocarbons (HCFCs) to continue doing so, as the price companies can get from the gas is about 70–90 times the cost of destroying them. It is more profitable for them to produce the gases, destroy them, and receive payments through the CDM than to change to an alternative business model.

Kyoto entered into force in 2005, but was set to expire at the end of 2012. In 2007, therefore, countries began negotiations on a successor treaty, again following the "ratcheting" logic of previous environmental treaties, heroically – perhaps stubbornly – attempting to push past the various difficulties that had emerged in the Kyoto process. These efforts came to a head in Copenhagen in December 2009.

The scale of the Copenhagen conference, as well as the expectations that preceded it, were reminiscent of the 1992 Earth Summit in Rio. Ambitious countries and activists alike framed the summit as a make-or-break opportunity to secure a global deal. Some 50,000 people attended the formal negotiations or the civil society forum nearby, including 115 heads of state or government, not to mention a bevy of celebrities and former leaders. After dragging along for nearly two weeks, the negotiations came to a dramatic conclusion on the final night when US President Barack Obama and Secretary of State Hillary Clinton burst into a private meeting of the heads of the Indian, Chinese, and Brazilian delegations and hammered out a rough agreement that would later be endorsed by the rest of the summit. Despite these efforts, no global deal was struck. Much blame was placed on China in the aftermath of the summit (the Chinese delegation did not come prepared to negotiate beyond the narrow instructions it had received from Beijing), but the truth was that few countries were able to offer the kinds of ambitious reductions that would have made a deal meaningful (Conrad 2012). In the end, delegates officially endorsed the goal of limiting the average temperature increase to 2 degrees Celsius and created a system through which countries could make pledges regarding actions they would take at the national level to achieve these goals. In the subsequent months, pledges came in, but even if these had been successfully implemented, they would have come up far short of the 2 degree goal (UNEP 2010).

Just as in the forest regime, voluntary targets took the place of binding commitments, which had proven not to be feasible to negotiate. The next meeting of the UNFCCC, in Cancún, was markedly different from Copenhagen in its tone. Mexico, the host, went to great lengths to find agreement between the key players well in advance of the meeting, and, after the Copenhagen debacle, governments were eager to be seen to be making progress. But perhaps the most important ingredient behind the "success" of Cancún was the reduction in expectations and ambitions that had followed Copenhagen. The Cancún Agreement essentially formalized the "pledge and review" system that was the de facto result of Copenhagen. A year later, in Durban, delegates managed to agree, in principle, to open negotiations on an agreement "with legal force" – a heavily debated and intentionally ambiguous phrase – that would include both developed and developing countries. In other words, to carry on the negotiations that had begun two years before the 1992 Earth Summit (Eckersley 2012).

In the meantime, Kyoto was set to expire on December 31, 2012. Just a month before, at multilateral negotiations in Doha, a weak agreement to extend the treaty to 2020 among some of the existing members was reached, but these countries accounted for just a fraction of global emissions. And despite the treaty's low ambitions, its results have been meager. Formally, most countries have met their official targets, many relying on the flexibility mechanisms. But if we look at real changes in national emissions, the only countries that have met their obligations in a meaningful way are the more environmentally oriented European states and Japan (see figure 4.10), which would likely have reduced emissions anyway (Japan, at any rate, has opted out of the extension to 2020). The post-Soviet states have also reduced emissions, but largely because their economies collapsed in the early 1990s. Some wealthy countries like Australia, Canada, and Switzerland have flagrantly increased their own emissions, even if flexibility mechanisms kept them in technical compliance, and the United States never joined. It is therefore hard to categorize Kyoto and its extension as anything but a failure. In terms of total GHGs

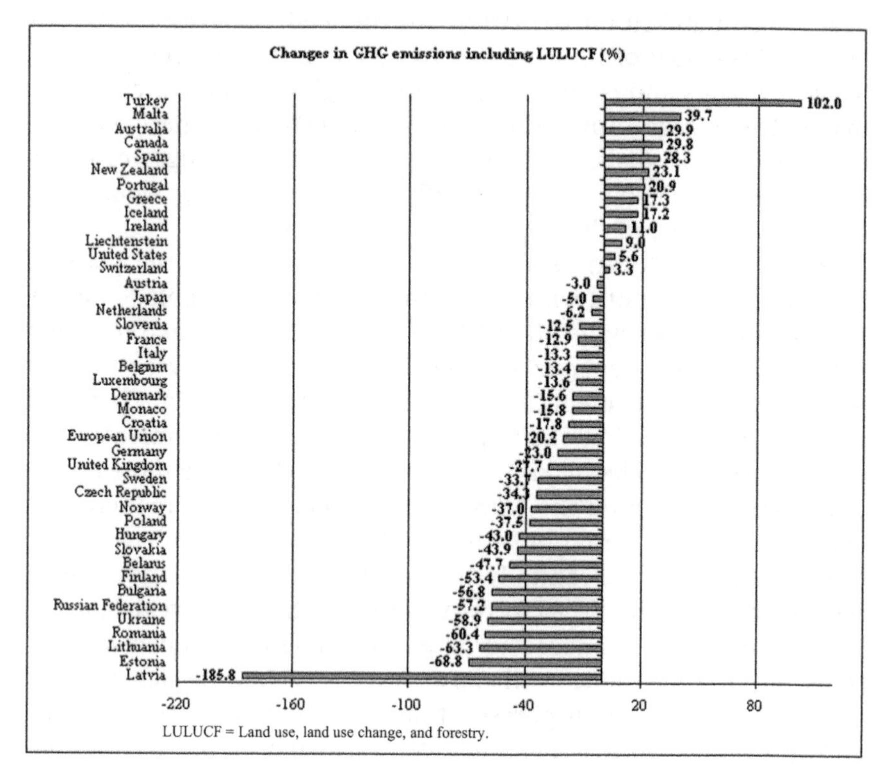

Figure 4.10 Change in greenhouse gas emissions of Annex 1 countries, 1990–2009

Source: UN Framework Convention on Climate Change Secretariat.

prevented, the UNFCCC estimates that actions under Kyoto prevented a total of 1,500 megatons of CO_2 eq from entering the atmosphere (UNFCCC 2011). This number is impressive, but negligible compared to the growth of the emerging markets. The year on year increase in China's emissions alone from 2009–10 and 2010–11 exceed this sum (UNFCCC 2011).

In the meantime, a host of parallel initiatives have appeared at various levels. At the intergovernmental level, in 1997 the European Union committed its member states to reductions beyond their Kyoto requirements, and it later mandated even deeper cuts. In 2006, the United States, Australia, Japan, South Korea, China, and India created an Asia-Pacific Partnership on Clean Development and Climate to facilitate technology exchange between them. While this initiative and related bilateral exchanges have led to some useful partnerships, they have not had an appreciable impact on the emission trajectories of the countries involved. The same can be said for the Major Economies Forum on Energy and Climate (MEF), an organization launched by the Bush administration that brings together 17 of the world's largest economies,[14] developed and emerging, to seek consensus without the cumbersome UN apparatus. This kind of "club" approach has been advocated as a more realistic way to address climate change (Victor 2011a), but it has yet to show results. Efforts by the G20 and the G8 to address the issue have similarly come to naught.

These international public initiatives have been accompanied by an enormous range of subnational and transnational initiatives. For example, several American states and Canadian provinces, led by California, have enacted regulations similar to those imposed by Kyoto, often cooperating regionally. At the municipal level, hundreds of mayors of 59 large cities have, with the support of the Clinton Global Initiative and the World Bank, convened a C40 Large Cities Climate Leadership Group to promote solutions in the world's largest metropolises. This group has implemented policies that will reduce GHG emissions by 250 megatons a year by 2020 (Bloomberg 2012). These figures can amount to substantial changes. In the United States, for example, Congressional inaction has stunted national efforts to limit emissions. But state- and city-level targets cover some 45 percent of US emissions, a figure equal to the annual emissions of Japan and Germany combined (Lutsey and Sperling 2008).

In China as well, intransigence at the level of international negotiations stands in contrast to ambitious experimentation at the national and regional levels. China's 11th Five Year Plan aimed to cut the carbon intensity of China's economy (the ratio of CO_2 emissions to GDP) by 20 percent by 2010, a goal it largely achieved. The current 12th Five Year Plan aims for a 17 percent reduction by 2015. This will still allow the total amount of emissions to grow considerably, but represents a serious effort that stands alongside other ambitious targets, like the aim to generate 20 percent of the country's energy from renewable sources by 2020, or the introduction of test-run cap-and-trade programs in some cities and regions in 2013.

Private initiatives have also emerged. On the NGO side, these include WWF's Climate Savers program, the Pew Center on Global Climate Change's Business Environmental Leadership Council, and Environmental Defense Fund's Partnership for Climate Action, all of which commit participating corporations to reduce their carbon emissions to some extent. The Business Roundtable's Climate RESOLVE program is a similar initiative from the business community. The Carbon Disclosure Initiative, also a business initiative but midwifed into being by the UK government, is a coalition of institutional investors with US$41 trillion under management that asks companies to report on their carbon footprints and identifies industry leaders.

The proliferation of climate governance institutions has been so vast that leading scholars now speak not of the "climate regime" but the "regime complex for climate change" (Keohane and Victor 2010; see table 4.4 and figure 4.11) or even the "transnational regime complex for climate change" (Abbott 2010). Recent efforts to map the universe of transnational climate governance (Bulkeley 2010; Hale and Roger 2011; Hoffmann 2011) reveal dozens of programs involving almost every country in the world (see figure 4.12).

Multipolarity

Climate change embodies a fundamental injustice. Rich countries are responsible for most of the GHGs currently in the atmosphere, and enjoy most of the benefits of these emissions in the form of higher living standards. As figure 4.13 shows, the legacy of industrialization in the rich world means that the EU and US alone are responsible for half of the gases currently warming the planet. China and India are, together, responsible for just 10 percent, even though they are home to over one-third of the world's population. Wealthy countries have been enjoying the luxury of emissions for 150 years now, and still enjoy higher per capita emissions than most poor countries. For these

Table 4.4 Components of the core climate regime

Regime component	Date	Description
Intergovernmental Panel on Climate Change	1988	Scientific monitoring and analysis
UN Framework Convention on Climate Change	1992	
Kyoto Protocol	1997	• Developed countries average 5.2% reduction below 1990 levels by 2012 • Clean Development Mechanism • Joint implementation
Bali Roadmap	2007	
Cancún Agreements	2010	

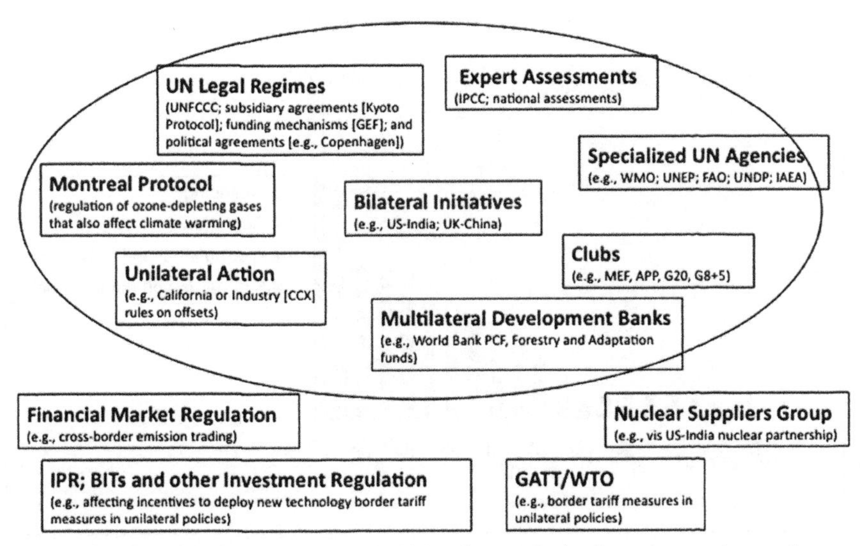

"Boxes show the main institutional elements and initiatives that comprise the climate change regime complex … Elements inside the oval represent forums where substantial rule making has occurred, focused on one or more of the tasks needed to manage climate change; elements outside are areas where climate rule making has required additional, supporting rules" (Keohane and Victor 2010: 5).

Figure 4.11 Regime complex for climate change from Keohane and Victor 2010

reasons, the developing world has long maintained that justice requires steep cuts in rich countries' emissions, with guarantees that poor countries can continue emitting in pursuit of their development goals. This idea of "common but differentiated responsibilities" is enshrined at the core of the UNFCCC.

But the distribution of emissions in 1992, when countries met in Rio to launch the UNFCCC, bears decreasing semblance to emissions today. As figure 4.14 shows, developing and emerging countries now emit more than the rich world. And the data in the graph, which end in 2008, do not capture the full extent of this shift. As this book went to press, one estimate put China on track to emit nearly twice as much as the US in 2012, which would put it on a par with the EU on a per capita basis, and on course to overtake the United States in per capita terms by the end of the decade (Olivier et al. 2012). And this comes despite a concerted effort by the Chinese government to improve energy efficiency.

Worse, nearly all future increases in emissions will come from the developing world. The International Energy Agency estimates that by 2035 the non-Annex I countries will emit nearly two-thirds of the world's total GHGs (see figure 4.15). And if emissions in fact reach those levels, the results will be nothing short of catastrophic. In other

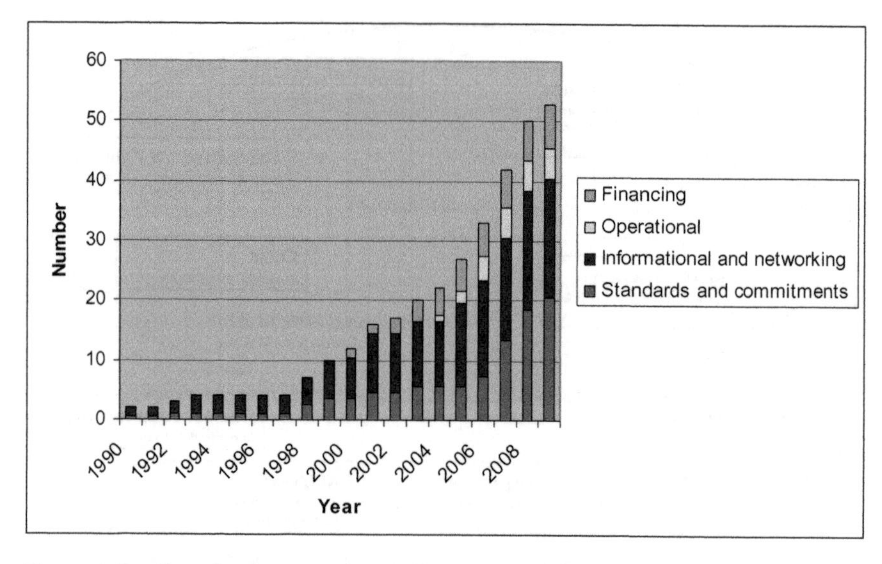

Figure 4.12 Growth of transnational climate governance by type, 1990–2010

Source: Hale and Roger 2011.

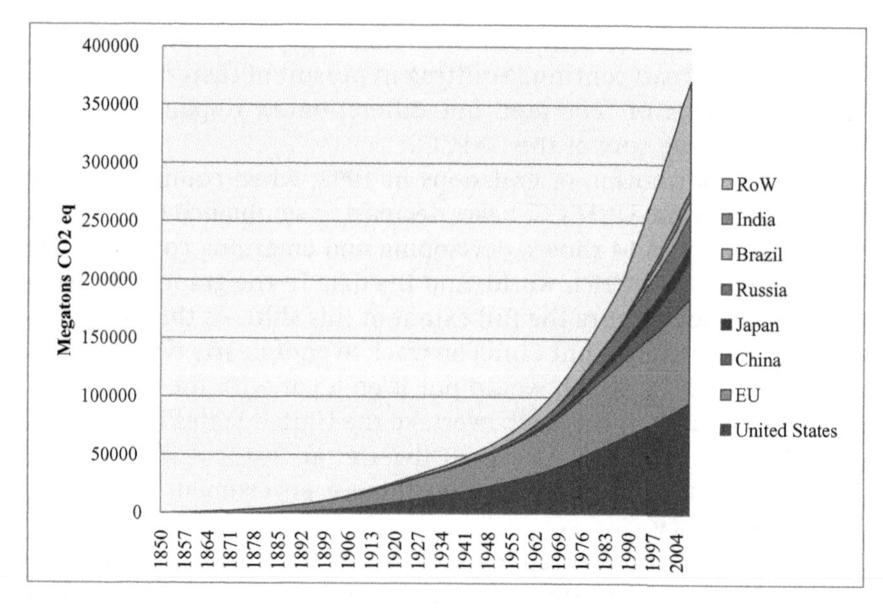

Figure 4.13 Cumulative greenhouse gas emissions, 1850–2008

Source: World Resources Institute.

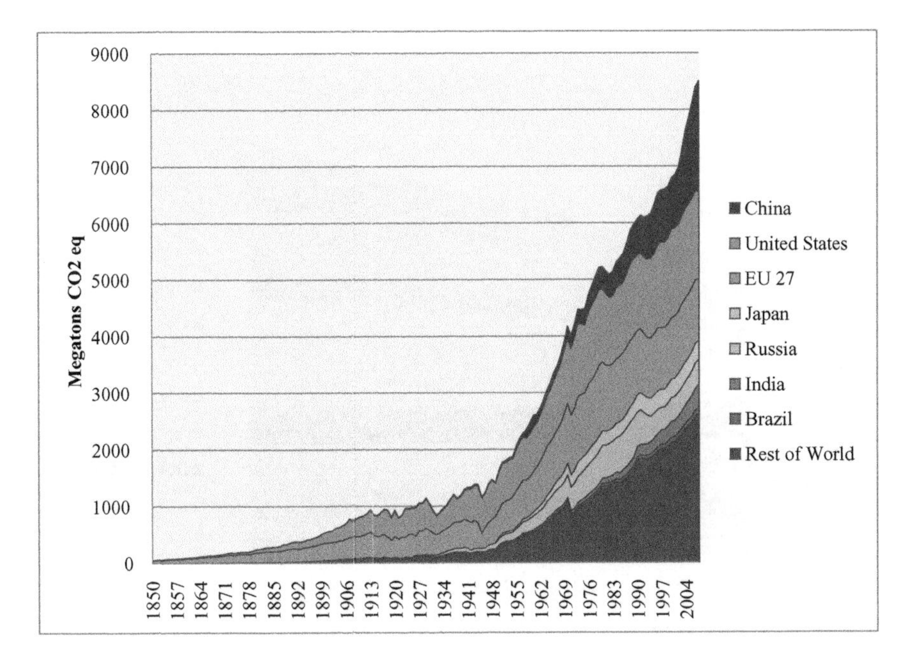

Figure 4.14 Greenhouse gas emissions, 1850–2008

Source: World Resources Institute.

words, the people who are relatively less responsible are the ones who must curtail their impact on the climate. The requirements of fairness are at odds with the requirements of maintaining a safe atmosphere. This distribution of emissions means that though the battle against climate change will be fought on many fronts, the most crucial decisions will be those made by large emerging markets like China, India, Brazil, and other industrializers. No global governance arrangement that excludes them will solve the problem, and so each is, in effect, a veto player. And yet these countries, on the merits of the historical justice argument, and in view of their ongoing efforts to make a better life for their citizens, have strongly resisted efforts to bind them to multilateral emissions targets. Agreement across the largest emitters is essential, but these countries have wildly divergent policy preferences.

Harder problems

In the 1970s policy analysts coined the term "wicked problems" to describe social challenges like poverty reduction or improving poor

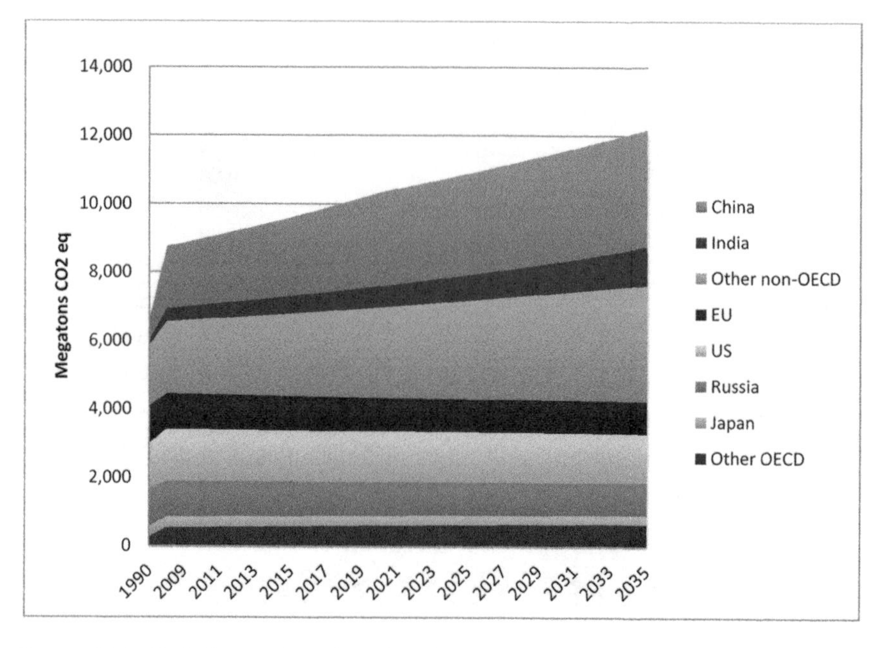

Figure 4.15 Emissions and projected emissions, 1990–2035

Source: International Energy Agency.

schools, problems characterized by "enormous interdependencies, uncertainties, circularities, and conflicting stakeholders implicated by any effort to develop a solution" (Lazarus 2009: 1159). Such challenges were so complex, containing so many interlinked social and economic processes, that they defied straightforward "solving." Instead, the best policy-makers could hope to do was to make an array of small policy interventions across various facets of the problem and hope that the general trajectory might be nudged in an upward direction. Social scientists now speak of climate change as a "super wicked problem," containing all the elements of a complex social challenge, but adding a few more as well (Levin et al. 2010).

First, almost every activity in the modern economy releases greenhouse gases. Heating, transportation, manufacturing, and agriculture are particularly climate-intensive. This means that any effort to solve climate change will necessitate changes, potentially costly ones, across many of the core systems of modern society. This creates a vast array of interests that could potentially organize to prevent change.

Second, the central role of energy in modern society has given fossil fuels a very particular political economy, concentrating wealth in some of the largest entities in the global economy. Depending on how the stock market is doing, about half of the ten largest companies in the world are oil companies.[15] With this economic heft comes the ability to defend one's interests. Oil, gas, coal, and electricity interests spent $2.3 billion lobbying the US federal government between 1998 and 2012 (OpenSecrets 2012). But this is not the only form of influence. In many oil-producing states, oil companies are owned by the state and form the most important source of government revenue. And even for net energy consumers like China, state-owned fossil fuel firms are among the most powerful actors in the domestic political process (Conrad 2012). Climate change cannot be mitigated without a wholesale shift away from fossil fuel usage, but some of the most influential companies in the world depend entirely on their continued exploitation.

Third, the costs of mitigating climate change are substantial. The IPCC estimates that the total cost of complying with the Kyoto Protocol will be approximately 0.05 percent of the GDP of the countries that have commitments (IPCC 2007). But Kyoto's "cheapness" is the product of its low ambitions. The global cost of the measures needed to ensure a safe climate in the future is of course difficult to tally, but the 2006 Stern Report estimated it at about 1 percent of global GDP per year (Stern 2006). This is a large figure, but significantly less than the 5 percent of GDP the report predicted that "business as usual" would cost the world each year. Even so, mustering 1 percent would be difficult under the best circumstances, but the nature of climate change entails a distribution of costs and benefits that makes it particularly difficult for governments to invest resources. Though the costs of mitigating climate change must be paid in the present, and are concentrated on powerful vested interests, the benefits of climate protection will accrue mostly to people who have not even been born yet. They will be diffused widely across the world, and will largely pass unnoticed by the beneficiaries. It therefore makes little difference, politically, that reports consistently show the cost of inaction to be far greater than the cost of action.

Fourth, time is running out. Unlike social challenges like the alleviation of poverty, which are never "solved" but rather ameliorated or managed, climate change advances over time. If the world does not act now – specifically, if emissions do not peak and then begin to recede in the next 10–15 years – catastrophic climate disruptions will occur. There is no second chance.

Fifth, every action to mitigate climate change taken today would have been cheaper to do yesterday, and will be more expensive tomorrow. As emissions grow, the amount of future reductions that will be required to undo the damage grows as well. If wealthy countries had managed to stick to the 1988 Toronto pledge to hold emissions at 1988 levels by 2005, the scale of the problem now facing developing countries and the world as a whole would be far less. In other words, the dynamic nature of climate change means that its "super-wickedness" is self-reinforcing; its difficulty delays action, but delaying action also makes it more difficult.

Institutional inertia

Unlike in the security or economic realms, where preexisting institutional structures have locked in formal decision-making rules that are now dysfunctional, climate change institutions have grown within the relatively weak and fragmented landscape of global environmental governance. Nonetheless, successful cooperation in the past has hampered cooperation in the present by giving policy-makers cognitive, institutional, and normative templates ill-suited to the problem of climate change. David Victor describes the perverse effects of institutional inertia eloquently in his book *Global Warming Gridlock*:

> when the global warming problem appeared on their radar screen, the world's top diplomats opened a toolbox that had all the wrong tools for the job. They thought global warming was just another environmental problem, but the standard tools of environmental diplomacy don't work well on problems, such as global warming, that require truly interdependent cooperation. The diplomats took a hard problem and made it even harder by choosing the wrong strategy. (2011a: 203)

Victor identifies several features of the UNFCCC process that are particularly ill-suited for solving climate change. First, the focus on targets and timetables – reduce X percent by X date – distances international agreements from both what governments will actually do and what they can actually control. While these agreements offer the illusion of solving the problem, the Kyoto experience suggests that governments are more than willing to sidestep their commitments when they find them too costly (see figure 4.10 above). Moreover, emissions outcomes are often the result of forces that governments only partially control, such as economic growth or collapse. A better approach would be to target *policies*, Victor argues; for example, removing subsidies from fossil fuels. Agreements that tied climate change mitigation to specific benefits, such as technology transfer, would be even more attractive.

Second, Victor criticizes the universal nature of the UNFCCC negotiations, another legacy of the ozone regime (see Hoffmann 2005). Only a few dozen countries emit enough GHGs to alter the composition of the atmosphere, he notes. An agreement among them alone would be sufficient to mitigate climate change. By including the other 170-odd countries in the world, the UNFCCC vastly increases the transaction costs of climate negotiations, and allows spoilers to reduce outcomes to a very low common denominator. Victor therefore advocates more of a club-based approach.

Third, and more controversially, the UNFCCC's attention to the "right" of poor countries to exploit the atmosphere as they develop has led to a bifurcation of voting blocs within the UNFCCC into "carbon haves" and "carbon have-nots" that bears less and less relation to reality. This distinction was necessary to secure the participation of the developing world and, in 1992, was certainly justified by both the historical responsibility of the wealthy world and its massive per capita consumption. But today many of the emerging and middle-income countries have increased emissions even as Europe and Japan have reduced theirs. Strikingly, Chinese emissions per capita nearly match those of the EU (7.2 tonnes per year and 7.5 tonnes per year, respectively) (Olivier et al. 2012). Moreover, the growing inequality within major developing countries makes the idea of a national average increasingly illusory. The per capita emissions of Beijing, Shanghai, and Tianjin are about three times more than those of Tokyo or Paris, and twice as big as the per capita emissions of London or New York. They are even larger than those of Los Angeles, though China's national average remains low (World Bank 2010a). Should urban Chinese really not be asked to contribute to the well-being of future generations?

Fourth, reinforcing these problems, the most pro-climate blocs of countries within the UNFCCC, such as the EU and the small island states, are also the ones most committed to the idea of formal multilateral procedures under the auspices of the UN. The EU has resisted efforts to shift climate discussions to alternative fora (like the MEF), because senior policy-makers continue to believe that the most effective and legitimate solution must be a universal one.

Finally Depledge (2006) describes a process of "ossification" in the climate regime, which she defines as the opposite of learning. Many international negotiations can be understood as a process not just of bargaining, but of mutual information exchange and joint learning, in which new information alters the course of discussions. In the UNFCCC talks, instead, Depledge finds that the entrenchment of political alliances, the maintenance of "taboo" topics, and the endless citation and repetition of previous agreements have come to dominate the process.

Fragmentation

As in forests, the failure of the core of the climate regime has caused many other actors and institutions to pile in (Zelli 2011; see figures 4.11 and 4.12, above). Many of these actions and institutions are helping to fill the gap left by ongoing gridlock in the UNFCCC, though collectively they do not add up to enough GHG reductions to substantially alter the trajectory of the planet. It is yet unclear, however, whether they can serve to catalyze deeper cooperation in the future, or if the diffusion of activity and political will creates conditions that make collective action more difficult.

Many observers of climate negotiations now advocate alternatives to the "global deal" envisioned in the multilateral process. Victor (2011a) suggests a club model in which a medium-sized group of the most important emitters agree to concrete policy actions that create mutual benefits. Falkner et al. (2010) suggest a "building blocks" approach that divides climate mitigation into several smaller pieces (e.g. an agreement on carbon sinks, another on transportation, etc.), with the idea that agreement is easier in more concrete, small-scale issues. And one of the present authors has advocated a more ambitious commitment to transnational governance in the climate realm, seeking to bring the actions of substate and nonstate actors to a higher level of scale and ambition (Hale 2011).

As noted above, these types of suggestions have provoked criticism from some of the most pro-climate groups and policy-makers. At the Bali climate conference in 2007, both the European Union and the G77 threatened to derail the MEF meeting unless the United States made firm commitments to the UNFCCC process. The German environment minister told the US delegation, "No result in Bali means no Major Economies Meeting" (quoted in Zelli 2011: 91). These countries fear that shifting the focus to nonmultilateral fora will allow countries to shirk their responsibilities. Importantly, the needs of the least developed countries are unlikely to be addressed outside the UNFCCC, but it is these countries that will be the most affected by climate change. For advocates of a "UN-plus" approach (Au et al. 2011), instead, this exclusive commitment to the UNFCCC risks making the ideal the enemy of the possible. A more fragmented response is likely a second-best outcome, but given ongoing gridlock, the best that can be hoped for.

It is probably too early to tell whether the fragmentation of the climate regime now impedes future negotiations. Certainly the other mechanisms of gridlock are themselves sufficient to stall progress. However, the issue highlights the trade-offs that gridlock imposes. Once "first best" solutions are off the table, global governance inevitably falls into compromises and adaptations that may themselves have implications for the future management of the global commons.

Conclusion: Increasingly Linked Problems, Increasingly Fragmented Governance

The advent of the Anthropocene means that environmental problems are increasingly global and systemic in nature, linked to one another, and, ultimately, more dangerous. These linkages and systemic qualities can be seen in just the few issues we have discussed in this chapter. One of the replacements for ozone-depleting CFCs are HCFCs, a similar chemical that does not destroy ozone. The ozone regime has facilitated the use of these chemicals, particularly in places like India and China, which benefited from the technology transfer arrangements embedded in the Montreal Protocol. Unfortunately, it turns out that HCFCs are powerful greenhouse gases. By making it easier for countries to use them, the ozone regime directly contributed to climate change. Ultimately, countries decided to phase out these products (by 2020 for rich countries, 2030 for developing countries), but the damage has already been done.

The linkages between climate and forests provide another example. Since 2008, the UNFCCC has increasingly recognized the role of reforestation and other land-use policies in absorbing carbon from the atmosphere and keeping it locked in the form of biomass. Countries now count policies to preserve forests as contributions to their climate goals. But what is good forestry policy from a carbon perspective is not necessarily good policy from the perspective of biodiversity (monoculture, plantation forests can lock in as much carbon as natural ones) or of the traditional users of forests.

Global problems like climate change and the systemic links that increasingly define most environmental issues reveal a tragic irony. Environmental problems are increasingly unified, but the institutions we have devised to govern them are increasingly fragmented. This is not a new observation. In the mid-1990s the UN Taskforce on Human

Settlement and Environment concluded that "institutional fragmentation and loss of policy coherence as a result of the number of separate environment-related intergovernmental processes had resulted in a loss of effectiveness in the work of the United Nations in the area of the environment" (quoted in Andresen 2001: 19). But it is a trend that grows ever more severe.

This gap was made crystal clear on the fortieth anniversary of the 1972 Stockholm summit, and the twentieth anniversary of the 1992 Rio summit. "Rio+20," as the event was known, brought together the usual bevy of diplomats, civil society groups, and businesses to try to save the world. A group of leading environmental scholars involved with the Earth Systems Governance project – an effort to evaluate the effectiveness of environmental policy on a global scale – noted the stakes of the event:

> our work indicated that incremental change – the main approach since the 1972 Stockholm Conference on the Human Environment – is no longer sufficient to bring about societal change at the level and with the speed needed to mitigate and adapt to Earth System transformation. Structural change in global governance is needed, both inside and outside the UN system and involving both public and private actors. (Biermann et al. 2012)

The authors minced no words about the scale of governance transformation that would be needed, in their view, to manage the global commons: "The world saw a major transformative shift in governance after 1945 that led to the establishment of the UN and numerous other organizations . . . We need similar changes today, a 'constitutional moment' in world politics and global governance" (Biermann et al. 2012).

But long before the delegates arrived in Rio in the summer of 2012, it was apparent that the outcomes would be far less than transformative. Countries made clear that they wanted a text to be agreed in advance of the Rio meeting, so that heads of state would not have to engage in the messy, last-minute negotiations that characterized Stockholm, Rio 1992, Copenhagen, or other major summits. This entailed a steep reduction in ambition for the summit. The final text included lots of exhortations, and very little substance. As the director of WWF International summarized the politics behind the summit, "With too few countries prepared to press for action, Brazilian president Dilma Rousseff chose to drive a process with no serious content – to the planet's detriment" (quoted in Clark and Leahy 2012). At the 1992 summit and in meetings like the 2009 Copenhagen conference, countries tried desperately to hash out agreements to global environmental cooperation, but found themselves thwarted by gridlock. At Rio+20 they scarcely even tried. One US official, quoted anonymously by *Foreign Policy*, described the negotiations as a "hopeless clusterfuck" (Rothkopf 2012). Despite this criticism, there were several small steps forward at Rio+20. For example, UNEP was given a universal membership, making its governing council more representative of the world as a whole. It was also given more stable funding from the regular UN budget, reducing its dependence on individual donors. But these reforms stopped short of making UNEP a full UN agency akin to the WHO or FAO, and seem unlikely to lead to significant results in the near to medium term.

The vapid intergovernmental outcome was not the only result of the conference. Some 209 partnerships were registered at Rio+20, action-oriented initiatives that bring national governments, cities, NGOs, companies, and other kinds of actors together around specific projects (UNCSD 2012).[16] Governments, companies, and civil society groups also made nearly 500 official "voluntary pledges" at the summit. Participants noted the sharp contrast between the unambitious intergovernmental process and the dynamic efforts of individual actors and small groups organized in partnerships.

This result would likely have pleased Elinor Ostrom, the political scientist who won the Nobel Prize for explaining the ability of community-based cooperation like the *zanjera* to solve collective action problems. Ostrom passed away on the eve of Rio+20, but in her last article (published, incredibly, on the day of her death), she noted: "Inaction in Rio would be disastrous, but a single international agreement would be a grave mistake. We cannot rely on singular global policies to solve the problem of managing our common resources" (Ostrom 2012). Instead, Ostrom called for "overlapping policies at city, subnational, national, and international levels," what she had referred to elsewhere as a "polycentric" approach to environmental governance (Ostrom 2009). This pluralistic form increasingly defines both individual areas of environmental governance, as well as the institutional architecture of environmental governance as a whole (Biermann et al. 2009). For some observers, the pluralization of environmental governance represents an effective path forward, bringing new actors and resources to a crucial problem (Abbott 2012). For others it is at most a second-best solution. But it is impossible to deny that it is the reality the world faces, as gridlock has ground intergovernmental environmental cooperation to a halt. It is also fascinating that the mix of public and private actors seen at events like Rio+20 bear such a strong resemblance to earlier phases of environmental cooperation, like the 1948 meeting in Fontainebleau that led to the creation of IUCN. It also mirrors the proliferation of institutional solutions in certain realms of economic governance, discussed in the previous chapters. We return to this question of pluralization in the conclusion to the book.

Before ending, however, it is worth considering how well this system addresses the vision laid out in Stockholm in 1972. A comprehensive evaluation of the complex system of global environmental governance must necessarily be somewhat impressionistic, but consider again the four functions Kennan laid out for effective environmental cooperation: unifying scientific knowledge, coordinating activities to avoid redundancy, setting appropriate standards, and enforcing rules for the global commons.

On the scientific front, the world has performed fairly well. On coordination and standard-setting, results are mixed at best, and rule enforcement has scarcely been attempted. At present it is difficult to see how a more polycentric system of global environmental governance will grow to fill these functions, though it may nonetheless represent the best possible route to addressing this complex web of problems.

5

Beyond Gridlock?

Harry Truman, who took over the US Presidency after Roosevelt died in the last days of World War II, was arguably the most influential architect of the postwar institutional infrastructure. Similarly, his successor, Dwight Eisenhower, the former general who had served as Supreme Commander of Allied Forces in Europe, was the driving force behind a more literal type of infrastructure: roads. As a young lieutenant, Eisenhower had traveled with a military convoy from Washington DC to San Francisco. His mission was to test America's road infrastructure against the needs of the new age of mechanized warfare introduced by World War I. It failed rather spectacularly. Eisenhower took some 62 days to cross the 3,521 miles, a pace of roughly 6 miles per hour (L. Snyder 2006). Today, Google Maps estimates the total journey time at 45 hours.

This improvement is in large part attributable to Eisenhower's interstate highway system, a national network of express roads inspired by the German autobahn, which Eisenhower had come to appreciate while invading that country. The interstate system was phenomenally successful, and not just in reducing journey times. While it is difficult to quantify its economic benefits precisely, it is widely seen as a fundamental building block of the US postwar boom. But perhaps even more importantly, no other infrastructure project has so transformed the United States. Car ownership skyrocketed,[1] the middle class left the cities, mid-century youth culture was given the space it needed to emerge, and the socioeconomic and cultural phenomenon known simply as the "suburbs" was born.

These changes radically altered the basic problem Eisenhower had been trying to solve – how to get from point A to point B – but not necessarily for the better. In the postwar years Americans bought more and more cars, and moved to communities in which a family needed at least one or two to get around. While the average American's mobility increased, so did traffic. For many years, the solution was simply to build ever more roads. But this did little to stem the problem. Indeed, the consensus among transportation planners today – what has been called the "fundamental principle of highway congestion" – is that building more roads actually makes the problem *worse* by encouraging more people to drive (Duranton and Turner 2011). Today, this literal gridlock has become a costly barrier to American mobility. The Texas Transportation Institute calculated that in 2010 traffic congestion made Americans sit in their cars 4.8 billion hours more than necessary and purchase an extra 1.9 billion gallons of fuel, costing them some $101 billion (Schrank et al. 2011). And while the United States is the historical leader in car dependency, today traffic is worse in Moscow, São Paolo, and Beijing than it is in Los Angeles (see Gyimesi et al. 2011).[2]

In other words, Eisenhower's national transport infrastructure has come to much the same conclusion as Truman's global institutional infrastructure. Both "interstate" systems were remarkably successful, so much so that they fundamentally altered the nature of the problems they set out to solve. And by doing so, they have ultimately undermined their own utility. In both cases, the result is gridlock.

This chapter asks what lies further down the road, and how we might get there. Just as drivers stuck in traffic might fantasize about flying cars that could take them over a traffic jam, many observers have imagined fix-all solutions to the dilemmas of global governance. Many are equally fantastical, and we do not engage with these panaceas here. Moreover, because gridlock is a phenomenon involving multiple pathways to the same result, any solution would have to be highly complex and multifaceted. Simple policy solutions for complex historically emergent problems on a global scale also tend to neglect the fact that any future trajectory is based on future social mobilization and uncertainty. Thus in what follows we conclude by reviewing the implications of gridlock and the trends that might strengthen or weaken it, and suggest where we might most productively invest in ameliorating it.

The first section synthesizes the arguments made in chapters 2–4, noting how the common pathways generating gridlock in global governance apply across widely different governance domains. The second section considers several negative implications of ongoing governance failures at the global level. Looking across issue areas, we lay out a series of trends that threaten to exacerbate gridlock and further weaken multilateralism. These include a return to great power rivalry, the possibility that failed states will incubate even greater global bads, and a shift to unsustainably technocratic governance, among others. These trends are real and could, in the face of ongoing gridlock, deepen.

The third section shifts from the systemic analysis that has guided this book, and considers instead how developments at the national level are likely to affect gridlock in the near future. There is potential for change in the domestic politics of a number of countries that weigh heavily on global affairs, we argue. Unfortunately, few of the domestic-level trends are cause for optimism. Both the United States and Europe are locked in their own internal forms of gridlock. China, which has benefited enormously from the postwar order, faces looming domestic challenges that will, at best, distract it from playing a more constructive role in global governance. And while emerging democratic countries such as India, Brazil, and South Africa offer some hope for a more just world order as their weight in global affairs grows, it remains unclear whether they will form a coherent force for global reform in the future.

In the fourth section we note several trends that might work against gridlock. These include the potential of social movements to uproot existing political constraints, as well as the capacity of existing actors to adapt and even radically reform the system through institutional innovation. While these forces have important potential to tackle many problems, we do not expect them to lead us out of gridlock in the short or medium term, given the strength of the gridlock mechanisms and their mutual reinforcement. Finally, we consider how the kinds of political forces that could undo gridlock might emerge, what constellations of power and interests they might face, in what institutional landscape, and how they might be able to build more effective solutions to transnational problems.

This book was not written to cast despair on the prospects for effective global governance, but it has suggested that a sober reading of the challenges before us and the likely effectiveness of the probable responses should give us pause. As such, it is a warning. Our argument is that gridlock is a dominant tendency within global governance today – but not an inevitable one. Though the mechanisms outlined constrain the potential agency of individuals, groups, and states to meet the need for global coordination, they do not render it impossible.

From Self-Reinforcing Interdependence to Gridlock

Immanuel Kant wrote in *Perpetual Peace*, published in 1795, that we are "unavoidably side by side." What he meant by this simple, eloquent phrase was that a violent challenge to law and justice in one place has consequences for many others and can be potentially experienced across the globe. While Kant dwelt on these matters and their implications at length, he could not have anticipated how profound his concerns would become. This book shows how our mutual interconnectedness and vulnerability have both grown rapidly. Even if it might once have been said that we lived in a world of relatively discrete communities and civilizations, this is certainly no longer true. Instead we live in a world of "overlapping communities of fate" where the trajectories of countries are deeply enmeshed with each other (Held 2004). The potential for violence to spill across borders, the changing structure of the world economy, and the degraded natural habitat we dwell in all signify that this interconnectedness is now part of everyday life and the social processes which join people in multiple ways. Against the backdrop of the production of carbon and its emissions in the atmosphere, the global division of labor and the dynamic character of the world economy, the emergence of multinational giants and the circulation of ideas and cultural artifacts across the world, the fate and fortunes of the world's citizens are thoroughly intertwined.

These dense patterns of self-reinforcing global interdependence have built on the foundations laid down following World War II. The successes have been extraordinary and were documented in the previous chapters: the prevention of a third world war, the development and expansion of a dynamic and rule-based global economic order, and the management of some environmental challenges – all facilitated by a complex system of international and transnational institutions. Out of this has emerged a multipolar world, shaped by increasingly complex patterns of interconnection and the assertion of agency and voice by new actors. This includes not only a greater number and diversity of states participating at the international negotiating table, but also global civil society advocates and pressure groups, which combine to constitute a thickening web of actors and agencies with a growing stake in global governance. We are truly "side by side" in ways that Kant could never have imagined. It is a world in which more issues require deeper cooperation from a wider array of actors with more divergent interests than ever before. Yet, despite a proliferation of institutions, these have not adapted sufficiently to the new constellation of global challenges. They have failed to prevent the institutional accomplishments of the immediate postwar years from ossifying into the inertial structures of the present. The result is a growing gap between the "demand" for governance and the capacity of states and intergovernmental organizations to "supply" it.

We have argued that this gridlock is the outcome of the four distinct but sometimes overlapping dynamics or "pathways": emerging multipolarity, institutional inertia, harder (complex 'intermestic') problems, and fragmentation. There is no single explanation for the development of these paths in any single sector of global governance, but there are common linkages. Current global governance problems are of a "second order" nature: they are not problems of international cooperation per se, but problems resulting from the historical process in which past systems of cooperation have evolved amidst changing circumstances. The complex narratives set out in chapters 2–4 present many explanations for why global institutions have seized up and have stopped working productively to address global challenges. Table 5.1 summarizes the narrative of gridlock by sector and by the four pathways to gridlock. Each pathway highlights a set of primary factors that explain why a particular area of governance has not made adequate progress on key issues. Of course, the table simplifies the complex historical reality described in previous chapters. Most issue areas have been explained and need to be explained by more than one pathway, as do the overlapping tendencies across security, the global economy, and the environment.

As we have stressed throughout the book, gridlock is shaped by an evolutionary logic. For example, the chapter on security highlights the role played by the postwar settlement in creating both the conditions of postwar economic and political successes and the circumstances wherein this settlement later became a structural impediment to institutional reform and resolving intermestic issues. The chapter on the global economy shows how the dramatic increase in economic integration has led to successive cycles of institution-building to solve particular problems, and how these changes generated even greater interdependence and new governance challenges. And the chapter on environment highlights how the diffusion of industrial production to a truly global scale has created new kinds of problems – fundamentally, the creation of a global commons – that has brought the world to a level of interdependence unforeseeable in 1945.

Table 5.1 Selected issue areas in which gridlock mechanisms predominate

		Sectors of global governance		
		Security	Economy	Environment
Pathways to gridlock	**Emerging multipolarity**	• Security Council reform • Conference on Disarmament • The Ottawa Process	• Structural imbalances • Doha Round of global trade talks	• Climate change • Forests
	Institutional inertia	• UN Security Council • Non-Proliferation Treaty/ nuclear disarmament • Small arms proliferation	• International Monetary Fund • Transnational financial standard-setting bodies	• Application of "convention and protocols" format to climate and forests
	Harder problems	• Terrorism • Failed states • Piracy • Cyber threats • Pandemics	• The macroprudential shift in financial regulation • "Deep integration" efforts within the global trade regime • Global corporate accountability	• Climate change • Forests
	Fragmentation	• R2P/Humanitarianism • The erosion of the state's monopoly on violence • Military capacity	• Global financial regulatory governance in various avatars • Global trade and finance rules interacting	• Weakness of UNEP • Proliferation of alternative climate fora • Use of transnational and private governance mechanisms (e.g. forests, climate)

Trends toward Deepening Gridlock

The analysis in the previous chapters has traced the forces of gridlock within three broad issue areas, finding considerable evidence within each of them that these have constrained the ability of the multilateral system to resolve global problems and meet pressing global needs. Now we turn from analyzing the past and present to considering how gridlock mechanisms might play out in the near future. We identify several trends in world politics that are likely to compound gridlock. The fact that these trends are themselves a consequence of gridlock underlines the systemic nature of our argument, as does the fact that these trends reach across the various issue areas that have thus far been discussed separately. Indeed, the potential for gridlock to ripple across spheres of global governance is one of its most concerning features.

The renewed salience of great power rivalry

For significant periods of history, world politics has been understood as the struggle between the great powers. Countries have been seen as unified actors pursuing their national interests in a competitive world of war and conquest. This view of world affairs, called "classic Realism," runs from Thucydides to Kissinger, and has served as a powerful tool for explaining and understanding geopolitics over the centuries. It has proven less insightful, however, to explain the world since 1945. As discussed in chapter 1, the development and persistence – indeed, the deepening – of international institutionalization in the decades after World War II did not sit comfortably with the Realist analysis (Keohane 1984). Thus arose the various theories of interdependence, institutional cooperation, domestic politics, and transnational actors that account for the more complex world of global politics we face today.

Just after the Cold War, it was tempting to think that the old world of realpolitik had drifted away. But world events quickly exposed the naivety of this position. The attacks of 9/11, the invasion of Afghanistan (2001), and the war in Iraq (2003), among other conflicts, revealed the continuing schisms and clashes of interests that pervaded geopolitics. The explosive growth of China, especially, prompted renewed attention to the balance of power. While it was of course impossible to understand the world of global politics only through the Realist lens, no serious observer doubted that the great powers, old and new, would continue to strive to achieve their goals on the world stage.

Despite the manifold achievements of multilateral governance in the postwar order, the logic of realpolitik was never far beneath the surface of global governance. Gridlock in the multilateral order, however, risks making great power rivalry the sole driver of world politics. As the ability of institutions to provide collective solutions diminishes, global politics may increasingly resemble the great power rivalries of, say, nineteenth-century Europe, in which relatively weak forms of institutionalization like the Concert of Europe swayed with shifts in the balance of power (Kissinger 1994).

The emergence of great powers and regional players in Asia – a process strongly facilitated by the postwar order – has put the relevance of great power politics beyond any doubt. Many of the features of the security challenges in the western Pacific would have been familiar to Bismarck, Metternich, or Richelieu, the geopolitical strategists par excellence of Europe in the early modern era. Five of the world's six largest armies[3] face each other across a series of contested territorial claims. Alliances link great powers to potentially volatile client states (e.g. China and North Korea, the United States and Taiwan). Across the region, nationalist sentiment among sectors of the public gives leaders incentives to grandstand and to avoid compromise. Meanwhile, regional institutions to build trust or share information are weak. The nineteenth century witnessed great power rivalry that manifested not only in the dramatic expansion of imperial conquest over the rest of the world, but also in the great wars of the first half of the twentieth century. Weakening multilateralism of the twenty-first century may contain seeds of similar antagonism and conflict, perhaps in forms that we cannot yet envisage.

One key source of conflict, though, may be an old one: access to natural resources. Many of the world's resources – oil, natural gas, forests, fishing stocks, fresh water supplies, rare earth minerals – are finite, and yet the rapid growth of the world economy creates ever greater demand for them. As Western living standards come within the reach of other parts of the world, a strain is inevitably placed on the resource base of the Earth. Resource conflicts and perhaps wars might be one result (see Klare 2002; Deligiannis 2012). Add to this the pressure on resources of a growing world population, estimated to rise from 7 billion today to over 10 billion by 2050, and a set of governance pressures are created that will be very hard to resolve.

Emerging multipolarity, institutional inertia, harder problems, and the fragmentation of governance capacity make a coherent response to global challenges more difficult, which makes it less likely that countries will find multilateral solutions satisfactory. This, in turn, makes unilateral actions politically tempting for many national leaders. But when great powers break with existing treaties and multilateral conventions to pursue unilateral paths (consider the war in Iraq, the use of military drones, or arms shipments to Syria, for instance), or stall international negotiations on key topics (climate change, world trade, nuclear proliferation), the achievements of the multilateral order look increasingly threadbare. This undermines the legitimacy of the multilateral system as a whole, potentially exacerbating gridlock. The institutional arrangements that once were in place to ensure great power participation in the multilateral order become cards that they can play to block censure and interference in their chosen foreign policy and security strategies.

There is no better case than the country that served as the chief architect of the postwar order. When the US under President Bush Jr bypassed the UN Security Council and opted for a "coalition of the willing" for the war in Iraq, he actively set aside the rule of international law and deeply held conventions in the multilateral order. By acting without a UN mandate, he demonstrated that the US would pursue its national security interests irrespective of UN institutional arrangements and legal requirements. The Bush administration adopted a similar position regarding the treatment of "enemy combatants," denying them the protections multilateral conventions provide to prisoners of war. And even after Bush Jr ceased to be US President, the country has maintained that the new nature of security threats necessitates violating international norms. President Obama has decided that an aggressive and growing drone program is needed to strike against terrorists in Pakistan, Yemen, Afghanistan, Iraq, and Somalia. Despite the objections posed by Pakistan that such strikes violate their national sovereignty (Nauman 2012), and in the face of fierce objections that such attacks are violations of human rights and even possibly war crimes (Carter 2012; Bowcott 2012), Obama has continued to order targeted killings – including of American citizens – in abrogation of international law.

In the context of the erosion of the rule of law and the weakening of the multilateral order there is a great danger that precedents created by unilateral action will be replicated by others, in ever increasing actions of arbitrary power. If the US can justify unilateralism why not also Russia, China, Israel, Iran, and other powers? It cannot coherently be argued that all states *bar one* must be bound by the rule of law and the constraints of multilateralism. Moreover, the current intense pattern of extrajudicial killings (organized, targeted killings), whether by terrorist groups or by those who launch drones across borders, compounds the anxiety about a breakdown of the rule of law. Against this background, strong leaders who offer to create stability and security can flourish. This easily becomes the basis for a spiraling of outlaw politics.

Failed states and global bads

There is a risk that ungovernable parts of the world could catalyze a vicious downward spiral of global ills (see Held et al. 2010). In the first instance, climate change has the capacity to wreak havoc on the world's natural systems and socioeconomic fabric. This is already happening in some parts of the world. But it will get worse as violent storms become more frequent, water access becomes a battleground, rising sea levels displace millions, mass migration becomes more common (as people seek refuge in temperate climates), and as death rates rise from disease in the world's poorest countries (largely because bacteria will spread more quickly, causing greater contamination of food and water). Those who will be the hardest hit will be, as is all too typical, the poorest and those already disadvantaged. The poor are extremely vulnerable to even minor shifts in natural and social conditions, exposing them to a diversity of hazards that lead to high infant mortality and low life expectancy. Thus, those at the bottom of the global income hierarchy risk being stuck there and will likely suffer continuing deterioration of their life chances, leading to the prospect of what Desmond Tutu has called "adaptation apartheid" (see Jones et al. 2009, p. 32).

These challenges are compounded by growing pressures that can arise from the combination of fragile and failing states with any of the intermestic security threats mentioned in chapter 2, such as terrorism, piracy, and the spread of weapons of mass destruction, as well as the increased polarization in income and wealth across the world. Against this background, the global order becomes increasingly vulnerable to a downward spiral of global crises.

Consider just one example. The horn of Africa has the unfortunate distinction of being one of the most climate-vulnerable regions of the world. Already prone to drought and food insecurity, Ethiopia, Eritrea, Somalia, and Djibouti will see rising temperatures and weather-related disruption that are poised to wreak havoc on the life chances of the region's 100 million inhabitants. Compounding these problems, and exacerbated by them, Somalia has no functional government, with power split between various local strongmen and the Shabab, an Islamic militia similar to Afghanistan's Taliban. Military conflicts between Eritrea and Ethiopia and Djibouti, and between these governments and various military groups in Somalia, are common. For many years the world was largely content to leave these problems to the region's residents, occasionally sending food aid to alleviate the worst of the regular famines. But in recent years the long-term cost of this neglect has become apparent. Some 8 percent of the world's sea trade must pass along the region's coast to reach the Suez Canal, putting it well within striking range of the pirate groups that thrive among the poverty and lawlessness (see chapter 2).

In addition, while the long-term effects of wars in Afghanistan, Iraq, and Libya cannot be fully known, Afghanistan and Libya in particular appear more likely to slip into a generalized cycle of violence and regional fragmentation than to cohere into functional states. Even as troops are withdrawn from Afghanistan it remains a highly volatile and violent country that continues to struggle to establish security. The lasting effects of this conflict are not confined only to the Afghanistan borders, however: the conflict has spilled over into Pakistan, exacerbating both internal and external tensions as well as threats to the peace and security of that country. Iraq continues to suffer from widespread violence (see terrorism in Iraq, chapter 2) and sectarian divides. Moreover, the war in Iraq has had numerous unintended consequences, such as the emboldenment of Iran. Libya, despite an ostensibly quick transition, remains fractured among militias with little, if any, rule of law. Neighboring Mali, which used to be a beacon of stability in Africa, has been undermined as a consequence of the NATO intervention in Libya, fueling a conflict with Islamist rebels that resulted in French intervention. In each of these cases, the countries and regions have become highly unstable. Violence in one country spills into others, resulting in unpredictable consequences that undermine regional, indeed global, peace and security.

Global markets run amuck

It is not only states, whether strong and unilateralist or weak and failed, that threaten to compound gridlock. Global markets, while emboldened by the policies that states pursue, also represent ongoing dynamic challenges. The continuing mismatch between the scope and size of global markets and the inadequacy of global regulation threatens to exacerbate multilateral weakness. The emergent neoliberalism of the 1980s onward emphasized the primacy of markets over politics and in so doing helped engender a system of often ad hoc and weak forms of global governance. As we saw in chapter 3, postwar international organizations sought to deal with an evolving economy by pursuing a liberalization agenda nearly at all costs, and new transnational governance institutions only tackled very specific problems as they emerged. The rapid liberalization of financial markets in particular shifted an enormous amount of decision-making from the public to the private sector. As markets "disembedded" from national regulatory constraints, global pressures developed to "open" international market flows with policies conducive to mobile firms but not necessarily to sustainable economic growth and development.

Competitive markets serve many useful functions, but they also come with the need for a continual adaptation of institutions and regulatory regimes which define the rules in which markets can and should operate. Under conditions of competition in which firms have great leverage over governmental decision-making, the very social infrastructure which makes advanced systems of production and exchange possible can be seen as costs, not assets. Environmental damage caused by modern production and consumption habits is all too often borne not by those that produce and consume a good, but by a much broader, diffuse population. Even the basic functions of entrepreneurialism and risk-taking that are arguably fundamental to the most dynamic aspects of capitalism are buttressed through a social safety net in which individuals, families, and communities are prepared to take risks. The business community often sees this logic well when it comes to institutions that socialize the costs of business failures, such as limited liability and bankruptcy provisions, but it is often less inclined to celebrate other institutions that have a publicly focused nonmarket orientation toward social and redistributive functions. The historic task of "reembedding" markets through effective regimes of rules and regulation was one of the greatest achievements of the modern nation-state (see Polanyi 1944). As we saw in chapter 3, the postwar order sought to enhance this achievement through a system of global economic governance in which economic volatility was managed through multilateral institutions (Ruggie 1982). However, this system has been increasingly bypassed or undermined by the expansive growth and far-reaching influence of capital, both corporate and financial. Since the introduction of floating exchange rates in the 1970s and the erosion of capital controls throughout the world, there has been a growing gap between global economic governance and global markets. Markets have been "disembedded" from regulatory structures, reversing some of the progress made in the postwar years and introducing higher levels of risk. The deregulation of markets has, moreover, socialized the cost of this risk in a manner that is disproportionately placed on the public, instead of squarely on the actors that instigate dysfunction and volatility (Palma 2009). When banks and investment houses fail now, the effects are felt across entire economic systems and the burden of recovery is equally diffuse – relying on revenues from taxpayers who were not connected to the problem in the first place.

Increasing technocracy, but at what cost?

Our enmeshed world is also an ever more complex world. Many of the "harder problems" this book has documented have an intricate technical character. To even understand issues such as swine flu, financial derivatives, or climate change, the boundaries of scientific knowledge must be pushed forward. In other words, the most important problems we face – globally, but also at the domestic and local levels – require more and more expertise. How to balance expert knowledge and popular opinion is a longstanding governance dilemma. All modern states have both technocratic and political organs that balance against each other. While political officials are almost always nominally dominant, technical bodies possess significant agenda-setting power, and are able to draw on their deeper knowledge of the issue to advance their preferred solutions. This is, of course, their job. Few would disagree that within a constitutional system it is right to empower bodies of experts sitting at some distance from political whims, be they courts, health and safety regulators, or central banks. Yet striking this balance is more difficult at the global level, because the "political" organs are typically weaker.

That said, delegation to international technocrats is not necessarily any more problematic than delegation to domestic ones. International bodies often possess unique levels of expertise and problem-solving capacities (especially relative to poorer governments) that make them valuable resources. The very fact that such bodies are not overly influenced by domestic political actors may give them even greater credibility. Indeed, Keohane, Macedo, and Moravcsik (2011) argue that such expertise is an important part of how international organizations can enhance the effectiveness of national-level democratic policy-making by injecting technically proficient outside advice into domestic policy discussions. Delegation to international technocratic bodies can also help domestic politicians achieve certain goals. If international bodies can make recommendations to states with the force of a requirement (for instance, in the case of IMF interventions to provide conditional liquidity to help ease credit crises, or an international decision to phase out certain productive operations that produce CFC aerosols), domestic politicians can use this as a cover for otherwise hard-to-sell policy packages. Hence, the frequent transfer of crucial decisions about regulation to transnational bodies.

Weakening multilateralism creates conditions under which we are likely to see a consolidation of technocratic elites. If global governance is gridlocked and significant aspects of the world become increasingly ungovernable, technocratic elites may well find more space to provide what they consider "depoliticized" solutions to issues of pressing concern. Such solutions, however, are not necessarily "neutral" in relation to distributional questions and may constrain future options and choices. These outcomes are particularly likely where politicians fail to agree on pressing issues, or are unable to create solutions in the face of institutional inertia. Furthermore, because there is a diversity of expertise operating in the global arena, room for expert maneuver can occur in many different sectors, from security to banking regulation to carbon offsetting schemes. While this may have short-term benefits in terms of problem-solving it can easily lead to further difficulties, occluding complex political considerations. Problems arise because technocratic solutions mask complex distributional questions and complex trade-offs which can only be legitimated ultimately by public discourse and political debate. In addition, purely technocratic governance is likely to exacerbate problems of fragmentation, as it facilitates a division of governance responsibilities among communities of experts. This is clearly the case in the realm of financial governance, for example, discussed in chapter 3.

National Trends and Gridlock

Thus far we have discussed gridlock as a general condition of global governance. But it is important also to consider its connections to domestic politics, particularly for the countries that weigh most heavily on global affairs. Such considerations are particularly vital as we imagine potential pathways out of gridlock, as changes at the domestic level have strong potential to lead countries to adopt new attitudes toward global cooperation. Of course, the question of how domestic shifts affect the likelihood of effective global governance in the future is too vast to address comprehensively here. Instead, we consider a few key trends in places we consider to have the most potential to reshape global affairs.

United States

Despite the radical transformations unleashed by the postwar order, which it had a leading role in building, the United States remains a dominant force within that system, and can be expected to remain so well into the future. Its economy is twice as large as China's in real terms (a more relevant gauge of national power than the purchasing power parity measures that are often breathlessly cited in the media). It accounts for over 40 percent of the world's military spending (China's share is 8 percent: see SIPRI, 2012). And it possesses a diplomatic apparatus and institutionalized position within a number of global governance bodies that give it considerable influence over a wide range of global issues, as noted in chapters 2–4. Strong US leadership at the global level, as occurred following World War II, could have the potential to greatly undo gridlock. Indeed, on a range of issues – climate change, nuclear proliferation, financial regulation – pundits and activists in the US and outside it, as well as other governments, have demanded that the United States summon the political will to exercise this potential leadership, sinking into frustration when it does not.

Just as might does not make right, the ability to solve a problem does not necessarily imply the existence of political institutions that allow a country to do so. A peculiar quality of US hegemony has been that, for most of its history, the United States has mattered more to other countries than other countries have mattered to the United States. This asymmetry can be observed across issue areas. Trade makes up a much smaller portion of US$ GDP than it does in the interconnected economies of Europe or the export powerhouses of Asia. On security, the physical isolation of the United States has given it a natural buffer unavailable to its allies around the world, who depend on US military guarantees for their security. And the country's vast size, resource abundance, wealth, and sophisticated technical institutions make it more resilient than most states in the face of threats like swine flu, cybercrime or food scarcity. To be sure, postwar globalization has eroded the "splendid isolation" of the United States in profound ways, making it far more dependent on the rest of the world than ever before, and prompting an unprecedented American engagement in global governance. The point is, rather, that this growing interdependence is highly unlikely, on its own, to prompt the United States to the higher level of leadership required to undo gridlock.

Related, there are also barriers to global cooperation within US domestic politics that are unlikely to dissipate in the near future. This book is about global gridlock, a specific condition of contemporary global governance, but the term is also increasingly applied to the government of the United States, and the US Congress in particular. Two of the most respected observers of Congress have recently published a book whose title bluntly states the situation: *It's Even Worse than It Looks: How the American Constitutional System Collided with the New Politics of Extremism* (Mann and Ornstein 2012). Most observers join Mann and Ornstein in blaming this deadlock on rising partisanship, which itself has many causes, including rising inequality, a gap between older and younger generations on social issues, the toxic role of interest group money in electioneering, decades of gerrymandering, and the shifting racial mix of the US population (see McCarty et al. 2006). Measures of political ideology now show that the most conservative Democrat in Congress is to the left of the most liberal Republican. In other words, the scope for compromise is extremely narrow (McCarty et al. 2006).

Importantly, these shifts have not simply made liberals more liberal and conservatives more conservative. Rather, they have pulled the Republican Party sharply to the right while leaving the Democratic Party essentially where it has been since the 1990s. A casualty of this shift is Richard Lugar, a Republican who served as Senator from Indiana from 1976 to 2012. Lugar was a key figure behind US arms control policy, galvanizing support in his party for strategic reductions with the Soviet Union, and for controlling warheads after the end of the Cold War. In 2012 he was denied a seventh term by a "Tea Party" challenger within his own party, who convinced Republican voters that Lugar had been overly accommodating toward the Democrats. Acknowledging defeat, Lugar pointed out the danger of entrusting politics to partisans: "They have worked to make it as difficult as possible for a legislator of either party to hold independent views or engage in constructive compromise. If that attitude prevails in American politics, our government will remain mired in the dysfunction we have witnessed during the last several years" (Lugar 2012).

As Lugar's defeat highlights, the important point for our purposes is the impact of this dysfunction on US foreign policy. Traditionally, this has been an area of relative consensus within American political elites, reflecting the unifying effects of national interests and the low salience of foreign policy in electoral politics. But global governance has always served as a bugbear for the Republican Party's isolationist wing – the same wing that prevented President Wilson from bringing the United States into the League of Nations that he designed. The party's rightward turn has given these voices renewed power. This turn is especially devastating for formal multilateral institutions. The US Constitution requires treaties to be ratified by two-thirds of the Senate. In an age of sharp partisanship, this has become a virtually insurmountable threshold.

Consider the fate of the Convention on the Law of the Sea. Concluded in 1982, the treaty has now been ratified by 162 countries. It lays out a set of common policies and guidelines, most of them quite technical, for defining international waters and managing their common use. The overwhelming expert consensus is that it is in the national interest of the United States to ratify this treaty, and in 2012 the Obama administration made a push to secure the two-thirds majority of the Senate needed to do so. It failed, despite having the support of the US military and every single former Secretary of State and Secretary of Defense, Democrat and Republican alike (Dempsey 2012). Given these obstacles to the ratification of a technical treaty related mainly to maritime navigation, imagine the political shift in US politics that would be required to obtain a US commitment to a substantive climate change program, or regulations regarding the use of drones in combat, or other far more difficult political issues. In short, in our view, it is unlikely in the near future that US politics will provide leadership out of gridlock at the global level.

Europe

The neoconservative writer Robert Kagan (2003) has popularized the idea of Europe as "Venus" to America's "Mars" – an attractive and pleasant continent, but ultimately passive in world affairs, too committed to its domestic social protections and peaceful integration to navigate geopolitics without America's protection. But a visitor from either of those planets, looking only at the observable data, would likely come to a different conclusion. The GDP of the 27 members of the European Union is larger than that of the United States. The EU trades more with China and the United States than either of those countries trade with each other, and it is much more important to global investment flows (both as a destination and a source) than the emerging economies combined. Europe accounts for a quarter of the world's military spending, half its official foreign aid, and it even gives more private charity abroad than the United States. It is also overrepresented in global institutions from the UN Security Council to the technical organizations that designate common product standards. As Andrew Moravcsik argues, by these measures Europe is the world's true "second superpower" (2010). Moreover, it is the polity most committed to effective multilateral governance, a commitment forged in its own history of violence and in the remarkable project of integration that followed. Could Europe prove both willing and able to move the world beyond gridlock?

At the time of writing the European project faces an economic crisis that perfectly encapsulates the barriers that Europe must overcome before it can play this role. It also, interestingly, reflects the logic of gridlock on a regional scale. On January 1, 1999, a new European currency, the euro, began taking over from the Deutsche mark, the franc, the lira, and the peso, among others; today it serves as the sole currency for 17 European countries. This created a fiction that, in effect, allowed countries like Greece to borrow money at rates more appropriate for Germany. And borrow they did, disregarding the weak fiscal rules that had accompanied the switch to the euro (rules that even the core euro countries broke). The resulting loans – not just to governments, but to private sector entities as well, especially in the construction sector – looked fine as long as the economy was performing well. But they could not continue forever, and the financial crisis of 2008–9 and the subsequent deleveraging made the fiction that Greek debt was just as valuable as German debt impossible to sustain.

Since 2009, European leaders have met over 20 times to try to resolve the crisis, declaring at each meeting a comprehensive solution. The markets have taken a different view, seeming to require ever greater bailout funds and loan guarantees. Tellingly, the most effective part of the EU response has not been these multilateral summits, but the efforts of the more independent and technocratic European Central Bank. The Bank provided emergency credit directly to commercial banks throughout the crisis, preventing the Euro from collapsing, just as a lender of last resort should. But these actions pushed the envelope of what is allowed under the Bank's mandate, and it possesses no power to go beyond crisis management and address the underlying issues.

As with the global governance of finance, existing institutions have been sufficient to prevent total disaster, but not to effectively manage the problem. The fundamental issue is that, unlike a nation-state, the eurozone does not have the ability to make fiscal transfers between its subordinate units. Many US states have little to teach Greece in terms of fiscal management, but they have not brought down the US dollar, in part because Washington's fiscal power implicitly distributes risk across the various states. For the eurozone to gain this power, it would have to delegate as much authority over budgets to Brussels as US states do to Washington. This would represent a far greater level of institutionalization than European publics have so far been willing to bear. In this way, the euro crisis parallels the logic of gridlock. An initial round of European cooperation – the creation of a currency union – has greatly increased interdependence, in terms of trade, migration, and crucially, debt. In purely functionalist terms, this new level of interdependence would require even more institutionalization – a fiscal union. But such a solution seems outside the realm of political possibility.

Which path Europe chooses out of the euro crisis will have crucial implications for its ability to confront gridlock at the global level. A messy disintegration of the euro would risk causing lasting economic damage and cast a pall over the EU's efforts to play a more cohesive and effective role in world affairs. Continuing to muddle through – doing the minimum to prevent catastrophe while leaving the fundamental problems unaddressed – is perhaps the most likely strategy. If this is the case, we should not expect Europe to play a more constructive role in the fight against gridlock in the near future (consider the Rio+20 at which the distractions of the euro crisis deprived global environmental governance of a key supporter when it was needed most). More optimistically, it is certainly within the realm of possibility that the present crisis will actually make possible a deeper level of regional institutionalization that over the long run makes Europe a stronger player in global affairs. Imagine that national governments in fact decide to grant Brussels the greater fiscal powers required to make the euro credible. Not only would this likely resolve many of the current financial woes facing the continent, it could also potentially catalyze deepening integration in foreign affairs. This is not, in our estimation, the most likely outcome, but it does contain a certain poetic hope, analogous to the US case: resolving a form of gridlock at the European level could significantly help resolve gridlock at the global level.

China

China's willingness and ability to engage in existing global governance structures is perhaps the most significant single factor affecting the continuance of the postwar order, an issue we have addressed throughout this book under the more general topic of emerging multipolarity. For observers outside the country, the issue is a reliable source of discontent. China has been criticized for its unwillingness to move its negotiating position at the Copenhagen climate summit (chapter 4), to allow its currency to trade at market rates (chapter 3), and to support efforts to apply various forms of pressure to Sudan, Syria, Iran, North Korea and other governments via the Security Council (chapter 2), among other examples. Robert Zoellick has called on China to act as a "responsible stakeholder" in the multilateral system, a concept that has gained significant traction in the Western discourse regarding China's rise (Zoellick 2005).

These critics all identify important ways in which China has hampered the resolution of global problems, but they are only one part of the story. Much of the public discussion of these issues in the West and in Japan ignores the many ways in which China already does participate in and contribute to global governance. While China's tough negotiating tactics and intransigence often frustrate its interlocutors, its record of compliance with the international commitments it has agreed to is in fact noteworthy. China's role in global environmental governance is often regarded as one of a monolith "veto player," blocking reform. Yet it has complied with all of the environmental treaties it has signed (Oksenberg and Economy 1998). Foreign companies often complain about the lack of enforcement of intellectual property rights in the country. However, this nonenforcement arguably stems more from the government's inability to control powerful economic interest groups than duplicity on the part of the government. Indeed, the central government has not only created a special court just to deal with foreign intellectual property rights concerns but has also taken dramatic steps to empower private arbitral tribunals to adjudicate commercial disputes between Chinese companies and foreign firms.[4] Such a high level of delegation to foreign, private authorities is extraordinary for a nominally communist, statist government, and represents how far China is willing to go to accommodate global governance when its interests are at stake.

This last point embodies the central truth: China's engagement in the global order is fundamentally pragmatic. In chapters 2 and 3 we noted how a stable global order and a liberalized world economy provided the conditions in which certain countries could take advantage of the opportunities afforded by the global economy and develop at a rapid rate. China is the most significant example of this growth model; in other words, it is one of the largest beneficiaries of the postwar order. This, then, is the ultimate reason why the rise of China has not led to a fundamental breakdown in the global order – that order serves Chinese interests more than it constrains them.

Will this alignment continue? Ironically, the "responsible stakeholder" moniker may have emerged at a time that will come to be regarded, in retrospect, as a high point in China's commitment to global governance. Much depends on the development of the Chinese economy. Over the past three decades, China has sustained an average growth rate of nearly 10 percent, lifting more people out of poverty in a shorter time than ever before. This extraordinary accomplishment was fueled, first, by the rationalization of the domestic economy in the 1980s – that is, the decollectivization of agriculture, the introduction of market pricing, and the reform of state-owned enterprises. But by the end of that decade these "low-hanging fruit" had been picked, and new strategies were required to sustain growth and develop the economy. Gradually, export-oriented manufacturing connected to foreign direct investment has filled that role (Wang 2006). Over the late 1990s and 2000s, China's favorable trade balance and currency controls gave the government a massive reserve of hard currency, and government control of the banking system effectively transferred wealth from consumers to state-owned enterprises and, ultimately, state-owned banks. This allowed for massive investment in infrastructure projects that has enabled domestic production at a scale never before seen.

But like the rationalizations of the early 1980s, neither the export model nor the investment model can generate 10 percent annual growth rates ad infinitum. And so there is a widespread consensus – including among China's top leaders – that China must rebalance its economy toward domestic consumption and private enterprise (see World Bank and Development Research Center 2012). This will not be easy. It runs against the interests of the economic groups that have grown to depend on the current growth model, such as the large state-owned enterprises. It impairs the ability of local governmental officials to direct the economy, and with it their own prospects for promotion and, all too frequently, corruption. And it means that China will likely grow on average more slowly in coming years than it has in the past.

All of these shifts will have profound implications for the political order. The Communist Party of China's legitimacy rests firmly on its economic record, but this will, inevitably, look less and less impressive as the rate of growth slows. If there is a sharp downturn, the implications could be devastating. This is not the place to speculate in any detail on the likely political trajectories that follow, but we submit that, in the medium term at least, none bode well for China's ability to make the kind of contribution to global governance that would move us beyond gridlock. Indeed, the opposite is quite likely. Let us assume, perhaps optimistically, that China moves in a more liberal direction, with top leaders summoning the political will to push difficult rebalancing on recalcitrant interest groups, and with politics growing more transparent and competitive. It seems likely that under such conditions political leaders would benefit from currying public favor in order to give themselves increased leverage against the old guard, particularly in the military. This could take the form of nationalist grandstanding, with negative implications for China's neighbors and global institutions alike.

Another possibility is that the conservative factions of the Communist Party resist economic and political reform until some breaking point is reached, for example, a massive default by municipal governments on their loans from state-owned banks and an ensuing collapse of municipal construction projects (it is estimated that Chinese municipalities hold as much as US$2.2 trillion in debt, equivalent to a third of the nation's GDP (Barboza 2011)). Such an event could have system-wide political repercussions, as these projects employ many of the migrant workers – rural laborers who come to the cities to work for meager wages, often under uncertain legality. Though the Chinese government is ferociously adept at dampening the destabilizing effects of local protests, it is unclear how the political system would be able to deal with a nationwide event.

The basic point is that, under a range of likely scenarios, the attention of China's leaders over the next decades is almost certain to be focused inward. This offers little hope for resolving gridlock, and indeed suggests several pathways through which it might be exacerbated.

The emerging democracies

Perhaps the greatest hope for global leadership away from gridlock lies with what we might call the emerging democracies. Countries like India, Brazil, South Africa, and Turkey (plus a number of medium-level powers around the world) are changing the way they operate in global affairs. Though their potential to generate effective global governance remains largely unrealized, a number of factors suggest that these countries could come to play a much larger, and constructive, role in the future.

First, the new democracies possess the demographic and institutional structures for long-term and sustainable – if not necessarily meteoric – growth. Unlike China, Russia, and the West, countries like Brazil, India, and South Africa possess young and growing populations. While poverty continues to prevent these countries from fully capitalizing on these human resources, health and education trends are broadly positive. Brazil in particular has shown how more robust social programs can stimulate not just rapid growth but widely distributed gains. Similarly, though political and legal institutions remain marred by corruption and inefficiency, a basic commitment to democracy and the rule of law generates a minimum threshold of predictability and stability over the long term.

Second, these countries have been advocates for alternative global orders that are more responsive to the needs of a broader swath of humanity. India was a leader of the Non-Aligned Movement during the Cold War, seeking to articulate a geopolitical alternative to East–West rivalry. It was also a key force behind the New International Economic Order, the attempt to remake the rules of the global economy mentioned in chapter 3. While neither attempt to steer global governance away from the preferences of the great powers proved successful, South-led initiatives of this kind are likely to be more important as these countries grow.

These foundations may yet lead to new groupings and organizations that build our mutual capacity to govern transnational problems. Brazil has been particularly active under presidents Lula da Silva and Rousseff. In 2010 it joined with Turkey to offer a surprise deal with Iran during a particularly tense moment in the standoff between the West and Tehran over the latter's nuclear program. In the wake of the 2011 Libyan intervention, it has suggested the concept of "Responsibility while Protecting" (RWP) to modify what it sees as the West's overly broad understanding of the Responsibility to Protect (Viotti 2011). The

Iranian intervention was widely condemned as naive in the West, and RWP has yet to take on a more concrete form, but both initiatives suggest a country that is engaged in solving global problems without the encumbrances of some of the other major powers (Rothkopf 2012).

Obviously, this potential is largely unrealized. Basic state capacity remains a problem; India still has fewer diplomats in total than the United States has in its New Delhi embassy alone (Stuenkel 2012). More fundamentally, politicians in each of these countries may face pressures that prevent them from realizing the potential, and increasing power will no doubt change these countries' preferences, and not necessarily for the better. But ultimately there is a choice to be made. In the next section, we take up the question of how this agency, should it be applied, might make the largest impact.

The Changed Global Landscape

The scenarios of deepening gridlock set out above describe a set of negative trends, international and domestic, that could significantly worsen the dilemma of gridlock. Yet, as noted, not all the forces at work are negative. There are significant examples of success in multilateral governance; many have been discussed in the preceding chapters. Politics at all levels is contested and this is no less true of the field of global governance. In the following section we lay out some countertendencies that could be built on to move beyond gridlock. Constant pressure from social movements, new networked political agents, coalitions of states and nonstate actors seeking innovations in transnational governance, and public and private partnerships are a breeding ground of productive experimentation and innovation in global governance.

It is important to recall what has made these positive trends possible. Gridlock is in large part due to the success of the multilateral order; that is, seeds fertilized by interstate cooperation have now grown to make further interstate cooperation more difficult. But the growth of interdependence and institutionalization has also led to changes that make possible new avenues of global collective action. Increasingly, these do not look like the "traditional" intergovernmental diplomatic negotiations that generated the initial postwar order. Past institutional structures and practices do not simply weigh, to adapt a phrase from Marx, like a mirage on the living (1852: ch. 1). The contested nature of power and governance at all levels reveals powerful countertrends which under the sign of crisis can produce "incidental consequences," as Habermas puts it (2012: 10–11), that can catalyze progress in the multilateral order.

A number of trends can be identified within the changed landscape of world politics. First, there has been a general trend of integration between national and international political arenas (Milner 1998; Slaughter 2004a). The relationship between national governments and international bodies is not unilinear, but rather overlapping and reflexive to pressures coming from all sides (domestic constituencies, IGOs, global civil society, etc.). The two distinct spheres of traditional politics – national and international – have merged in some key respects. This has been well documented throughout this book in the discussions of self-reinforcing interdependence and illustrated by numerous examples of overlapping communities of fate that now exist in various governance sectors. As we have seen, a significant variety of institutional arrangements have been created in response to this trend, and this has included substantial innovation and change resulting in diverse forms of multi-actor, multisectoral and multilevel governance.

The integration of national and international politics has also had an impact on our understanding of politics. The manner in which politics is conceived in the contemporary world can no longer be focused only on Realist state-centric modes of analysis (Keohane and Nye 1974; Putnam, 1988; Moravcsik 1997; Slaughter 2004a). While this shift in perception has had its critics (Gilpin 2002), the realities of politics today gives little support for seeing the nature and form of global governance through the lens of the unitary state acting alone, despite the resilience of great power politics. The greatest issues now confronting the world are not delineated and distributed neatly along national boundaries, and neither is the debate on how to solve them. The diffusion and growth of transborder governance arrangements reflect this integration of politics in significant ways. Recognition of this trend means that we can begin the move away from gridlock informed by a complex understanding of the enmeshment of the national, international, and transnational. Any other starting point simplifies the character of the form and nature of global politics and masks the nature of political relationships in the contemporary world.

A second trend that can be observed since 1945 is the emergence of powerful nonstate actors in the development of transborder governance. Nonstate actors such as INGOs, MNCs, and even individuals have always been active agents in political debate, but the manner in which they influence international politics has changed in significant ways. While these actors had varying degrees of influence in international politics in earlier periods, their impact came largely through lobbying their national governments. In this mode of political influence, nonstate actors aggregate and articulate domestic interests to the state, shaping the preferences of a state which in turn determine the state's behavior in international politics.

Although the direct relationship between nonstate actors and the state remains an important link for political participation, nonstate actors now also influence international politics more directly (Haas 1991; Keck and Sikkink 1998; Betsil and Corell 2008). Through direct lobbying of global governance bodies, nonstate actors shape political debate internationally, in turn influencing the behaviour of states from both above and below. This can be seen across the sectors we have discussed. The Ottawa process for a landmine treaty is perhaps the most prominent example of nonstate actors participating in security governance with marked success, and banks have started to lobby the Basel Committee on Banking Supervision directly on issues such as capital reserve requirements when they find national policies contrary to their interest. This trend in general is strongest, however, in environmental governance where INGOs have become such important actors that their influence has been called "functionally equivalent to diplomats," since they perform "many of the same functions as state delegates" such as interest aggregation and articulation, negotiation and submitting policy recommendations (Hale and Held 2011: 9; Betsill and Corell 2008). The emergence of nonstate actors certainly creates a more complex governance system than one comprised of traditional principal–agent relationships between states and purely intergovernmental organizations. This can pose potential problems of fragmentation, but it also broadens the platform for political deliberation and debate (Risse-Kappen 1995; Anheier et al. 2006; Betsill and Corell 2008).

Third, there has been a shift in how regulation and governance are enforced. The diverse forms of global governance produce equally diverse regulation that is intended to shape the behavior of states. This requires, first and foremost, the participation of states in regulatory structures, but it also requires that states comply with the result of negotiations even if it is against their own self-interest. Traditionally, compliance in international agreements is linked to the possibility of punitive measures (i.e. sanctions) that penalize violators in order to ensure appropriate conduct. Increasingly, however, trends can be detected that ensure that rules are enforced through alternative means such as voluntary based arrangements and initiatives, as well as international standards that are adhered to by actors because of their reputational and coordinative effects (see Kerwer 2005). Norm diffusion and capacity-building can be an even more powerful tool for behavioral change than punitive measures (Chayes and Chayes 1995). This approach seeks to do more than just punish violators by building the capacity and incentives for actors to comply with established international standards. Institutions such as the UN Global Compact and the International Network for Environmental Compliance and Enforcement are good examples of the voluntary and informal regulation that is growing in global governance bodies (see Hale and Held 2011). Similarly, transparency initiatives such as the Carbon Disclosure Project use information disclosure to build market incentives for pro-social behavior without employing coercion. These innovations in compliance schemes are positive steps in developing more effective governance; they indicate a range of productive experiments in new methods of creating rules and systems of enforcement which a diversity of public and private actors can both engage with and uphold. Self-evidently, however, they are not sufficient in and of themselves to solve the problem of compliance and enforcement as a spiral of global bads continues to form.

Fourth, overlapping with the trends mentioned above, there has been a proliferation of new types of global governance institutions in the postwar era, and especially since the end of the Cold War (Hale and Held 2011). These are not multilateral, state-to-state institutions, but instead combine various actors under varying degrees of institutionalization. New forms of governance include "transgovernmental networks" of ostensibly domestic officials who collaborate with their peers across borders (Slaughter 2004b), multi-stakeholder initiatives that bring public and private actors together to address common problems, and purely private institutions like voluntary corporate regulations or the private arbitral tribunals that provide contract adjudication for most transborder commerce. In some areas of global governance these kinds of institutions rank among the most important. The case of global finance, discussed above, stands out in this regard, but other examples include global health governance (e.g. the Global Fund, the GAVI alliance, and polio eradication efforts, see Hanefield 2011; Harmer and Bruen 2011; Koenig-Archibugi 2011) and standard-setting (Büthe and Mattli 2011).

In aggregate, these new institutions have contributed to the growing polycentricism observed in many areas of global governance, particularly in the economic and environmental realms (see chapters 3 and

4, respectively). In security, in contrast, states seem to be reluctant to cede their central role, even as the challenges they face erode their monopoly over the use of force.

A polycentric approach can have advantages and disadvantages. On the one hand, it can mean that more issues are addressed in meaningful ways – through specialized bodies qualified to regulate and govern a specific issue area. It can also represent a pathway around gridlock in multilateral institutions. On the other hand, it can exacerbate institutional fragmentation. More importantly, in many areas of global governance it is by no means clear that institutional innovation alone is sufficient to fill the governance gap gridlock leaves in its wake. At best these new institutional forms represent a partial solution (Hale and Held 2011).

Pathways through Gridlock

Within this changed landscape of global politics there are several ongoing trends that may affect the chances of continued gridlock into the future. Among these are popular protest movements that seek to change the nature and form of the global order. The early twenty-first century has been marked by punctuated moments of social activism ranging from global protests against the wars in Afghanistan and Iraq, demonstrations against the Bretton Woods organizations and significant protests against the WTO, to similar types of actions at various environmental summits that have taken place throughout the world. These demonstrations have included diverse voices across national identities as well as across socioeconomic classes (see Pleyers 2010). At any given protest in Washington DC one might find a parent with a child holding a picket sign alongside the anarchistic "black bloc" that strives to disrupt summits. The general trend that has emerged is a powerful expression of grassroots popular movements that follow, in real time, the negotiations and forums held on the global issues that we have discussed throughout this volume. This layer of involvement has been catalyzed and accelerated by the revolution in information technology. Contemporary activism seeks to capitalize on IT innovation and uses technology for coordination and messaging which ultimately reaches conventional media outlets and, in turn, reaches mobile phones, computer screens, and household television sets throughout the world.

More recently, this form of activism can be seen in two prominent examples. The Occupy Wall Street movement that spread first across the US in 2011, then globally, is one illustration of how bottom-up networking and alternative politics have gained prominence in global debate. Thousands of individuals gathered, initially on the streets of Manhattan and later across the world to protest the perceived corruption of financial and equity trading and the gross inequalities that such activity is associated with. "Occupy," as the movement became known, began as an amorphous social movement rallying against the disproportionate political influence of the world's financial elite. It enjoyed several months of high-profile protest and countless acts of civil disobedience until its influence gradually waned. While Occupy had an impact on public opinion and the agenda of debate across many Western countries, this did not translate into an effective challenge to the political power of financial capital, much less to more effective governance of financial risk at the global level.

On the other side of the world a set of revolutions unfolded which in fact inspired elements of the Occupy movement. The popular uprisings known as the Arab Spring catalyzed latent opposition to dictatorial regimes that had long maintained power through repressive and coercive threats of violence. What started in Tunisia, as a single act of self-immolation, quickly spread to Egypt and Libya – culminating in regime changes in one way or another in all three countries – and beyond. While the movements in these countries often had mixed ends, they were all accelerated in significant measure by common means – the diffusion of communication technologies and the power of social media. The same is true for the spread of protest in other parts of the Middle East stretching from Jordan to Bahrain. The Arab Spring shook the power structures of the postcolonial regimes that dominated Middle East politics for over 40 years. Yet, these horizontal movements of change are rarely in themselves sufficient to resolve power transitions, where well-established elites (economic, social, religious, military) find ways to diffuse them and retain key elements of control of the political agenda. Moreover, the technological advances that created the space for broad and effective populist movements are not simply neutral tools for popular mobilization. They have also been deployed in order to enhance state-led capacities of surveillance and – if need be – repression (Ulrichsen and Held 2011).

Irrespective of the ends of the Occupy and Arab Spring movements, the transformative effects of technology and social media are significant enabling conditions. Advances in technology have made it easier for hundreds of thousands of individuals to organize in a coordinated manner that affects political structures in meaningful ways. Surely, the world has yet to see the full impact these technologies will have on politics, just as it would have been impossible to foresee the impact of Gutenberg's printing press a mere decade after its invention. This relates to one possible scenario for politics beyond gridlock; that a grassroots voice organized and articulated in quintessentially popular ways can come to influence established institutional structures. The opportunities offered by such technology alone are, of course, limited and unpredictable. This technology has allowed for greater coordination in organizing a political movement of rebellion, but it in itself lacks the capacity to translate protest into new stable institutional arrangements. If this is true at the national level in a country like the US (faced with Occupy) or Egypt (faced with the movements of the Arab Spring) then it is even more true at the global level which necessarily involves state, regional, and global actors.

A second trend is the small way in which institutions are adapting to the challenges we have laid out. Gridlock does not imply total failure to meet second-order problems. For example, some institutions have accommodated emerging multipolarity by expanding their representative base; that is, by expanding the active number of participants in order to enhance the collective bargaining power and influence of marginalized states. The shift from a focus on the G5/7 to the G20 is one such example. The G20 architects sought to overcome problems of institutional inertia in the G5/7 by broadening it to include new rising powers in order to ensure both greater geographic and demographic balance. Such instances of adaptation have involved a degree of rapprochement from leading states whereby they have yielded elements of their exclusive privilege in order to foster greater inclusion and, thus, greater buy-in by a larger range of states into problem-solving at the global level. In addition, it entails that each state at the negotiating table recognizes that it cannot resolve the challenges ahead on its own without the support, collaboration, and cost-sharing of other key parties.

In other global areas, the economic and the environmental, we find similar trends. Adaptation was a dominant strategy during the most recent global financial crisis, which featured states temporarily adjusting their fiscal and monetary policies in loose coordination with one another in order to avoid a deepening of the crisis. In the environmental realm, adaptation has primarily taken the form of institutional pluralization. Unable to achieve their conservation goals in the major interstate fora, environmental advocates have created a range of transnational governance mechanisms that seek to advance the same goals by different means. However, strategies of rapprochement and institutional innovation also reach clear limits if the sovereign interests of great powers are at stake or if the structural integrity of the system is in question.

Adaptation strategies do very little to alter or reform the core governance schemes of key international institutions, such as the balance of power in the Security Council or the IMF. Rather, they focus on changes in the way participants cope with and manage the structural constraints codified in the system. Adaptation can include elements of institutional innovation and change, but for the most part it does not fundamentally change the rules of the game. Still, within these small adjustments to gridlock, we can perhaps see seeds that could be nurtured into more meaningful reforms.

A third trend of developments which might overcome gridlock involves reform of the organizational principles and structures of global governance. Institutional reform of the kind needed to resolve gridlock has, obviously, not been achieved, and this book has argued why it is especially difficult now. But this does not mean that it has not been tried. Indeed, efforts to alter radically the international system have been pursued repeatedly, and these efforts have had some positive impacts. Think, for example, of the Non-Aligned Movement or the New International Economic Order. Perhaps even more importantly, they remind us what a functional system of multilateral institutions might look like.

Breaking through gridlock cannot be achieved without representative and effective global governance institutions that have the capacity to create credible regulatory frameworks and to invest directly in the provision of global public goods and the mitigation of global public bads. Developing these institutions is not, as this book shows, unprecedented. The manifold political and legal transformations since 1945 have gone some distance toward reshaping the interstate system and providing stepping stones to both a universal constitutional order and reformed international institutions. The G20 signifies a shift away from the control of the multilateral order by the small clubs: the G1 (the USA), the G5 and the G7/8. It is, as we have argued, an important innovation which seeks to extend the representative base of international discussions and negotiations to a wider range of countries. However, as of writing, the G20 has neither a permanent secretariat nor institutional base and thus is far from a robust organizational structure capable of following through and implementing collective decisions. Nevertheless, it is an indication that global governance has neither been representative nor sufficiently coordinated and thus needs reform.

As the contemporary multi-actor, multilevel global system has outgrown the geopolitical settlement of 1945, there needs to be decisive change in both its representative and financial base if it is to be "fit for purpose" in the decades ahead. One cannot call a state a modern state, it is important to note, if it does not embed two principles: the principles of impartial representation and a depersonalized taxation system. If a system of representation and taxation depend on the whims and the voluntary contributions of the powerful and rich, then these principles are clearly absent. The significance of this is that the state then is reduced to a dependent relation on powerful elites and ruling groups and will necessarily reflect their interests. Since 1945 both the UN and the Bretton Woods organizations, along with many other international bodies, have been in a similar structural position; that is to say, they have been dependent on the power and resources, above all, of the 1945 victors. As a result, neither the principles of impartial representation nor impartial financing were embedded. This was not a problem when the main question was how to incentivize great power participation at the pinnacles of global governance and to secure their place in the international system. But what was once the basis of a helpful solution to a problem now constitutes the ground of institutional inertia and the failure to break down forces of gridlock.

Initiatives to make global governance more representative in the key decision-making structures of global power, above all the Security Council and the Bretton Woods institutions, have largely stalled. Despite reforms in the governance of the global economy – the transition from GATT to the WTO, the reform of the Basel Committee, and the redistribution of voting shares in the IMF – US and European powers remain firmly lodged. The reform process needs acceleration if the principles of impartial representation and a more impartial financing of international and transnational bodies are to be secured. This would require both the institutionalization of equitable representation and new resource flows to invest directly in the provision of global public goods. The character of political institutions is all too typically determined by the source(s) of their revenue. Effective global institutions thus need to be funded by new streams of resource flows for them to function in a manner which is no longer dependent on a small group of powerful interests. There have been various proposals for a financial transaction tax (FTT) that include the Tobin Tax, the Robin Hood Tax, and the G20 FTT. And while these proposals have not been implemented, other forms of FTT have been, as by 2011 there were 40 countries with FTTs. Additionally, there is increasing discussion and pressure for an EU FTT and continued debate on a global equivalent (Griffith-Jones and Persaud 2012). What these discussions recognize is that new forms of revenue can be put at the service of global problem-solving in a manner that does not put more demands on leading states, and breaks the pure dependency relation with them. Designing, yielding and directing new global revenue sources also strengthens the resolve for effective multilateral governance and encourages states and civil society organizations to problem-solve across issue areas, as was revealed by the discussion of the usefulness of a FTT at the 2012 World AIDS Summit.

The political space needed for the development of more effective and accountable global governance must be made by all those participating in existing institutions, but it would require more concessions from the leading states than from any others, difficult as this is to envisage now. The decision-making processes of many existing international bodies would need to be restructured in such a way that principles of impartiality and political equality are entrenched in their institutional design. The mechanisms for representation in international institutions could no longer be tilted in permanent favor of the 1945 victors, creating more room for the enfranchisement of other states, but also for the voices of nonstate stakeholders in global civil society. But even if broader representation is needed to accommodate shifting conditions, this enfranchisement runs the risk of exacerbating problems of emerging multipolarity. As we have seen throughout this book, the growing number and diversity of actors has proven anathema to effective governance. If each state is committed to its national interest and empowered through sovereignty to defend it without regard for the implications for others, then simply increasing the number of voices at the table will further slow multilateral mechanisms. For this reason, broadening representation must be matched with an equal shift away from absolutist sovereignty and, especially, de jure or de facto veto powers, such as those possessed by the P-5 or the virtual veto power the US enjoys in the IFIs. Instead, moves to broaden representation should be implemented in tandem with shifts toward qualified majoritarian decision-making systems, as exist in the European Union or in many national legislatures, for example. Meeting the challenge of a greater diversity of voices by including them in the participatory structure of institutions will fail unless fair procedures are in place to translate a greater plurality of voices into binding decisions.

Politics beyond Gridlock

Whether there is the political will to shift beyond gridlock is the most pressing question now in the global domain. Can the 1945 multilateral order be reforged to confront the deeper level of interdependence we now face? The crucial tests ahead include finding solutions to urgent problems concerning financial market regulation, global economic imbalances, climate change, the prevention of nuclear proliferation, and investing in capabilities more broadly to cope with global goods and bads. These tests are for the here and now, not some remote future. We face a choice between an effective and representative rule-based multilateral order, or the further development of gridlock and descent into the negative scenarios outlined above.

It should not be forgotten that the international order has been rebuilt before. The codification of the United Nations was the first step in the creation of a framework of rules embedding rights and responsibilities in the international order, as were the Bretton Woods institutions, and their successors. These developments were the result of crisis and can be thought of as "crisis innovations": international institutions and governance preceded by devastation and human destruction. Here and elsewhere one can observe that some of the most violent and catastrophic moments of human history have been followed by transformative institutional developments. While at present we are not facing an immediate catastrophe on the scale of World War II, we are facing a cumulative series of crises, some of which, like nuclear proliferation and climate change, could profoundly alter the basis of human life. Yet, despite the overwhelming significance of these problems, there has not yet been a pathway out of gridlock. Thus, the challenge is to find a way out of this institutional malaise without an engulfing crisis to act as a catalyst for change.

The key question is, therefore, how a politics can be developed that moves beyond gridlock. The distinctive pathways through gridlock outlined above – networking/alternative politics, adaptation and institutional reform – provide a general account of trends that might help overcome current forms of gridlock, but they in themselves do not explain how such a transformation could occur. While catastrophic crises have allowed for paradigm changes in institutional development in the past, the challenge is to develop a form of politics today that can provide an equivalent catalyst, that is to say, that can provide a way forward without a return to horrendous pressures and disastrous losses.

The new landscape of politics discloses one or two useful insights in this regard. Extensive global governance changes and developments reveal a compelling truth – that transformations in global governance today are rarely determined solely by top-down politics whereby powerful leaders or states exclusively dictate the rules of the game. The growth of the network society and horizontal communication across borders has given rise to strong and effective bottom-up political pressures that shape and influence global policy in substantial ways. Movement beyond gridlock, accordingly, needs to grow out of a symbiotic exchange between bottom-up and top-down politics. It is no longer acceptable that debate and policy formation is monopolized by powerful and exclusive clubs at the global level. And yet, leading powers of the world order are also needed to implement and embed the changes advocated through bottom-up politics. The interplay of bottom-up and top-down politics appears in many ways inevitable in any transformation of global governance arrangements. That said, there is still considerable room for failure. While the integration of bottom-up pressures may be inevitable, success is not.

Political change, whether at local, national or global levels, can be driven by economic, political or social actors. While there is no general rule about why and when political and social agents are likely to mobilize for change, there is rarely any political transformation unless there are interests at stake and agents willing and able to act (see Archibugi and Held 2011: 448–9). Throughout chapters 2–4 analysis has shown how there are numerous interests at stake in and across the diverse sectors of security, global economy, and the environment, and many voices and forces pressing for and against gridlock. While the vested interests are clear in sectors like security for preserving institutional inertia, there are numerous groups and agents pressing for the reform of security institutions. Likewise, throughout the global economy there are not just clashes of competitive interests but movements and forces pressing for institutional change. As for the environment, it has virtually been defined by the emergence of social movements pressing hard on sustainability issues for the last 40 years. Across all three sectors, not just interests but ideologies which define competing conceptions of the future are articulated again and again. While the gap remains huge between the forces of change and the changes needed to break gridlock, the sketch below offers clues as to which agents and actors might be most effective in bridging this chasm.

When considering possible scenarios of continued gridlock we discussed how political leaders who pursue unilateralism can undermine the multilateral order. However, it is also possible that strong leaders of a benign character could emerge who seek to bolster global governance and the rule of law at the international level. Rothkopf (2012), for example, has suggested that the current failure of leadership may inspire a new generation of leaders to try harder. A strong leader who advocates reform represents one example of an agent in the public domain that can potentially lead beyond gridlock. This form of leadership would, arguably, be most effective coming from either an already entrenched power in the global order – such as a head of state from one of the P-5 countries – and/or from an emerging market economy. As states remain the most powerful voices in global governance, attempts made by or on behalf of a leading state could have a significant impact. It is, of course, important to recognize the constraints placed on state leaders as they vie for continued support from domestic constituencies, and to bear in mind that, on our current assessment (see above), the prospects for the development and consolidation of such leadership does not look good at the present time.

More formal interest aggregation and articulation bodies such as political parties could also emerge as powerful voices in the reform of global governance. While political parties remain primarily organizations for structuring domestic politics, they are increasingly unable to limit their platforms to domestic concerns only. The World Economic Forum and the World Social Forum constitute alternative political platforms formed and exercised across national boundaries. The EU and the European Parliament remain perhaps the best example of how politics can be organized across national borders involving representation, debate and policy-making. Similarly, trade unions and the labor movement represent another group that aggregates interests across borders and advocates policy in global governance bodies. The labor movement has demonstrated some ability to do this by arguing for standardized labor and wage requirements in the ILO and for fair trade practices in the WTO. While these groups differ in significant ways, they all have in common the function of representing transnational interests in global governance bodies. This common thread between them could very well be influential in attempts to move away from gridlock in the years ahead.

MNCs have, moreover, considerable voice and influence in world politics and could be agents for change in the future. They have proven exceptionally adept at lobbying for their interests, both at the national and international levels. And while they are locked into the pursuit of changes that serve their interests, it is also true that they depend on global public goods as much as the rest of us. Without regularized standards and arbitration bodies, for example, the business of MNCs would be near impossible to conduct. Thus, while their influence remains limited to date – focused largely on private commercial concerns – their capacity for affecting governance bodies is something that could be a catalyst for broad reform of global governance more generally. All MNCs depend on well-ordered markets, minimal disruption from global bads such as climate change and pandemics, and public goods that provide a global infrastructure of education, health, communication, and transportation. In acting to support these, MNCs could play a role on behalf of effective and accountable reform. The role of large insurance and financial companies in pressing for more action on climate change, for example, represents a positive step forward, even as the efforts of these same companies to block effective financial regulation demonstrate the drawbacks of their agency.

The networking and alternative politics described earlier is a potential pathway through gridlock, enhanced by social media and communication technologies. More specifically, this form of politics can be thought of as the toolkit for hundreds of thousands of individuals across the globe who express their grievances and demands through social activism. As forms of media grow, and access to them, so too does the influence of diverse social movements around the world. In areas such as environmental politics and antiwar campaigns, social movements already exhibit some influence in global politics. Thus, it is possible that a transnational coalition of political groupings could emerge to further contest the trajectory of globalization and governance failures. By coalescing around causes that seek to bolster effective and impartial multilateral governance, transnational social movements have the potential to pressure individual states and the international community as a whole toward resolving the problems of gridlock.

Elsewhere, there are other voices that have the potential to help initiate a reform agenda, such as those advocating on behalf of marginalized groups. These groups most often come from underdeveloped and impoverished states and are the most vulnerable to the consequences of gridlock. They are most affected by violent conflicts in fragile and failing states, they have few safety nets to protect them from global economic crises, and they often feel the effects of climate change in the most significant ways. Having their voices heard is, of course, the biggest challenge and one that continues to explain the marginalization of their interests. Often their voice is only heard when it is adopted and refracted by other individuals and groups. These advocates play a major role in global civil society that continues to gain entry into global governance debates and policy formation.

Yet gaining entry into policy debates and determining policy are two very different things. As this book has shown, access alone is no guarantee of influence on policy and outcomes.

Gridlock means that it is highly unlikely that the multilateral order can survive in its current form. Something has to give if the global challenges described in this book are to be met. The political space for the development of a post-gridlock politics has to be made. In some measure, it is possible to detect that a certain space is being created by the activities of all those who are engaged in the struggle for alternative politics, the adaptation of institutions and their reform. Those who are pushing in this direction are seeking greater coordination and accountability of the leading forces of globalization; the opening up of IGOs to key stakeholders and participants; the pursuit of greater equity in the decision-making structures of global governance arrangements; the protection of human rights and fundamental freedoms; the promotion of sustainable development across generations; and the pursuit of peaceful dispute settlement in leading geopolitical conflicts. The pathways out of gridlock can start from these stepping stones. They can begin, in other words, from the new landscape of global politics, existing pathways through gridlock, and from the plurality of agents and agencies seeking to affect change in the global order.

Moreover, the project starts from the many achievements of multilateralism (from the foundation of the UN system to the development of the WTO), international law (from the human rights regime to the establishment of the ICC) and multilayered governance (from networks of central banks to the dense web of global policy-making fora). Since 1945 there has been a significant entrenchment of universal values concerning the equal dignity and worth of all human beings in international rules and regimes; the reconnection of international law and morality, with sovereignty no longer cast merely as effective power but increasingly as legitimate authority defined in terms of maintaining human rights and democratic values; the establishment of complex governance systems, regional and global; and the growing recognition that the public good – whether conceived as financial stability, environmental protection, or global justice – requires coordinated multilateral action if it is to be achieved in the long term. These developments need to be and can be built upon. The stakes are high, but so too are the potential gains for multilateralism and global governance if the aspirations to move beyond gridlock are realized.

There is no "silver bullet," or to put it in the terms used hitherto, no easily accessible coalition of political forces or institutional innovations capable of resolving gridlock on many of the issues set out in table 5.1, never mind resolving gridlock as a whole. While this gives rise to caution and some justified pessimism about progress, it is important that this be put in context. Global politics since 1989 has shown that spontaneous and dramatic political transformations can and do take place. Moreover, a breakthrough in negotiations and policy in any one of the areas of any one sector (security, global economy, environment) could catalyze a paradigm shift in the way the world community conducts the business of governance; a single successful act of reform could become a model for the resolution of other pressing global governance issues. For instance, a breakthrough on representation in the Security Council, or the World Bank, or the IMF could help create a more impartial approach to global challenges such that no particular national interest can trump the development of global public goods or the mitigation of public bads. Breaking the deadlock in global negotiations in trade, financial market reform, climate change or nuclear proliferation could have the same learning impact on other areas. In other words, we need to learn how the 1945 paradigm of multilateralism, that was so effective in shaping the postwar era, can be replaced by another fit to meet the demands of the twenty-first century. This is a task both for research and for policy-makers as well as political and social agents coming together to meet the challenges of individual gridlock mechanisms.

It is important to recall why progress on these issues remains so fundamental. Unresolved global challenges such as nuclear proliferation, global inequality, global infectious diseases, environmental degradation, and financial crises not only risk affecting the life chances and life expectancy of men, women, and children across the world in the future, but do so now in numerous ways. At the core of daily human insecurity, as well as the uncertainty created by risks ranging from new forms of terrorism to nuclear war or accelerating climate change, lie fundamental issues of survival, freedom, the rule of law, and social justice. In the aftermath of World War II the institutional breakthroughs that occurred provided the momentum for decades of global economic growth and geopolitical stability sufficient for the transformation of the world economy: the shift from the Cold War to a multipolar order, and the rise of new communication and networked societies. What worked then does not work anymore as gridlock freezes problem-solving capacity in global governance. The search for a politics beyond gridlock, in theory and in practice, is a hugely significant task – nationally and globally.

Notes

Introduction

1 As we outline in chapter 3, an International Trade Organization was proposed alongside the Bretton Woods organizations, but countries proved unwilling in the 1940s to commit themselves to hard rules on tariff reductions.
2 The mechanisms we posit are not new, but the combination of them, and their common roots in the trajectory of the postwar multilateral project, have not been recognized by scholars or policy-makers. We do not go as far as some scholars in the "historical institutionalist" field (e.g. Greif 2006), who question the utility of any general social scientific theory of institutions. We do, however, contend that it is intellectually productive for political scientists to apply such theories to specific historical moments.

1 Gridlock

1 We are not the only ones to make use of Lorenzetti's work for contemporary politics, see Skinner 1986; Prantl, forthcoming.
2 Ikenberry also emphasizes that the democratic and open nature of the domestic political systems of the leading states increased information about their motives and decision-making processes, thus making the commitments embodied in the postwar order more credible.
3 Which they characterized as multiple channels and linkages across societies, an absence of hierarchy between issue areas, and the circumscribed returns to the traditional measure of state power, military force. See Keohane and Nye 1977.
4 The firm also nearly collapsed in 2008–9 during the global financial crisis, only to be bailed out by the US government – a vivid reminder of the importance of the continued institutional support that states provide to even the largest and most iconic enterprises.
5 Measured as FDI inflows aggregated across the entire world, in US dollars at current prices and current exchange rates. Source is UNCTADstat.
6 Authors' calculation, based on subtracting annual 1970 figures from 2011 figures, divided by 1970 figures. GDP figures are based on real annual GDP, measured in US dollars at current prices and current exchange. Source for all data is UNCTADstat.

7 For example, in the case of the US, as more manufacturing jobs shifted to places like Mexico, Eastern Europe, and East Asia, there were fewer and fewer workers in the rich countries to combat this shift. In the US in 2011, only 11.8 percent of salaried workers belonged to a union, compared to over 20 percent in 1983 (the first year for which comparable data are available) (Bureau of Labor Statistics 2012). These changes reduced the political power of organized labor in wealthy countries, and so removed one of the key barriers to further globalization.
8 Authors' calculation based on GDP in current US dollar terms. Data source is the World Bank World Development Indicators.
9 Francis Fukuyama (2011) recently put forward a similar view.
10 Some point out that while multipolarity may be increasing in terms of the economic importance of emerging economies, it is kept relatively in check by the forces of institutional inertia, our other pathway to gridlock discussed above. Under this guise, the importance of the historical reemergence of countries like China and India as economic powerhouses is less significant than it would otherwise seem, because existing multilateral institutions have already "locked in" a position of relative dominance for Europe and the United States (see e.g. Wade 2011). There may indeed be instances when the institutional inertia pathway "countervails" the multipolarity pathway to gridlock. However it is unlikely that multilateral institutions will enjoy as many functional capabilities, or as much legitimacy for that matter, if rising multipolarity isn't accommodated in some way. Moreover, these interactive effects between gridlock mechanisms only underscore our point that the emergence of gridlock in our contemporary historical moment can be best conceived as a problem exhibiting characteristics of equifinality: there are multiple paths to the same outcome – many paths lead to gridlock.

2 Security

1 The OAS grew from the International Union of American Republics created in 1890.
2 Venezuela is set to become the fifth full member state, pending the ratification of its membership by Paraguay. Other associate member states include Bolivia, Chile, Colombia, Ecuador, and Peru, with Mexico and New Zealand participating as observer states of the agreement.
3 As Bassiouni (2008) has pointed out, there are a number of difficulties in differentiating an "internationalized" intrastate armed conflict from a non-internationalized one. See also Mundy 2011.
4 Furthermore, others point to the difficulties associated with measurement as such. Sambanis (2004: 835) points out, for example, that the number of civil wars occurring in the world between 1960 and 1993 ranges from 58 to 116 depending on what kind of definition of civil wars is applied.
5 The end of the Cold War also transformed the qualitative form of civil wars, in terms of the social technology of warfare, by decreasing the number of irregular (guerrilla) forms of warfare. See Balcells and Kalyvas 2010.
6 The UNDP *Human Development Report*'s initial articulation of human security included two distinct elements: "(1) Safety from chronic threats such as

hunger, disease and repression. (2) Protection from sudden and hurtful disruptions in the patterns of daily life – whether in jobs, in homes or in communities": that is, freedom from want and freedom from fear (see UNDP 1994 and Alkire 2003 for reference).

7 An additional 279 civilian deaths are counted though not attributed to any party (UNAMA 2012).

8 Kupchan's framework includes three distinct phases in the creation of a zone of stable peace: (1) rapprochement, (2) creation of security communities, (3) creation of a security union (2010: 28–37).

9 "Nothing in this Treaty shall be interpreted as affecting the inalienable right of all the Parties to the Treaty to develop research, production and use of nuclear energy for peaceful purposes . . ." (NPT text).

10 Article X, paragraph II is the clause included in the original text establishing the review process for the treaty and extension procedures by a majority vote of states party, either indefinitely or for some specified period of time.

11 This figure includes those deaths that result from SALW in nonconflict settings.

12 Terrorism in Colombia is an altogether different brand from that of networks such as al-Qaeda; fueled by guerrillas, paramilitaries, and drug lords, terrorism in Colombia stands out as an example of a consequence arising from a state's loss of the monopoly on the legitimate use of violence. This trend, more generally, will be explored later.

3 Economy

1 The expansion of the franchise to urban workers in 1832 had a decisive impact on shifting the balance of power toward industrial interests, and repeals of legislation such as the Corn Laws in England signified the new power bloc centered around the emerging industrial property owning class.

2 Interestingly, the nonofficial nature of the appointments allowed for de facto American participation in the committees through US businessmen, even though the United States itself was not a member of the League.

3 Under the prewar, liberal economic system, these policy options were much more limited: central banks rarely intervened, and demands for government intervention to secure full employment were also dampened by the fact that voting power was concentrated among wealthy elites, and labor was largely unorganized.

4 For an excellent history of the different positions and negotiation context at the time, see Bordo 1993: 31–4; also Helleiner 1994b.

5 A full discussion of the role of development assistance in growth falls beyond the scope of the present study.

6 For an extended discussion, see Bordo 1993.

7 This is a replication of Lane and Milesi-Ferretti 2007: 25.

8 Such a plan arguably reflected not only changes in macroeconomic thinking at the time, but also changes in the relative structural importance of financial institutions in the economy. After all, if there is one thing that banks hate more than recession, it is inflation, as it erodes the differential between the credit they lend out and its future value in repayment. See Gowan 1999; Konings 2008.

9 Transnational governance institutions can be understood as rule-making institutions which are organized above the level of the state but which are not strictly composed of state representatives, and which don't usually possess coercive authority (see Kahler and Lake 2008: 269–70). Note that some international relations scholars use the term "transgovernmental" to refer to relationships between state actors which are not executives/cabinets, a usage begun by Keohane and Nye 1974.
10 To be sure, national financial crises have important domestic drivers. Yet a central remit of many, if not most, existing global governance institutions is to prevent or at least to seriously mitigate crises.
11 WTO, "Statement by Murasoli Maran, Seattle Ministerial Conference," WT/MIN(99)/ST/17, 1999; cited in Scott and Wilkinson 2011.
12 Despite the bargaining advantages that a formal multilateral institution like the WTO offers, there are nevertheless many informal channels by which negotiation actually takes place. Bohne offers a comprehensive empirical study of these informal channels, including proposals for reform (see Bohne 2010: 68–74, 200–1).
13 Calculation by authors based on 2004–9 figures in IMF 2012: 190 (table A1), 205.
14 As of 2012 the figure stands at 27 million (ILO 2012: 9). Though, as the ILO's recent global labor market research indicates, since 2009 labor force participation has plummeted, with many workers leaving the formal labor market altogether, partially masking the official unemployment statistics and making the situation more alarming than it first appeared (ILO 2012: 10).
15 To be sure, many important national regulatory dynamics were at play. See FCIC 2011; Turner 2009.
16 On the legitimacy of the G20's governance structure in comparison with other multilateral institutions, as well as a critique of its effectiveness, see Vestergaard and Wade 2012.
17 See Ho 2002; Kerwer 2005. One model that persisted in the late 1990s especially was the widespread use of international standards and codes as a metric for evaluating financial safety and soundness. This metric was used both by the International Monetary Fund, as part of its monitoring criteria, and by financial markets themselves. See Alexander et al. 2006: 42, 229.
18 The CMIM was signed on December 28, 2009 and took effect on March 24, 2010.
19 The fact that European financial regulatory initiatives increasingly depart from global norms and practices as well only accelerates this trend – a point also raised by Sohn 2012: 17. See Young and Park 2013, for an explication of financial regulatory divergences across countries.
20 It might be contended that there is a trade-off between a broad base for a multilateral institution and its effectiveness. Yet some have persuasively argued that institutions such as the G20 achieve neither, and call for extensive membership reform (Vestergaard and Wade 2012).
21 Lagarde, quoted in Curry 2011.
22 Joseph Stiglitz, quoted in Thornton 2006: 50.
23 The US has actually shown some leadership on the issue, for example proposing an ambitious "cap" on countries' current account balances, at 4 percent

of GDP, but this was rejected as unrealistic by the Japanese and Germans (see J. Cho 2010).

24 See Wu Xiaoling, Vice Chairman of the Financial and Economic Committee under the National People's Congress, quoted in Jeong and Kim 2010.

25 Although, as Caporaso and Tarrow (2009) point out, institutionalizing embeddedness has been more successful in the European Union.

26 Official figures surely understate the true level of inequality as many wealthy individuals hide their income for tax purposes.

27 Another case along similar lines to what we outline below is the Equator Principles, which are a set of standards for promoting more environmentally and socially responsible bank lending practices. Modeled after the World Bank's International Finance Corporation (the private sector financing division of the World Bank), the Equator Principles emerged after a transnational network of NGOs had criticized international banks severely for funding large industrial projects which had disastrous impacts. See Wright 2012.

28 UN Agencies involved included the Office of the High Commissioner for Human Rights, UNEP, ILO, UNDP, UNIDO, United Nations Office on Drugs and Crime, UN Entity for Gender Equality and the Empowerment of Women.

29 For some critics, this is in fact worse than nothing. Soederberg argues, for example, that the Compact depoliticizes struggles to tame transnational corporations and serves to legitimate their growing presence. In doing so, the Global Compact "discredits the drive to tame corporate behavior through legally binding codes" (Soederberg 2007). As Rasche (2009) reminds us, the Global Compact is intended to be a necessary supplement to fundamentally incomplete state and nonstate regulatory approaches.

4 Environment

1 While it is certainly true that by catalyzing industrialization, globalization deepens environmental challenges, this is not the only effect. Vogel (1995) points out that international trade can in some cases lead to *cleaner* forms of production than those that existed previously. To the extent that multinational firms manufacturing goods in a developing country impose higher environmental standards than are required, de facto or de jure, domestically (which they are often compelled to do by shareholders or customers in the home country), they may in fact enhance environmental practices in the countries in which they work. This dynamic is important, though the general macrohistorical connection between globalization, industrialization, and environmental degradation is difficult to deny.

2 Aits are small, riverine islands formed by accumulating sediments; the term is used particularly with regard to the River Thames.

3 Interestingly, the same euphemism is used today in Beijing, where the government insists the frequent hazes are nothing more than harmless water vapor. This claim has little basis in reality, as the North China plain is distinctly arid for much of the year, and is given to weather conditions similar to those in London in which prevailing winds trap pollutants over the city.

4 For a more detailed version of this argument see Held et al. 1999: ch. 8.

5 For a more contemporary account of orchestration as a strategy employed by IGOs, see Abbott and Snidal 2009.
6 Similar pollution events had not been uncommon in the intervening century. "Smog" entered English usage some decades earlier, but the horrific toll of the 1952 incident gave the term new significance. The event was also called the "Big Smoke," a name sometimes used to describe London itself.
7 The magnitude of this shift can be seen in the creation of a special day for environmental consciousness. In 1969 US Senator Gaylord Nelson of Wisconsin proposed a national day of education and activism on environmental issues. Inspired by the tactics of grassroots groups protesting the Vietnam War (which were themselves inspired by the civil rights movement), Nelson proposed a series of "teach-ins" at which activists would hold small events in their communities to educate their neighbors about environmental issues. On April 22, 1970, some 300,000 Americans took direct part in these activities (McCormick 1989: 47), one of the largest social demonstrations in the nation's history. Today Earth Day is celebrated around the world.
8 In another example of the role private actors play in environmental governance, the Ford Foundation funded the transition costs between the Stockholm conference and the creation of the UNEP secretariat, maintaining Strong and his team.
9 Indeed, opposition from conservative figures in the Reagan administration nearly prevented US participation in the 1985 Vienna Convention. It was the timely intervention of industry leaders – albeit at the behest of environmentalists – that convinced the government to proceed. See Benedick 1998.
10 On the importance of the ozone hole for creating public concern, see Liftin 2010; UNEP 2010.
11 The report continued, "There is now a need to consolidate and extend relevant legal principles in a new charter to guide state behaviour in the transition to sustainable development. It would provide the basis for, and be subsequently expanded into, a Convention, setting out the sovereign rights and reciprocal responsibilities of all states on environmental protection and sustainable development. The charter should prescribe new norms for state and interstate behaviour needed to maintain livelihoods and life on our shared planet."
12 This was in addition to an agreement to negotiate a convention on desertification in the future.
13 The organizations included FAO, ITTO, Convention on Biological Diversity secretariat, UNDP, UNEP, World Bank, UN Department of Economic and Social Affairs, and the Center for International Forestry Research.
14 Specifically, Australia, Brazil, Canada, China, European Union, France, Germany, India, Indonesia, Italy, Japan, Korea, Mexico, Russia, South Africa, United Kingdom, and United States.
15 The exact ranking fluctuates with the stock market, but ExxonMobil, PetroChina, Royal Dutch Shell, Chevron, Petrobras, and BHP Billiton are typically found in the top ten (Forbes 2012).
16 A similar spate of partnerships came out of the "Rio+10" conference in 2002, which was similarly lacking in "hard" outcomes. See Witte et al. 2003; Hale and Mauzerall 2004; Andonova 2007.

5 Beyond Gridlock?

1 In 1945 there were 222 cars for every 1,000 Americans. By 1960 that number had climbed to 410, nearly twice as many. In 2009 it stood at 828 (US Department of Energy 2012).

2 Traffic congestion is only one problem in this regard, and we have not mentioned the many ancillary issues of smog, traffic fatalities, dependence on politically volatile oil, the health effects of a sedentary lifestyle, and climate change, to name just a few.

3 In order, these are the armies of China, United States, North Korea, Russia, and South Korea. India has the world's third largest active military force (see CIA 2012).

4 Distrustful of Chinese courts, firms prefer these private bodies as dispute resolution fora. Under Chinese law, the decisions of these private entities are binding in Chinese courts, and all judicial decisions to deny the enforcement of an arbitral award are automatically reviewed by a higher court.

References

Abbott, K. W. 2010. "The Transnational Regime Complex for Climate Change." Transnational Climate Governance Workshop. Durham: Durham University.

Abbott, K. W. 2012. "Engaging the Public and the Private in Global Sustainability Governance." *International Affairs* 88(3).

Abbott, K. W. and Snidal, D. 2000. "Hard and Soft Law in International Governance." *International Organization* 54(3).

Abbott, K. W. and Snidal, D. 2009. "Strengthening International Regulation through Transnational Governance: Overcoming the Orchestration Deficit." *Vanderbilt Journal of Transnational Law* 42.

Abdelal, R. 2007. *Capital Rules: The Construction of Global Finance.* Cambridge, MA: Harvard University Press.

Acemoglu, D. and Robinson, J. A. 2012. *Why Nations Fail: The Origins of Power, Prosperity, and Poverty.* New York: Random House.

Acemoglu, D., Johnson S. and Robinson J. A. 2005. "Institutions as the Fundamental Cause of Long-Run Growth." In P. Aghion and S. Durlauf (eds), *Handbook of Economic Growth.* Amsterdam: North-Holland.

Alexander, K., Dhumale, R. and Eatwell, J. 2006. *Global Governance of Financial Systems: The International Regulation of Systemic Risk.* Oxford: Oxford University Press.

Alkire, S. 2003. "A Conceptual Framework for Human Security." Working Paper 2. Centre for Research on Inequality, Human Security and Ethnicity, Oxford.

Alter, K. J. and Meunier, S. 2009. "The Politics of International Regime Complexity." *Perspectives on Politics* 7(1).

Andersen, S. O. and Sarma, K. M. 2005. *Protecting the Ozone Layer: The United Nations History.* London: Earthscan.

Anderson, K. and Martin, W. 2005. *Agriculture Trade Reform and the Doha Development Agenda.* Washington, DC: World Bank.

Andonova, L. B. 2007. "Globalization, Agency, and Institutional Innovation: The Rise of Public-Private Partnerships in Global Governance." MS.

Andresen, S. 2001. "Global Environmental Governance: UN Fragmentation and Co-ordination." In O. S. Stokke and Ø. B. Thommessen (eds), *Yearbook of International Co-operation on Environment and Development 2001/2002.* London: Earthscan.

Andriamananjara, S. 2002. "On the Size and Number of Preferential Trading Arrangements." *Journal of International Trade and Economic Development* 11(3).

Anheier, H. K., Kaldor, M. and Glasius, M. (eds). 2006. *Global Civil Society 2006/7*. London: Sage.

Annan, K. 1999a. Address to World Economic Forum in Davos. Reproduced in "Secretary-General Proposes Global Compact on Human Rights, Labour, Environment," UN Press Release SG/SM/6881. At http://www.un.org/News/Press/docs/1999/19990201.sgsm6881.html (accessed Oct. 2012).

Annan, K. 1999b. "Two Concepts of Sovereignty." *The Economist*, Sept. 16.

AP (Associated Press). 2011. "Libyan Estimate: At Least 30,000 Died in the War." *Guardian*, Sept. 8. At http://www.guardian.co.uk/world/feedarticle/9835879 (accessed Dec. 2012).

Archibugi, D. and Held, D. 2011. "Cosmopolitan Democracy: Paths and Agents." *Ethics and International Affairs* 25(4).

Arrighi, G. 2007. *Adam Smith in Beijing: Lineages of the Twenty-First Century*. London: Verso.

Arrighi, G. and Moore, J. 2001. "Capitalist Development in World Historical Perspective." In R. Albittron, M. Itoh, R. Westra and A. Zuege (eds), *Phases of Capitalist Development: Booms, Crises and Globalization*. New York: Palgrave.

Atkins, R. and Peel, Q. 2011. "G20 Strikes Compromise on Global Imbalances." *Financial Times*, Feb. 20.

Au, B. et al. 2011. *Beyond a Global Deal: A UN+ Approach to Climate Governance*. Berlin: Global Governance 2020.

Axelrod, R. and Keohane, R. 1985. "Achieving Cooperation under Anarchy: Strategies and Institutions." *World Politics* 38(1).

Babb, S. 2012. "The Washington Consensus as Transnational Policy Paradigm: Its Origins, Trajectory and Likely Successor." *Review of International Political Economy*, iFirst: 1–30.

Babb, S. and Buira, A. 2005. "Mission Creep, Mission Push, and Discretion: The Case of IMF Conditionality." In A. Buira (ed.), *The IMF and the World Bank at Sixty*. London: Anthem Press.

Baker, A. 2013. "The New Political Economy of the Macroprudential Ideational Shift." *New Political Economy* 18(1).

Balcells, L. and Kalyvas, S. 2010. "International System and Technologies of Rebellion: How the End of the Cold War Shaped Internal Conflict." *American Political Science Review* 104(3).

Baldwin, R. 2010. "Understanding the GATT's Wins and the WTO's Woes." *Policy Insight* 49. At http://www.cepr.org/pubs/policyinsights/PolicyInsight49.pdf (accessed Oct. 2012).

Ban Ki-moon. 2009. "Implementing the Responsibility to Protect: Report of the UN Secretary-General." UN doc. A/63/677, United Nations, Jan. 12.

Barboza, D. 2011. "Building Boom in China Stirs Fears of Debt Overload." *New York Times*, July 6.

Bartley, T. 2003. "Certifying Forests and Factories: States, Social Movements, and the Rise of Private Regulation in the Apparel and Forest Principles." *Politics and Society* 31(3).

Bassiouni, M. C. 2008. "The New Wars and the Crisis of Compliance with the Law of Armed Conflict by Non-State Actors." *Journal of Criminal Law and Criminology* 98(3).

BBC. 2005. "Counting the Civilian Cost in Iraq." BBC News, June 6. At http://news.bbc.co.uk/1/hi/world/middle_east/3672298.stm (accessed Oct. 2012).

BBC. 2010. "Stuxnet Worm Hits Iran Nuclear Plant Staff Computers." BBC News, Sept. 26. At http://www.bbc.co.uk/news/world-middle-east-11414483 (accessed Oct. 2012).

BBC. 2012. "Higgs Boson-Like Particle Discovery Claimed at LHC." BBC News, July 4. At http://www.bbc.co.uk/news/world-18702455 (accessed Oct. 2012).

Becker, J. and Shane, S. 2012. "Secret 'Kill List' Proves a Test of Obama's Principles and Will." *New York Times*, May 29. At http://www.nytimes.com/2012/05/29/world/obamas-leadership-in-war-on-al-qaeda.html?_r=1&pagewanted=all (accessed Oct. 2012).

Beebe, S. D. and Kaldor, M. 2010. *The Ultimate Weapon is No Weapon*. New York: Public Affairs.

Bell, M. L. and Davis, D. 2001. "Reassessment of the Lethal London Fog of 1952: Novel Indicators of Acute and Chronic Consequences of Acute Exposure to Air Pollution." *Environmental Health Perspectives* 109.

Benedick, R. E. 1998. *Ozone Diplomacy: New Directions in Safeguarding the Planet*. Cambridge, MA: Harvard University Press.

Benedictow, O. J. 2004. *The Black Death, 1346–1353: The Complete History*. Woodbridge: Boydell Press.

Berensmann, K. and Brandi, C. 2011. "The Financial Crisis and International Trade: The Consequences for Developing Countries." German Development Institute Briefing Paper 13.

Bernhagen, P. and Mitchell, N. J. 2010. "The Private Provision of Public Goods: Corporate Commitments and the United Nations Global Compact." *International Studies Quarterly* 54.

Besinger, K. 2008. "A GM Failure Could Mean a World of Hurt." *Los Angeles Times*, Dec. 7.

Best, J. 2008. "Hollowing Out Keynesian Norms: How the Search for a Technical Fix Undermined the Bretton Woods Regime." In J. G. Ruggie (ed.), *Embedding Global Markets: An Enduring Challenge*. Cheltenham: Ashgate.

Betsill, M. M. and Corell, E. (eds). 2008. *NGO Diplomacy: The Influence of Nongovernmental Organizations in International Environmental Negotiations*. Cambridge, MA: MIT Press.

Biermann, F., Pattberg, P., van Asselt, H. and Zelli, F. 2009. "The Fragmentation of Global Governance Architectures: A Framework for Analysis." *Global Environmental Politics* 9(4): 14–40.

Biermann, F., Pattberg, P., van Asselt, H. and Zelli, F. 2012. "Navigating the Anthropocene: Improving Earth System Governance." *Science* 335(6074).

BIS (Bank for International Settlements). 2011. *81st Annual Report*. Basel: Bank for International Settlements.

Blanchard, O. and Milesi-Ferretti, G. 2009. "Global Imbalances: In Midstream." IMF Staff Position Note 09/29, Dec.

Bloom, D. E. 1995. "International Public Opinion on the Environment." *Science* 269(5222): 354–8.

Bloomberg, M. 2012. "Innovation Hotbeds." *Financial Times*, Sept. 12.

Boardman, R. 1981. *International Organization and the Conservation of Nature*. London: Macmillan.

Bohne, E. 2010. *The World Trade Organization: Institutional Development and Reform*. London: Palgrave Macmillan.

Bordo, M. D. 1993. "The Bretton Woods International Monetary System: A Historical Overview." In M. D. Bordo and B. Eichengreen (eds), *Retrospectives on the Bretton Woods System: Lessons for International Monetary Reform*. Chicago: University of Chicago Press.

Bordo, M., Eichengreen, B., Klingebiel, M. and Martinez-Peria, M. S. 2001. Web Appendix for "Is the Crisis Problem Growing More Severe?" *Economic Policy* 32 (Spring). At http://www.economic-policy.org/pdfs%5CWeb Appendices%5Cbordo.pdf (accessed Oct. 2012).

Borio, C. and Disyatat, P. 2011. "Global Imbalances and the Financial Crisis: Link or No Link?" BIS Working Paper 346 (May).

Bornman, J. F. and van der Leun, J. C. 1998. "Appendix: Frequently Asked Questions." *Journal of Photochemistry and Photobiology B: Biology* 46: I–IV.

Botzem, S. 2012. *The Politics of Accounting Regulation*. Cheltenham: Edward Elgar.

Bowcott, O. 2012. "Drone Strikes Threaten 50 Years of International Law, Says UN Rapporteur." *Guardian*, June 21. At http://www.guardian.co.uk/world/2012/jun/21/drone-strikes-international-law-un?newsfeed=true (accessed Oct. 2012).

Bown, C. 2009. *Self-Enforcing Trade: Developing Countries and WTO Dispute Settlement*. Washington, DC: Brookings Institution Press.

Bowsky, W. M. 1964. "The Impact of the Black Death upon Sienese Government and Society." *Speculum* 39(1).

BP. 2012. *Statistical Review of World Energy 2012*. At http://www.bp.com/sectionbodycopy.do?categoryId=7500&contentId=7068481 (accessed Dec. 2012).

Bradsher, K. and Barboza, D. 2006. "Pollution from Chinese Coal Casts a Global Shadow." *New York Times*, June 11.

Braumoeller, B. 2003. "Causal Complexity and the Study of Politics." *Political Analysis* 11.

Bremmer, I. 2012. *Every Nation for Itself: Winners and Losers in a G-Zero World*. London: Penguin.

Brenner, R. 2002. *The Boom and the Bubble: The US in the World Economy*. London: Verso.

Breslin, S. 2012. "The 'China Model' and the Global Crisis: From Friedrich List to a Chinese Mode of Governance?" *International Affairs* 87(6).

Bulkeley, H. 2010. "Transnational Climate Governance: What Does the Database Tell Us?" Transnational Governance Workshop. Durham, UK.

Bull, H. 1977. *The Anarchical Society*. London: Macmillan.

Bureau of Labor Statistics. 2012. "Union Members 2011." News release, Jan. 27. At http://www.bls.gov/news.release/pdf/union2.pdf (accessed Oct. 2012).

Burnham, G., Lafta, R., Doocy, S., and Roberts, L. 2006. "Mortality after the 2003 Invasion of Iraq: A Cross-Sectional Cluster Sample Survey." *The Lancet*, 368 (9545): 1421–8. At http://www.brussellstribunal.org/pdf/lancet111006.pdf (accessed Oct. 2012).

Burnheim, J. 1986. *Is Democracy Possible?* Cambridge: Polity.

Büthe, T. 2010. "Private Regulation in the Global Economy: A (P)Review." *Business and Politics* 12(3).

Büthe, T. and Mattli, W. 2011. *The New Global Rulers: The Privatization of Regulation in the World Economy.* Princeton: Princeton University Press.

Calhoun, C. and Derlugian, G. (eds). 2011. *The Deepening Crisis: Governance Challenges after Neoliberalism.* New York: New York University Press.

Caporaso, J. and Tarrow, S. 2009. "Polanyi in Brussels: Supranational Institutions and the Transnational Embedding of Markets." *International Organization* 63(4).

Carr, E. H. 1946. *The Twenty Years' Crisis, 1919–1939: An Introduction to the Study of International Relations.* Rev. edn. London: Macmillan. Originally published 1939.

Carter, J. 2012. "A Cruel and Unusual Record." *New York Times*, June 24. At http://www.nytimes.com/2012/06/25/opinion/americas-shameful-human-rights-record.html?_r=1 (accessed Oct. 2012).

Carvalho, F. J. C. and Kregel, J. 2007. *Who Rules the Financial System?* Rio de Janeiro: IBase.

Cashore, W., Auld, G. and Newsom, D. 2004. *Governing through Markets: Forest Certification and the Emergence of Non-State Authority.* New Haven: Yale University Press.

Cassese, A. 1986. *International Law in a Divided World.* Cambridge: Polity.

Cassese, A. 1988. *Violence and Law in the Modern Age.* Cambridge: Polity.

Cassese, A. 1991. "Violence, War and the Rule of Law in the International Community." In D. Held (ed.), *Political Theory Today*. Cambridge: Polity.

CEIP (Carnegie Endowment for International Peace). 1920. *The Proceedings of the Hague Peace Conferences.* New York: Oxford University Press.

Cerny, P. G. 1994. "The Dynamics of Financial Globalization: Technology, Market Structure and Policy Response." *Policy Sciences* 27.

CGFS (Committee on the Global Financial System). 2008. "Central Bank Operations in Response to the Financial Turmoil." CGFS Papers 31 (July).

Chayes, A., and Chayes, A. H. 1995. *The New Sovereignty: Compliance with International Regulatory Agreements.* Cambridge, MA: Harvard University.

Cheung, W., Fung, S. and Tsai, S.-C. 2010. "Global Capital Market Interdependence and Spillover Effect of Credit Risk: Evidence from the 2007–2009 Global Financial Crisis." *Applied Financial Economics* 20(1–2).

Chin, G. 2011. "Global Imbalances: Beyond the 'MAP' and G20 Stovepiping." Centre for International Governance Innovation, Oct. 18. At http://www.cigionline.org/publications/2011/10/global-imbalances-beyond-%E2%80%9Cmap%E2%80%9D-and-g20-stovepiping-0 (accessed Oct. 2012).

Chinn, M. D. and Ito, H. 2008. "A New Measure of Financial Openness." *Journal of Comparative Policy Analysis* 10(3): 309–22.

Cho, J. 2010. "Geithner Calls for '4%' Rule but Comes under Fire." *Korea Times*, Oct. 22.

Cho, S. 2004. "A Bridge Too Far: The Fall of the Fifth WTO Ministerial Conference in Cancún and the Future of Trade Constitution." *Journal of International Economic Law* 7(2).

Cho, S. 2010. "The Demise of Development in the Doha Round Negotiations." *Texas International Law Journal* 45.

Chwieroth, J. 2010. *Capital Ideas: The IMF and the Rise of Financial Liberalization.* Princeton: Princeton University Press.

CIA (Central Intelligence Agency). 2012. *The World Factbook.* Washington, DC: CIA. At https://www.cia.gov/library/publications/the-world-factbook/ (accessed Nov. 2012).

Clark, I. 1989. *The Hierarchy of States: Reform and Resistance in the International Order.* Cambridge: Cambridge University Press.

Clark, P. and Leahy, J. 2012. "Rio+20 Declaration Lacking on Pledges," *Financial Times*, June 22.

Clarke, I. 1999. *Globalization and International Relations Theory.* Oxford: Oxford University Press.

Clarke, M. 2010. "Nuclear Disarmament and the 2010 NPT Review Conference." *Global Policy* 1(1).

Clavin, P. and Wessels, J. W. 2005. "Transnationalism and the League of Nations: Understanding the Work of Its Economic and Financial Organisation." *Contemporary European History* 14(4): 465–92.

Coase, R. H. 1960. "The Problem of Social Cost." *Journal of Law and Economics* 3: 1–44.

Cohen A. J. et al. 2004. "Urban Air Pollution." In M. Ezzati et al. (eds), *Comparative Quantification of Health Risks*, vol. 2. Geneva: World Health Organization.

Cohen, J. and Sabel, C. 1997. "Directly Deliberative Polyarchy." *European Law Journal* 3(4).

Cohen, R. 2010. "Reconciling Responsibility to Protect with IDP Protection." Brookings, Mar. 25. At http://www.brookings.edu/research/articles/2010/03/25-internal-displacement-cohen (accessed Oct. 2012).

Computer Weekly. 2010. "UN Rejects International Cybercrime Treaty." Apr. 20. At http://www.computerweekly.com/news/1280092617/UN-rejects-international-cybercrime-treaty (accessed Dec. 2012).

Conrad, B. 2012. "China in Copenhagen: Reconciling the 'Beijing Climate Revolution' and the 'Copenhagen Climate Obstinacy.'" *China Quarterly* 210: 435–55.

Cooper, M. 2011. "Complexity Theory after the Financial Crisis." *Journal of Cultural Economy* 4(4).

Council on Foreign Relation. 2012. "The Global Health Regime." At http://www.cfr.org/health-science-and-technology/global-health-regime/p22763 (accessed Dec. 2012).

Crafts, N. and Toniolo, G. 1996. *Economic Growth in Europe since 1945.* Cambridge: Cambridge University Press.

Crimaldi, L. 2011. "Nation's Fight against Cyber Intruders Goes Local." At http://www.msnbc.msn.com/id/43828271/ns/technology_and_science-security/t/nations-fight-against-cyber-intruders-goes-local/ (accessed Oct. 2012).

Crotty, J. 2009. "Structural Causes of the Global Financial Crisis: A Critical Assessment of the 'New Financial Architecture.'" *Cambridge Journal of Economics* 33.

Crouch, C. *The Strange Non-Death of Neoliberalism*. Cambridge: Polity.

CSD (Commission on Sustainable Development). 1992. *Agenda 21*. Rio de Janeiro.

Curry, B. 2011. "G20 Pressed to Agree on Global Imbalances." *Globe and Mail*, Feb. 16.

Dallaire, R. 2004. "Shake Hands with the Devil: The Failure of Humanity in Rwanda." New York: Carroll & Graf.

Das, D. K. 2008. "A Kiss of Life for the Withering Doha Round of the Multilateral Trade Negotiations?" *Global Economic Review: Perspectives on East Asian Economies and Industries* 37(2).

Das, D. K. 2012. "How Did the Asian Economy Cope with the Global Financial Crisis and Recession? A Revaluation and Review." *Asia Pacific Business Review* 18(1).

Davies, H. and Green, D. 2008. *Global Financial Regulation: The Essential Guide*. Cambridge: Polity.

Davis, C. 2004. "International Institutions and Issue Linkage: Building Support for Agricultural Trade Liberalization." *American Political Science Review* 98(1).

Davis, C. 2006. "Do WTO Rules Create a Level Playing Field? Lessons from the Experience of Peru and Vietnam." In J. Odell (ed.), *Negotiating Trade: Developing Countries in the WTO and NAFTA*. Cambridge: Cambridge University Press.

Davis, D. L., Bell, M. L. and Fletcher, T. 2002. "A Look Back at the London Smog of 1952 and the Half Century Since." *Environmental Health Perspectives* 110(12).

De Cordoba, S. F. and Vanzetti, D. 2005. "Now What? Searching for a Solution in WTO Industrial Tariff Negotiations." In UNCTAD, *Coping with Trade Reforms: A Developing-Country Perspective on the WTO Industrial Tariff Negotiations*. Geneva: UNCTAD.

Dee, P. 2008. "The Economic Effects of PTAs." *Australian Journal of International Affairs* 62(2).

Deligiannis, T. 2012. "The Evolution of Environment-Conflict Research: Toward a Livelihood Framework." *Global Environmental Politics* 12(1).

Dempsey, M. 2012. "Statement of General Martin E. Dempsey, USA Chairman Joint Chiefs of Staff, before the Senate Committee on Foreign Relations, Law of the Sea." May 23. At http://www.foreign.senate.gov/imo/media/doc/General_Dempsey_Testimony%20(2012-05-23)%20(Final).pdf (accessed Dec. 2012).

Depledge, Joanna. 2006. "The Opposite of Learning: Ossification in the Climate Change Regime." *Global Environmental Politics* 6(1): 1–22.

Deva, S. 2006. "Global Compact: A Critique of the UN's 'Public-Private' Partnership for Promoting Corporate Citizenship." *Syracuse Journal of International Law and Communication* 34.

de Waal, A. 1994. "Humanitarianism Unbound?" *African Rights*. At http://www.netnomad.com/DeWaal.html (accessed Oct. 2012).

de Waal, A. 2011. Public talk. Department of International Development, London School of Economics.

Dickson, D. M. 2008. "Farm Tariffs Sink World Trade Talks." *Washington Post*, July 30.

Di John, J. 2010. "The Concept, Causes and Consequences of Failed States: A Critical Review of the Literature and Agenda for Research with Specific Reference to Sub-Saharan Africa." *European Journal of Development Research* 22(1).

Dimitrov, R. 2005. "Hostage to Norms: States, Institutions and Global Forest Politics." *Global Environmental Politics* 5(4).

Dinstein, Y. 1993. "Rules of War." In J. Krieger (ed.), *The Oxford Companion to Politics of the World*. Oxford: Oxford University Press.

Dobusch, L. and Quack, S. 2012. "Framing Standards, Mobilizing Users: Copyright versus Fair Use in Transnational Regulation." *Review of International Political Economy*. DOI: 10.1080/09692290.2012.662909.

Donnelly, J. 1998. *International Human Rights*. 2nd edn. Boulder: Westview Press.

Dos Santos, T. 1970. "The Structure of Dependence." *American Economic Review* (May).

Dreher, A. 2006. "Does Globalization Affect Growth? Evidence from a New Index of Globalization." *Applied Economics* 38(10).

Dreher, A., Gaston, N. and Martens, P. 2008. *Measuring Globalization: Gauging Its Consequences*. New York: Springer.

Drezner, D. 2012. "The Irony of Global Economic Governance: The System Worked." Council on Foreign Relations Working Paper, Washington, DC.

Duffield, M. 1998. "Post-modern Conflict: Warlords, Post-adjustment States and Private Protection." *Civil Wars* 1(1).

Duffield, M. 2001. *Global Governance and the New Wars: The Merging of Development and Security*. London: Zed Books.

Duranton, G. and Turner, M. A. 2011. "The Fundamental Law of Road Congestion: Evidence from US Cities." *American Economic Review* 101(6).

Easterly, William. 2006. *The White Man's Burden: Why the West's Efforts to Aid the Rest Have Done So Much Ill And So Little Good*. New York: Penguin.

Eckersley, R. 2012. "Moving Forward in the Climate Negotiations: Multilateralism or Minilateralism?" *Global Environmental Politics* 12(2).

Economist. 1998. "A Survey of Human Rights." *The Economist*, Dec. 5.

Efstathopoulos, C. 2012. "Leadership in the WTO: Brazil, India and the Doha Development Agenda." *Cambridge Review of International Affairs* 25(2).

Eichengreen, B. (ed.). 1995. *Europe's Postwar Recovery*. Cambridge: Cambridge University Press. DOI: http://dx.doi.org/10.1017/CBO9780511759314.

Eichengreen, B. 2006. "Global Imbalances: The New Economy, the Dark Matter, the Savvy Investor and the Standard Analysis." Berkeley Working Paper. University of California, Mar.

Eichengreen, B. and Uzan, M. 1990. "The 1933 World Economic Conference as an Instance of Failed International Cooperation." Berkeley Department of Economics Working Paper 90–149. University of California.

Eichengreen, B., Gullapilla, R. and Panizza, U. 2011. "Capital Account Liberalization, Financial Development and Industry Growth: A Synthetic View." *Journal of International Money and Finance* 30(6): 1090–106.

Eisenhower, D. 1954. President Eisenhower's News Conference, April 7. *Public Papers of the Presidents*, p. 382. At https://www.mtholyoke.edu/acad/intrel/pentagon/ps11.htm (accessed Oct. 2012).

Ellis, L. and Smith, K. 2007. "The Global Upward Trend in the Profit Share." BIS Working Paper 231. Bank for International Settlements, Basel.
Enzenberger, H. M. 1993. *Civil Wars: From L.A. to Bosnia.* New York: New Press.
EPA (Environmental Protection Agency). 2012. "40 Years of Achievements, 1970–2010." At: http://www.epa.gov/40th/achieve.html (accessed Oct. 2012).
Evans, T. 1997. *Democratization and Deliberation.* New Haven: Yale University Press.
Evron, Y. 2007. "China's Anti-Terrorism Policy." *Strategic Assessment* 10(3). At http://www.inss.org.il/publications.php?cat=21&incat=&read=1387&print=1 (accessed Oct. 2012).
Falk, R. 2011. "Libya after Gaddafi: A Dangerous Precedent?" Aljazeera, Oct. 22. At http://www.aljazeera.com/indepth/opinion/2011/10/201110221327583002 19.html (accessed Oct. 2012).
Falkner, R. 2012. "Global Environmentalism and the Greening of International Society." *International Affairs* 88: 503–22.
Falkner, R., Stephan, H. and Vogler, J. 2010. "International Climate Policy after Copenhagen: Towards a 'Building Blocks' Approach." *Global Policy* 1(3).
Fall, P. and Zahran, M. 2010. "United Nations Corporate Partnerships: The Role and Functioning of the Global Compact." United Nations Joint Inspection Unit, Geneva.
FAO (Food and Agriculture Organization). 2010. *Global Forest Resources Assessment 2010.* Rome. At http://www.fao.org/docrep/013/i1757e/i1757e.pdf (accessed Dec. 2012).
FAO (Food and Agriculture Organisation). 2012. *State of the World's Forests 2012.* At http://www.fao.org/docrep/016/i3010e/i3010e00.htm (accessed Dec. 2012).
FCIC (Financial Crisis Inquiry Commission). 2011. *The Financial Crisis Inquiry Report: Final Report of the National Commission on the Causes of the Financial and Economic Crisis in the United States.* New York: Public Affairs.
Fenn, J. 2004. "The Nuclear Weapons Bazaar." *Middle East* (334).
Flick, C. 1980. "The Movement for Smoke Abatement in 19th-Century Britain." *Technology and Culture* 21(1).
Forbes. 2012. "The Forbes 500 List." At http://www.forbes.com (accessed Dec. 2012).
Fox, S. 1986. *The American Conservation Movement: John Muir and His Legacy.* Madison: University of Wisconsin Press.
Fritsch, S. 2008. "The UN Global Compact and the Global Governance of Corporate Social Responsibility: Complex Multilateralism for a More Human Globalisation?" *Global Society* 22(1).
FSC (Forest Stewardship Council). 2012. "Facts and Figures for 2012." At http://ic.fsc.org/facts-figures.19.htm (accessed Dec. 2012).
Fukuyama, F. 2011. *The Origins of Political Order.* New York: Farrar, Straus, & Giroux.
Gagnon, J. 2012. "Global Imbalances and Foreign Asset Expansion by Developing-Economy Central Banks." Policy Brief. Peterson Institute for International Economics, Jan.
Gallagher, K. P. 2008. "Understanding Developing Country Resistance to the Doha Round." *Review of International Political Economy* 15(1).

Gallagher, P. 2005. *The First Ten Years of the WTO.* Cambridge: Cambridge University Press.
Garber, P. M. 1993. "The Collapse of the Bretton Woods Fixed Exchange Rate System." In M. D. Bordo and B. Eichengreen (eds), *Retrospectives on the Bretton Woods System: Lessons for International Monetary Reform.* Chicago: University of Chicago Press.
General Motors. 1956. "Annual Report 1995." *GM Folks* 19(4). At http://www.carofthecentury.com/gm's_annual_report_1955.htm (accessed Oct. 2012).
George, A. L. and Craig, G. A. 1995. "Balance of Power, 1815–1914." In G. A. Craig and A. L. George, *Force and Statecraft: Diplomatic Problems of Our Time.* Oxford: Oxford University Press.
Gereffi, G. and Lee, J. 2012. "Why the World Suddenly Cares about Global Supply Chains." *Journal of Supply Chain Management* 48(3).
Germain, R. 2001. "Global Financial Governance and the Problem of Inclusion." *Global Governance* 7.
Germain, R. 2004. "Globalising Accountability within the International Organization of Credit: Financial Governance and the Public Sphere." *Global Society* 18(3).
Germain, R. 2011. "The Financial Stability Board." In T. Hale and D. Held (eds), *Handbook of Transnational Governance.* Cambridge: Polity.
Gill, B. (ed.). 2011. *Globalization in Crisis.* New York: Routledge.
Gillis, M. 2009. "Disarmament, a Basic Guide." New York: United Nations Office for Disarmament Affairs. At www.un.org/disarmament/HomePage/ODAPublications/AdhocPublications/PDF/guide.pdf.
Gilpin, R. 1981. *War and Change in World Politics.* Cambridge: Cambridge University Press.
Gilpin, R. 2002. "A Realist Perspective on International Governance." In D. Held and A. McGrew (eds), *Governing Globalization.* Cambridge: Polity.
Gleditsch, N. P., Wallensteen, P., Eriksson, M., Sollenberg, M. and Strand, H. 2002. "Armed Conflict 1946–2001: A New Dataset." *Journal of Peace Research* 39(5): 615–37.
Global Compact. 2007. "After the Signature: A Guide to Reengagement in the United Nations Global Compact." At http://www.unglobalcompact.org/docs/news_events/8.1/after_the_signature.pdf (accessed Oct. 2012).
Global Compact. 2008. "630 Companies Delisted as Part of Integrity Measures." Press release, June 25. At http://www.unglobalcompact.org/newsandevents/news_archives/2008_06_25.html (accessed Oct. 2012).
Global Compact. 2010. "Blueprint for Corporate Sustainability Leadership." UN Global Compact Office, New York, June.
Global Compact Office. 2011. "A Response from the Global Compact Office to United Nations Corporate Partnerships: The Role and Functioning of the Global Compact JIU/REP/2010/9." UN Global Compact, Mar. 24.
Goodman, J. B. and Pauly, L. W. 1993. "The Obsolescence of Capital Controls? Economic Management in an Age of Global Markets." *World Politics* 46(1).
Goose, S. and Docherty, B. 2012. "White Phosphorous: The New Napalm?" Human Rights Watch, June 8. At http://www.hrw.org/news/2012/06/08/white-phosphorous-new-napalm (accessed Oct. 2012).

Gorman, S. and Barnes, J. E. 2011. "Cyber Combat: Act of War," *Wall Street Journal*, May 31. At http://online.wsj.com/article/SB10001424052702304563104576355623135782718.html (accessed Oct. 2012).

Gourinchas, P.-O. and Rey, H. 2005. "From World Banker to World Venture Capitalist: US External Adjustment and the Exorbitant Privilege." NBER Working Paper 11563. National Bureau of Economic Research, Cambridge, MA.

Gowan, P. 1999. *The Global Gamble: Washington's Faustian Bid for World Dominance.* London: Verso.

Grant, R. W. and Keohane, R. O. 2005. "Accountability and Abuses of Power in World Politics." *American Political Science Review* 99(1).

Greif, A. 2006. *Institutions and the Path to the Modern Economy: Lessons from Medieval Trade.* Cambridge: Cambridge University Press.

Griesgraber, J. M. 2009. "Reforms for Major New Roles of the International Monetary Fund? The IMF Post-G20 Summit." *Global Governance* 15.

Griffith-Jones, S. and Persaud, A. 2012. "Why Critics Are Wrong about a Financial-Transaction Tax." EuropeanVoice.com. At http://www.europeanvoice.com/article/2012/march/why-critics-are-wrong-about-a-financial-transaction-tax/73843.aspx (accessed Oct. 2012).

Guerrieri, P. 2006. "The Doha Round and the Future of the Multilateral Trading Regime." *International Spectator* 41(1).

Gyimesi, K., Vincent, C. and Lamba, N. 2011. "Frustration Rising: IBM 2011 Commuter Pain Survey." IBM.

Haas, P. M. 1991. "Policy Responses to Stratospheric Ozone Depletion." *Global Environmental Change* 1.

Haas, P. M. 1992. "Banning Chlorofluorocarbons: Epistemic Community Efforts to Protect Stratospheric Ozone." *International Organization* 46: 187–224.

Haas, P. M. 2004. "Addressing the Global Governance Deficit." *Global Environmental Politics* 4(3).

Habermas, J. 2012. *The Crisis of the European Union: A Response.* Cambridge: Polity.

Hagen, E. 2008. "Global Compact Clears Ill-Reputed Companies." Global Compact Critics blog, May 28. At http://globalcompactcritics.blogspot.com/2008_05_01_archive.html (accessed Oct. 2012).

Haldane, A. and May, R. 2011. "Systemic Risk in Banking Ecosystems." *Nature* 469.

Hale, D. and Hale, L. 2008. "Reconsidering Revaluation – the Wrong Approach to the US-Chinese Trade Imbalance." *Foreign Affairs* 87(1).

Hale, T. 2011. "A Climate Coalition of the Willing." *Washington Quarterly* (Winter).

Hale, T. 2012. "The Rule of Law in the Global Economy: Explaining Institutional Diversity in Commercial Dispute Resolution." Dissertation, Department of Politics, Princeton University.

Hale, T. and Held, D. 2011. *Handbook of Transnational Governance.* Cambridge: Polity.

Hale, T. and Mauzerall, D. 2004. "Thinking Globally and Acting Locally: Can the Johannesburg Partnerships Coordinate Action on Sustainable Development?" *Journal of Environment and Development* 13(3).

Hale, T. and Roger, C. 2011. "Orchestration and Transnational Climate Governance." European Consortium of Political Research Joint Session, St Gallen.

Hanefield, J. 2011. "The Global Fund to Fight AIDS, Malaria, and Tuberculosis." In T. Hale and D. Held (eds), *Handbook of Transnational Governance*. Cambridge: Polity.

Hardin, G. 1968. "The Tragedy of the Commons." *Science* 162(1243).

Harmer, A. and Bruen, C. 2011. "Global Alliance for Vaccines and Immunisation." In T. Hale and D. Held (eds), *Handbook of Transnational Governance*. Cambridge: Polity.

Harvey, D. 2005. *A Brief History of Neoliberalism*. Oxford: Oxford University Press.

Held, D. 1995. *Democracy and the Global Order*. Cambridge: Polity.

Held, D. 2004. *Global Covenant*. Cambridge: Polity Press.

Held, D. 2010. *Cosmopolitanism: Ideals and Realities*. Cambridge: Polity.

Held, D. and Kaya, A. 2007. *Global Inequality: Patterns and Explanations*. Cambridge: Polity.

Held, D. and McGrew, A. 2002. *Governing Globalization*. Cambridge: Polity.

Held, D. and McGrew, A. 2007. *Globalization/Anti-globalization*. Cambridge: Polity.

Held, D. and Young, K. 2011. "Crisis in Parallel Worlds: The Governance of Global Risks in Finance, Security, and the Environment." In C. Calhoun and G. Derlugian (eds), *The Deepening Crisis: Governance Challenges after Neoliberalism*. New York: New York University Press.

Held, D., McGrew, A., Goldblatt, D. and Perraton, J. 1999. *Global Transformations: Politics, Economics and Culture*. Cambridge: Polity.

Held, D., Kaldor, M. and Quah, D. 2010. "The Hydra-Headed Crisis." *Global Policy*, Feb. 28. At http://www.globalpolicyjournal.com/articles/global-governance/hydra-headed-crisis (accessed Oct. 2012).

Helleiner, E. 1994a. "Freeing Money: Why Have States Been More Willing to Liberalize Capital Controls than Trade Barriers?" *Policy Sciences* 27(4): 299–318.

Helleiner, E. 1994b. *States and the Reemergence of Global Finance*. Ithaca: Cornell University Press.

Helleiner, E. 2008. "The Evolution of the International Monetary and Financial System." In John Ravenhill (ed.), *Global Political Economy*. Cambridge: Cambridge University Press.

Helleiner, E. 2010. "What Role for the New Financial Stability Board? The Politics of International Standards after the Crisis." *Global Policy* 1(3): 282–90.

Helleiner, E. and Pagliari, S. 2009a. "Crisis and the Reform of International Financial Regulation." In E. Helleiner, S. Pagliari and H. Zimmermann (eds), *Global Finance in Crisis*. London: Routledge.

Helleiner, E. and Pagliari, S. 2009b. "Towards a New Bretton Woods? The First G20 Leaders' Summit and the Regulation of Global Finance." *New Political Economy* 14(2).

Helleiner, E. and Pagliari, S. 2011. "The End of an Era in International Financial Regulation? A Post-Crisis Research Agenda." *International Organization* 65(1).

Hinsley, F. H. 1963. *Power and the Pursuit of Peace*. Cambridge: Cambridge University Press.

Ho, Daniel. 2002. "Compliance and International Soft Law: Why Do Countries Implement the Basel Accord?" *Journal of International Economic Law* 5.

Hobbes, T. 1968. *Leviathan*, ed. C. B. Macpherson. Harmondsworth: Penguin.

Hobsbawm, E. 1994. *Age of Extremes: The Short Twentieth Century 1914–1991*. London: Michael Joseph.

Hoekman, B. and Mattoo, A. 2011. "Services Trade Liberalization and Regulatory Reform: Re-invigorating International Cooperation." World Bank Policy Research Working Paper 5517.

Hoffmann, M. 2005. *Ozone Depletion and Climate Change*. Albany: State University of New York Press.

Hoffmann, M. 2011. *Climate Governance at the Crossroads: Experimenting with a Global Response after Kyoto*. Oxford: Oxford University Press.

Holt, V. K. and MacKinnon, M. G. 2008. "The Origins and Evolution of US Policy towards Peace Operations." *International Peacekeeping* 15(1).

Howard, M. 1981. *War and the Liberal Conscience*. Oxford: Oxford University Press.

Hu Xiaodi. 2002. Statement by Mr. Hu Xiaodi, Ambassador for Disarmament Affairs of China, at the Plenary of the 2003 Session of the Conference on Disarmament, Geneva, July 31. Ministry of Foreign Affairs of the People's Republic of China. At http://www.fmprc.gov.cn/eng/wjb/zzjg/jks/jkxw/t26399.htm (accessed Oct. 2012).

Huang, Y. 2010. "Facing the Problem of Global Imbalance." *China Daily*, Dec. 2.

Humphreys, D. 1996. *Forest Politics: The Evolution of International Cooperation*. London: Earthscan.

Humphreys, D. 2006. *Logjam: Deforestation and the Crisis of Global Governance*. London: Earthscan.

Huntington, S. P. 1968. *Political Order in Changing Societies*. New Haven: Yale University Press.

IAEA. 2013. "IAEA Says DPRK Nuclear Test 'Deeply Regrettable.'" At http://www.iaea.org/newscenter/pressreleases/2013/prn201301.html (accessed Feb. 2013).

icasualties.org. 2012a. "Operation Enduring Freedom/Afghanistan." At http://icasualties.org/ (accessed Oct. 2012).

icasualties.org. 2012b. "Operation Iraqi Freedom." At http://icasualties.org/ (accessed Oct. 2012).

ICC (International Criminal Court). 2012. "Situations and Cases." At http://www.icc-cpi.int/Menus/ICC/Situations+and+Cases/ (accessed Oct. 2012).

ICG (International Crisis Group). 2011. "Security in Afghanistan." At http://www.crisisgroup.org/en/publication-type/key-issues/country/security-in-afghanistan.aspx (accessed Oct. 2012).

ICRC (International Committee of the Red Cross). 2010. "The ICRC's Mandate and Mission." Oct. 29. At http://www.icrc.org/eng/who-we-are/mandate/overview-icrc-mandate-mission.htm (accessed Oct. 2012).

ICTJ (International Center for Transitional Justice). 2009. "Transitional Justice in the Former Yugoslavia." At http://ictj.org/publication/transitional-justice-former-yugoslavia (accessed Oct. 2012).

ICTSD (International Centre for Trade and Sustainable Development). 2008. "Daily Update." WTO Mini-Ministerial, Geneva. *Bridges* (6) (July 26).

IFC Review. 2011. "IMF's Strauss-Kahn: Global Imbalances Pre-crisis Worries Returned." Feb. 11. At http://www.ifcreview.com/viewarticle.aspx?articleId=2514&areaId=45 (accessed Oct. 2012).

Ikenberry, G. J. 2001. *After Victory.* Princeton: Princeton University Press.

Ikenberry, G. J. 2004. "Liberal Hegemony or Empire? American Power in the Age of Unipolarity." In D. Held and M. Koenig-Archibugi (eds), *American Power in the 21st Century.* Cambridge: Polity.

ILO (International Labour Organization). 2009. "Migrant Working Girls, Victims of the Global Crisis." ILO press release, June 10.

ILO (International Labour Organization). 2010. *Global Wage Report 2010/2011: Wage Politics in Times of Crisis.* Geneva: International Labour Office.

ILO (International Labour Organization). 2011. *Trends Econometric Models.* Geneva: International Labour Office.

ILO (International Labour Organization). 2012. *Global Employment Trends 2012.* Geneva: International Labour Office.

ILO (International Labour Organization) and World Bank. 2012. *Inventory of Policy Responses to the Financial and Economic Crisis.* Washington, DC: ILO and World Bank.

IMF (International Monetary Fund). 2005. "Global Imbalances: A Saving and Investment Perspective." *World Economic Outlook* (Sept.).

IMF (International Monetary Fund). 2007. "Reaping the Benefits of Financial Globalization." Discussion Paper. At www.imf.org/external/np/res/docs/2007/0607.htm (accessed Dec. 2012).

IMF (International Monetary Fund). 2009a. "Initial Lessons of the Crisis." IMF Policy Paper, Feb. 6. At www.imf.org/external/pp/longres.aspx?id=4315 (accessed Dec. 2012).

IMF (International Monetary Fund). 2009b. *World Economic Outlook: Crisis and Recovery.* Washington, DC: IMF.

IMF (International Monetary Fund). 2011a. "G-20 Moves Forward to Tackle Global Imbalances." *IMF Survey*, Apr. 16. At http://www.imf.org/external/pubs/ft/survey/so/2011/new041611a.htm (accessed Oct. 2012).

IMF (International Monetary Fund). 2011b. *World Economic Outlook: Slowing Growth, Rising Risks.* Washington, DC: International Monetary Fund.

IMF (International Monetary Fund). 2012. *World Economic Outlook: Rebalancing Growth.* Washington, DC: International Monetary Fund.

IMO (International Maritime Organization). 2011a. "International Shipping Facts and Figures: Information Resources on Trade, Safety, Security, and the Environment." At http://www.imo.org/KnowledgeCentre/ShipsAndShippingFactsAndFigures/TheRoleandImportanceofInternationalShipping/Pages/TheRoleAndImportanceOfInternationalShipping.aspx (accessed Oct. 2012).

IMO (International Maritime Organization). 2011b. "Piracy Situation 'Unacceptable' Says UN Secretary-General Ban Ki-moon." Briefing, Feb. 4. At http://www.imo.org/MediaCentre/PressBriefings/Pages/04-2011-WMD-launch.aspx (accessed Oct. 2012).

IPCC (Intergovernmental Panel on Climate Change). 1990. "Preface to the IPCC Overview." At http://www.ipcc.ch/ipccreports/1992%20IPCC%20Supplement/

IPCC_1990_and_1992_Assessments/English/ipcc_90_92_assessments_far_overview.pdf (accessed Oct. 2012).
IPCC (Intergovernmental Panel on Climate Change). 2007. "Mitigation Costs across Sectors and Macro-Economic Costs." At http://www.ipcc.ch/publications_and_data/ar4/wg3/en/tssts-ts-11-2-mitigation-costs.html (accessed Oct. 2012).
IUCN (International Union for the Conservation of Nature). 1948. Constitution. Geneva.
Ismail, F. 2009. "An Assessment of the WTO Doha Round July-December 2008 Collapse." *World Trade Review* 8(4).
Ivanova, Maria. 2005. "Assessing UNEP as Anchor Institution for the Global Environment: Lessons for the UNEO Debate." Yale Center for Environmental Law and Policy. Working Paper 05/01.
Ivanova, Maria. 2007. "Designing the United Nations Environment Programme: A Story of Compromise and Confrontation." *International Environmental Agreements: Politics, Law and Economics* 7(4): 337–61.
Jaleel, A. 2008. "Why Are There So Many Preferential Trade Areas? A Political Economy Perspective." *Global Economic Review* 37(1).
Jeong, K.-Y. and Kim, E. 2010. "The Global Financial Crisis: New Implications and Perspectives for Emerging Economies." *Global Economic Review* 39(1).
Johnson, C. 1982. *MITI and the Japanese Miracle: The Growth of Industrial Policy, 1925–1975*. Palo Alto: Stanford University Press.
Johnson, S. (ed.). 1993. *The Earth Summit: the United Nations Conference on Environment and Development (UNCED)*. London: Graham & Trotman.
Joint Forum. 2003. "Initiatives by the BCBS, IAIS and IOSCO to Combat Money Laundering and the Financing of Terrorism." Bank for International Settlements. Basel, June.
Joint Forum. 2005. "Initiatives by the BCBS, IAIS and IOSCO to Combat Money Laundering and the Financing of Terrorism." Rev. and updated version. Bank for International Settlements. Basel, Jan.
Jones, A., LaFleur, V. and Purvis, N. 2009. "Double Jeopardy: What the Climate Crisis Means for the Poor." In L. Brainard, A. Jones and N. Purvis (eds), *Climate Change and Global Poverty: A Billion Lives in the Balance*. Washington, DC: Brookings Institution Press.
Kagan, R. 2003. *Of Paradise and Power: America and Europe in the New World Order*. New York: Knopf.
Kahler, M. and Lake, D. 2008. "Economic Integration and Global Governance: Why So Little Supranationalism?" In Walter Mattli and Ngaire Woods (eds), *The Politics of Global Regulation*. Princeton: Princeton University Press.
Kaldor, M. 1998a. *New and Old Wars*. Cambridge: Polity.
Kaldor, M. 1998b. "Reconceptualizing Organized Violence." In D. Archibugi, D. Held and M. Köhler (eds), *Reimagining Political Community*. Cambridge: Polity.
Kalyvas, S. 2001. "New and Old Wars: A Valid Distinction?" *World Politics* 54(1).
Kant, I. 2007. *Perpetual Peace* (1795). Minneapolis: Filiquarian.
Kaplan, R. 1994. *Balkan Ghosts: A Journey through History*. New York: Vintage.
Kapstein, E. 1992. "Between Power and Purpose: Central Bankers and the Politics of Regulatory Convergence." *International Organization* 46(1).

Kaufman, J. 2008. "China's Health Care System and Avian Influenza Preparedness." *Journal of Infectious Diseases* 197.
Keck, M. E. and Sikkink, K. 1998. *Activists beyond Borders*. Ithaca: Cornell University Press.
Kell, G. 2003. "The Global Compact: Origins, Operations, Progress, Challenges." *Journal of Corporate Citizenship* 11.
Kennan, G. F. 1970. "To Prevent a World Wasteland: A Proposal." *Foreign Affairs* 48(3): 401–13.
Keohane, R. O. 1980. "The Theory of Hegemonic Stability and Changes in International Economic Regimes." In O. Holsti, R. Siverson and A. George (eds), *Change in the International System*. Boulder: Westview Press.
Keohane, R. O. 1982. "The Demand for International Regimes." *International Organization* 36: 325–55.
Keohane, R. O. 1984. *After Hegemony: Cooperation and Discord in the World Political Economy*. Princeton: Princeton University Press.
Keohane, R. O. and Martin, L. 1995. "The Promise of Institutionalist Theory." *International Security* 20(1).
Keohane, R. O. and Nye, J. 1977. *Power and Interdependence: World Politics in Transition*. Boston: Little, Brown.
Keohane, R. O., and Nye, J. S. 1974. "Transgovernmental Relations and International Organizations." *World Politics* 27(1).
Keohane, R. O. and Ostrom, E. (eds). 1995. *Local Commons and Global Interdependence*. New York: Sage.
Keohane, R. O., Moravcsik, A. and Macedo, S. 2009. "Democracy-Enhancing Multilateralism." *International Organization* 63: 1–31.
Keohane, R. O. and Victor, D. G. 2010. "The Regime Complex for Climate Change." Discussion Paper 2010-33. Harvard Project on International Climate Agreements, Cambridge, MA.
Kerwer, D. 2005. "Rules That Many Use: Standards and Global Regulation." *Governance* 18(4).
Keynes, J. M. 1920. *The Economic Consequences of the Peace*. London: Harcourt, Brace & Howe.
Keynes, J. M. 1936. *The General Theory of Employment, Interest and Money*. New York: Classic Books America.
Khanna, P. 2008. *The Second World*. London: Random House.
Khanna, P. 2011. *How to Run the World: Charting a Course to the Next Renaissance*. London: Random House.
Kindleberger, C. 1973. *The World in Depression: 1929–1939*. 1st edn. Berkeley: University of California Press.
Kindleberger, C. 1986. *The World in Depression 1929–1938*. Rev. and enlarged edn. Berkeley: University of California Press.
Kingsolver, B. 2001. "A Pure, High Note of Anguish." *Los Angeles Times*, Sept. 23.
Kissinger, H. 1994. *Diplomacy*. New York: Simon & Schuster.
Klare, M. 2002. *Resource Wars: The New Landscape of Global Conflict*. New York: Henry Holt.
Koenig-Archibugi, M. 2004. "Transnational Corporations and Public Accountability." *Government and Opposition* 39(2).

Koenig-Archibugi, M. 2011. "Global Polio Eradication Initiative." In T. Hale and D. Held (eds), *Handbook of Transnational Governance*. Cambridge: Polity.

Kohli, Atul. 2004. *State-Directed Development: Political Power and Industrialization in the Global Periphery*. Cambridge: Cambridge University Press.

Konings, M. 2008. "American Finance and Empire in Historical Perspective." In L. Panitch and M. Konings (eds), *American Empire and the Political Economy of Global Finance*. Basingstoke: Palgrave Macmillan.

Koremenos, B., C. Lipson and D. Snidal. 2001. "The Rational Design of International Institutions." *International Organization* 55(4): 761–99.

Krasner, S. 1984. "Approaches to the State: Alternative Conceptions and Historical Dynamics." *Comparative Politics* 16(2): 223–46.

Krasner, S. D. 1999. *Sovereignty: Organized Hypocrisy*. Princeton: Princeton University Press.

Krueger, A. B. 2012. "The Rise and Consequences of Inequality in the United States." Remarks as prepared for delivery, Jan. 12. At http://www.whitehouse.gov/sites/default/files/krueger_cap_speech_final_remarks.pdf (accessed Oct. 2012).

Kupchan, C. A. 2010. *How Enemies Become Friends: The Sources of Stable Peace*. Princeton: Princeton University Press.

Laborde, D. 2008. "Looking for a Meaningful Duty Free Quota Free Market Access Initiative in the Doha Development Agenda." Issue Paper No. 4. International Centre for Trade and Sustainable Development, Geneva.

Lacina B. and Gleditsch, N. P. 2005. "Monitoring Trends in Global Combat: A New Dataset of Battle Deaths." *European Journal of Population* 21(2–3).

Laeven, L. and Valencia, F. 2010. "Resolution of Banking Crises: The Good, the Bad, and the Ugly." IMF Working Paper 10/146.

Lampe, M. 2011. "Explaining Nineteenth-Century Bilateralism: Economic and Political Determinants of the Cobden–Chevalier Network." *Economic History Review* 64(2): 644–68.

Lander, M. 2011. "US Troops to Leave Iraq by Year's End, Obama Says." *New York Times*, Oct. 21. At http://www.nytimes.com/2011/10/22/world/middleeast/president-obama-announces-end-of-war-in-iraq.html (accessed Oct. 2011).

Lane, P. R. and Milesi-Ferretti, G. M. 2007. "The External Wealth of Nations Mark II." *Journal of International Economics* 73.

Lawrence, C. 2011. "Virus Infects Program That Controls US Drones." CNN, Oct. 10. At http://articles.cnn.com/2011-10-10/us/us_drone-program-virus_1_computer-virus-drones-uavs?_s=PM:US (accessed Oct. 2012).

Lazarus, R. J. 2009. "Super Wicked Problems and Climate Change: Restraining the Present to Liberate the Future." *Cornell Law Review* 94(5).

Leander, A. 2005. "The Power to Construct International Security: On the Significance of Private Military Companies. *Millennium: Journal of International Studies* 33(3).

Leander, A. 2009. "Securing Sovereignty by Governing Security through Markets." In R. Adler-Nissen and T. Gammeltoft-Hansen (eds), *Sovereignty Games: Instrumentalizing State Sovereignty in Europe and Beyond*. London: Palgrave.

Lee, D. 2012. "Global Trade Governance and the Challenges of African Activism in the Doha Development Agenda Negotiations." *Global Society* 26(1).

Leeson, R. 2003. *Ideology and the International Economy: The Decline and Fall of Bretton Woods.* Basingstoke: Palgrave-Macmillan.

Levin, K., Cashore, B., Bernstein, S. and Auld, G. 2010. "Playing It Forward: Path Dependency, Progressive Incrementalism, and the 'Super Wicked' Problem of Global Climate Change." At http://environment.research.yale.edu/documents/downloads/0-9/2010_super_wicked_levin_cashore_bernstein_auld.pdf (accessed Oct. 2012).

Li, M. and Chen, G. 2010. "China's Search for a Multilateral World: Dilemmas and Desires." *International Spectator* 45(4).

Lieber, K. A. and Press, D. G. 2006. "The Rise of US Nuclear Primacy." *Foreign Affairs*, Mar.–Apr. At http://www.foreignaffairs.com/articles/61508/keir-a-lieber-and-daryl-g-press/the-rise-of-us-nuclear-primacy (accessed Oct. 2012).

Liftin, K. T. 1994. *Ozone Discourses.* New York: Columbia University Press.

Lin, J., Hinh Ding and Im, F. 2010. "US–China External Imbalance and the Global Financial Crisis." *China Economic Journal* 3(1).

Lipset, S. M. 1959. "Some Social Requisites of Democracy." *American Political Science Review* 53.

Lockyer, A. 2011. "Foreign Intervention and Warfare in Civil Wars." *Review of International Studies* 37.

Lugar, R. 2012. "Prepared Statement of Senator Richard G. Lugar on the Concluded Indiana Senate Primary." At http://www.nytimes.com/2012/05/09/us/politics/prepared-statement-of-senator-richard-g-lugar-on-the-concluded-indiana-senate-primary.html?pagewanted=all (accessed Dec. 2012).

Lutsey, N. and Sperling D. 2008. "America's Bottom-Up Climate Change Mitigation Policy." *Energy Policy* 36(2), 673–85.

Macey, J. 2003. "Regulatory Globalization as a Response to Regulatory Competition." *Emory Law Journal* 52.

Maddison, A. 2001. *The World Economy: A Millennial Perspective.* Paris: OECD.

Mahoney, J. 2000. "Path Dependence in Historical Sociology." *Theory and Society* 29(4).

Malhi, Y., Roberts, T. J., Betts, R. A., Killeen, T. J., Li, W. and Nobre, C. A. 2008. "Climate Change, Deforestation, and the Fate of the Amazon." *Science* 319(5860): 169–72.

Mann, T. E. and Ornstein, N. J. 2012. *It's Even Worse than It Looks: How the American Constitutional System Collided with the New Politics of Extremism.* New York: Basic Books.

Mansbach, R. and Rafferty, K. 2008. *Introduction to Global Politics.* New York: Routledge.

Marshall, G. 1947. "The Marshall Plan Speech." Harvard University, June 5. At http://www.nato.int/docu/speech/1947/s470605a_e.htm (accessed Oct. 2012).

Marx, K. 1852. "The Eighteenth Brumaire of Louis Bonaparte." *Die Revolution* (New York) 1.

Masciandaro, D. 2011. "International Association of Insurance Supervisors." In T. Hale and David Held (eds), *Handbook of Transnational Governance: Institutions and Innovations.* Cambridge: Polity.

Mason, R. J. 1999. "Whither Japan's Environmental Movement? An Assessment of Problems and Prospects at the National Level." *Pacific Affairs* 72(2): 187–207.

McCarty, N., Poole, K. and Rosenthal, H. 2006. *Polarized America: The Dance of Ideology and Unequal Riches*. Cambridge, MA: MIT Press.

McCormick, J. 1989. *The Global Environmental Movement*. New York: Wiley.

McNeill, W. 1982. *The Pursuit of Power*. Oxford: Blackwell.

Mearsheimer, J. 1995. "The False Promise of International Institutions." *International Security* 19(3).

Medical News Today. 2008. "25 Years of Pollution Monitoring in the UK Shows a Fall in the Presence of Toxins in Ambient Air." At http://www.medicalnewstoday.com/releases/94021.php (accessed Oct. 2012).

Melik, J. 2012. "Interpol Clamps Down on Illegal Logging." BBC, Sept. 11. At http://www.bbc.co.uk/news/business-19541718 (accessed Oct. 2012).

Milesi-Ferretti, G. M. and Tille, C. 2011. "The Great Retrenchment: International Capital Flows during the Global Financial Crisis." *Economic Policy* 26(66).

Milner, H. 1987. "Resisting the Protectionist Temptation: Industry and the Making of Trade Policy in France and the US in the 1970s." *International Organization* 41(4): 639–65.

Milner, H. 1998. "Rationalizing Politics: The Emerging Synthesis of International, American, and Comparative Politics." *International Organization* 52(4).

Ministry of the Environment, Government of Japan. 2012. "Minamata Disease: The History and Measures." At http://www.env.go.jp/en/chemi/hs/minamata 2002/ch2.html (accessed Oct. 2012).

Montgomerie, J. 2009. "The Pursuit of (Past) Happiness? Middle-Class Indebtedness and American Financialisation." *New Political Economy* 14(1).

Moravcsik, A. 1997. "Taking Preferences Seriously: A Liberal Theory of International Relations." *International Organization* 51(4).

Moravcsik, A. 2010. "Europe, the Second Superpower." *Current History* (Mar.): 91–8.

Moggridge, D. (ed). 1980. *The Collected Writings of John Maynard Keynes*, vol. 26: *Activities 1941–1946: Shaping the Post-War World, Bretton Woods and Reparations*. Cambridge: Cambridge University Press.

Moschella, M. 2012. "Designing the Financial Stability Board: A Theoretical Investigation of Mandate, Discretion, and Membership." *Journal of International Relations and Development* (May).

Moschella, M. and Tsingou, E. (eds). 2013. *Great Expectations, Slow Transformation: Incremental Change in Financial Governance*. Colchester: ECPR Press.

Mosley, L. and Uno, S. 2007. "Racing to the Bottom or Climbing to the Top? Economic Globalization and Labor Rights." *Comparative Political Studies* 40(8).

MSF (Médecins sans Frontières). 2012. "Libya: Detainees Tortured and Denied Medical Care." At http://www.doctorswithoutborders.org/press/release.cfm?id=5744 (accessed Oct. 2012).

Mueller, J. 1990. "The Obsolescence of Major War." *Security Dialogue* 21(3).

Mulgan, G., Ali, R. and Tucker, S. 2007. "Social Innovation: What It Is, Why It Matters and How It Can Be Accelerated." Said Business School, Oxford. At http://www.sbs.ox.ac.uk/centres/skoll/research/Documents/Social%20 Innovation.pdf (accessed Oct. 2012).

Multilateral Fund. 2012. "Welcome to the Multilateral Fund for the Implementation of the Montreal Protocol." At http://www.multilateralfund.org/default.aspx (accessed Oct. 2012).

Mundy, J. 2011. "Deconstructing Civil Wars: Beyond the New Wars Debate." *Security Dialogue* 42.

Nanto, D. K. 2009. "The Global Financial Crisis: Analysis and Policy Implications." Congressional Research Service, July 2.

Narlikar, A. 2010. *Deadlock in Multilateral Negotiations.* Cambridge: Cambridge University Press.

Narlikar, A. and Odell, J. 2006. "The Strict Distributive Strategy for a Bargaining Coalition: The Like-Minded Group in the World Trade Organization." In J. Odell (ed.), *Negotiating Trade: Developing Countries in the WTO and NAFTA.* Cambridge: Cambridge University Press.

NATO (North Atlantic Treaty Organization). 2011. "Member Countries." At http://www.nato.int/cps/en/natolive/topics_52044.htm (accessed Oct. 2012).

Nauman, Q. 2012. "Pakistan Condemns US Drone Strikes." Reuters, June 4. At http://www.reuters.com/article/2012/06/04/us-pakistan-usa-drones-idUSBRE8530MS20120604 (accessed Oct. 2012).

Nesvetailova, A. and Palan, R. 2009. "The End of Liberal Finance? Towards a Changing Paradigm of Global Financial Governance." *Millennium* 38(3).

Nissanke, M. 2012. "Introduction: Transmission Mechanisms and Impacts of the Global Financial Crisis on the Developing World." *Journal of Development Studies* 48(6).

Nölke, A. 2011. "International Accounting Standards Board." In T. Hale and D. Held (eds), *Handbook of Transnational Governance: Institutions and Innovations.* Cambridge: Polity.

North, D. 1981. *Structure and Change in Economic History.* New York: Norton.

North, D. 1990. *Institutions, Institutional Change and Economic Performance.* Cambridge: Cambridge University Press.

OAS (Organization of American States). 2012. "Who We Are." At http://www.oas.org/en/about/who_we_are.asp (accessed Oct. 2012).

Obama, B. 2011. Remarks by President Obama in address to the United Nations General Assembly. At http://www.whitehouse.gov/the-press-office/2011/09/21/remarks-president-obama-address-united-nations-general-assembly (accessed Oct. 2012).

OCHA (Office for the Coordination of Humanitarian Affairs). 2012. "Introduction to Humanitarian Principles and Civil-Military Coordination Fundamentals." New York: United Nations.

Odell, J. 1979. "The US and the Emergence of Flexible Exchange Rates." *International Organization* 33(1).

Odell, J. 2007. "Growing Power Meets Frustration in the Doha Round's First Four Years." In L. Crump and J. Maswood (eds), *Developing Countries and Global Trade Negotiations.* London: Routledge.

Odell, J. 2009. "Breaking Deadlocks in International Institutional Negotiations: The WTO, Seattle and Doha." *International Studies Quarterly* 53(2).

OECD (Organisation for Economic Co-operation and Development). 2011. *Divided We Stand: Why Inequality Keeps Rising*. Paris: OECD.

Oksenberg, M. and Economy, E. 1998 "China's Accession to and Implementation of International Environmental Accords 1978–95." In E. Brown Weiss and H. Jacobson (eds), *Engaging Countries: Strengthening Compliance with International Environmental Accords*. Cambridge, MA: MIT Press.

Olivier, J. G., Janssens-Maenhout, G. and Peters, J. A. 2012. *Trends in Global CO2 Emissions: 2012 Report*. The Hague: PBL Netherlands Environmental Assessment Agency.

Olson, M. 1965. *The Logic of Collective Action: Public Goods and the Theory of Groups*. Cambridge: Harvard University Press.

O'Neal, J. and Russett, B. 1997. "The Classical Liberals Were Right: Democracy, Interdependence and Conflict, 1950–1985." *International Studies Quarterly* 41(2).

OPCW (Organization for the Prohibition of Chemical Weapons). 2012. "Convention on the Prohibition of the Development, Production, Stockpiling and Use of Chemical Weapons and on their Destruction (Chemical Weapons Convention)." At http://www.opcw.org/chemical-weapons-convention/ (accessed Oct. 2012).

OpenSecrets. 2012. "Lobbying Database." At http://www.opensecrets.org/lobby/index.php (accessed Oct. 2012).

Osiander, A. 1994. *The States of Europe: 1640–1990*. Oxford: Clarendon Press.

Osiander, A. 2001. "Sovereignty, International Relations, and the Westphalian Myth." *International Organization* 55(2).

Ostrom, E. 1990. *Governing the Commons: The Evolution of Institutions for Collective Action*. Cambridge: Cambridge University Press.

Ostrom, E. 2009. "Beyond Markets and States: Polycentric Governance of Complex Economic Systems." Prize Lecture, Dec. 8. At http://www.nobelprize.org/nobel_prizes/economics/laureates/2009/ostrom_lecture.pdf (accessed Oct. 2012).

Ostrom, E. 2012. "Green from the Grassroots." Project Syndicate, June 12. At http://www.project-syndicate.org/commentary/green-from-the-grassroots (accessed Oct. 2012).

Ovodenko, A. and Keohane, R. O. 2012. "Institutional Diffusion in International Environmental Affairs." *International Affairs* 88(3).

Owen, T. 2004. "Human Security – Conflict, Critique and Consensus: Colloquium Remarks and a Proposal for a Threshold-Based Definition." *Security Dialogue* 35(3).

Owens, P. 2012. "Human Security and the Rise of the Social." *Review of International Studies* 38.

Palma, J. G. 2009. "The Revenge of the Market on the Rentiers: Why Neo-liberal Reports of the End of History Turned Out to be Premature." *Cambridge Journal of Economics* 33(4).

Palmer, G. 1992. "The Earth Summit: What Went Wrong at Rio?" *Washington University Law Quarterly* 70(4): 1005–28.

Panitchpakdi, S. 2008. Speech at the Executive Session of the Trade and Development Board on Financing for Development. 45th Executive Session, Geneva, Nov. 13.

Pennay, P., Scobie, R., Feifei, Z. and Bin, Z. 2010. "Economic Observer Exclusive: Interview with Director General of the WTO Pascal Lamy." *Economic Observer*, June 3. At http://www.eeo.com.cn/ens/feature/2010/06/03/171706.shtml (accessed Dec. 2012).

Paris, R. 2001. "Human Security: Paradigm Shift or Hot Air?" *International Security* 26(2).

Parson, Edward A. 1993. "Protecting the Ozone Layer." In P. M. Haas, R. O. Keohane and M. A. Levy (eds), *Institutions for the Earth: Sources of Effective International Environmental Protection*. Cambridge, MA: MIT Press.

Pattberg, P. 2005. "The Forest Stewardship Council: Risk and Potential of Private Forest Governance." *Journal of Environment and Development* 14(3).

Pattberg, P. 2011. "The Forest Stewardship Council." In T. Hale and D. Held (eds), *Handbook of Innovation in Transnational Governance*. Cambridge: Polity.

Payne, R. 1995. "Freedom and the Environment." *Journal of Democracy* 6(3).

PEFC (Programme for the Endorsement of Forest Certification). 2012. "About PEFC." At http://www.pefc.org/about-pefc/who-we-are (accessed Dec. 2012).

Percy, S. 2007. "Mercenaries: Strong Norm, Weak Law." *International Organization* 61(2).

Perlroth, N. 2012. "Researchers Find Clues in Malware." New York Times, May 30. At http://www.nytimes.com/2012/05/31/technology/researchers-link-flame-virus-to-stuxnet-and-duqu.html (accessed Oct. 2012).

Picciotto, S. 2011. *Regulating Global Corporate Capitalism*. Cambridge: Cambridge University Press.

Pinto, S., Macdonald, K. and Marshall, S. 2011. "Rethinking Global Market Governance: Crisis and Reinvention?" *Politics and Society* 39(3).

Pleyers, G. 2010. *Alter-Globalization*. Cambridge: Polity.

Polanyi, K. 1944. *The Great Transformation*. Boston: Beacon.

Ponte, S., Gibbon, P. and Vestergaard, J. (eds). 2011. *Governing through Standards: Origins, Drivers and Limitations*. London: Palgrave.

Potoski, M. and Prakash, A. 2005. "Green Clubs and Voluntary Governance: ISO14001 and Firms' Regulatory Compliance." *American Journal of Political Science* 49(2).

Prantl, J. (ed.).Forthcoming. *Effective Multilateralism*. Basingstoke: Palgrave Macmillan.

Przeworski, A. and Limongi, F. 1997. "Modernization: Theories and Facts." *World Politics* 49(2).

Putnam, R. D. 1988. "Diplomacy and Domestic Politics: The Logic of Two Level Games." *International Organization* 42(3).

Quah, Danny. 2008. "Where in the World Is Asian Thrift and the Global Savings Glut?" EconoMonitor, Roubini Global Economics, Nov. 22.

Rachman, G. 2010. *Zero-Sum World: Power and Politics after the Crash*. London: Atlantic Books.

Ragin, C. 1987. *The Comparative Method: Moving beyond Qualitative and Quantitative Strategies*. Berkeley: University of California Press.
Randall, L. 1997. *The Political Economy of Latin America in the Postwar Period*. Austin: University of Texas Press.
Rapkin, D. and Strand, J. 2006. "Reforming the IMF's Weighted Voting System." *World Economy* 29(3).
Rasche, A. 2009. "'A Necessary Supplement': What the United Nations Global Compact Is and Is Not." *Business and Society* 48(4).
Raustiala, K. and Victor, D. G. 2004. "The Regime Complex for Plant Genetic Resources." *International Organization* 58: 277–309.
Ravenhill, J. 2008. "The Move to Preferential Trade on the Western Pacific Rim: Some Initial Conclusions." *Australian Journal of International Affairs* 62(2).
Ravenhill, J. and Jiang, Y. 2009. "China's Move to Preferential Trading: A New Direction in China's Diplomacy." *Journal of Contemporary China* 18(58).
Rees, M. 2003. *Our Final Century*. New York: Arrow Books.
Reuters. 2011. "Update 2: Trichet Warns of Widening Global Imbalances." June 19.
Rischard, J.-F. 2002. *High Noon: Twenty Global Problems, Twenty Years to Solve Them*. New York: Basic Books.
Risse, T. 2004. "Beyond Iraq: The Crisis of the Transatlantic Security Community." In D. Held and M. Koenig-Archibugi (eds), *American Power in the 21st Century*. Cambridge: Polity.
Risse-Kappen, T. 1995. *Bringing Transnational Relations Back In: Non-State Actors, Domestic Structures and International Institutions*. Cambridge: Cambridge University Press.
Rodrik, D. 2006a. "Goodbye Washington Consensus, Hello Washington Confusion?" *Journal of Economic Literature* 44 (Dec.).
Rodrik, D. 2006b. "The Social Cost of Foreign Exchange Reserves." *International Economic Journal* 20(3).
Rodrik, D. 2007. "Saving Globalization from Its Cheerleaders." 1(2).
Rodrik, D. 2010. "Diagnostics before Prescription." *Journal of Economic Perspectives* 24(3).
Rodrik, D. and Subramanian, A. 2009. "Why Did Financial Globalization Disappoint?" *IMF Staff Papers* 56(1).
Rosenau, J. N. 1997. *Along the Domestic-Foreign Frontier: Exploring Governance in a Turbulent World*. Cambridge: Cambridge University Press.
Rothkopf, David. 2012. "For Multilateralism, Is This the Dark Moment before the Dawn?" *Foreign Policy*, June 18.
Rowland, W. 1973. *The Plot to Save the World*. Toronto: Clarke, Irwin.
Rubin, H. 2011. "Future Global Shocks: Pandemics." International Futures Programme, OECD, Jan. 14. At www.oecd.org/dataoecd/58/1/46889985.pdf (accessed Oct. 2012).
Rüdig, W. 1991. "Green Party Politics around the World," *Environment: Science and Policy for Sustainable Development* 33(8).
Ruggie, J. G. 1982. "International Regimes, Transactions, and Change: Embedded Liberalism in the Postwar Economic Order." *International Organization* 36.

Ruggie, J. G. (ed.). 1993. *Multilateralism Matters: The Theory and Praxis of an Institutional Form*. New York: Columbia University Press.

Ruggie, J. G. 2001. "The Global Compact as Learning Network." *Global Governance* 7.

Ruggie, J. G. 2003. "Taking Embedded Liberalism Global: The Corporate Connection." In D. Held and M. Koenig-Archibugi (eds), *Taming Globalization: Frontiers of Governance*. Cambridge: Polity.

Ruggie, J. G. 2004. "Reconstituting the Global Public Domain: Issues, Actors, and Practices." *European Journal of International Relations* 10(4).

Ruggie, J. G. 2007. "Business and Human Rights: The Evolving International Agenda." *American Journal of International Law* 101(4).

Rupert, M. 1995. *Producing Hegemony: The Politics of Mass Production and American Global Power*. Cambridge: Cambridge University Press.

Sambanis, N. 2004. "What Is Civil War? Conceptual and Empirical Complexities of an Operational Definition." *Journal of Conflict Resolution* 48(6).

Sands, P. and Peel, J. 2012. *Principles of International Environmental Law*. Cambridge: Cambridge University Press.

Sarkees, M. R. and Wayman, F. 2010. *Resort to War: 1816–2007*. Washington, DC: CQ Press.

Seabrooke, L. 2006. "The Bank for International Settlements." *New Political Economy* 11(1).

Sell, S. and Prakash, A. 2004. "Using Ideas Strategically: The Contest between Business and NGO Networks in Intellectual Property Rights." *International Studies Quarterly* 48(1).

Schelling, T. C. 1980. *The Strategy of Conflict*. Cambridge, MA: Harvard University Press. Originally published 1960.

Schott, J. (ed.). 2000. *The WTO after Seattle*. Washington, DC: Institute for International Economics.

Schrank, D., Lomax, T. and Eisele, D. 2011. "TTI's 2011 Urban Mobility Report." At http://d2dtl5nnlpfr0r.cloudfront.net/tti.tamu.edu/documents/mobility-report-2011.pdf (accessed Oct. 2012).

Schwartz, H. 2009. *Subprime Nation: American Power, Global Capital, and the Housing Bubble*. Ithaca: Cornell University Press.

Scott, J. 1909. *The Hague Peace Conferences of 1899 and 1907*. Baltimore: Johns Hopkins University Press.

Scott, J. and Wilkinson, R. 2011. "The Poverty of the Doha Round and the Least Developed Countries." *Third World Quarterly* 32(4).

Sethi, P. 2003. "Global Compact Is Another Exercise in Futility." *Financial Express*, Sept. 7.

Shadlen, K. 2005. "Exchanging Development for Market Access? Deep Integration and Industrial Policy under Multilateral and Regional-Bilateral Trade Agreements." *Review of International Political Economy* 12(5).

Shadlen, K. 2008. "Globalization, Power, and Integration: The Political Economy of Regional and Bilateral Trade Agreements in the Americas." *Journal of Development Studies* 44.

Shiller, R. J. 2005. *Irrational Exuberance*. Princeton: Princeton University Press.

SIPRI (Stockholm International Peace Research Institute), 2010. *SIPRI 2010 Yearbook*. Oxford: Oxford University Press.

Skinner, Q. 1986. "Ambrogio Lorenzetti: The Artist as Political Philosopher." *Proceedings of the British Academy* 72.

Slaughter, A.-M. 2004a. "Disaggregated Sovereignty: Towards the Public Accountability of Global Government Networks." *Government and Opposition* 39(2).

Slaughter, A.-M. 2004b. *A New World Order*. Princeton: Princeton University Press.

Snyder, L. T. 2006. "President Dwight Eisenhower and America's Interstate Highway System." *American History* (June).

Snyder, T. 2010. *Bloodlands: Europe between Hitler and Stalin*. New York: Basic Books.

Social Enterprise. 2011. "Vibrant Sector Defies Downturn with Powerful Growth." SE100 News, July 11. At http://www.socialenterpriselive.com/section/se100/management/20110711/vibrant-sector-defies-downturn-powerful-growth (accessed Oct. 2012).

Soederberg, S. 2007. "Taming Corporations or Buttressing Market-Led Development? A Critical Assessment of the Global Compact." *Globalizations* 4(4).

Sohn, I. 2012. "Toward Normative Fragmentation: An East Asian Financial Architecture in the Post-Global Crisis World." *Review of International Political Economy* 19(4). DOI: 10.1080/09692290.2011.613350.

Sohn, I. 2013. "Between Confrontation and Assimilation: China and the Fragmentation of Global Financial Governance." *Journal of Contemporary China*.

Sokolski, H. D. 2004. "Taking Proliferation Seriously." In H. D. Sokolski (ed.), *Getting MAD: Nuclear Mutual Assured Destruction, Its Origins and Practice*. At http://www.strategicstudiesinstitute.army.mil/pubs/display.cfm?pubid=585 (accessed Oct. 2012).

START (National Consortium for the Study of Terrorism and Responses to Terrorism). 2011. "Global Terrorism Database." Data file. At http://www.start.umd.edu/gtd (accessed Oct. 2012).

Steffen, W. et al. 2004. *Global Change and the Earth System: A Planet under Pressure*. New York: Springer.

Steffen, W., Grinevald, J., Crutzen, P. and McNeill, J. 2011. "The Anthropocene: Conceptual and Historical Perspectives." *Philosophical Transactions of the Royal Society A* 369(1938).

Steinberg, R. 2002. "In the Shadow of Law or Power? Consensus-Based Bargaining and Outcomes in the GATT/WTO." *International Organization* 56(2): 339–74.

Stern Review. 2006. "The Economics of Climate Change: Executive Summary." HM Treasury, London. At http://www.hm-treasury.gov.uk/d/Executive_Summary.pdf (accessed Oct. 2012).

Stiglitz, J. E. 2012. *The Price of Inequality: How Today's Divided Society Endangers Our Future*. London: Norton.

Stone, P. 1973. *Did We Save the World at Stockholm?* London: Earth Island.

Strange, S. 1988. *States and Markets*. Oxford: Blackwell.

Stuenkel, O. 2012. "How Many Diplomats Does an Emerging Power Need?" *Post-Western World*, Oct. 14. At: http://www.postwesternworld.com/2012/10/14/how-many-diplomats-does-an-emerging-power-need/ (accessed Dec. 2012).

Sundaram, J. and Rodriguez, F. 2011. "Structural Causes and Consequences of the 2008–2009 Financial Crisis." In C. Calhoun and G. Derlugian (eds), *The Deepening Crisis: Governance Challenges after Neoliberalism*. New York: New York University Press.

Takahashi, M. A. 2012. "Migratory Bird Treaties' Issues and Potentials: Are They Valuable Tools or Just Curios in the Box?" *Environmental Law* 42.

Taylor, J. 2007. *Global Financial Warriors: The Untold Story of International Finance in the Post-9/11 World*. London: Norton.

Terborgh, A. G. 2003. "The Post-war Rise of World Trade: Does the Bretton Woods System Deserve Credit?" Mimeo, LSE Department of Economic History, Sept.

Tesner. S. and Kell, G. 2000. *The United Nations and Business: A Partnership Recovered*. New York: St Martin's Press.

Thakur, R. C. 2010. *The Responsibility to Protect: Norms, Laws, and the Use of Force in International Politics*. London: Routledge.

Thérien, J.-P. 2012. "Human Security: The Making of a UN Ideology." *Global Society* 25(2).

Thornton, P. 2006. "Stiglitz Doubts IMF Will Make Headway on Global Imbalances." *Independent*, Sept. 8.

TNC (The Nature Conservancy). 2012. "Facts about Rainforests." At http://www.nature.org/ourinitiatives/urgentissues/rainforests/rainforests-facts.xml (accessed Dec. 2012).

Toyne, P., O'Brien, C. and Nelson, R. 2002. "The Timber Footprint of the G8 and China." WWF International, June. At http://www.wwf.org.uk/filelibrary/pdf/g8timberfootprint.pdf (accessed Oct. 2012).

Truman, H. 1945. Address to the United Nations Conference in San Francisco. Apr. 25. At http://trumanlibrary.org/publicpapers/viewpapers.php?pid=17 (accessed Oct. 2012).

Truman, H. 1949. Inaugural Address. Jan 20. At http://www.trumanlibrary.org/calendar/viewpapers.php?pid=1030 (accessed Dec. 2012).

Tsebelis, G. 2002. *Veto Players: How Political Institutions Work*. Princeton: Princeton University Press.

Tsingou, E. 2010. "Global Financial Governance and the Developing Anti-Money Laundering Regime: What Lessons for International Political Economy?" *International Politics* 47(6).

Turner, A. 2009. *The Turner Review: A Regulatory Response to the Global Banking Crisis*. London: Financial Services Authority.

UIA (Union of International Associations). 2011. *Yearbook of International Organizations*. Leiden: Brill.

UIA (Union of International Associations). 2012. *Yearbook of International Organizations*. Leiden: Brill.

Ulrichsen, K. and Held, D. 2011. "The Arab 1989 Revisited." openDemocracy, Sept. 27. At http://www.opendemocracy.net/kristian-coates-ulrichsen-david-held/arab-1989-revisited (accessed Oct. 2012).

UN (United Nations). 1945. Charter of the United Nations. At http://www.un.org/en/documents/charter/ (accessed Oct. 2012).

UN (United Nations). 1971. UN General Assembly Resolution 2758. At http://www.un.org/documents/ga/res/26/ares26.htm (accessed Oct. 2012).

UN (United Nations). 2004. "Report of the Open-Ended Working Group on the Question of Equitable Representation On and Increase in the Membership of the Security Council and Other Matters Related to the Security Council: Joint Debate." At http://www.un.org/en/ga/62/plenary/screport/bkg.shtml (accessed Oct. 2012).

UN (United Nations). 2005. "The Treaty on the Non-Proliferation of Nuclear Weapons." At http://www.un.org/en/conf/npt/2005/npttreaty.html (accessed Oct. 2012).

UN (United Nations). 2009. Resolution A/RES/63/308 adopted by the General Assembly, The Responsibility to Protect. At http://www.un.org/en/ga/63/resolutions.shtml (accessed Oct. 2012).

UN (United Nations). 2011. "S/RES/1973 Resolution 1973 Adopted by the Security Council at its 6498th meeting, on 17 March 2011." At http://www.un.org/Docs/sc/unsc_resolutions11.htm (accessed Oct. 2012).

UN (United Nations). 2012. "Meetings Conducted/Actions Taken by the Security Council." At http://www.un.org/Depts/dhl/resguide/scact.htm (accessed Oct. 2012).

UNAMA (UN Assistance Mission in Afghanistan). 2012. "Afghanistan Annual Report 2011: Protection of Civilians in Armed Conflict." At http://www.unhcr.org/refworld/docid/4f2fa7572.html (accessed Oct. 2012).

UNCSD (UN Conference on Sustainable Development). 2012. "Partnerships at Rio+20." At http://www.uncsd2012.org/partnerships.html (accessed Dec. 2012).

UNCTAD (UN Conference on Trade and Development). 2002. *World Investment Report 2002: Transnational Corporations and Export Competitiveness.* New York: UNCTAD.

UNCTAD (UN Conference on Trade and Development). 2009. *World Investment Report 2009: Transnational Corporations, Agricultural Production and Development.* At http://unctad.org/en/docs/wir2009_en.pdf (accessed Oct. 2012).

UN DESA (UN Department of Economic and Social Affairs). 1973. *Multinational Corporations in World Development.* New York: United Nations. At http://unctc.unctad.org/data/e73iia11a.pdf (accessed Oct. 2012).

UNDP (UN Development Programme). 1994. *Human Development Report: New Dimensions of Human Security.* At http://hdr.undp.org/en/reports/global/hdr1994/ (accessed Oct. 2012).

UNDP (UN Development Programme). 2010. *Human Development Report 2010: The Real Wealth of Nations, Pathways to Human Development.* New York: UNDP.

UNECE (United Nations Economic Commission for Europe). 2006. *Strategies and Policies for Air Pollution Abatement.* Geneva: United Nations.

UNEP (United Nations Environment Programme). 2009. *Key Achievements of the Montreal Protocol to Date.* Nairobi: UNEP.

UNEP (United Nations Environment Programme). 2010. *The Emissions Gap Report: Are the Copenhagen Accord Pledges Sufficient to Limit Global Warming to 2° C or 1.5° C?* Nairobi: UNEP.

UNEP (United Nations Environment Programme). 2012. Ecolex Database. At www.ecolex.org (accessed Dec. 2012).

UNESCO. 2004. "The COE International Convention on Cybercrime before Its Entry into Force." At http://portal.unesco.org/culture/en/ev.php-URL_ID=19556&URL_DO=DO_TOPIC&URL_SECTION=201.html (accessed Dec. 2012).

UNFCCC (United Nations Framework Convention on Climate Change). 2011. "Compilation and Synthesis of Fifth National Communications." At http://unfccc.int/resource/docs/2011/sbi/eng/inf01.pdf (accessed Dec. 2012).

UNFCCC (United Nations Framework Convention on Climate Change). 2012. "CDM in Numbers." At http://cdm.unfccc.int/Statistics/index.html (accessed Dec. 2012).

UNOCHA (UN Coordinator for Humanitarian Affairs). 2012. "Human Security." At http://ochaonline.un.org/humansecurity/ (accessed Oct. 2012).

UN Security Council. 1950. "Resolution 84 (1950) of 7 July 1950." S/RES/84. At http://www.unhcr.org/refworld/docid/3b00f1e85c.html (accessed Oct. 2012).

UN Security Council. 2001. "Security Council Resolution 1386 (2001) on the Situation in Afghanistan." S/RES/1386, Dec. 20. At http://www.unhcr.org/refworld/docid/3c4e94571c.html (accessed Oct. 2012).

US Census Bureau. 2012. "World Population." At http://www.census.gov/population/international/data/worldpop/table_population.php (accessed Oct. 2012).

US Department of Energy. 2012. *Transportation Energy Data Book.* At http://cta.ornl.gov/data/index.shtml (accessed Oct. 2012).

US SIF (Forum for Sustainable and Responsible Investment). 2011. "Sustainable and Responsible Investing." At http://ussif.org/resources/factsheets_resources/documents/10mediaquestions2011_final.pdf (accessed Oct. 2012).

Valenzuela, J. S. and Valenzuela, A. 1978. "Modernization and Dependency: Alternative Perspectives in the Study of Latin American Development." *Comparative Politics* (July).

Vestergaard, J. and Wade, R. 2012. "Establishing a New Global Economic Council: Governance Reform at the G20, the IMF and the World Bank." *Global Policy* 3(3).

Viana, V. et al. (eds). 1996. *Certification of Forest Products: Issues and Perspectives.* Washington, DC: Island Press.

Victor, D. 2011a. *Global Warming Gridlock.* Cambridge: Cambridge University Press.

Victor, D. 2011b. "Why the UN Can Never Stop Climate Change." *Guardian*, Apr. 4.

Viotti, M. 2011. "Letter dated 9 November 2011 from the Permanent Representative of Brazil to the United Nations addressed to the Secretary-General." At http://www.un.int/brazil/speech/Concept-Paper-%20RwP.pdf (accessed Dec. 2012).

Vogel, D. 1995. *Trading Up: Consumer and Environmental Regulation in a Global Economy.* Cambridge, MA: Harvard University Press.

Vogel, D. 2008. "Private Global Business Regulation." *Annual Review of Political Science* 11: 261–82.

Wade, R. 1990. *Governing the Market.* Princeton: Princeton University Press.

Wade, R. 2003a. *Governing the Market.* Princeton: Princeton University Press.

Wade, R. 2003b. "The Invisible Hand of the American Empire." *Ethics and International Affairs* 17(2).

Wade, R. 2009. "From Global Imbalances to Global Reorganizations." *Cambridge Journal of Economics* 33.

Wade, R. 2010. "After the Crisis: Industrial Policy and the Developmental State in Low-Income Countries." *Global Policy* 1(2).

Wade, R. 2011. "Emerging World Order? From Multipolarity to Multilateralism in the G20, the World Bank and the IMF." *Politics and Society* 39(3).

Wade, R. 2012. "Marginalizing the United Nations as a Forum for Debate about the Financial Crisis: The West's Success." *Le Monde Diplomatique*, Aug.

Walter, A. 2011. "Global Economic Governance after the Crisis: The G2, the G20, and Global Imbalances." Bank of Korea Working Paper.

Walter, A. Forthcoming. "The Mismanagement of Global Imbalances: Why Did Multilateralism Fail?" In J. Prantl (ed.), *Effective Multilateralism*. Basingstoke: Palgrave Macmillan.

Wang, H. 2006. *China's New Order: Society, Politics, and Economy in Transition*. Cambridge, MA: Harvard University Press.

Wara, M. W. and Victor, D. G. 2008. "A Realistic Policy on International Carbon Offsets." Working Paper 74. Program on Energy and Sustainable Development, Freeman Spogli Institute for International Studies, Stanford University.

WCED (World Commission on Environment and Development). 1987. *Report: Our Common Future*. Document A/42/427. New York: United Nations.

Weber, C. L., Peters, G. P., Guan, D. and Hubacek, K. 2008. "The Contribution of Chinese Exports to Climate Change." *Energy Policy* 36(9).

Weber, M. 1964. *The Theory of Economic and Social Organization*. New York: Free Press.

Weiss, T. 2003. "The Illusion of UN Security Council Reform." *Washington Quarterly* 26(4).

Weiss, T. 2009. *What's Wrong with the United Nations and How to Fix It*. Cambridge: Polity.

Weiss, T. and Thakur, R. 2010. *Global Governance and the UN*. Bloomington: Indiana University Press.

Wesley, M. 2008. "The Strategic Effects of Preferential Trade Agreements." *Australian Journal of International Affairs* 62(2).

Westad, A. O. 2006. *The Global Cold War: Third World Interventions and the Making of Our Times*. Cambridge: Cambridge University Press.

Wettestad, J. 2002. "The Convention on Long-Range Transboundary Air Pollution." In E. L. Miles et al. (eds), *Environmental Regime Effectiveness: Confronting Theory with Evidence*. Cambridge, MA: MIT Press.

White House. 2002. "The National Security Strategy of the United States of America." Washington, DC: The White House.

Wilkinson, R. and Pickett, K. 2010. *The Spirit Level: Why Greater Equality Makes Societies Stronger*. New York: Bloomsbury.

Williams, O. 2004. "The UN Global Compact: The Challenge and the Promise." *Business Ethics Quarterly* 14.

Williamson, J. 1990. "What Washington Means by Policy Reform." In J. Williamson (ed.), *Latin American Adjustment: How Much Has Happened?* Washington, DC: Institute for International Economics.

Witte, J. M., Streck, C. and Benner, T. 2003. "The Road from Johannesburg: What Future for Partnerships in Global Environmental Governance?" In T. Benner, C. Streck and J. M. Witte (eds), *Progress or Peril? Networks and Partnerships in Global Environmental Governance.* Berlin: Global Public Policy Institute.

Wöbse, A.-K. 2008. "Oil on Troubled Waters? Environmental Diplomacy in the League of Nations." *Diplomatic History* 32(4).

Woods, N. 2010. "Global Governance after the Financial Crisis: A New Multilateralism or the Last Gasp of the Great Powers?" *Global Policy* 1(2).

World Bank. 2009a. *Development Policy Lending Retrospective: Flexibility, Customization, and Results.* Washington, DC: World Bank.

World Bank. 2009b. *Global Monitoring Report 2009: A Development Emergency.* Washington, DC: IBRD/World Bank.

World Bank. 2010a. "Cities and Climate Change: An Urgent Agenda." Dec. At http://siteresources.worldbank.org/INTUWM/Resources/340232-1205330656272/CitiesandClimateChange.pdf (accessed Dec. 2012).

World Bank. 2010b. *Global Monitoring Report 2010: The MDGs after the Crisis.* Washington, DC: World Bank.

World Bank. 2010c. "Results Profile: China Poverty Reduction." At http://www.worldbank.org/en/news/2010/03/19/results-profile-china-poverty-reduction (accessed Oct. 2012).

World Bank. 2011. *World Development Report: Conflict, Security and Development.* Washington, DC: World Bank.

World Bank. 2012. "Introduction to the Inequality in Focus Series." At http://siteresources.worldbank.org/EXTPOVERTY/Resources/Inequality_in_Focus_April2012.pdf#page=1&view=FitH,400 (accessed Oct. 2012).

World Bank and Development Research Center of the State Council. 2012. "China 2030: Building a Modern, Harmonious, and Creative High-Income Society." Washington, DC.

World Bank Group. 2011. "Vulnerability, Risk Reduction, and Adaptation to Climate Change: Philippines." At http://sdwebx.worldbank.org/climateportal/doc/GFDRRCountryProfiles/wb_gfdrr_climate_change_country_profile_for_PHL.pdf (accessed Oct. 2012).

World Economic Forum. 2012. "Outlook on the Global Agenda 2012." World Economic Forum, Davos.

Wright, C. 2012. "The Impact of the Equator Principles on Lending Policies and Practices." *Global Environmental Politics* 12(1).

WTO (World Trade Organization). 2006. "Talks Suspended: 'Today There Are Only Losers.'" Press release, July 24. At http://www.wto.org/english/news_e/news06_e/mod06_summary_24july_e.htm (accessed Oct. 2012).

WTO (World Trade Organization). 2007. *World Trade Report 2007: Six Decades of Multilateral Trade Cooperation: What Have We Learnt?* Geneva: WTO.

WTO (World Trade Organization). 2008. "Lamy Presents 'Package of Elements' from Consultations with Ministers." Press release, July 26. At http://www.wto.

org/english/news_e/news08_e/meet08_chair_26july08_e.htm (accessed Oct. 2012).

WTO (World Trade Organization). 2011a. "Members Support Lamy's Proposed Three-Speed Search for Doha Outcome in December." Press release, May 31. At http://www.wto.org/english/news_e/news11_e/tnc_infstat_31may11_e.htm (accessed Oct. 2012).

WTO (World Trade Organization). 2011b. *World Trade Report 2011.* At http://www.wto.org/english/res_e/booksp_e/anrep_e/world_trade_report11_e.pdf (accessed Oct. 2012).

WTO (World Trade Organization). 2012. *World Trade Report 2012.* Geneva: WTO.

WWF. 2007. "Deforestation and Climate Change." At http://awsassets.panda.org/downloads/intro_factsheet_27nov07_lr.pdf (accessed Oct. 2012).

WWF. 2012. "Factsheet: FSC in China." At http://awsassets.panda.org/downloads/fsc_in_china_fact_sheet.pdf (accessed Dec. 2012).

Wyler, L. S. 2008. "Weak and Failing States: Evolving Security Threats and US Policy." CRS Report for Congress RL34253. Washington, DC: Congressional Research Service, Library of Congress.

Yeuh, L. 2010. "The US, China, and Global Imbalances." *China Economic Journal* 3(1).

Young, K. 2011a. "China's Ascendance in International Finance: External versus Internal Sources of Its Changing Policy Stance." *21st Century International Review* 2(2).

Young, K. 2011b. "The Rise of Regulatory Standards in Banking and Their Limits." In S. Ponte, P. Gibbon and J. Vestergaard (eds), *Governing through Standards: Origins, Drivers and Limitations.* London: Palgrave Macmillan.

Young, K. 2012. "Transnational Regulatory Capture? An Empirical Examination of Transnational Lobbying over the Basel Committee on Banking Supervision." *Review of International Political Economy* 19(4).

Young, K. and Park, S. 2013. "Regulatory Opportunism: Cross-National Patterns in National Banking Regulatory Responses Following the Global Financial Crisis." *Public Administration.*

Zakaria, F. 2008a. *The Post-American World.* New York: Norton.

Zakaria, F. 2008b. "The Rise of the Rest." *Newsweek*, May 12.

Zelli, F. 2011. "The Fragmentation of the Global Climate Governance Architecture." *Wiley Interdisciplinary Reviews: Climate Change* 2(2): 255–70.

Zimmern, A. 1936. *The League of Nations and the Rule of Law.* London: Macmillan.

Zoellick, R. 2005. "Whither China: From Membership to responsibility?" *NBR Analysis* 16(4).

Index

Page numbers in *italics* refer to figures and tables.